INJUSTICE

GROUND ZERO

VOLUME 1

INJU
GROUN

BRIAN BUCCELLATO CHRISTOPHER SEBELA
Writers

POP MHAN   TOM DERENICK   DANIEL SAMPERE
JUAN ALBARRAN   MARCO SANTUCCI   JHEREMY RAAPACK
Artists

REX LOKUS   J. NANJAN   MARK ROBERTS
Colorists

WES ABBOTT
Letterer

BEN OLIVER
Collection and series cover artist

STICE

D ZERO

VOLUME 1

SUPERMAN created by JERRY SIEGEL and JOE SHUSTER
By special arrangement with the Jerry Siegel Family

BASED ON THE VIDEO GAME *INJUSTICE: GODS AMONG US*

JIM CHADWICK Editor – Original Series
SUSIE ESPARZA
ROB LEVIN Assistant Editors – Original Series
JEB WOODARD Group Editor – Collected Editions
PAUL SANTOS Editor – Collected Edition
STEVE COOK Design Director – Books
LOUIS PRANDI Publication Design

BOB HARRAS Senior VP – Editor-in-Chief, DC Comics
PAT McCALLUM Executive Editor, DC Comics

DIANE NELSON President
DAN DiDIO Publisher
JIM LEE Publisher
GEOFF JOHNS President & Chief Creative Officer
AMIT DESAI Executive VP – Business & Marketing Strategy,
Direct to Consumer & Global Franchise Management
SAM ADES Senior VP & General Manager, Digital Services
BOBBIE CHASE VP & Executive Editor, Young Reader & Talent Development
MARK CHIARELLO Senior VP – Art, Design & Collected Editions
JOHN CUNNINGHAM Senior VP – Sales & Trade Marketing
ANNE DePIES Senior VP – Business Strategy, Finance & Administration
DON FALLETTI VP – Manufacturing Operations
LAWRENCE GANEM VP – Editorial Administration & Talent Relations
ALISON GILL Senior VP – Manufacturing & Operations
HANK KANALZ Senior VP – Editorial Strategy & Administration
JAY KOGAN VP – Legal Affairs
JACK MAHAN VP – Business Affairs
NICK J. NAPOLITANO VP – Manufacturing Administration
EDDIE SCANNELL VP – Consumer Marketing
COURTNEY SIMMONS Senior VP – Publicity & Communications
JIM (SKI) SOKOLOWSKI VP – Comic Book Specialty Sales & Trade Marketing
NANCY SPEARS VP – Mass, Book, Digital Sales & Trade Marketing
MICHELE R. WELLS VP – Content Strategy

INJUSTICE: GROUND ZERO VOLUME 1

Published by DC Comics. Compilation and all new material
Copyright © 2017 DC Comics. All Rights Reserved. Originally
published in single magazine form in INJUSTICE GROUND
ZERO 1-6. Copyright © 2016, 2017 DC Comics. All Rights
Reserved. All characters, their distinctive likenesses and related
elements featured in this publication are trademarks of DC
Comics. The stories, characters and incidents featured in this
publication are entirely fictional. DC Comics does not read or
accept unsolicited submissions of ideas, stories or artwork.

DC Comics, 2900 West Alameda Ave., Burbank, CA 91505
Printed by LSC Communications, Kendallville, IN, USA. 11/24/17.
First Printing. ISBN: 978-1-4012-7387-3

Library of Congress Cataloging-in-Publication Data is available.

PEFC Certified

Printed on paper from
sustainably managed
forests, controlled
sources

PEFC/29-31-337

www.pefc.org

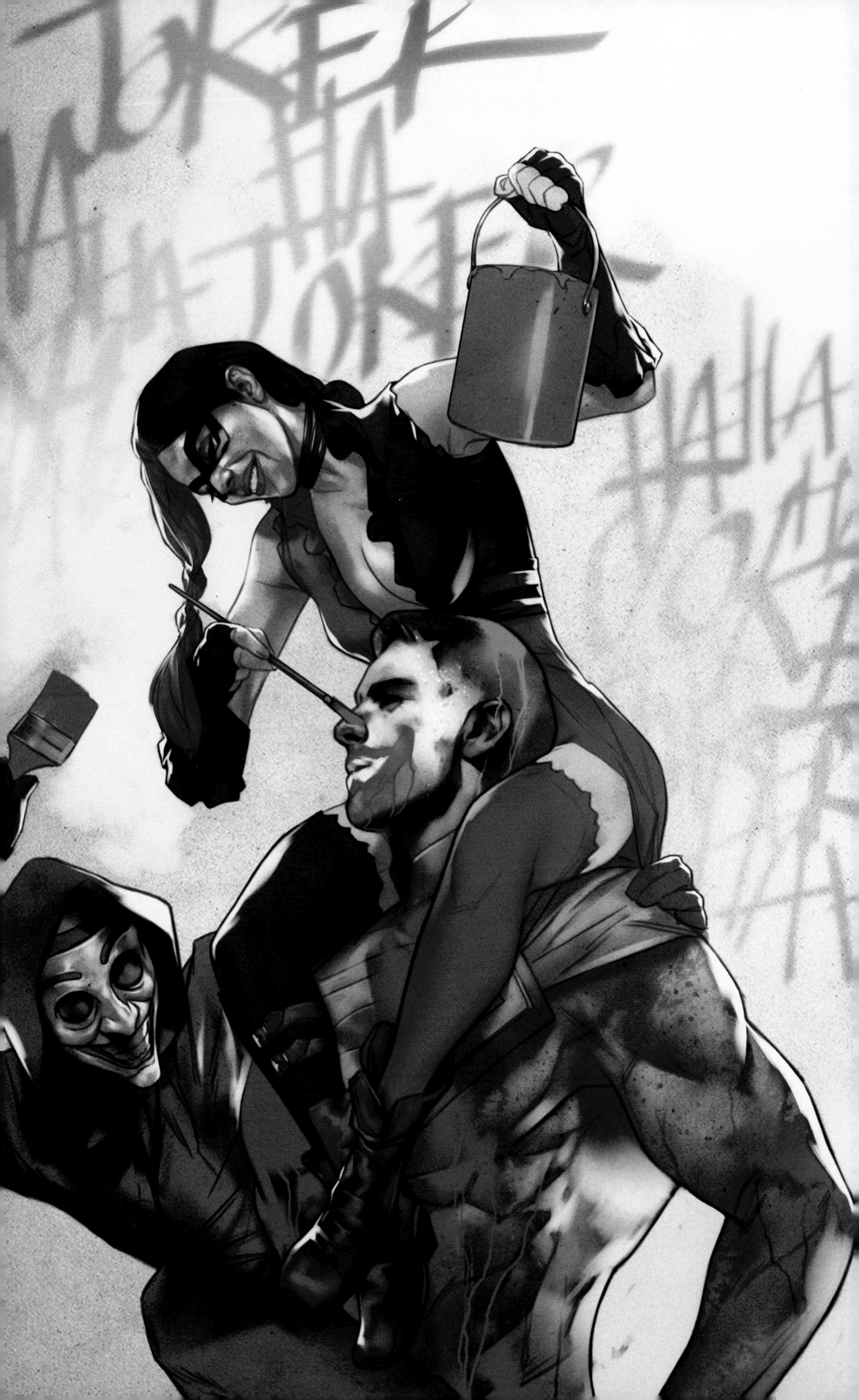

"All Bad Things Must End: Part 1" **Pop Mhan** Artist **Rex Lokus** Colorist
"All Bad Things Must End: Part 2" **Tom Derenick** Artist **Rex Lokus** Colorist

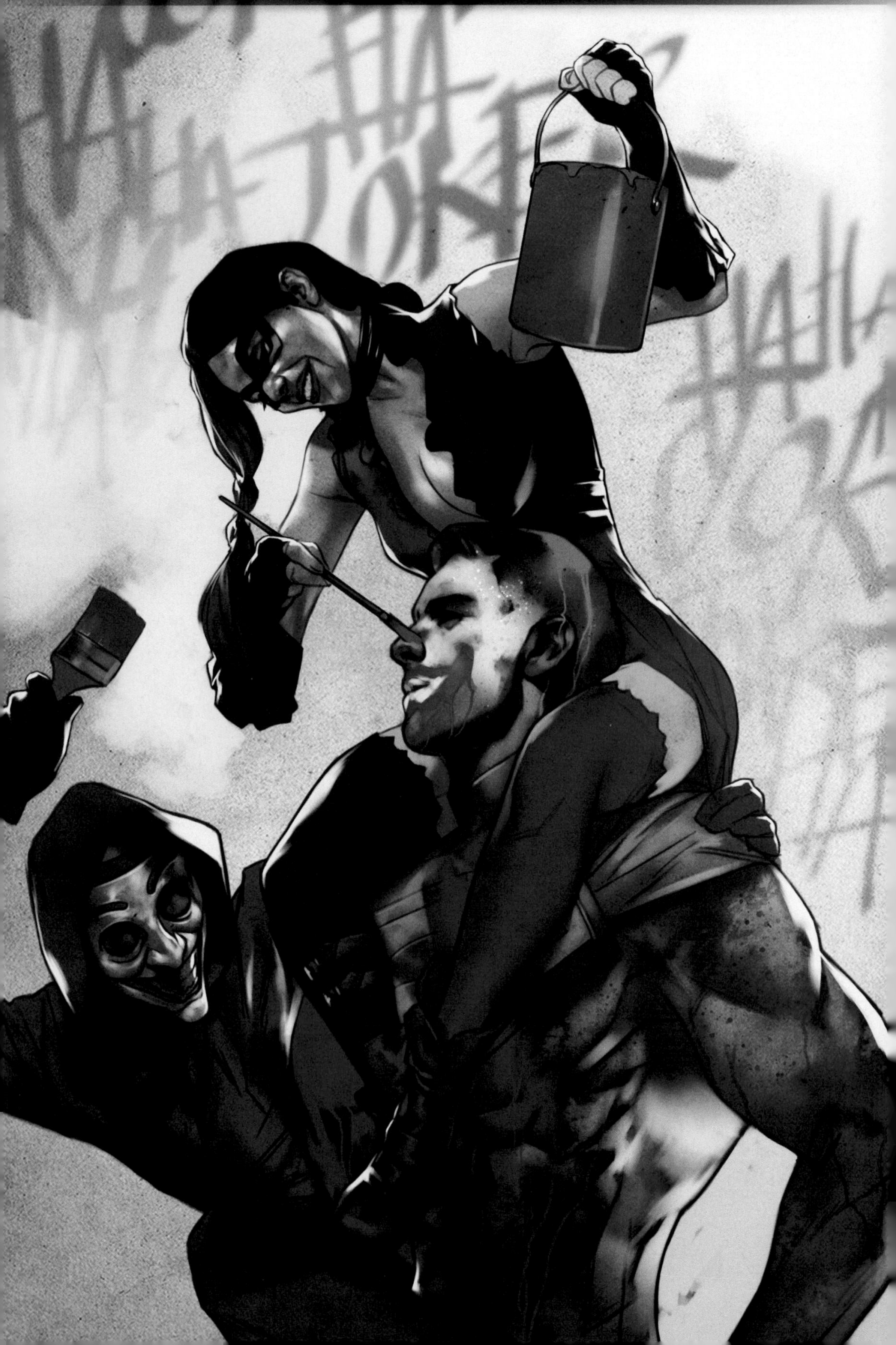

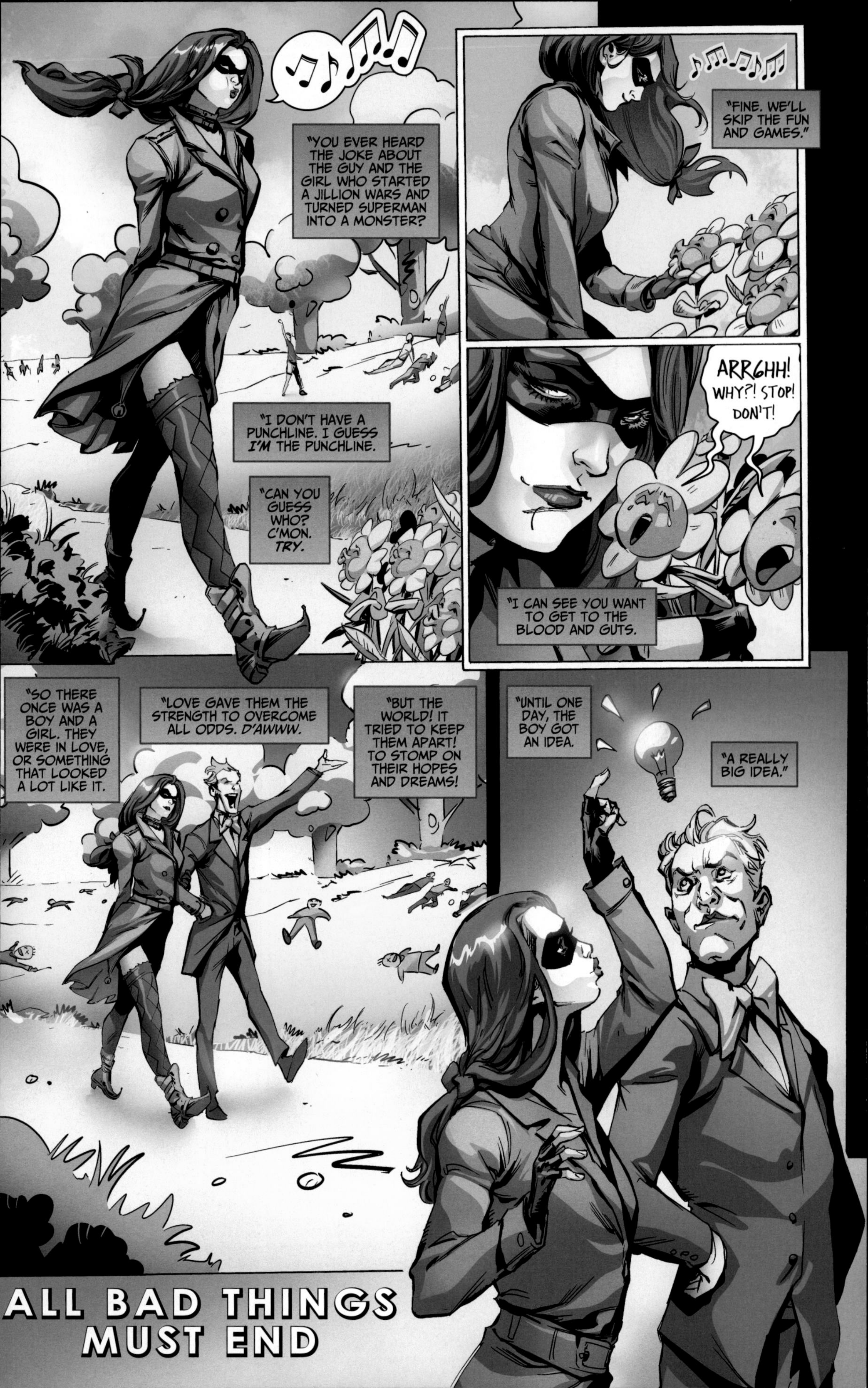
"YOU EVER HEARD THE JOKE ABOUT THE GUY AND THE GIRL WHO STARTED A JILLION WARS AND TURNED SUPERMAN INTO A MONSTER?
"I DON'T HAVE A PUNCHLINE. I GUESS *I'M* THE PUNCHLINE.
"CAN YOU GUESS WHO? C'MON. *TRY.*
"FINE. WE'LL SKIP THE FUN AND GAMES."
ARRGHH! WHY?! STOP! DON'T!
"I CAN SEE YOU WANT TO GET TO THE BLOOD AND GUTS.
"SO THERE ONCE WAS A BOY AND A GIRL. THEY WERE IN LOVE, OR SOMETHING THAT LOOKED A LOT LIKE IT.
"LOVE GAVE THEM THE STRENGTH TO OVERCOME ALL ODDS. D'AWWW.
"BUT THE WORLD! IT TRIED TO KEEP THEM APART! TO STOMP ON THEIR HOPES AND DREAMS!
"UNTIL ONE DAY, THE BOY GOT AN IDEA.
"A REALLY BIG IDEA."
ALL BAD THINGS MUST END

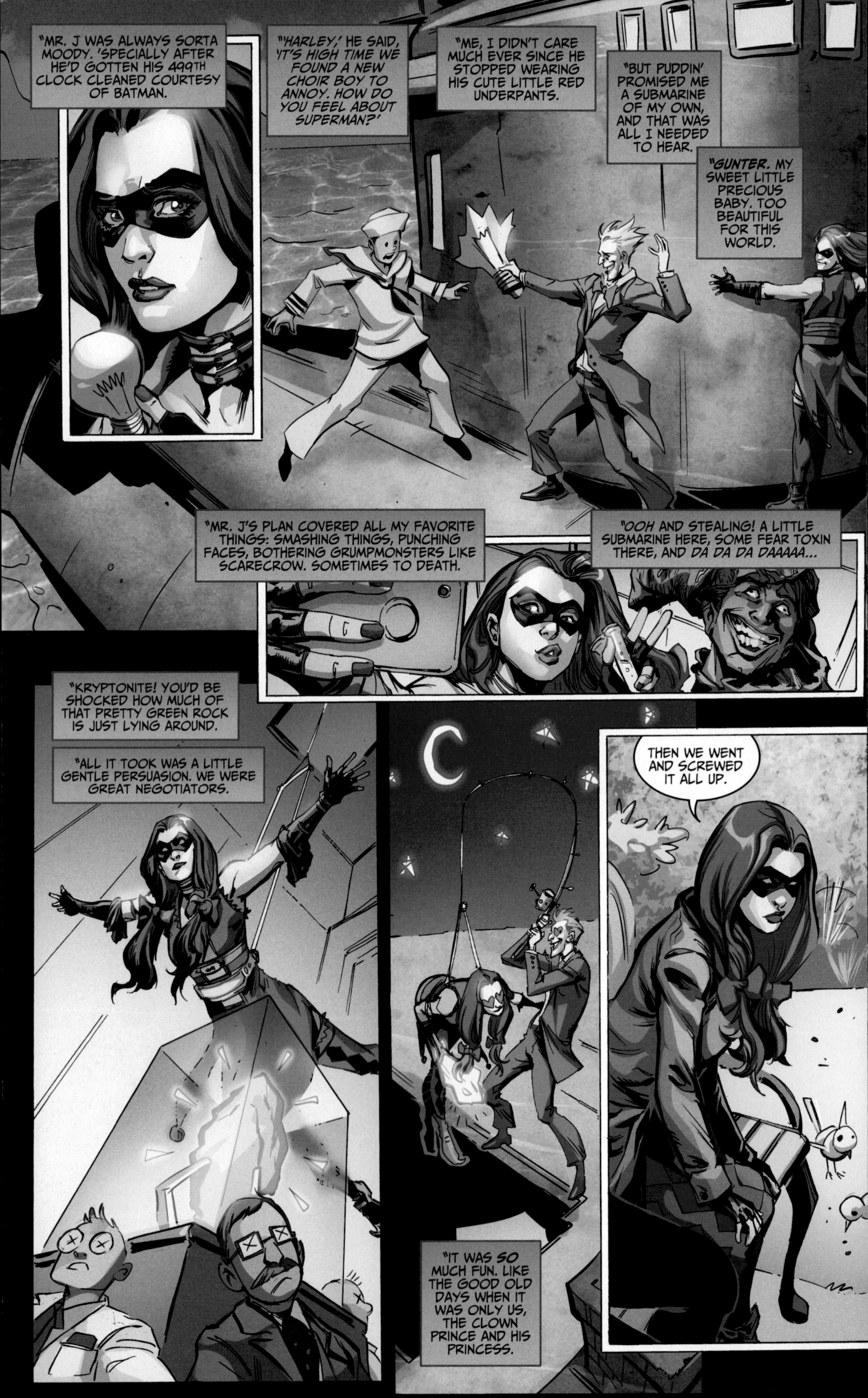
"MR. J WAS ALWAYS SORTA MOODY. 'SPECIALLY AFTER HE'D GOTTEN HIS 499TH CLOCK CLEANED COURTESY OF BATMAN.
"'HARLEY,' HE SAID, 'IT'S HIGH TIME WE FOUND A NEW CHOIR BOY TO ANNOY. HOW DO YOU FEEL ABOUT SUPERMAN?'
"ME, I DIDN'T CARE MUCH EVER SINCE HE STOPPED WEARING HIS CUTE LITTLE RED UNDERPANTS.
"BUT PUDDIN' PROMISED ME A SUBMARINE OF MY OWN, AND THAT WAS ALL I NEEDED TO HEAR.
"GUNTER. MY SWEET LITTLE PRECIOUS BABY. TOO BEAUTIFUL FOR THIS WORLD.
"MR. J'S PLAN COVERED ALL MY FAVORITE THINGS: SMASHING THINGS, PUNCHING FACES, BOTHERING GRUMPMONSTERS LIKE SCARECROW. SOMETIMES TO DEATH.
"OOH AND STEALING! A LITTLE SUBMARINE HERE, SOME FEAR TOXIN THERE, AND DA DA DA DAAAAA...
"KRYPTONITE! YOU'D BE SHOCKED HOW MUCH OF THAT PRETTY GREEN ROCK IS JUST LYING AROUND.
"ALL IT TOOK WAS A LITTLE GENTLE PERSUASION. WE WERE GREAT NEGOTIATORS.
"IT WAS SO MUCH FUN. LIKE THE GOOD OLD DAYS WHEN IT WAS ONLY US, THE CLOWN PRINCE AND HIS PRINCESS.
THEN WE WENT AND SCREWED IT ALL UP.

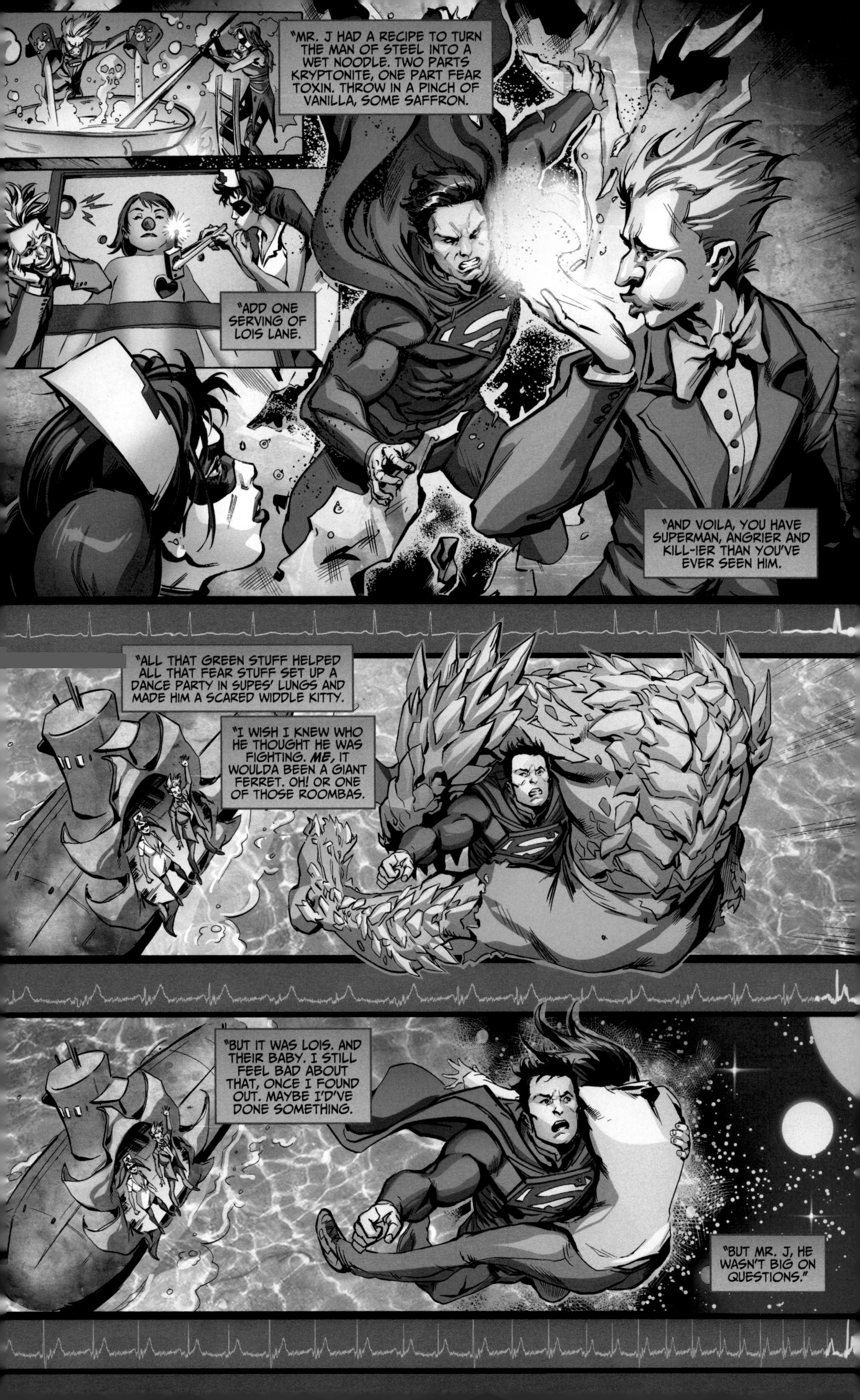
"MR. J HAD A RECIPE TO TURN THE MAN OF STEEL INTO A WET NOODLE. TWO PARTS KRYPTONITE, ONE PART FEAR TOXIN. THROW IN A PINCH OF VANILLA, SOME SAFFRON.
"ADD ONE SERVING OF LOIS LANE.
"AND VOILA, YOU HAVE SUPERMAN, ANGRIER AND KILL-IER THAN YOU'VE EVER SEEN HIM.
"ALL THAT GREEN STUFF HELPED ALL THAT FEAR STUFF SET UP A DANCE PARTY IN SUPES' LUNGS AND MADE HIM A SCARED WIDDLE KITTY.
"I WISH I KNEW WHO HE THOUGHT HE WAS FIGHTING. *ME,* IT WOULDA BEEN A GIANT FERRET. OH! OR ONE OF THOSE ROOMBAS.
"BUT IT WAS LOIS. AND THEIR BABY. I STILL FEEL BAD ABOUT THAT, ONCE I FOUND OUT. MAYBE I'D'VE DONE SOMETHING.
"BUT MR. J, HE WASN'T BIG ON QUESTIONS."

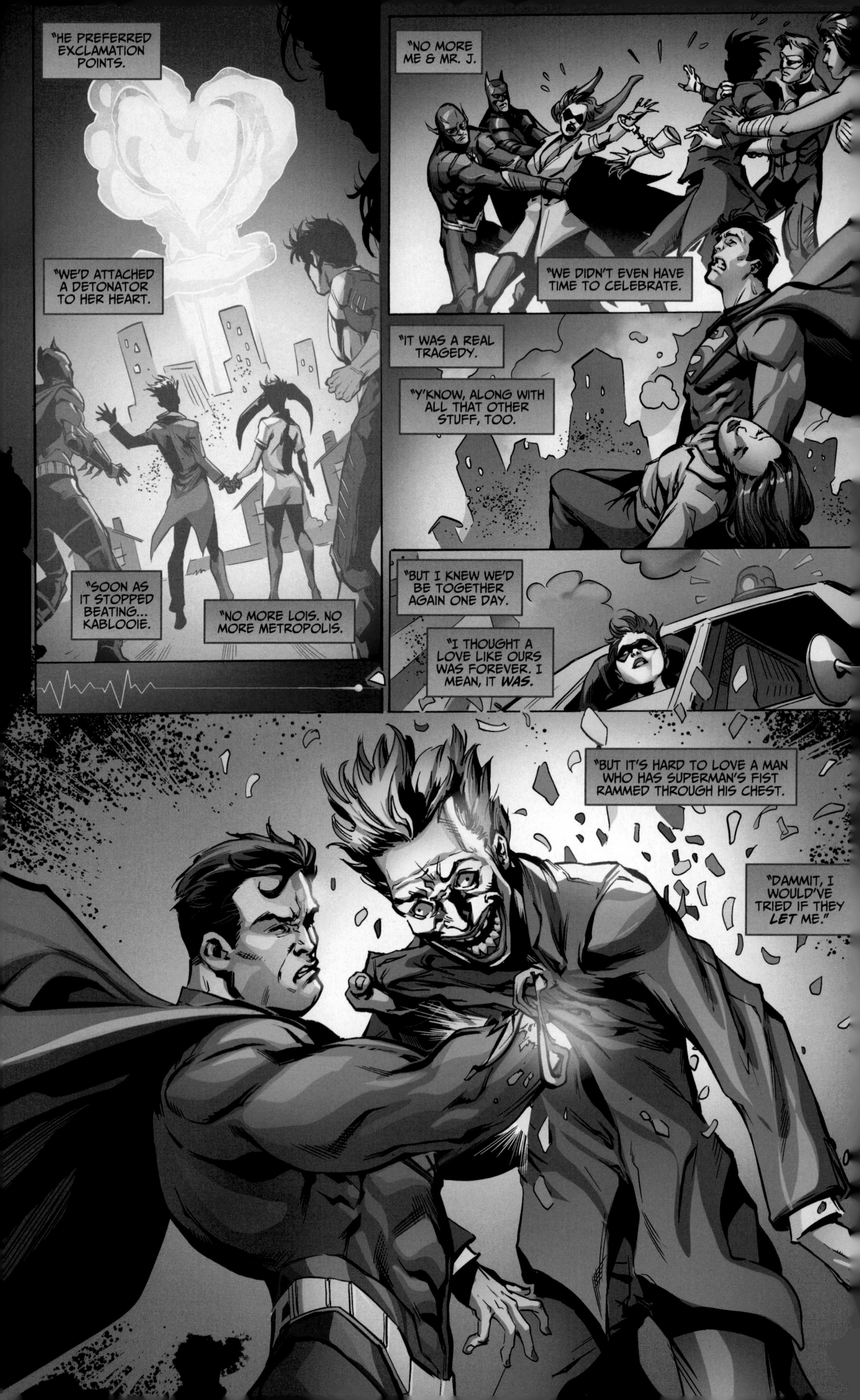
"HE PREFERRED EXCLAMATION POINTS.
"WE'D ATTACHED A DETONATOR TO HER HEART.
"SOON AS IT STOPPED BEATING... KABLOOIE.
"NO MORE LOIS. NO MORE METROPOLIS.
"NO MORE ME & MR. J.
"WE DIDN'T EVEN HAVE TIME TO CELEBRATE.
"IT WAS A REAL TRAGEDY.
"Y'KNOW, ALONG WITH ALL THAT OTHER STUFF, TOO.
"BUT I KNEW WE'D BE TOGETHER AGAIN ONE DAY.
"I THOUGHT A LOVE LIKE OURS WAS FOREVER. I MEAN, IT *WAS*.
"BUT IT'S HARD TO LOVE A MAN WHO HAS SUPERMAN'S FIST RAMMED THROUGH HIS CHEST.
"DAMMIT, I WOULD'VE TRIED IF THEY *LET* ME."

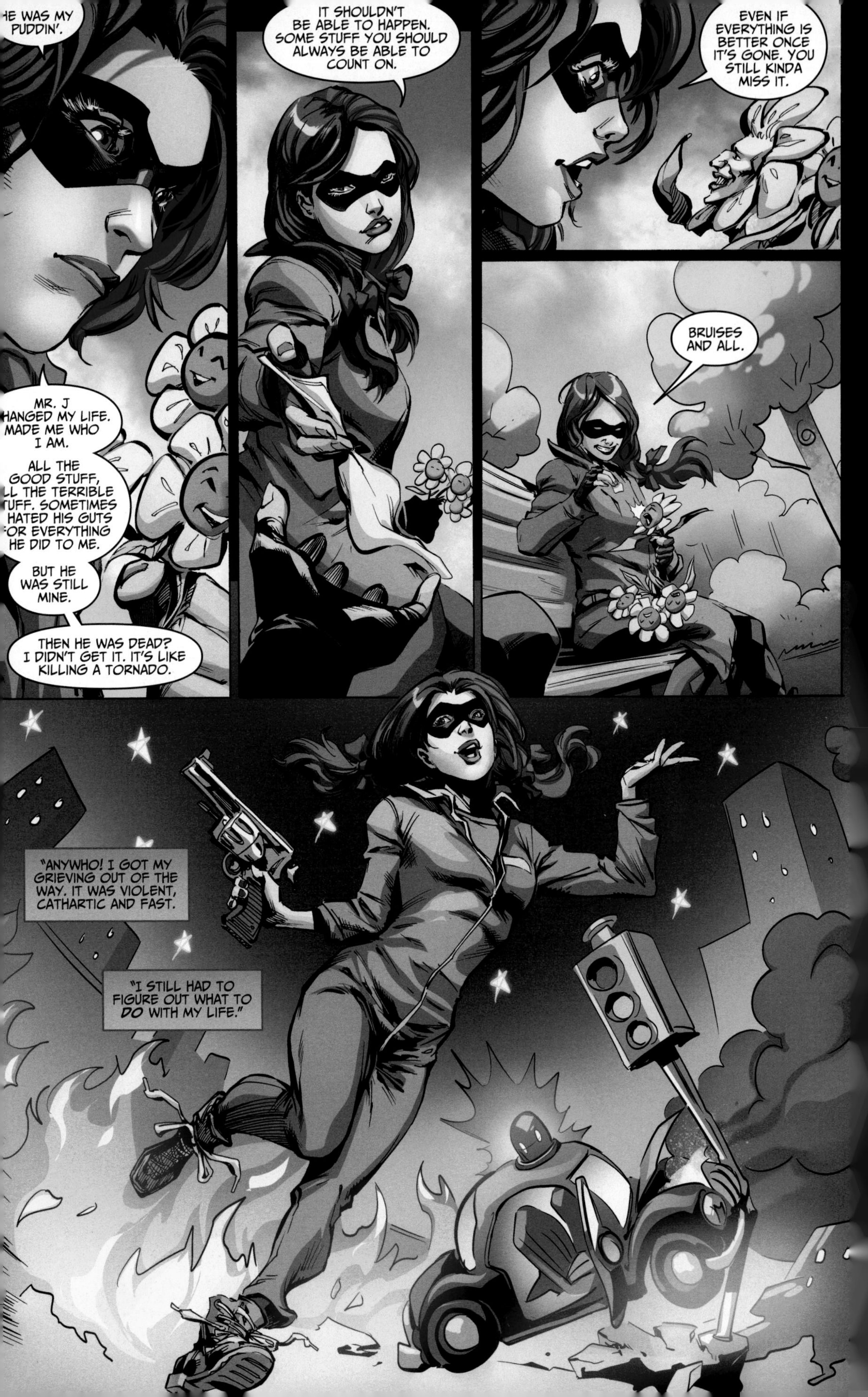
HE WAS MY PUDDIN'.
IT SHOULDN'T BE ABLE TO HAPPEN. SOME STUFF YOU SHOULD ALWAYS BE ABLE TO COUNT ON.
EVEN IF EVERYTHING IS BETTER ONCE IT'S GONE. YOU STILL KINDA MISS IT.
MR. J CHANGED MY LIFE. MADE ME WHO I AM.
ALL THE GOOD STUFF, ALL THE TERRIBLE STUFF. SOMETIMES I HATED HIS GUTS FOR EVERYTHING HE DID TO ME.
BUT HE WAS STILL MINE.
THEN HE WAS DEAD? I DIDN'T GET IT. IT'S LIKE KILLING A TORNADO.
BRUISES AND ALL.
"ANYWHO! I GOT MY GRIEVING OUT OF THE WAY. IT WAS VIOLENT, CATHARTIC AND FAST.
"I STILL HAD TO FIGURE OUT WHAT TO DO WITH MY LIFE."

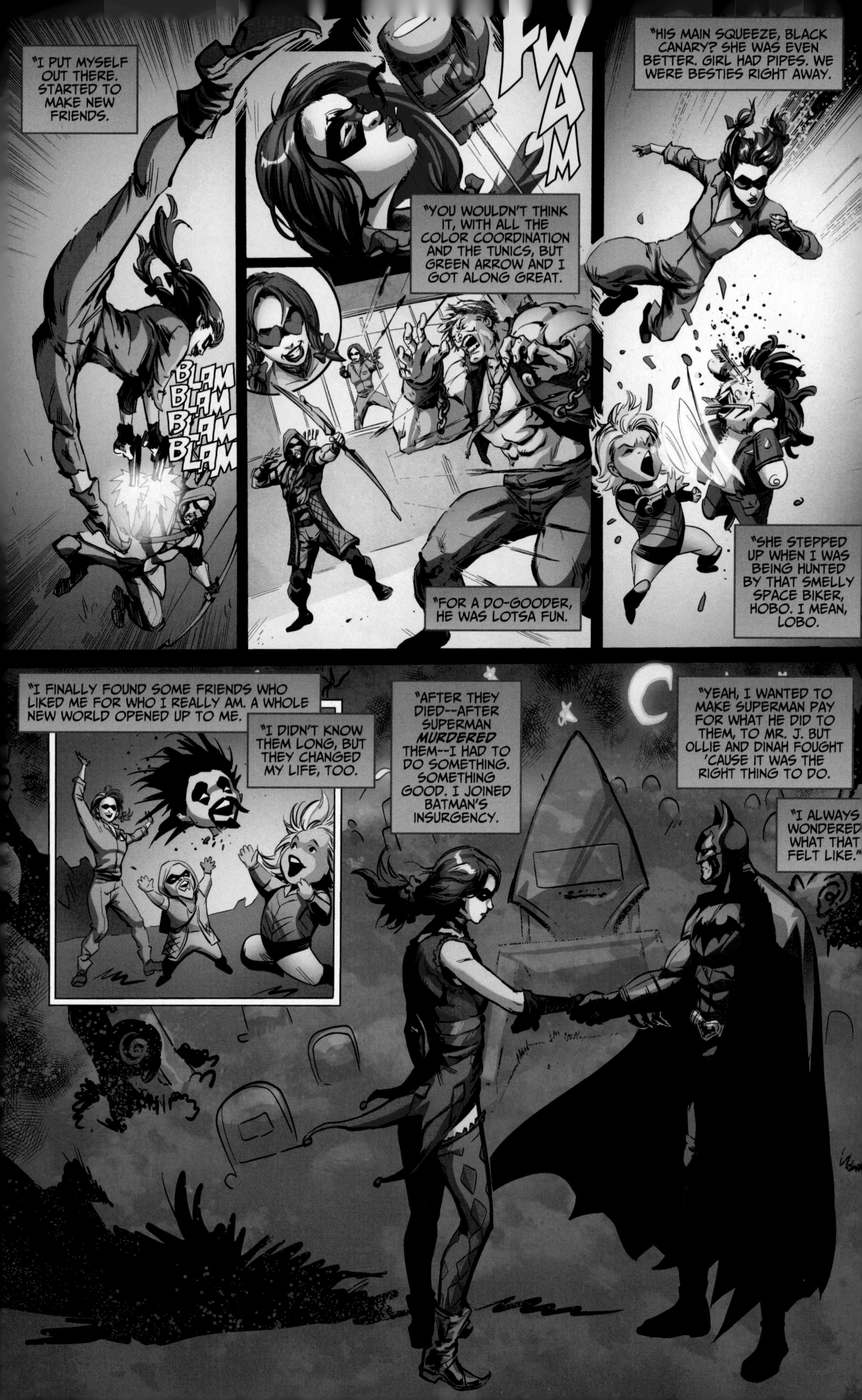

"I PUT MYSELF OUT THERE. STARTED TO MAKE NEW FRIENDS.
BLAM BLAM BLAM BLAM
FWAM
"YOU WOULDN'T THINK IT, WITH ALL THE COLOR COORDINATION AND THE TUNICS, BUT GREEN ARROW AND I GOT ALONG GREAT.
"FOR A DO-GOODER, HE WAS LOTSA FUN.
"HIS MAIN SQUEEZE, BLACK CANARY? SHE WAS EVEN BETTER. GIRL HAD PIPES. WE WERE BESTIES RIGHT AWAY.
"SHE STEPPED UP WHEN I WAS BEING HUNTED BY THAT SMELLY SPACE BIKER, HOBO. I MEAN, LOBO.
"I FINALLY FOUND SOME FRIENDS WHO LIKED ME FOR WHO I REALLY AM. A WHOLE NEW WORLD OPENED UP TO ME.
"I DIDN'T KNOW THEM LONG, BUT THEY CHANGED MY LIFE, TOO.
"AFTER THEY DIED--AFTER SUPERMAN MURDERED THEM--I HAD TO DO SOMETHING. SOMETHING GOOD. I JOINED BATMAN'S INSURGENCY.
"YEAH, I WANTED TO MAKE SUPERMAN PAY FOR WHAT HE DID TO THEM, TO MR. J. BUT OLLIE AND DINAH FOUGHT 'CAUSE IT WAS THE RIGHT THING TO DO.
"I ALWAYS WONDERED WHAT THAT FELT LIKE."

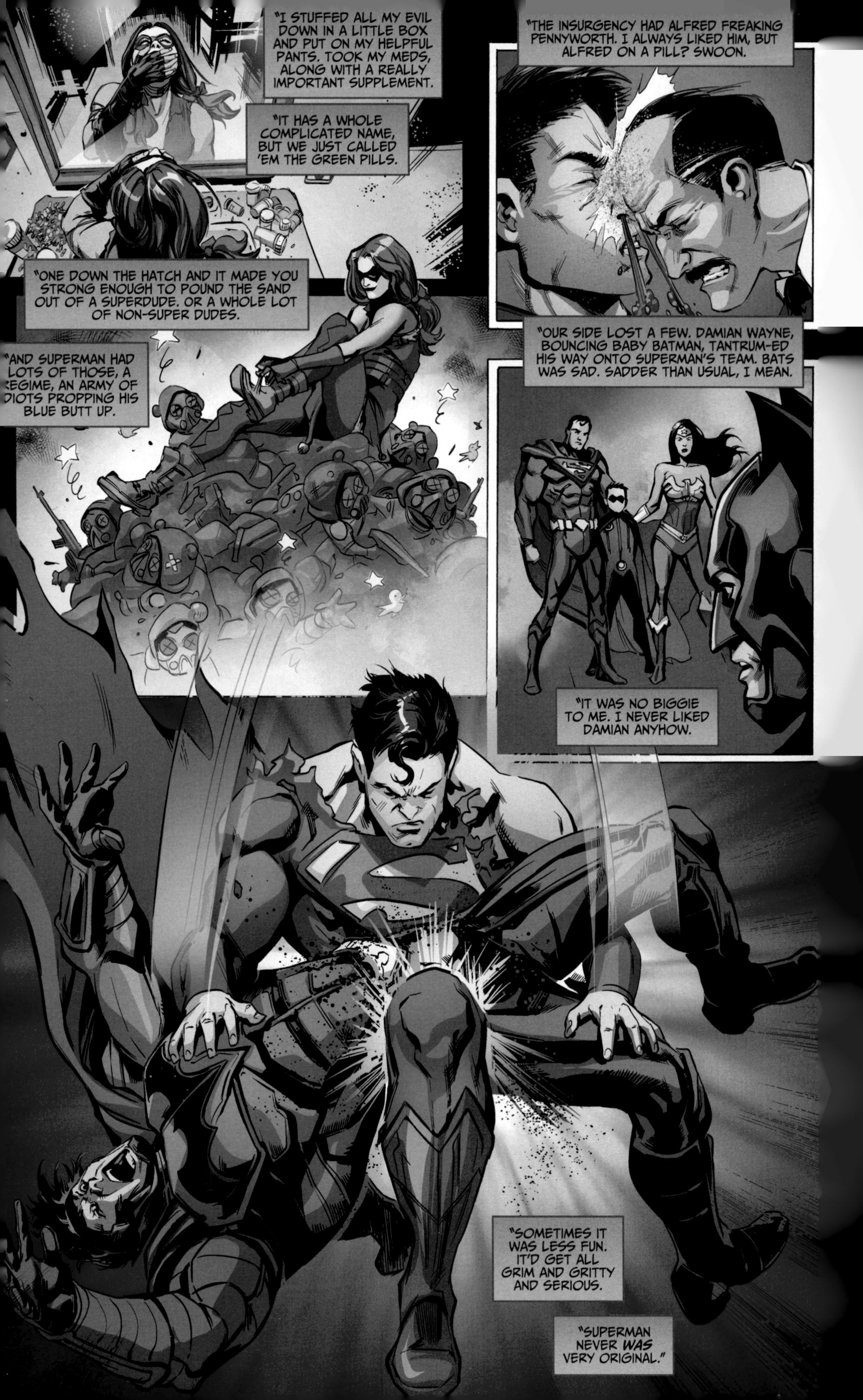
"I STUFFED ALL MY EVIL DOWN IN A LITTLE BOX AND PUT ON MY HELPFUL PANTS. TOOK MY MEDS, ALONG WITH A REALLY IMPORTANT SUPPLEMENT.
"IT HAS A WHOLE COMPLICATED NAME, BUT WE JUST CALLED 'EM THE GREEN PILLS.
"THE INSURGENCY HAD ALFRED FREAKING PENNYWORTH. I ALWAYS LIKED HIM, BUT ALFRED ON A PILL? SWOON.
"ONE DOWN THE HATCH AND IT MADE YOU STRONG ENOUGH TO POUND THE SAND OUT OF A SUPERDUDE. OR A WHOLE LOT OF NON-SUPER DUDES.
"AND SUPERMAN HAD LOTS OF THOSE, A REGIME, AN ARMY OF IDIOTS PROPPING HIS BLUE BUTT UP.
"OUR SIDE LOST A FEW. DAMIAN WAYNE, BOUNCING BABY BATMAN, TANTRUM-ED HIS WAY ONTO SUPERMAN'S TEAM. BATS WAS SAD. SADDER THAN USUAL, I MEAN.
"IT WAS NO BIGGIE TO ME. I NEVER LIKED DAMIAN ANYHOW.
"SOMETIMES IT WAS LESS FUN. IT'D GET ALL GRIM AND GRITTY AND SERIOUS.
"SUPERMAN NEVER WAS VERY ORIGINAL."

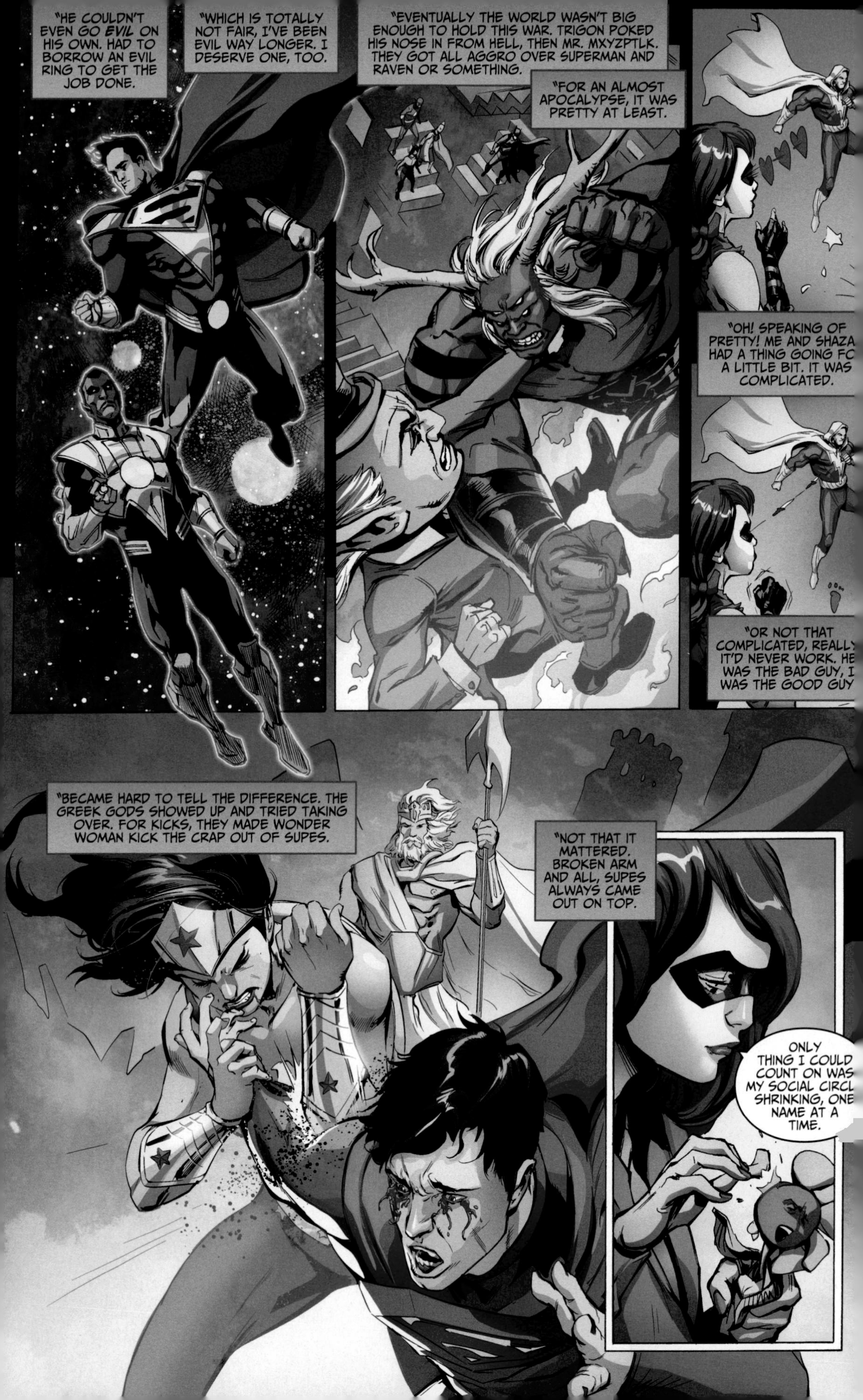
"HE COULDN'T EVEN GO *EVIL* ON HIS OWN. HAD TO BORROW AN EVIL RING TO GET THE JOB DONE.
"WHICH IS TOTALLY NOT FAIR, I'VE BEEN EVIL WAY LONGER. I DESERVE ONE, TOO.
"EVENTUALLY THE WORLD WASN'T BIG ENOUGH TO HOLD THIS WAR. TRIGON POKED HIS NOSE IN FROM HELL, THEN MR. MXYZPTLK. THEY GOT ALL AGGRO OVER SUPERMAN AND RAVEN OR SOMETHING.
"FOR AN ALMOST APOCALYPSE, IT WAS PRETTY AT LEAST.
"OH! SPEAKING OF PRETTY! ME AND SHAZA HAD A THING GOING FO A LITTLE BIT. IT WAS COMPLICATED.
"OR NOT THAT COMPLICATED, REALLY IT'D NEVER WORK. HE WAS THE BAD GUY, I WAS THE GOOD GUY
"BECAME HARD TO TELL THE DIFFERENCE. THE GREEK GODS SHOWED UP AND TRIED TAKING OVER. FOR KICKS, THEY MADE WONDER WOMAN KICK THE CRAP OUT OF SUPES.
"NOT THAT IT MATTERED. BROKEN ARM AND ALL, SUPES ALWAYS CAME OUT ON TOP.
ONLY THING I COULD COUNT ON WAS MY SOCIAL CIRCL SHRINKING, ONE NAME AT A TIME.

TRIED AGAIN. HUNG OUT WITH SOME COOL CHICKS. WE USED TO HATE EACH OTHER. THEN WE HAD A WHOLE TEAM THING GOING. BONDED SUPER TIGHT.

"BUT THAT WORE OFF. I MEAN, TALK ABOUT HOLIER THAN THOU. NO THANKS.

"WHAT I NEEDED WAS MY OWN THING. I HAD TO BE IN CHARGE. BUT WHO?

"THE JOKER CLAN. THEY WERE MISGUIDED DUMMIES. KINDA REMINDED ME OF ME A LONG TIME AGO. VERY PROBLEMATIC.

"THEY NEEDED SOMEONE TO NUDGE THEM IN THE RIGHT DIRECTION, TAKE THE BURDEN OF THINKING OFF THE TABLE.

"I'D DONE MORE WITH LESS. I HAD BIG PLANS FOR MY CREW.

"DON'T GET ME WRONG, I WAS STILL WAY TIGHT WITH THE INSURGENCY. A DEEP COVER OPERATIVE. BATMAN'S SECRET WEAPON.

...IF WE CAN PULL THE PARALLEL DIMENSION VERSIONS OF THEM THROUGH, WE CAN USE THEM TO--

HEY. HEY, BATS. WHAT'CHA DOIN'? NEED SOME HELP?

"ALL I'D EVER WANTED TO DO WAS SMASH HIS FACE INTO PASTE. NOW? BEST FRIENDS.

EVERYTHING ABOUT THE FACTORY IS IN THERE. THEY'RE MAKING GREEN PILLS AND I WANT YOU TO RAID IT.

TAKE AS LONG AS YOU NEED TO.

"LIFE IS FUNNY, RIGHT?"

SLAM

O CAPTAIN MY CAP--

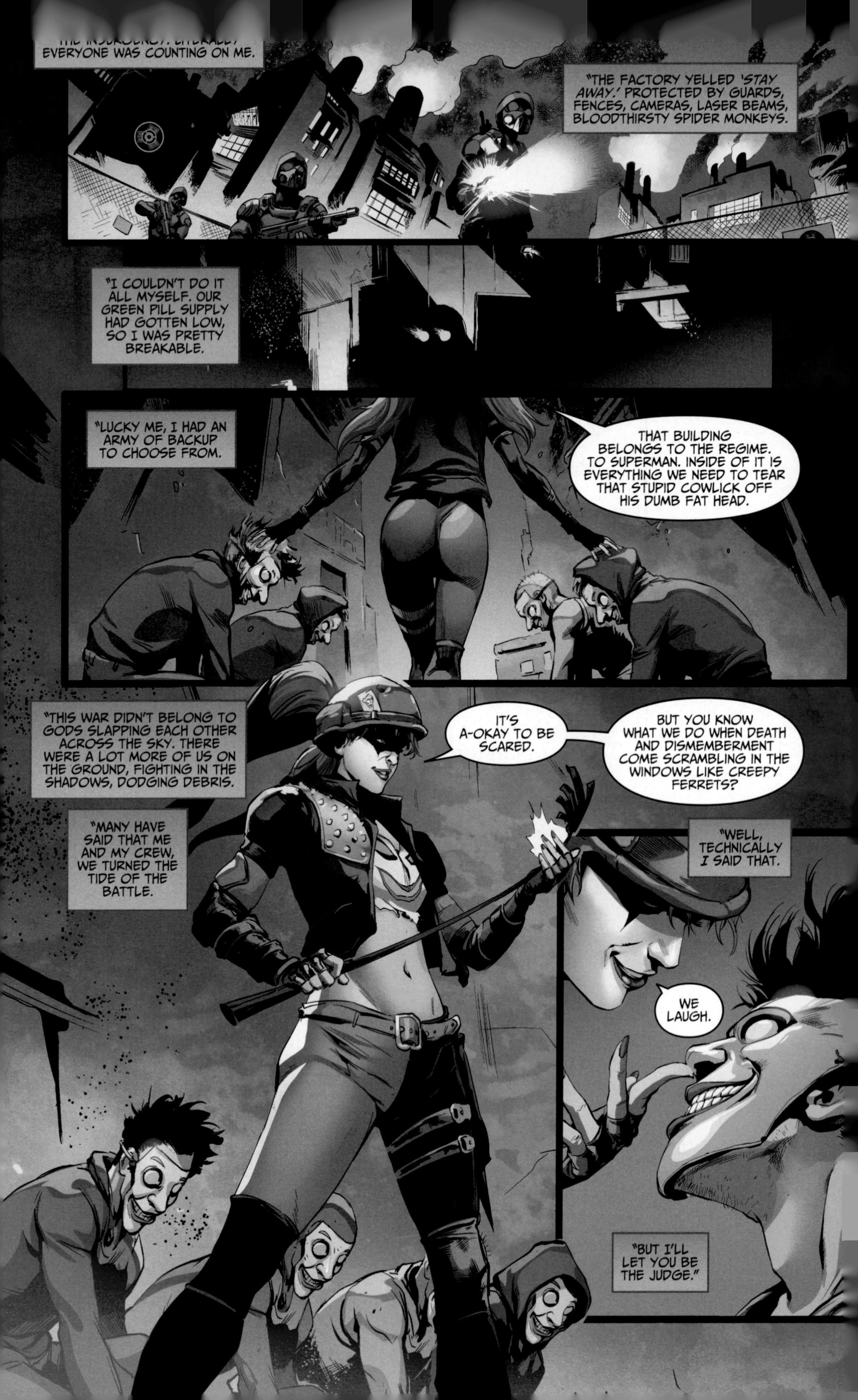
EVERYONE WAS COUNTING ON ME.
"THE FACTORY YELLED 'STAY AWAY.' PROTECTED BY GUARDS, FENCES, CAMERAS, LASER BEAMS, BLOODTHIRSTY SPIDER MONKEYS.
"I COULDN'T DO IT ALL MYSELF. OUR GREEN PILL SUPPLY HAD GOTTEN LOW, SO I WAS PRETTY BREAKABLE.
"LUCKY ME, I HAD AN ARMY OF BACKUP TO CHOOSE FROM.
THAT BUILDING BELONGS TO THE REGIME. TO SUPERMAN. INSIDE OF IT IS EVERYTHING WE NEED TO TEAR THAT STUPID COWLICK OFF HIS DUMB FAT HEAD.
"THIS WAR DIDN'T BELONG TO GODS SLAPPING EACH OTHER ACROSS THE SKY. THERE WERE A LOT MORE OF US ON THE GROUND, FIGHTING IN THE SHADOWS, DODGING DEBRIS.
"MANY HAVE SAID THAT ME AND MY CREW, WE TURNED THE TIDE OF THE BATTLE.
IT'S A-OKAY TO BE SCARED.
BUT YOU KNOW WHAT WE DO WHEN DEATH AND DISMEMBERMENT COME SCRAMBLING IN THE WINDOWS LIKE CREEPY FERRETS?
"WELL, TECHNICALLY I SAID THAT.
WE LAUGH.
"BUT I'LL LET YOU BE THE JUDGE."

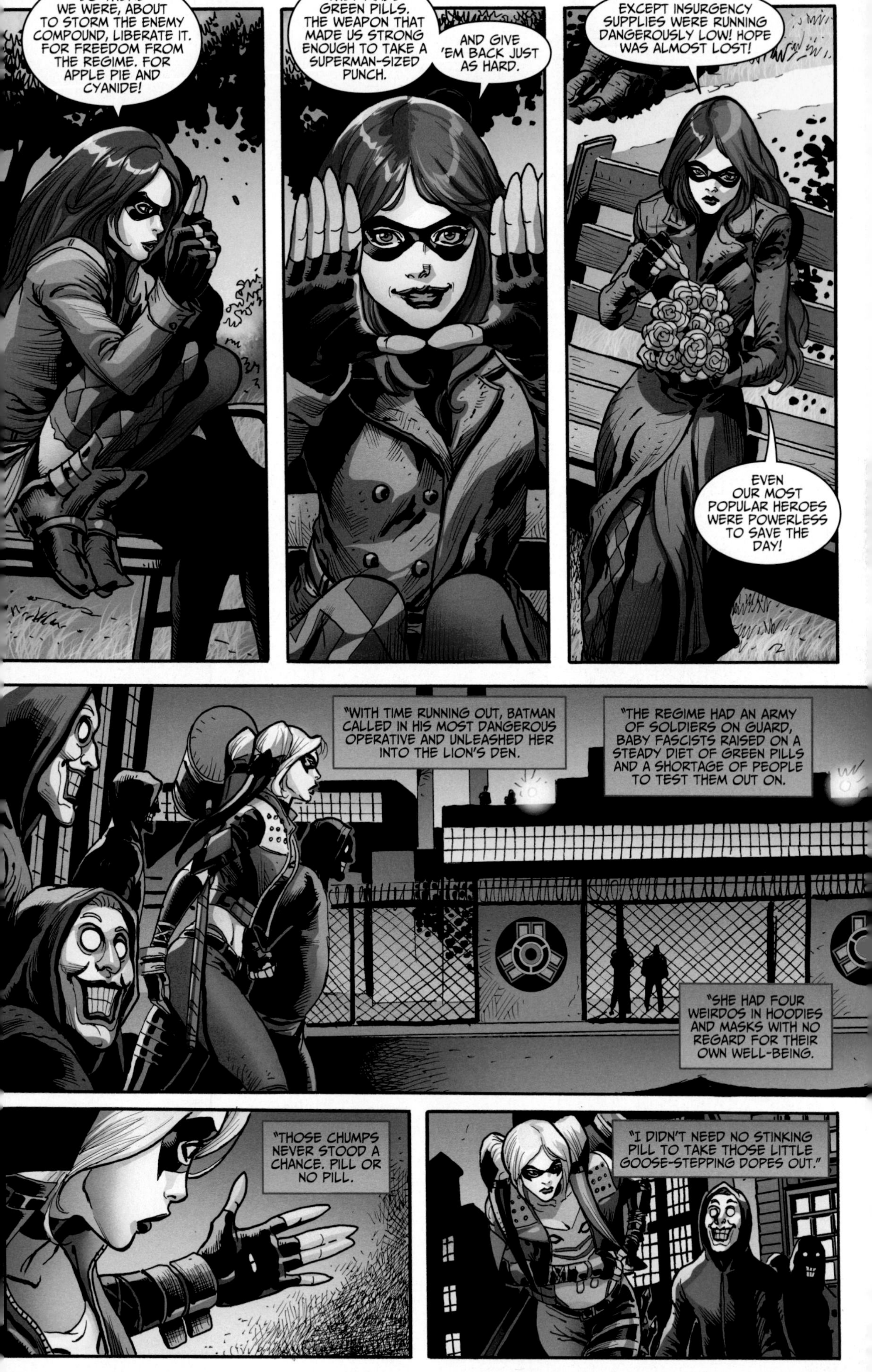
SO THERE WE WERE, ABOUT TO STORM THE ENEMY COMPOUND, LIBERATE IT. FOR FREEDOM FROM THE REGIME. FOR APPLE PIE AND CYANIDE!
THEY MADE GREEN PILLS. THE WEAPON THAT MADE US STRONG ENOUGH TO TAKE A SUPERMAN-SIZED PUNCH.
AND GIVE 'EM BACK JUST AS HARD.
EXCEPT INSURGENCY SUPPLIES WERE RUNNING DANGEROUSLY LOW! HOPE WAS ALMOST LOST!
EVEN OUR MOST POPULAR HEROES WERE POWERLESS TO SAVE THE DAY!
"WITH TIME RUNNING OUT, BATMAN CALLED IN HIS MOST DANGEROUS OPERATIVE AND UNLEASHED HER INTO THE LION'S DEN.
"THE REGIME HAD AN ARMY OF SOLDIERS ON GUARD, BABY FASCISTS RAISED ON A STEADY DIET OF GREEN PILLS AND A SHORTAGE OF PEOPLE TO TEST THEM OUT ON.
"SHE HAD FOUR WEIRDOS IN HOODIES AND MASKS WITH NO REGARD FOR THEIR OWN WELL-BEING.
"THOSE CHUMPS NEVER STOOD A CHANCE. PILL OR NO PILL.
"I DIDN'T NEED NO STINKING PILL TO TAKE THOSE LITTLE GOOSE-STEPPING DOPES OUT."

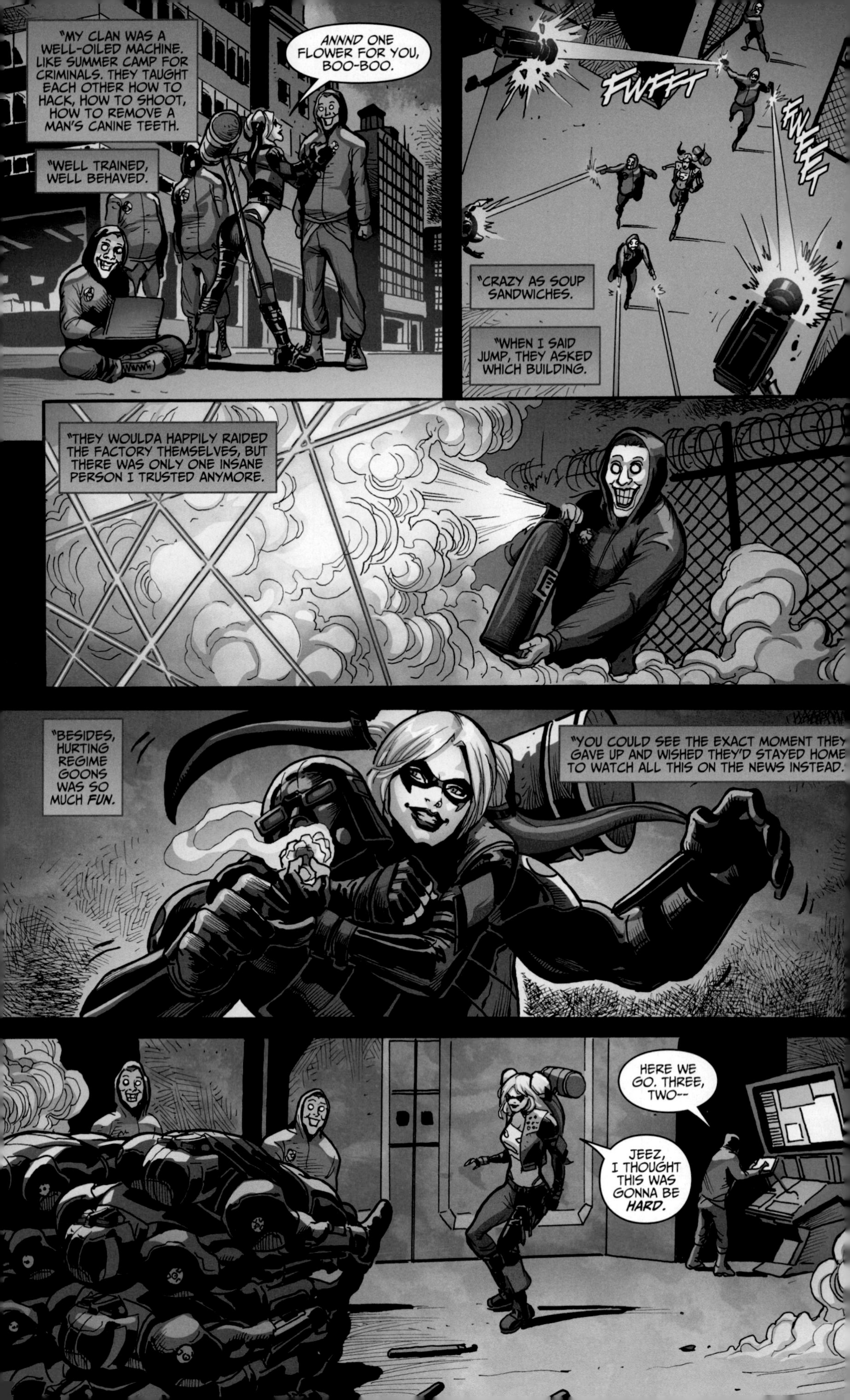
"MY CLAN WAS A WELL-OILED MACHINE. LIKE SUMMER CAMP FOR CRIMINALS. THEY TAUGHT EACH OTHER HOW TO HACK, HOW TO SHOOT, HOW TO REMOVE A MAN'S CANINE TEETH.
ANNND ONE FLOWER FOR YOU, BOO-BOO.
"WELL TRAINED, WELL BEHAVED.
FWFFT
FWFFFT
"CRAZY AS SOUP SANDWICHES.
"WHEN I SAID JUMP, THEY ASKED WHICH BUILDING.
"THEY WOULDA HAPPILY RAIDED THE FACTORY THEMSELVES, BUT THERE WAS ONLY ONE INSANE PERSON I TRUSTED ANYMORE.
"BESIDES, HURTING REGIME GOONS WAS SO MUCH FUN.
"YOU COULD SEE THE EXACT MOMENT THEY GAVE UP AND WISHED THEY'D STAYED HOME TO WATCH ALL THIS ON THE NEWS INSTEAD.
HERE WE GO. THREE, TWO--
JEEZ, I THOUGHT THIS WAS GONNA BE HARD.

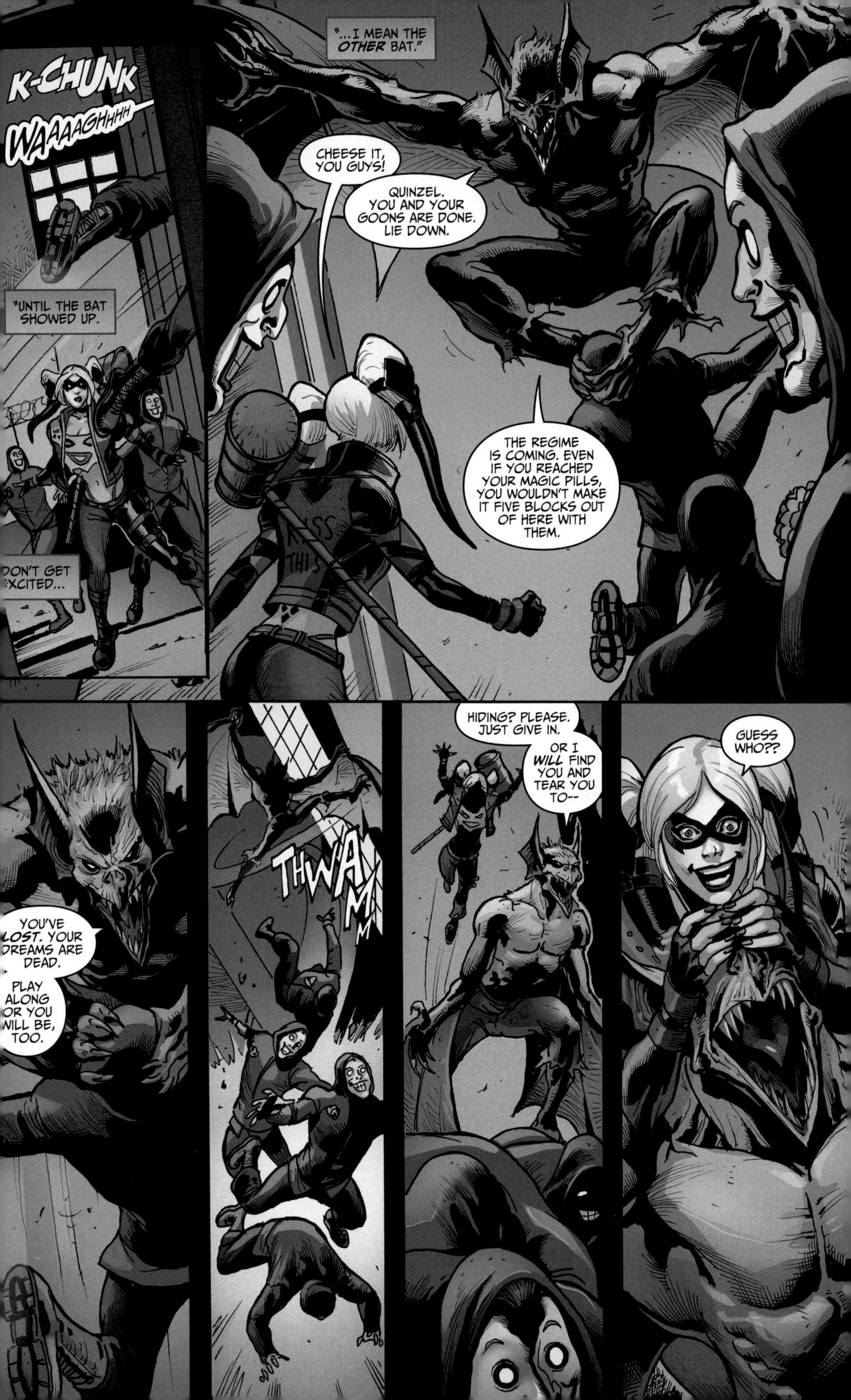
K-CHUNK
WAAAAGHHHH
"UNTIL THE BAT SHOWED UP.
DON'T GET EXCITED...
"...I MEAN THE OTHER BAT."
CHEESE IT, YOU GUYS!
QUINZEL. YOU AND YOUR GOONS ARE DONE. LIE DOWN.
THE REGIME IS COMING. EVEN IF YOU REACHED YOUR MAGIC PILLS, YOU WOULDN'T MAKE IT FIVE BLOCKS OUT OF HERE WITH THEM.
YOU'VE LOST. YOUR DREAMS ARE DEAD.
PLAY ALONG OR YOU WILL BE, TOO.
THWAM
HIDING? PLEASE. JUST GIVE IN.
OR I WILL FIND YOU AND TEAR YOU TO--
GUESS WHO??

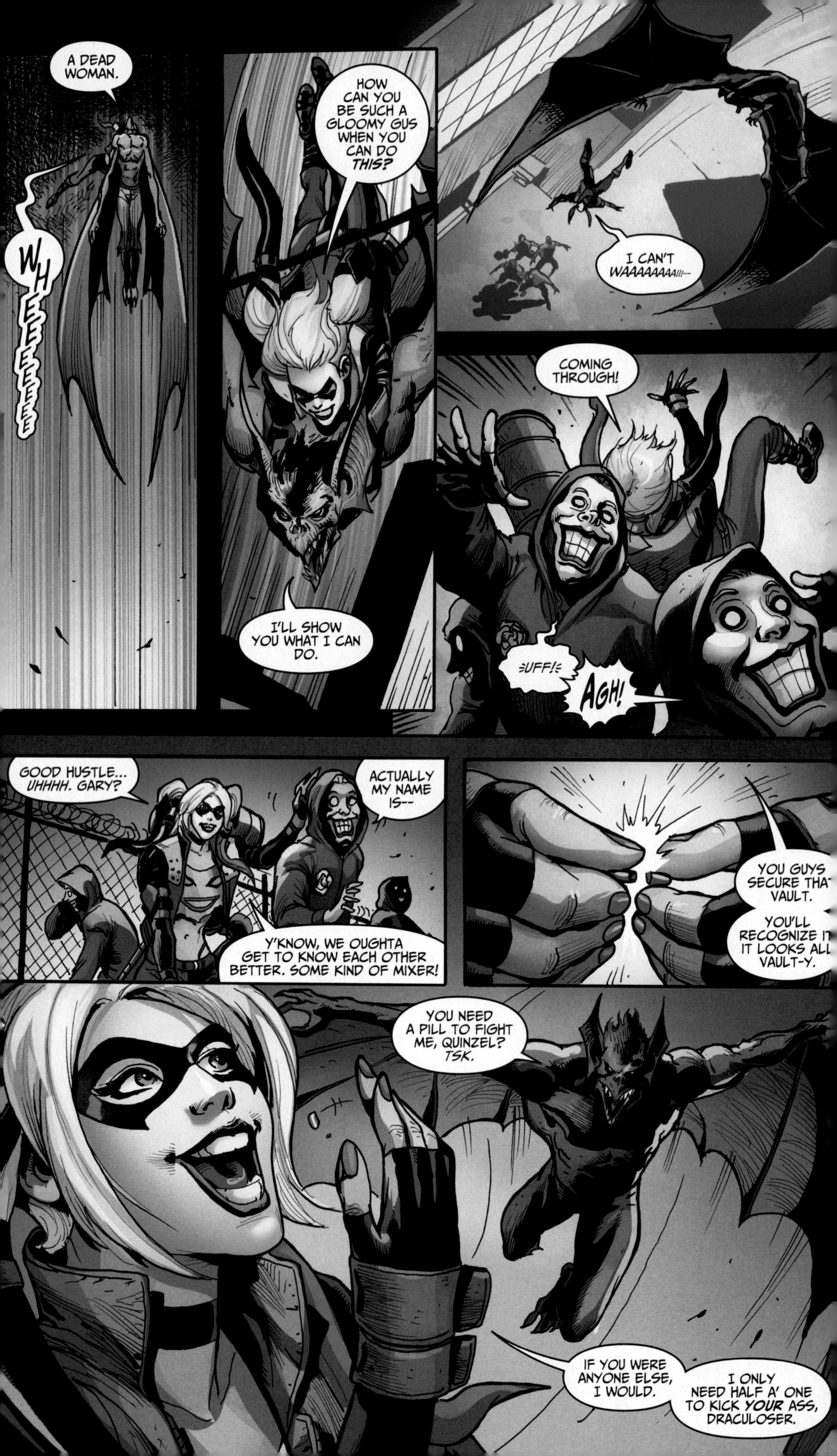
A DEAD WOMAN.
WHEEEEEEEE
HOW CAN YOU BE SUCH A GLOOMY GUS WHEN YOU CAN DO *THIS?*
I'LL SHOW YOU WHAT I CAN DO.
I CAN'T *WAAAAAAAA!!!--*
COMING THROUGH!
UFF!
AGH!
GOOD HUSTLE... *UHHHH.* GARY?
ACTUALLY MY NAME IS--
Y'KNOW, WE OUGHTA GET TO KNOW EACH OTHER BETTER. SOME KIND OF MIXER!
YOU GUYS SECURE THAT VAULT.
YOU'LL RECOGNIZE IT. IT LOOKS ALL VAULT-Y.
YOU NEED A PILL TO FIGHT ME, QUINZEL? *TSK.*
IF YOU WERE ANYONE ELSE, I WOULD.
I ONLY NEED HALF A' ONE TO KICK *YOUR* ASS, DRACULOSER.

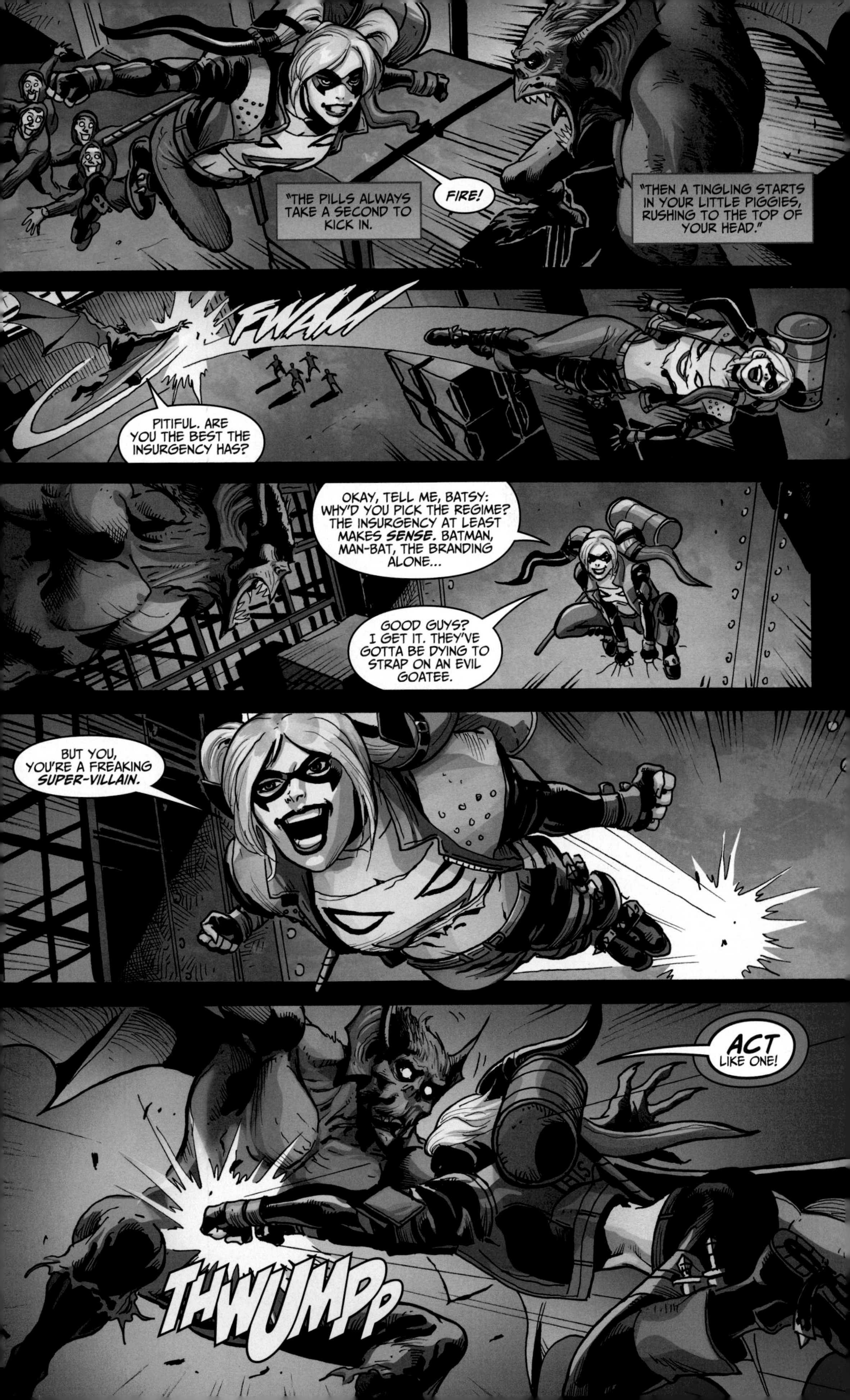
"THE PILLS ALWAYS TAKE A SECOND TO KICK IN.
FIRE!
"THEN A TINGLING STARTS IN YOUR LITTLE PIGGIES, RUSHING TO THE TOP OF YOUR HEAD."
FWAM
PITIFUL. ARE YOU THE BEST THE INSURGENCY HAS?
OKAY, TELL ME, BATSY: WHY'D YOU PICK THE REGIME? THE INSURGENCY AT LEAST MAKES SENSE. BATMAN, MAN-BAT, THE BRANDING ALONE...
GOOD GUYS? I GET IT. THEY'VE GOTTA BE DYING TO STRAP ON AN EVIL GOATEE.
BUT YOU, YOU'RE A FREAKING SUPER-VILLAIN.
ACT LIKE ONE!
THWUMPP

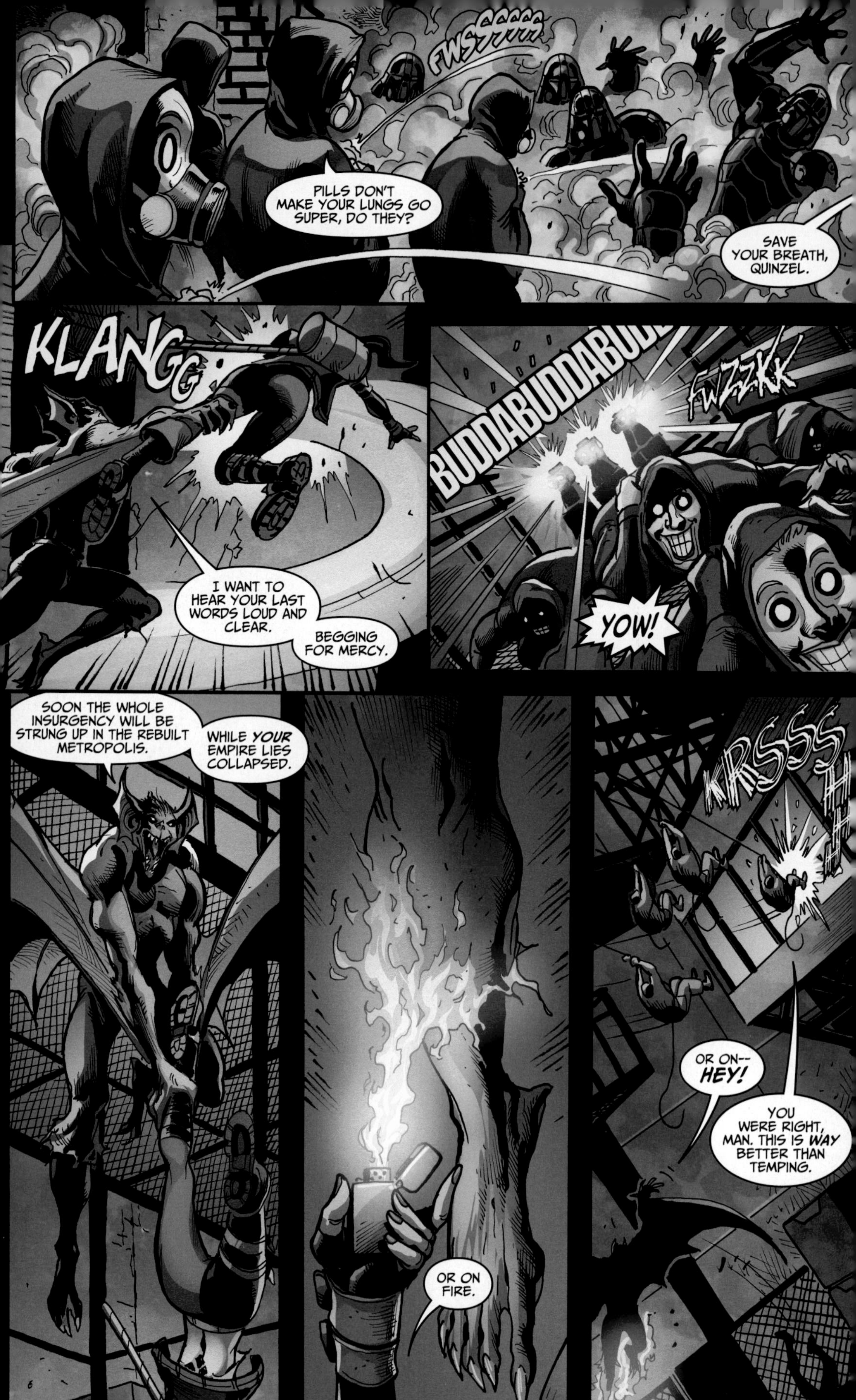
FWSSSSSS
PILLS DON'T MAKE YOUR LUNGS GO SUPER, DO THEY?
SAVE YOUR BREATH, QUINZEL.
KLANGG
I WANT TO HEAR YOUR LAST WORDS LOUD AND CLEAR.
BEGGING FOR MERCY.
BUDDABUDDABUDD
FWZZKK
YOW!
SOON THE WHOLE INSURGENCY WILL BE STRUNG UP IN THE REBUILT METROPOLIS.
WHILE YOUR EMPIRE LIES COLLAPSED.
OR ON FIRE.
KRSSSH
OR ON-- HEY!
YOU WERE RIGHT, MAN. THIS IS WAY BETTER THAN TEMPING.

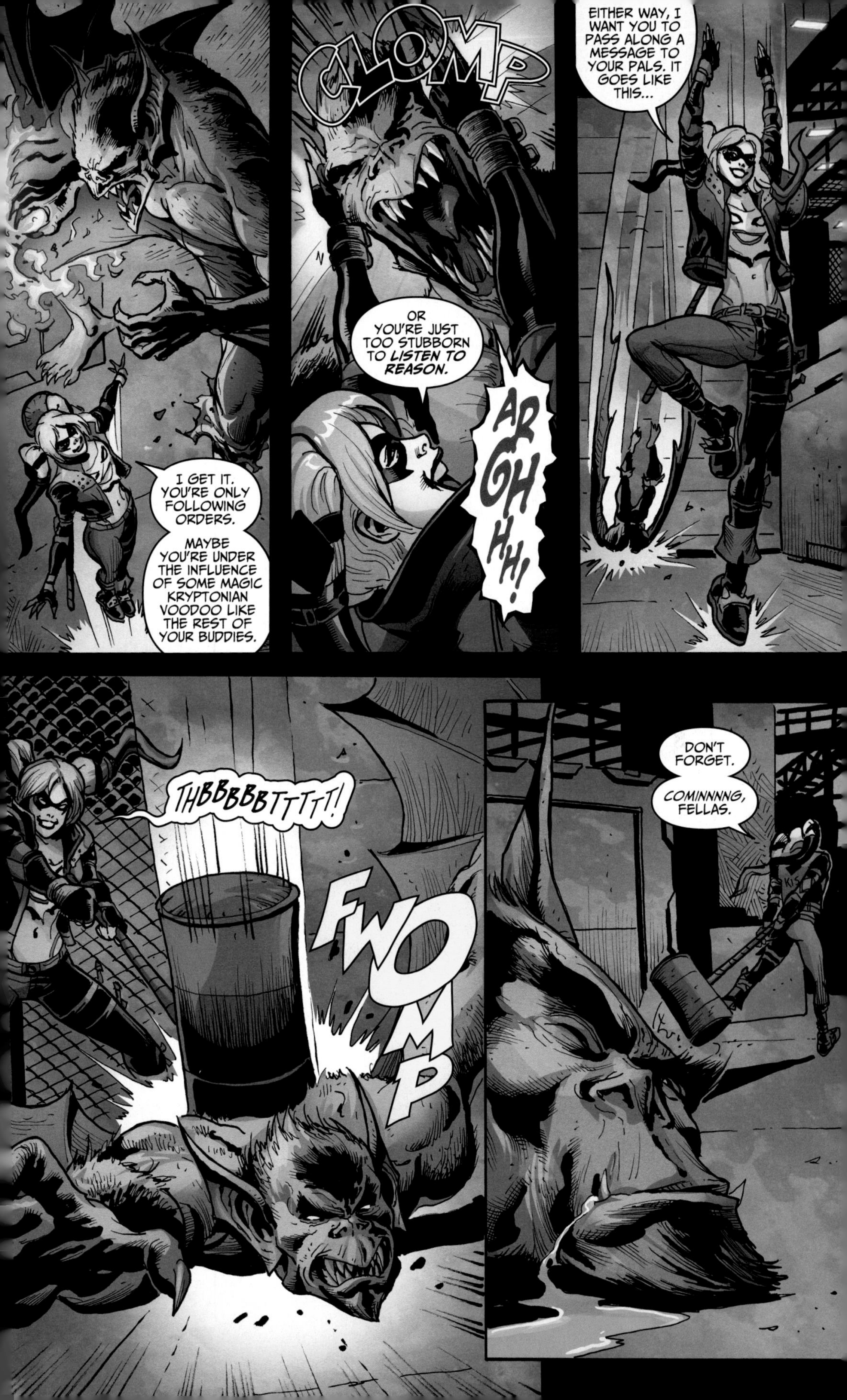
I GET IT. YOU'RE ONLY FOLLOWING ORDERS.
MAYBE YOU'RE UNDER THE INFLUENCE OF SOME MAGIC KRYPTONIAN VOODOO LIKE THE REST OF YOUR BUDDIES.
CLOMP
OR YOU'RE JUST TOO STUBBORN TO *LISTEN TO REASON.*
ARGHHH!
EITHER WAY, I WANT YOU TO PASS ALONG A MESSAGE TO YOUR PALS. IT GOES LIKE THIS...
THBBBBBTTTTT!
FWOMP
DON'T FORGET.
COMINNNNG, FELLAS.

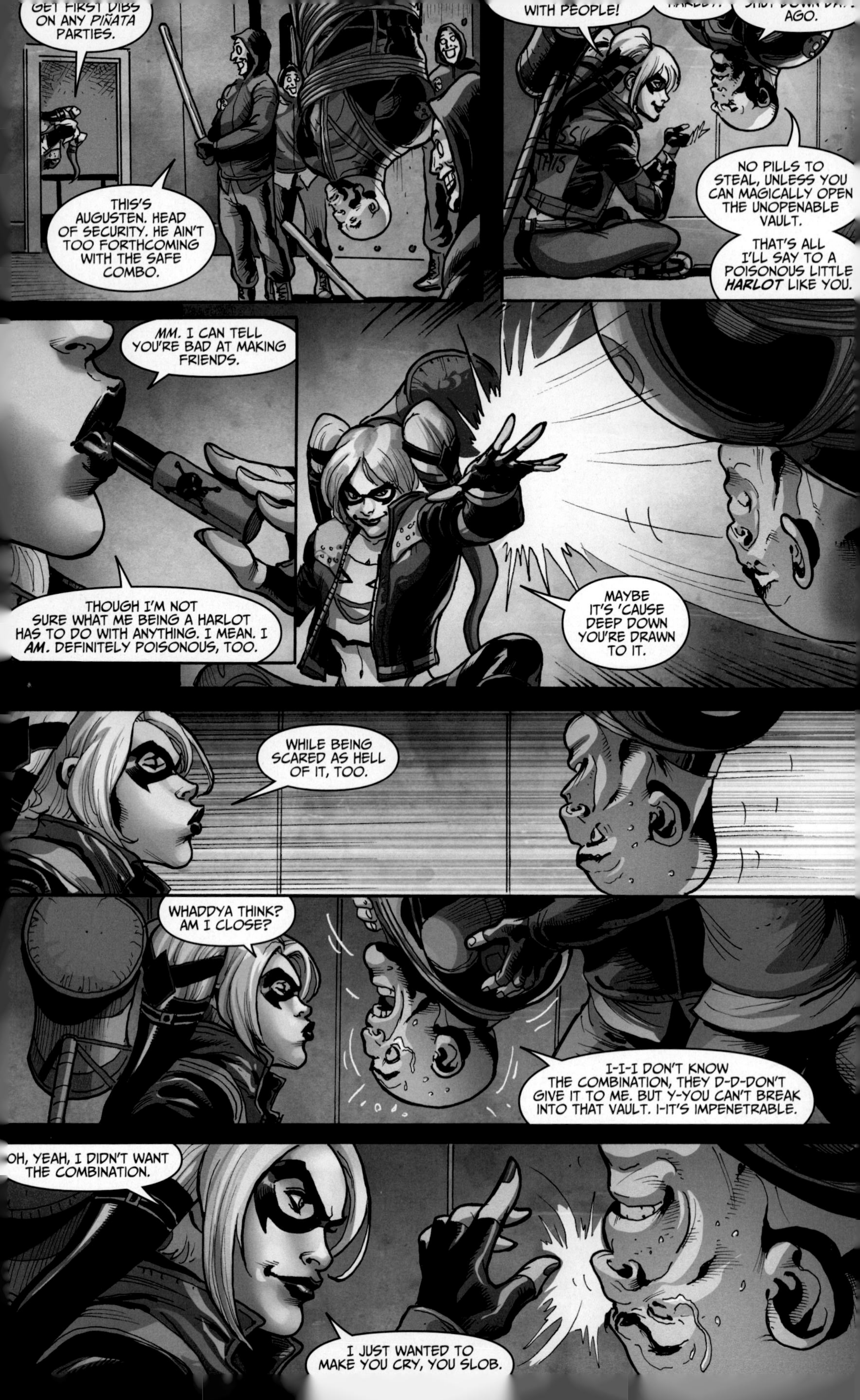
GET FIRST DIBS ON ANY PIÑATA PARTIES.
THIS'S AUGUSTEN. HEAD OF SECURITY. HE AIN'T TOO FORTHCOMING WITH THE SAFE COMBO.
WITH PEOPLE!
AGO.
NO PILLS TO STEAL, UNLESS YOU CAN MAGICALLY OPEN THE UNOPENABLE VAULT.
THAT'S ALL I'LL SAY TO A POISONOUS LITTLE HARLOT LIKE YOU.
MM. I CAN TELL YOU'RE BAD AT MAKING FRIENDS.
THOUGH I'M NOT SURE WHAT ME BEING A HARLOT HAS TO DO WITH ANYTHING. I MEAN. I AM. DEFINITELY POISONOUS, TOO.
MAYBE IT'S 'CAUSE DEEP DOWN YOU'RE DRAWN TO IT.
WHILE BEING SCARED AS HELL OF IT, TOO.
WHADDYA THINK? AM I CLOSE?
I-I-I DON'T KNOW THE COMBINATION, THEY D-D-DON'T GIVE IT TO ME. BUT Y-YOU CAN'T BREAK INTO THAT VAULT. I-IT'S IMPENETRABLE.
OH, YEAH, I DIDN'T WANT THE COMBINATION.
I JUST WANTED TO MAKE YOU CRY, YOU SLOB.

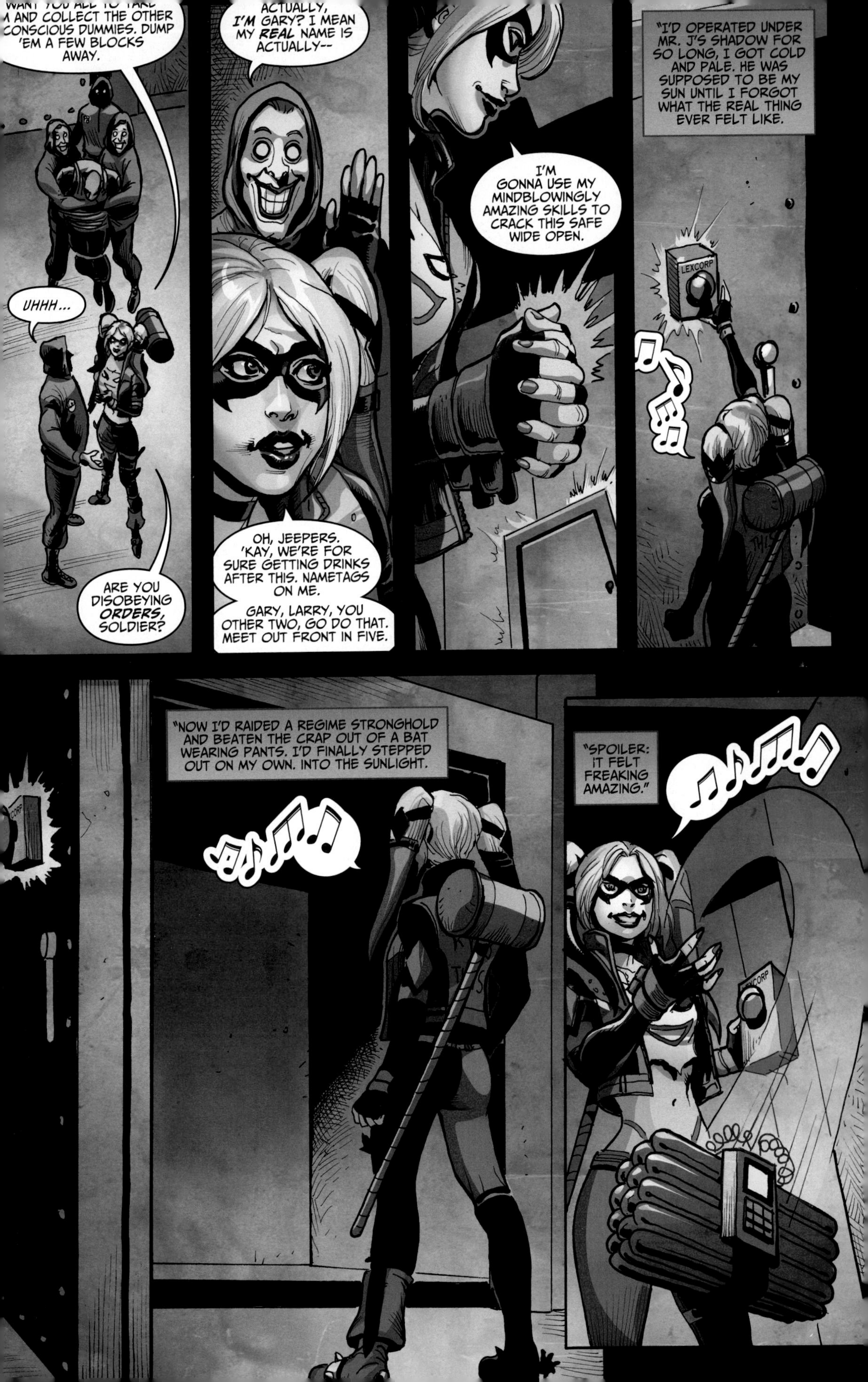
WANT YOU ALL TO TAKE
M AND COLLECT THE OTHER CONSCIOUS DUMMIES. DUMP 'EM A FEW BLOCKS AWAY.
UHHH...
ARE YOU DISOBEYING ORDERS, SOLDIER?
ACTUALLY, I'M GARY? I MEAN MY REAL NAME IS ACTUALLY--
OH, JEEPERS. 'KAY, WE'RE FOR SURE GETTING DRINKS AFTER THIS. NAMETAGS ON ME.
GARY, LARRY, YOU OTHER TWO, GO DO THAT. MEET OUT FRONT IN FIVE.
I'M GONNA USE MY MINDBLOWINGLY AMAZING SKILLS TO CRACK THIS SAFE WIDE OPEN.
"I'D OPERATED UNDER MR. J'S SHADOW FOR SO LONG, I GOT COLD AND PALE. HE WAS SUPPOSED TO BE MY SUN UNTIL I FORGOT WHAT THE REAL THING EVER FELT LIKE.
LEXCORP
"NOW I'D RAIDED A REGIME STRONGHOLD AND BEATEN THE CRAP OUT OF A BAT WEARING PANTS. I'D FINALLY STEPPED OUT ON MY OWN. INTO THE SUNLIGHT.
"SPOILER: IT FELT FREAKING AMAZING."

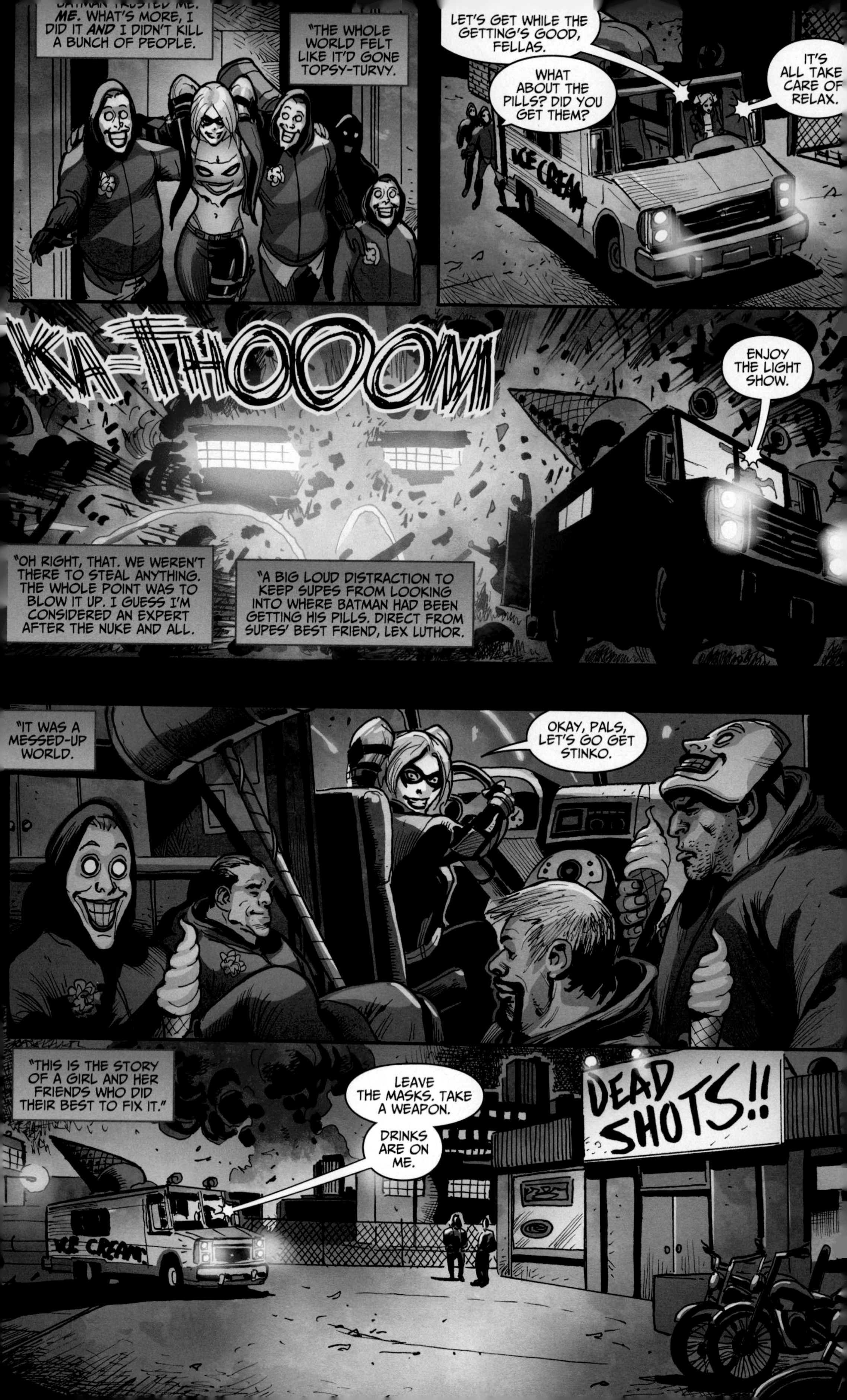
ME. WHAT'S MORE, I DID IT AND I DIDN'T KILL A BUNCH OF PEOPLE.
"THE WHOLE WORLD FELT LIKE IT'D GONE TOPSY-TURVY.
LET'S GET WHILE THE GETTING'S GOOD, FELLAS.
WHAT ABOUT THE PILLS? DID YOU GET THEM?
IT'S ALL TAKE CARE OF. RELAX.
ICE CREAM
KA-THOOOOM
ENJOY THE LIGHT SHOW.
"OH RIGHT, THAT. WE WEREN'T THERE TO STEAL ANYTHING. THE WHOLE POINT WAS TO BLOW IT UP. I GUESS I'M CONSIDERED AN EXPERT AFTER THE NUKE AND ALL.
"A BIG LOUD DISTRACTION TO KEEP SUPES FROM LOOKING INTO WHERE BATMAN HAD BEEN GETTING HIS PILLS. DIRECT FROM SUPES' BEST FRIEND, LEX LUTHOR.
"IT WAS A MESSED-UP WORLD.
OKAY, PALS, LET'S GO GET STINKO.
"THIS IS THE STORY OF A GIRL AND HER FRIENDS WHO DID THEIR BEST TO FIX IT."
LEAVE THE MASKS. TAKE A WEAPON.
DRINKS ARE ON ME.
DEAD SHOTS!!
ICE CREAM

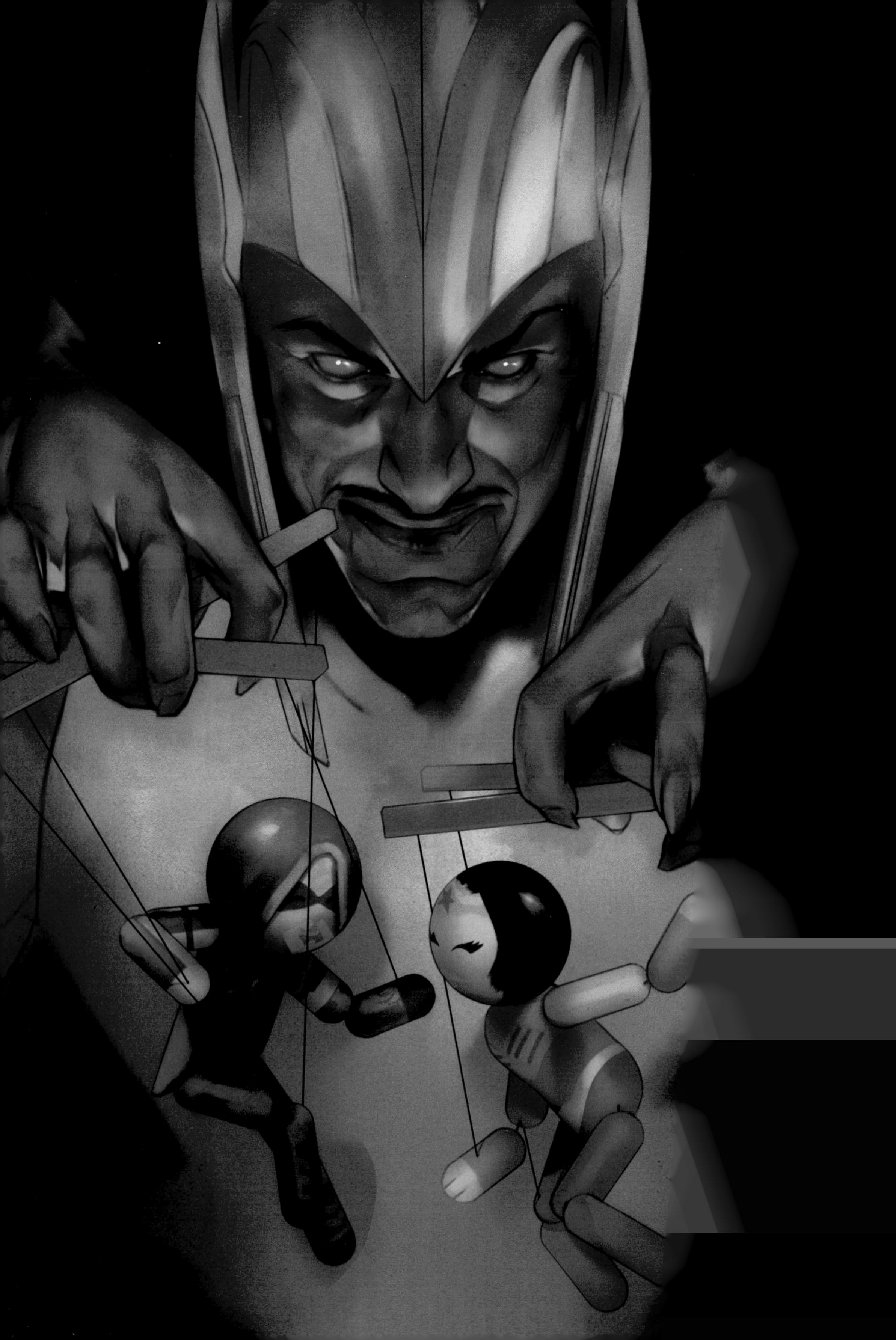

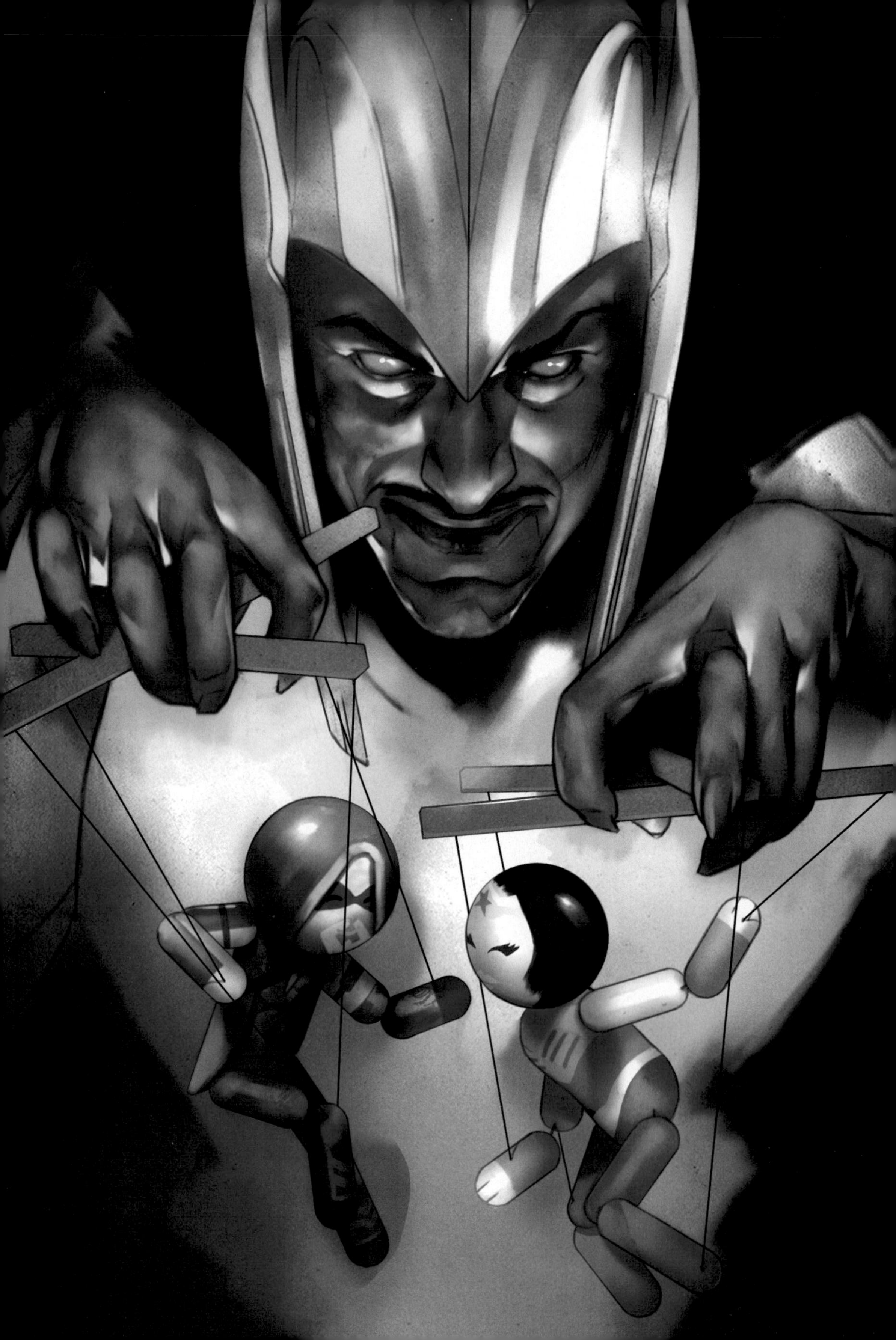

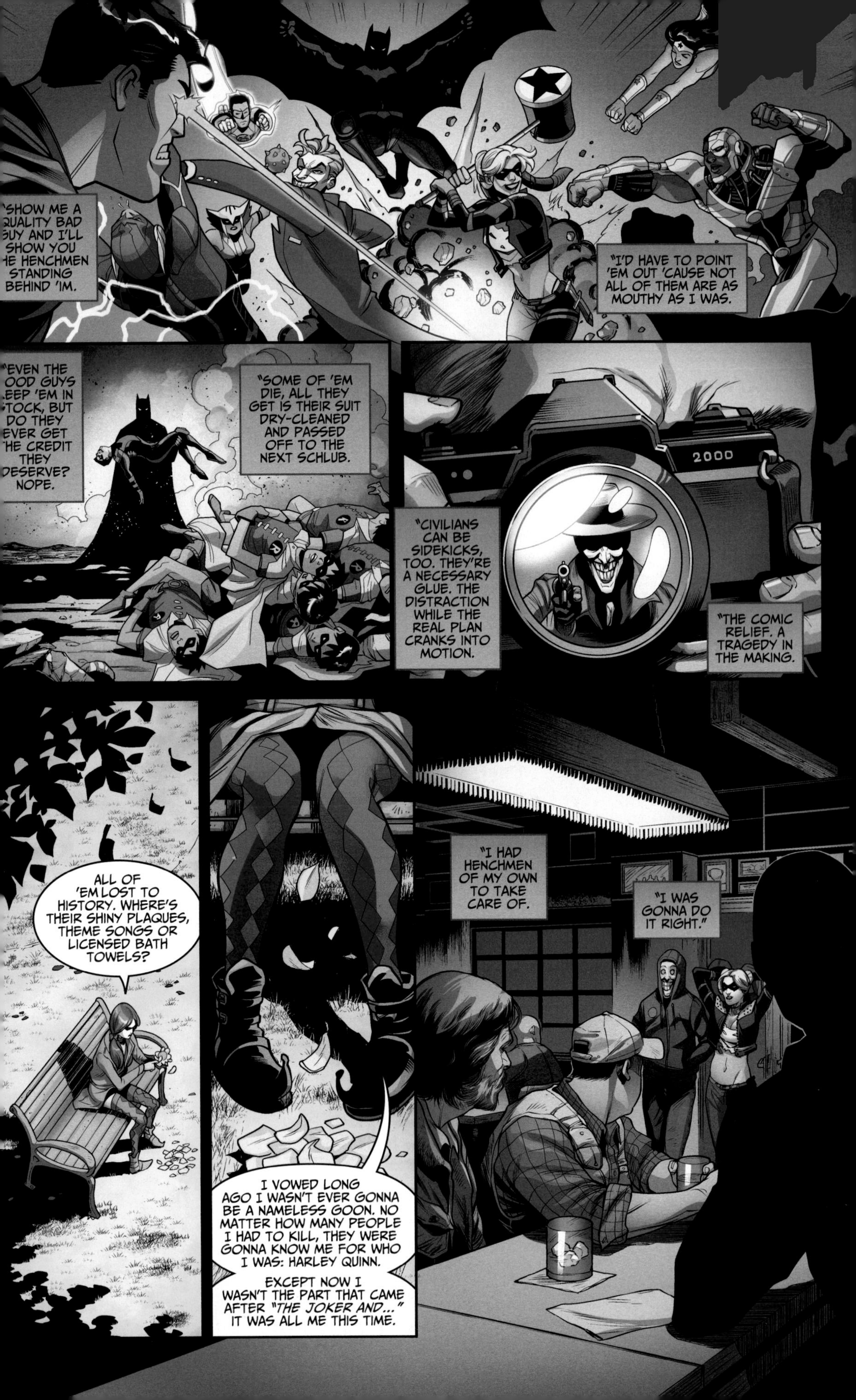
"SHOW ME A QUALITY BAD GUY AND I'LL SHOW YOU HE HENCHMEN STANDING BEHIND 'IM.
"I'D HAVE TO POINT 'EM OUT 'CAUSE NOT ALL OF THEM ARE AS MOUTHY AS I WAS.
"EVEN THE OOD GUYS EEP 'EM IN TOCK, BUT DO THEY EVER GET HE CREDIT THEY DESERVE? NOPE.
"SOME OF 'EM DIE, ALL THEY GET IS THEIR SUIT DRY-CLEANED AND PASSED OFF TO THE NEXT SCHLUB.
2000
"CIVILIANS CAN BE SIDEKICKS, TOO. THEY'RE A NECESSARY GLUE. THE DISTRACTION WHILE THE REAL PLAN CRANKS INTO MOTION.
"THE COMIC RELIEF. A TRAGEDY IN THE MAKING.
ALL OF 'EM LOST TO HISTORY. WHERE'S THEIR SHINY PLAQUES, THEME SONGS OR LICENSED BATH TOWELS?
I VOWED LONG AGO I WASN'T EVER GONNA BE A NAMELESS GOON. NO MATTER HOW MANY PEOPLE I HAD TO KILL, THEY WERE GONNA KNOW ME FOR WHO I WAS: HARLEY QUINN.
EXCEPT NOW I WASN'T THE PART THAT CAME AFTER "THE JOKER AND..." IT WAS ALL ME THIS TIME.
"I HAD HENCHMEN OF MY OWN TO TAKE CARE OF.
"I WAS GONNA DO IT RIGHT."

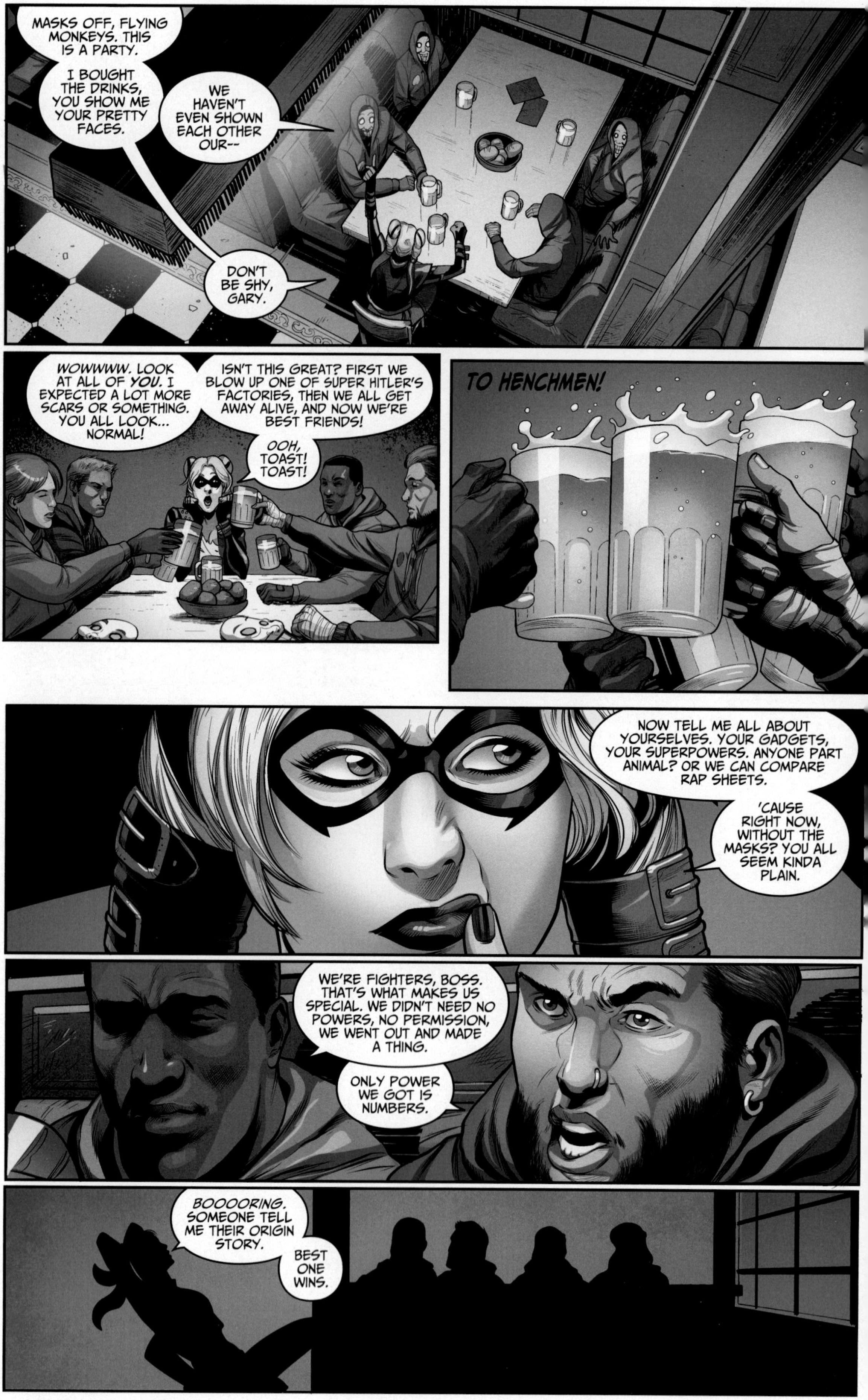
MASKS OFF, FLYING MONKEYS. THIS IS A PARTY.
I BOUGHT THE DRINKS, YOU SHOW ME YOUR PRETTY FACES.
WE HAVEN'T EVEN SHOWN EACH OTHER OUR--
DON'T BE SHY, GARY.
WOWWWW. LOOK AT ALL OF YOU. I EXPECTED A LOT MORE SCARS OR SOMETHING. YOU ALL LOOK... NORMAL!
ISN'T THIS GREAT? FIRST WE BLOW UP ONE OF SUPER HITLER'S FACTORIES, THEN WE ALL GET AWAY ALIVE, AND NOW WE'RE BEST FRIENDS!
OOH, TOAST! TOAST!
TO HENCHMEN!
NOW TELL ME ALL ABOUT YOURSELVES. YOUR GADGETS, YOUR SUPERPOWERS. ANYONE PART ANIMAL? OR WE CAN COMPARE RAP SHEETS.
'CAUSE RIGHT NOW, WITHOUT THE MASKS? YOU ALL SEEM KINDA PLAIN.
WE'RE FIGHTERS, BOSS. THAT'S WHAT MAKES US SPECIAL. WE DIDN'T NEED NO POWERS, NO PERMISSION, WE WENT OUT AND MADE A THING.
ONLY POWER WE GOT IS NUMBERS.
BOOOORING. SOMEONE TELL ME THEIR ORIGIN STORY.
BEST ONE WINS.

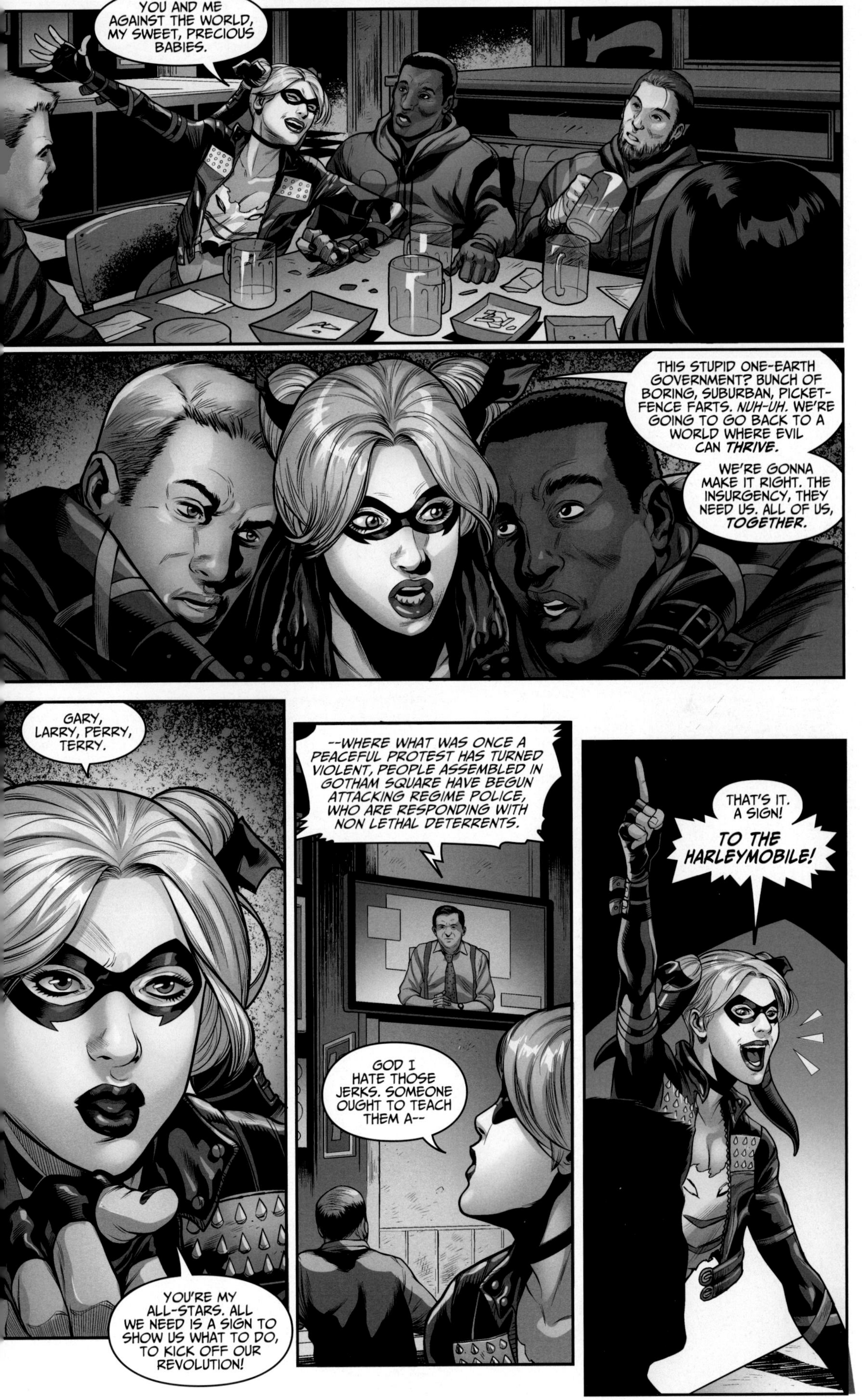

YOU AND ME AGAINST THE WORLD, MY SWEET, PRECIOUS BABIES.
THIS STUPID ONE-EARTH GOVERNMENT? BUNCH OF BORING, SUBURBAN, PICKET-FENCE FARTS. NUH-UH. WE'RE GOING TO GO BACK TO A WORLD WHERE EVIL CAN THRIVE.
WE'RE GONNA MAKE IT RIGHT. THE INSURGENCY, THEY NEED US. ALL OF US, TOGETHER.
GARY, LARRY, PERRY, TERRY.
YOU'RE MY ALL-STARS. ALL WE NEED IS A SIGN TO SHOW US WHAT TO DO, TO KICK OFF OUR REVOLUTION!
--WHERE WHAT WAS ONCE A PEACEFUL PROTEST HAS TURNED VIOLENT, PEOPLE ASSEMBLED IN GOTHAM SQUARE HAVE BEGUN ATTACKING REGIME POLICE, WHO ARE RESPONDING WITH NON LETHAL DETERRENTS.
GOD I HATE THOSE JERKS. SOMEONE OUGHT TO TEACH THEM A--
THAT'S IT. A SIGN!
TO THE HARLEYMOBILE!

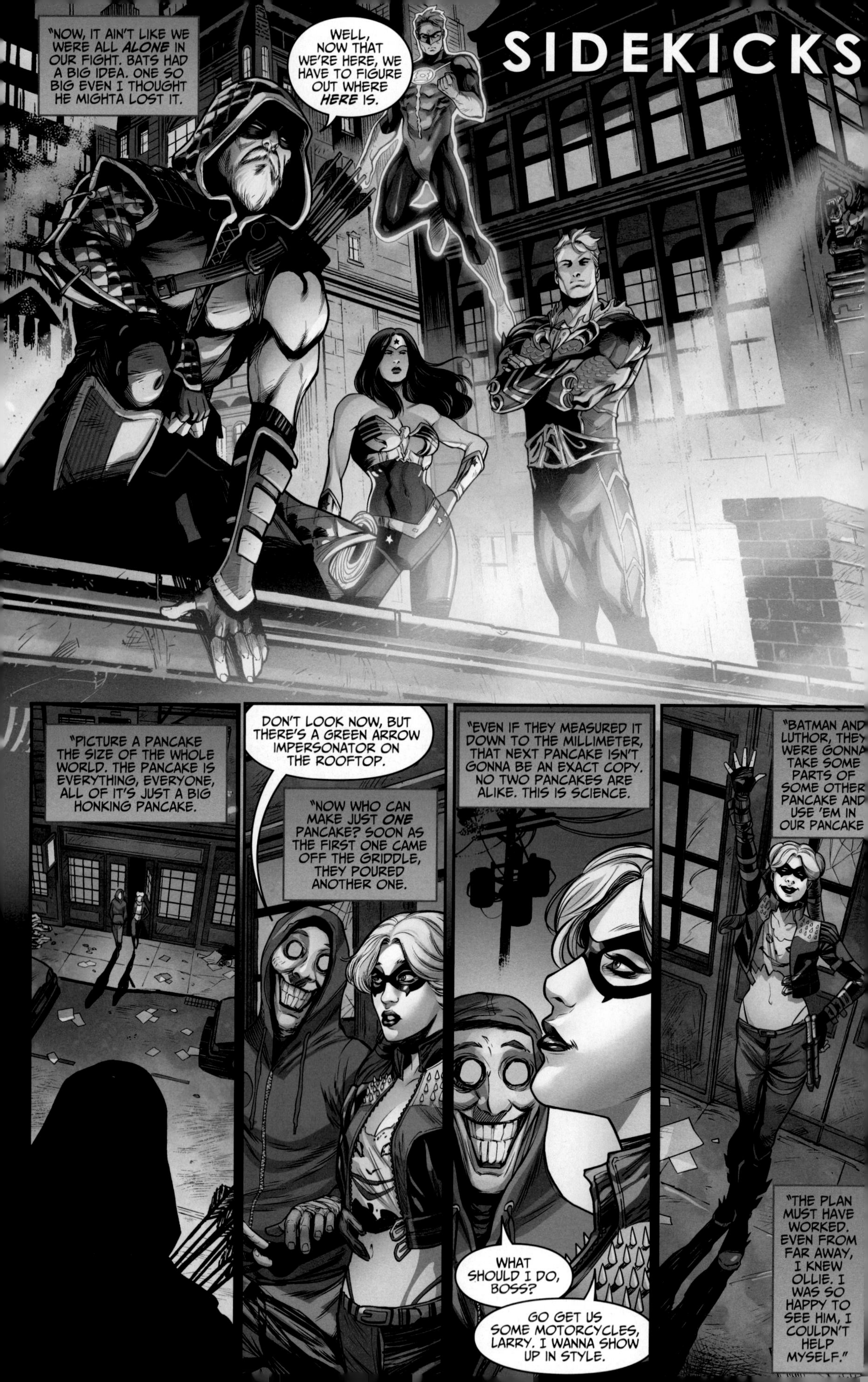
SIDEKICKS
"NOW, IT AIN'T LIKE WE WERE ALL ALONE IN OUR FIGHT. BATS HAD A BIG IDEA. ONE SO BIG EVEN I THOUGHT HE MIGHTA LOST IT.
WELL, NOW THAT WE'RE HERE, WE HAVE TO FIGURE OUT WHERE HERE IS.
"PICTURE A PANCAKE THE SIZE OF THE WHOLE WORLD. THE PANCAKE IS EVERYTHING, EVERYONE, ALL OF IT'S JUST A BIG HONKING PANCAKE.
DON'T LOOK NOW, BUT THERE'S A GREEN ARROW IMPERSONATOR ON THE ROOFTOP.
"NOW WHO CAN MAKE JUST ONE PANCAKE? SOON AS THE FIRST ONE CAME OFF THE GRIDDLE, THEY POURED ANOTHER ONE.
"EVEN IF THEY MEASURED IT DOWN TO THE MILLIMETER, THAT NEXT PANCAKE ISN'T GONNA BE AN EXACT COPY. NO TWO PANCAKES ARE ALIKE. THIS IS SCIENCE.
WHAT SHOULD I DO, BOSS?
GO GET US SOME MOTORCYCLES, LARRY. I WANNA SHOW UP IN STYLE.
"BATMAN AND LUTHOR, THEY WERE GONNA TAKE SOME PARTS OF SOME OTHER PANCAKE AND USE 'EM IN OUR PANCAKE.
"THE PLAN MUST HAVE WORKED. EVEN FROM FAR AWAY, I KNEW OLLIE. I WAS SO HAPPY TO SEE HIM, I COULDN'T HELP MYSELF."

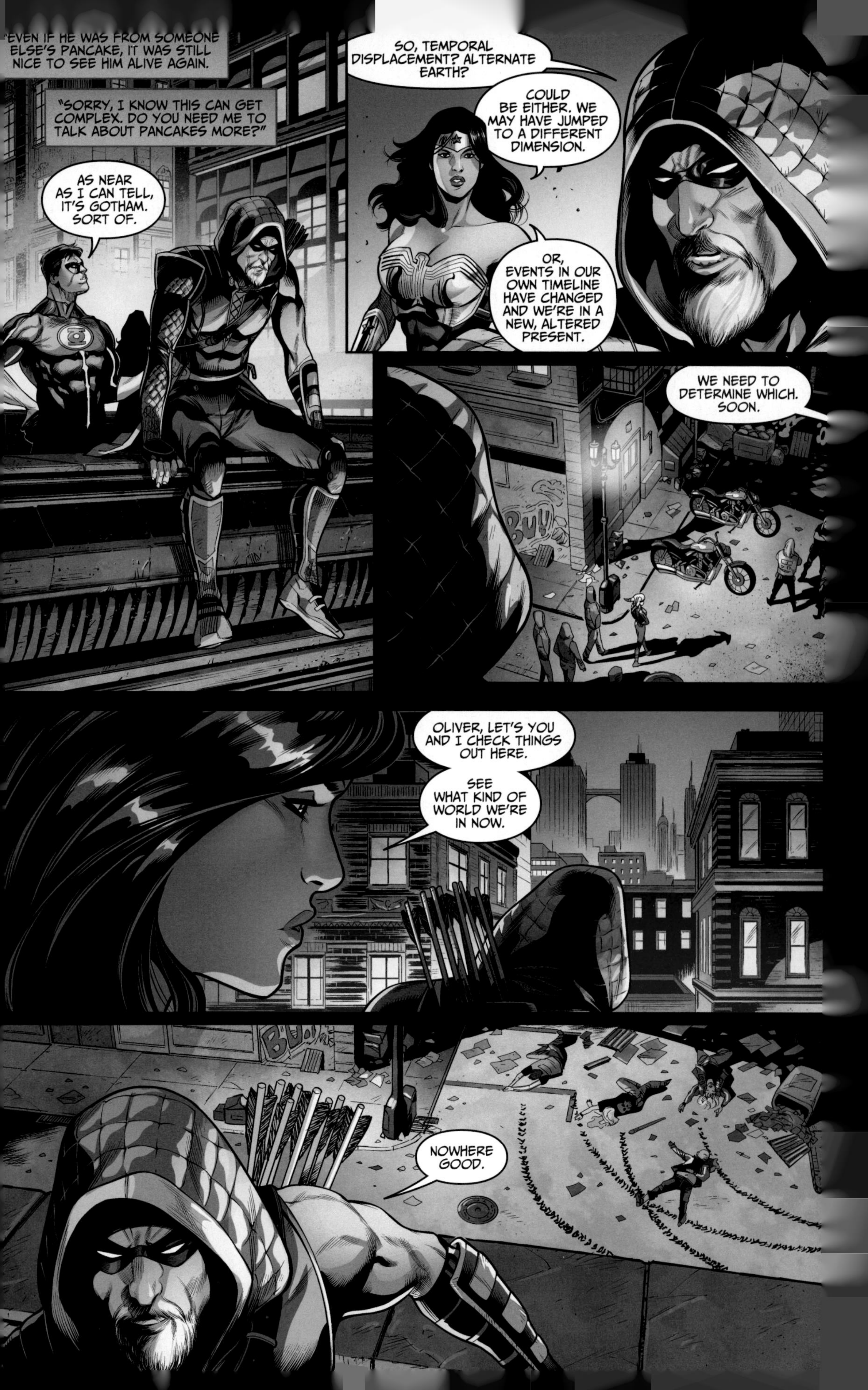
EVEN IF HE WAS FROM SOMEONE ELSE'S PANCAKE, IT WAS STILL NICE TO SEE HIM ALIVE AGAIN.
"SORRY, I KNOW THIS CAN GET COMPLEX. DO YOU NEED ME TO TALK ABOUT PANCAKES MORE?"
AS NEAR AS I CAN TELL, IT'S GOTHAM. SORT OF.
SO, TEMPORAL DISPLACEMENT? ALTERNATE EARTH?
COULD BE EITHER. WE MAY HAVE JUMPED TO A DIFFERENT DIMENSION.
OR, EVENTS IN OUR OWN TIMELINE HAVE CHANGED AND WE'RE IN A NEW, ALTERED PRESENT.
WE NEED TO DETERMINE WHICH. SOON.
OLIVER, LET'S YOU AND I CHECK THINGS OUT HERE.
SEE WHAT KIND OF WORLD WE'RE IN NOW.
NOWHERE GOOD.

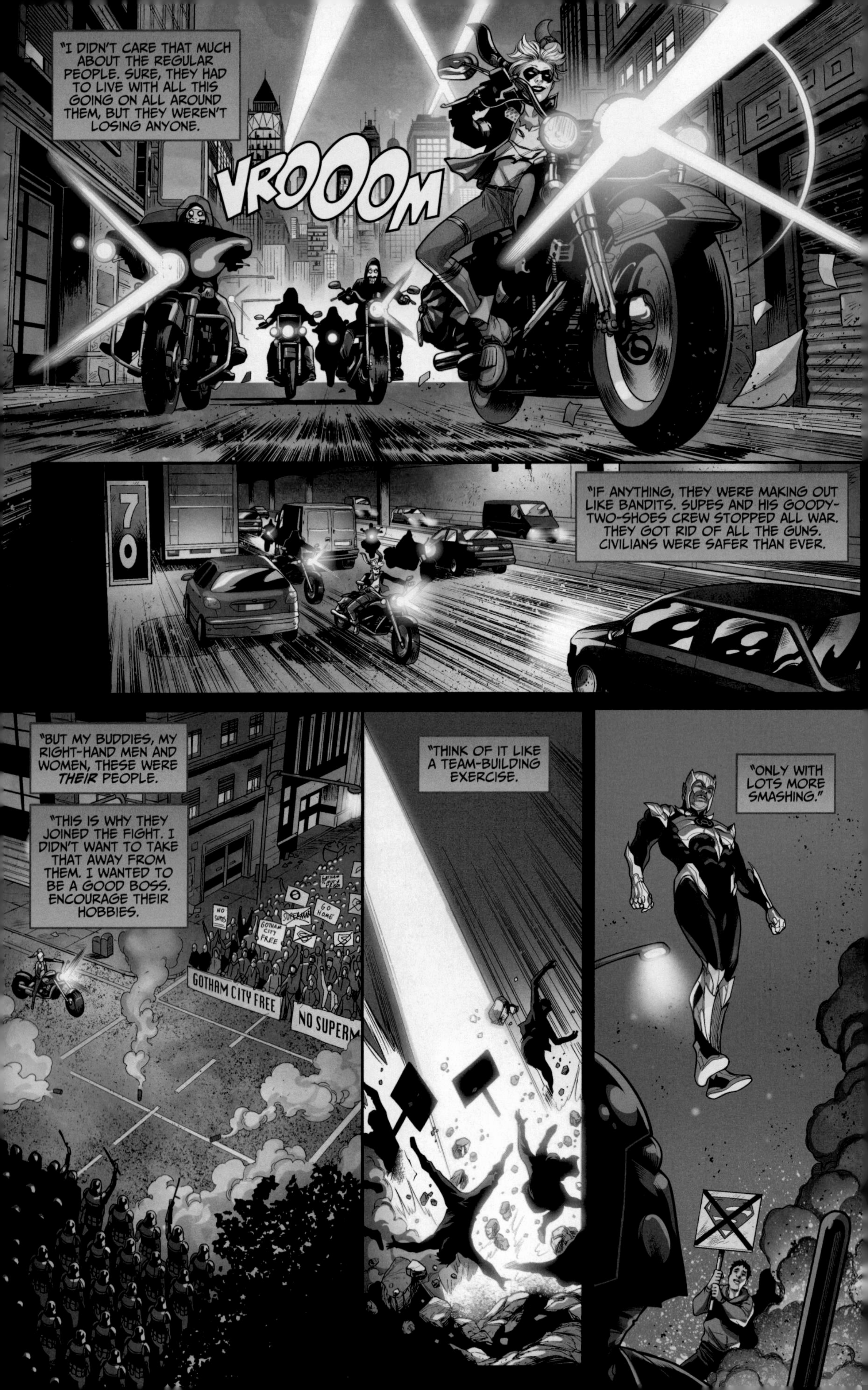
"I DIDN'T CARE THAT MUCH ABOUT THE REGULAR PEOPLE. SURE, THEY HAD TO LIVE WITH ALL THIS GOING ON ALL AROUND THEM, BUT THEY WEREN'T LOSING ANYONE.
VROOOM
70
"IF ANYTHING, THEY WERE MAKING OUT LIKE BANDITS. SUPES AND HIS GOODY-TWO-SHOES CREW STOPPED ALL WAR. THEY GOT RID OF ALL THE GUNS. CIVILIANS WERE SAFER THAN EVER.
"BUT MY BUDDIES, MY RIGHT-HAND MEN AND WOMEN, THESE WERE *THEIR* PEOPLE.
"THIS IS WHY THEY JOINED THE FIGHT. I DIDN'T WANT TO TAKE THAT AWAY FROM THEM. I WANTED TO BE A GOOD BOSS. ENCOURAGE THEIR HOBBIES.
GO HOME
NO SUPES
GOTHAM CITY FREE
GOTHAM CITY FREE
NO SUPERM
"THINK OF IT LIKE A TEAM-BUILDING EXERCISE.
"ONLY WITH LOTS MORE SMASHING."

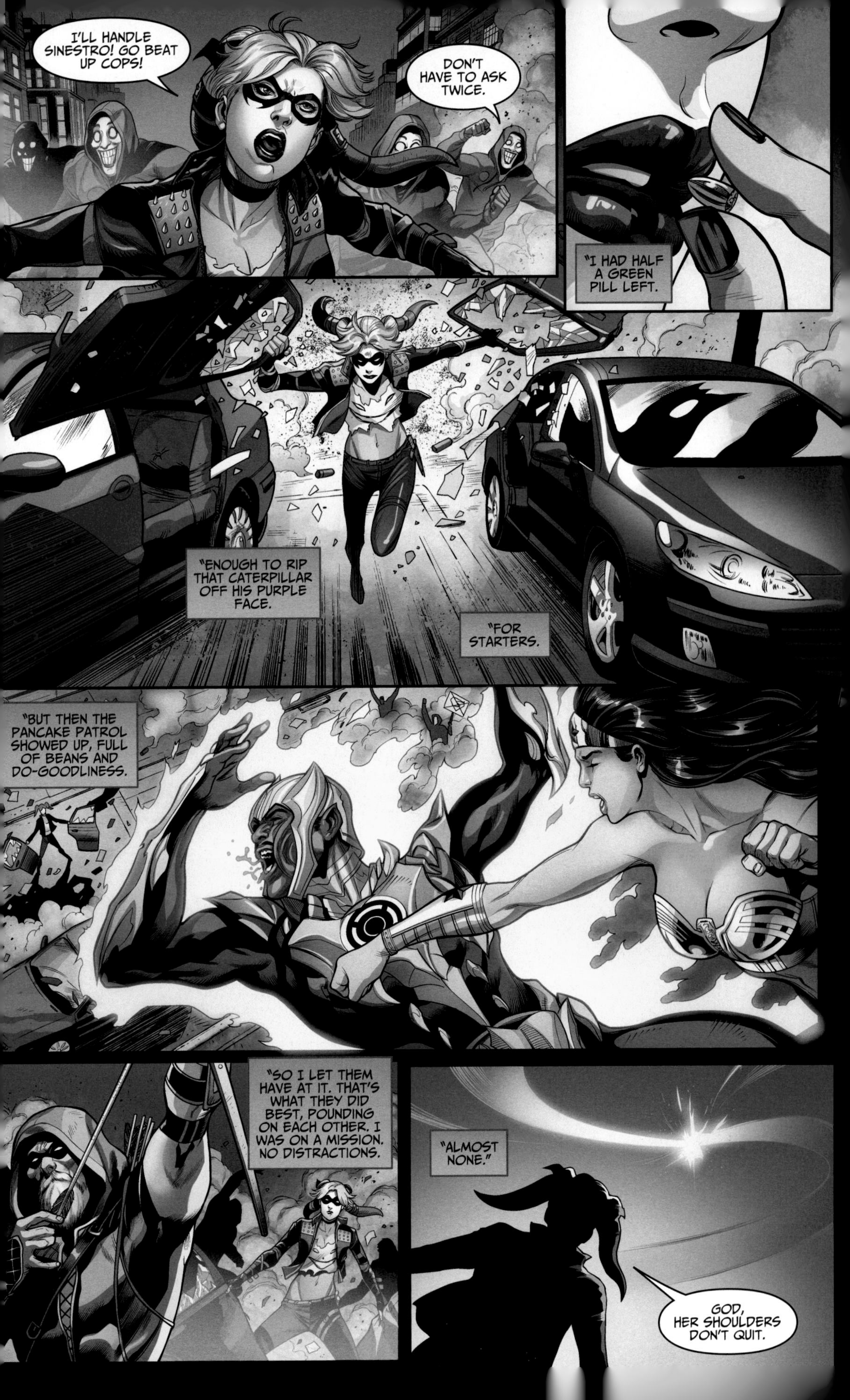
I'LL HANDLE SINESTRO! GO BEAT UP COPS!
DON'T HAVE TO ASK TWICE.
"I HAD HALF A GREEN PILL LEFT.
"ENOUGH TO RIP THAT CATERPILLAR OFF HIS PURPLE FACE.
"FOR STARTERS.
"BUT THEN THE PANCAKE PATROL SHOWED UP, FULL OF BEANS AND DO-GOODLINESS.
"SO I LET THEM HAVE AT IT. THAT'S WHAT THEY DID BEST, POUNDING ON EACH OTHER. I WAS ON A MISSION. NO DISTRACTIONS.
"ALMOST NONE."
GOD, HER SHOULDERS DON'T QUIT.

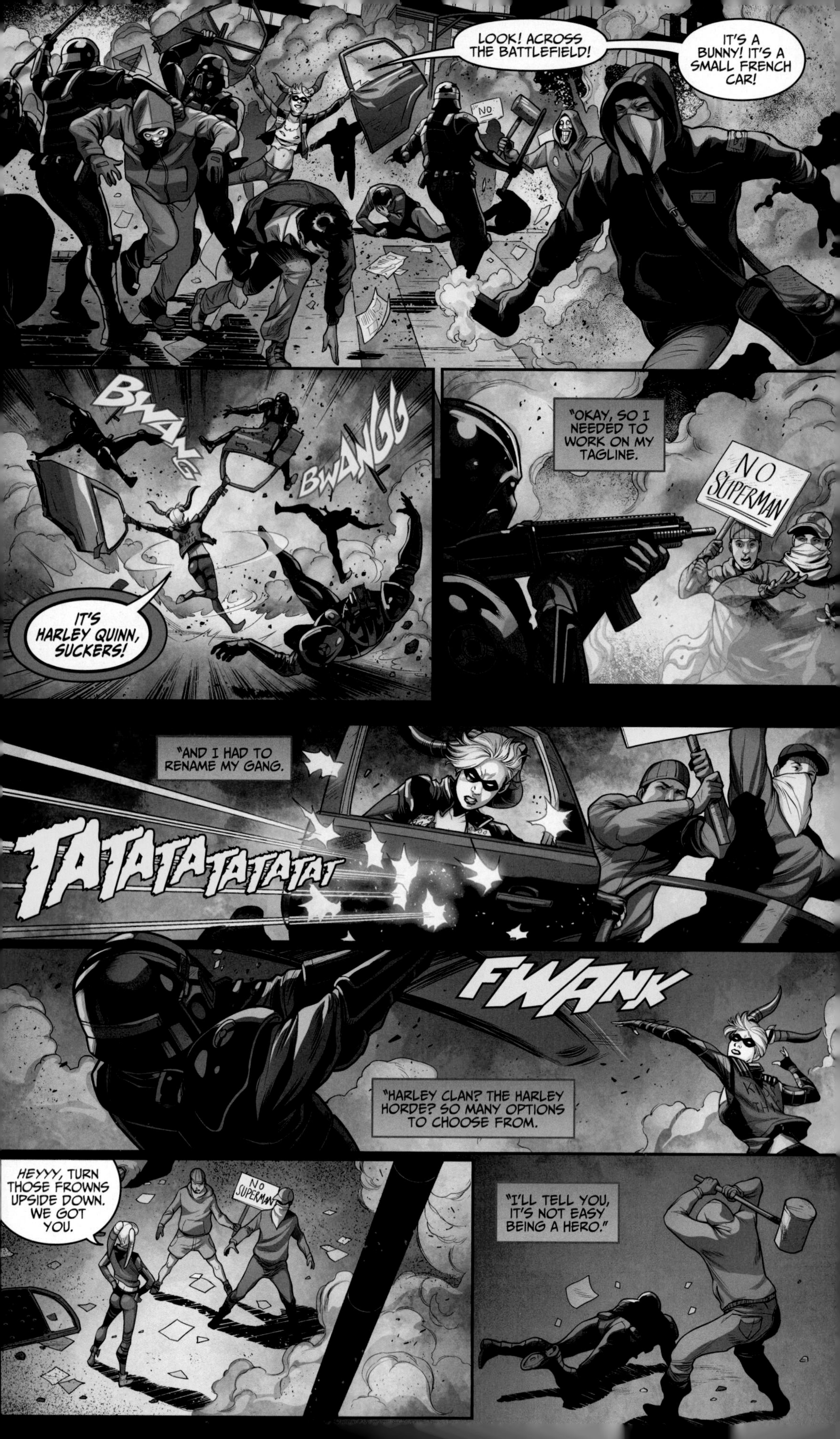

LOOK! ACROSS THE BATTLEFIELD!
IT'S A BUNNY! IT'S A SMALL FRENCH CAR!
NO
BWANG
BWANGG
IT'S HARLEY QUINN, SUCKERS!
"OKAY, SO I NEEDED TO WORK ON MY TAGLINE.
NO SUPERMAN
"AND I HAD TO RENAME MY GANG.
TATATATATATAT
FWANK
"HARLEY CLAN? THE HARLEY HORDE? SO MANY OPTIONS TO CHOOSE FROM.
HEYYY, TURN THOSE FROWNS UPSIDE DOWN. WE GOT YOU.
NO SUPERMAN
"I'LL TELL YOU, IT'S NOT EASY BEING A HERO."

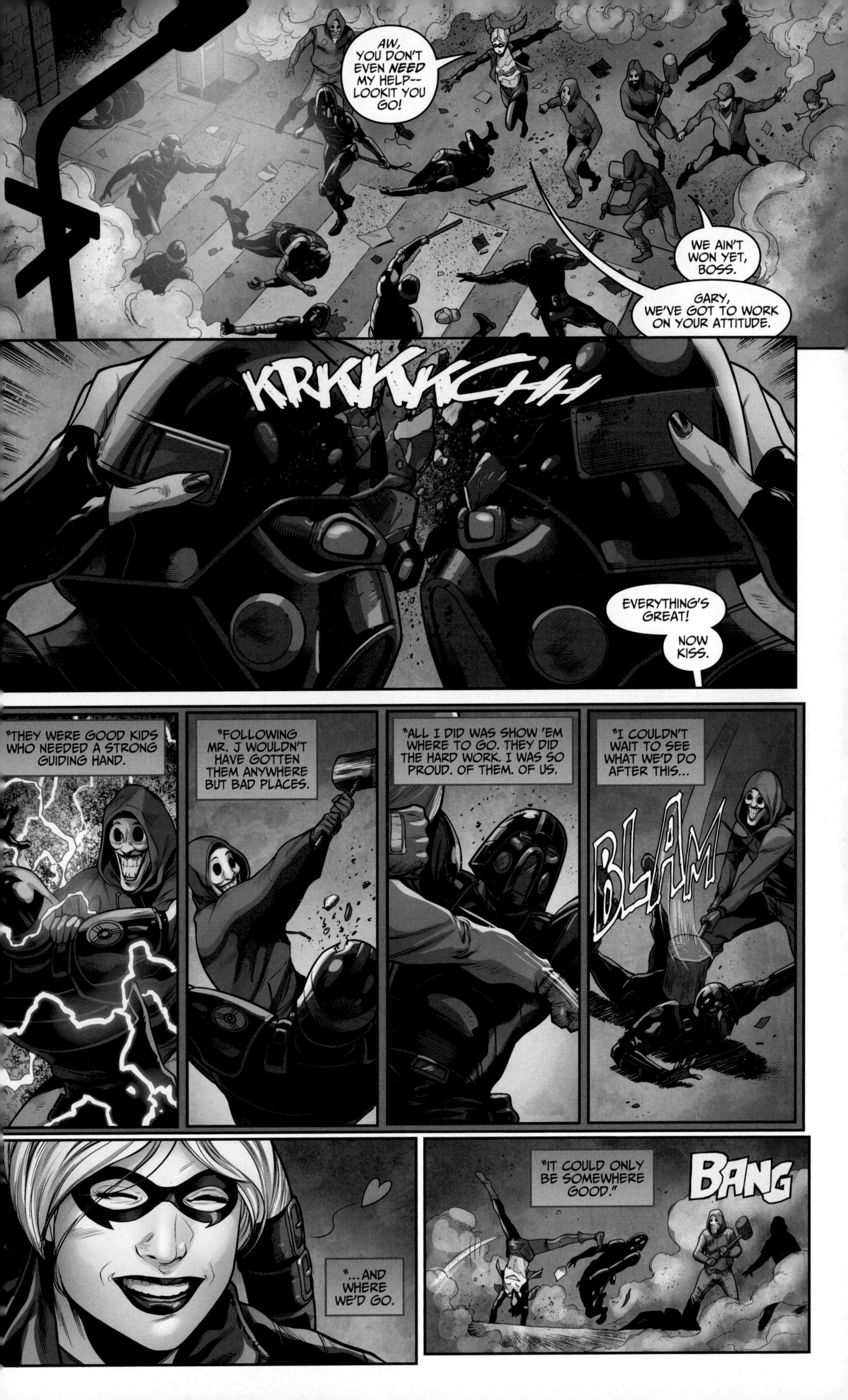
AW, YOU DON'T EVEN NEED MY HELP-- LOOKIT YOU GO!
WE AIN'T WON YET, BOSS.
GARY, WE'VE GOT TO WORK ON YOUR ATTITUDE.
KRKKKCHH
EVERYTHING'S GREAT!
NOW KISS.
"THEY WERE GOOD KIDS WHO NEEDED A STRONG GUIDING HAND.
"FOLLOWING MR. J WOULDN'T HAVE GOTTEN THEM ANYWHERE BUT BAD PLACES.
"ALL I DID WAS SHOW 'EM WHERE TO GO. THEY DID THE HARD WORK. I WAS SO PROUD. OF THEM. OF US.
"I COULDN'T WAIT TO SEE WHAT WE'D DO AFTER THIS...
BLAM
"...AND WHERE WE'D GO.
"IT COULD ONLY BE SOMEWHERE GOOD."
BANG

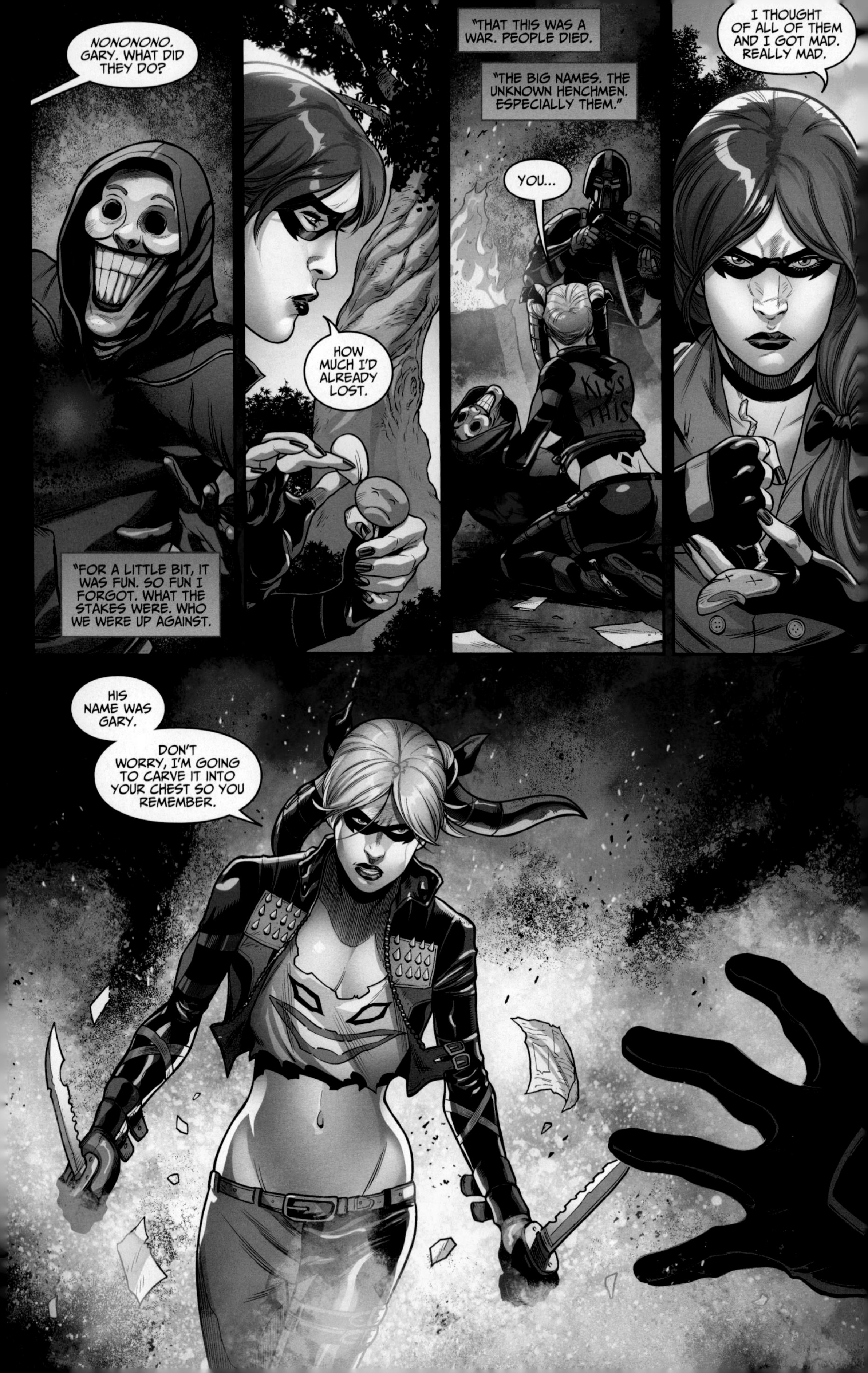

NONONONO. GARY. WHAT DID THEY DO?
"FOR A LITTLE BIT, IT WAS FUN. SO FUN I FORGOT. WHAT THE STAKES WERE. WHO WE WERE UP AGAINST.
HOW MUCH I'D ALREADY LOST.
"THAT THIS WAS A WAR. PEOPLE DIED.
"THE BIG NAMES. THE UNKNOWN HENCHMEN. ESPECIALLY THEM."
YOU...
KISS THIS
I THOUGHT OF ALL OF THEM AND I GOT MAD. REALLY MAD.
HIS NAME WAS GARY.
DON'T WORRY, I'M GOING TO CARVE IT INTO YOUR CHEST SO YOU REMEMBER.

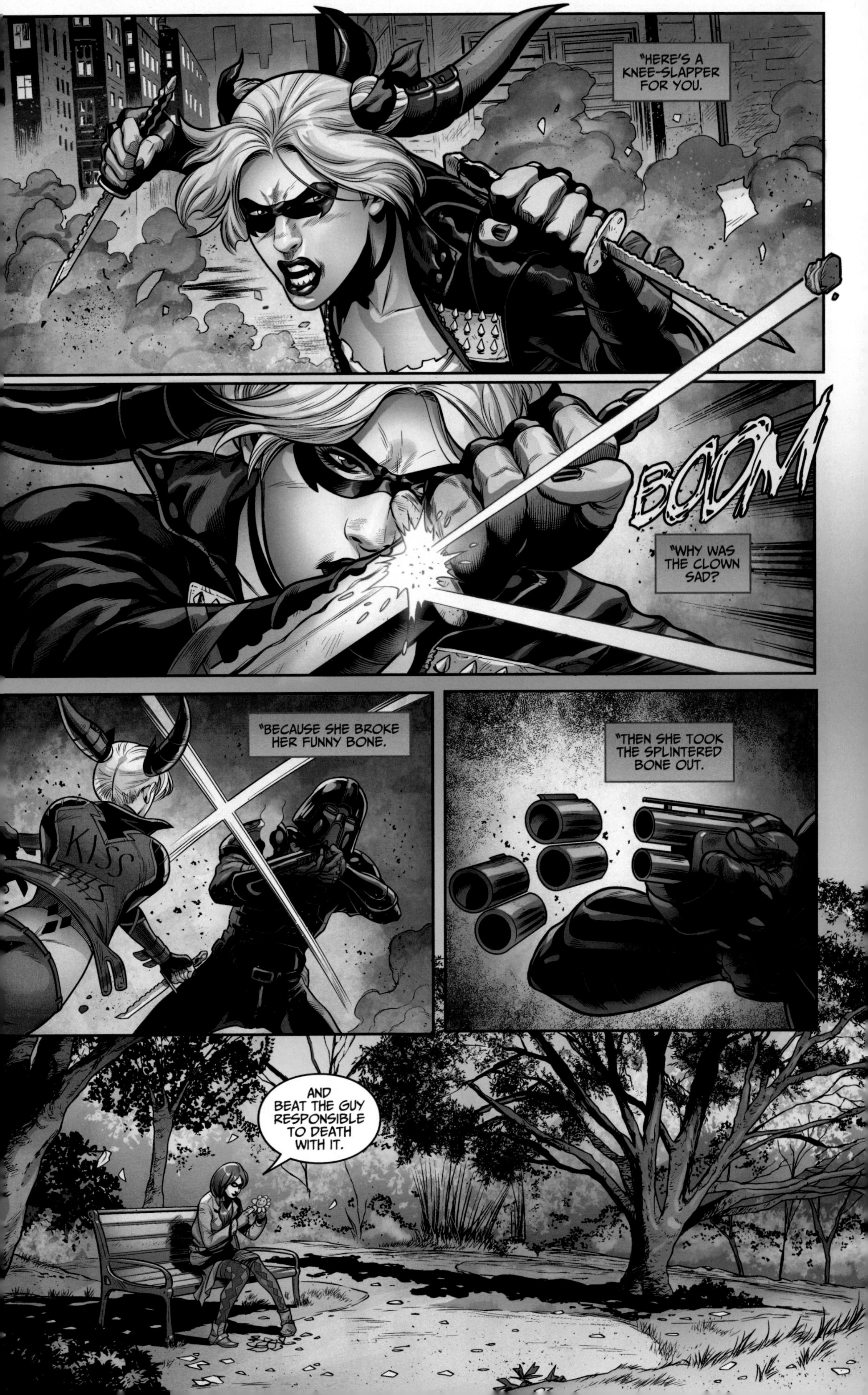
"HERE'S A KNEE-SLAPPER FOR YOU.
BOOM
"WHY WAS THE CLOWN SAD?
"BECAUSE SHE BROKE HER FUNNY BONE.
"THEN SHE TOOK THE SPLINTERED BONE OUT.
AND BEAT THE GUY RESPONSIBLE TO DEATH WITH IT.

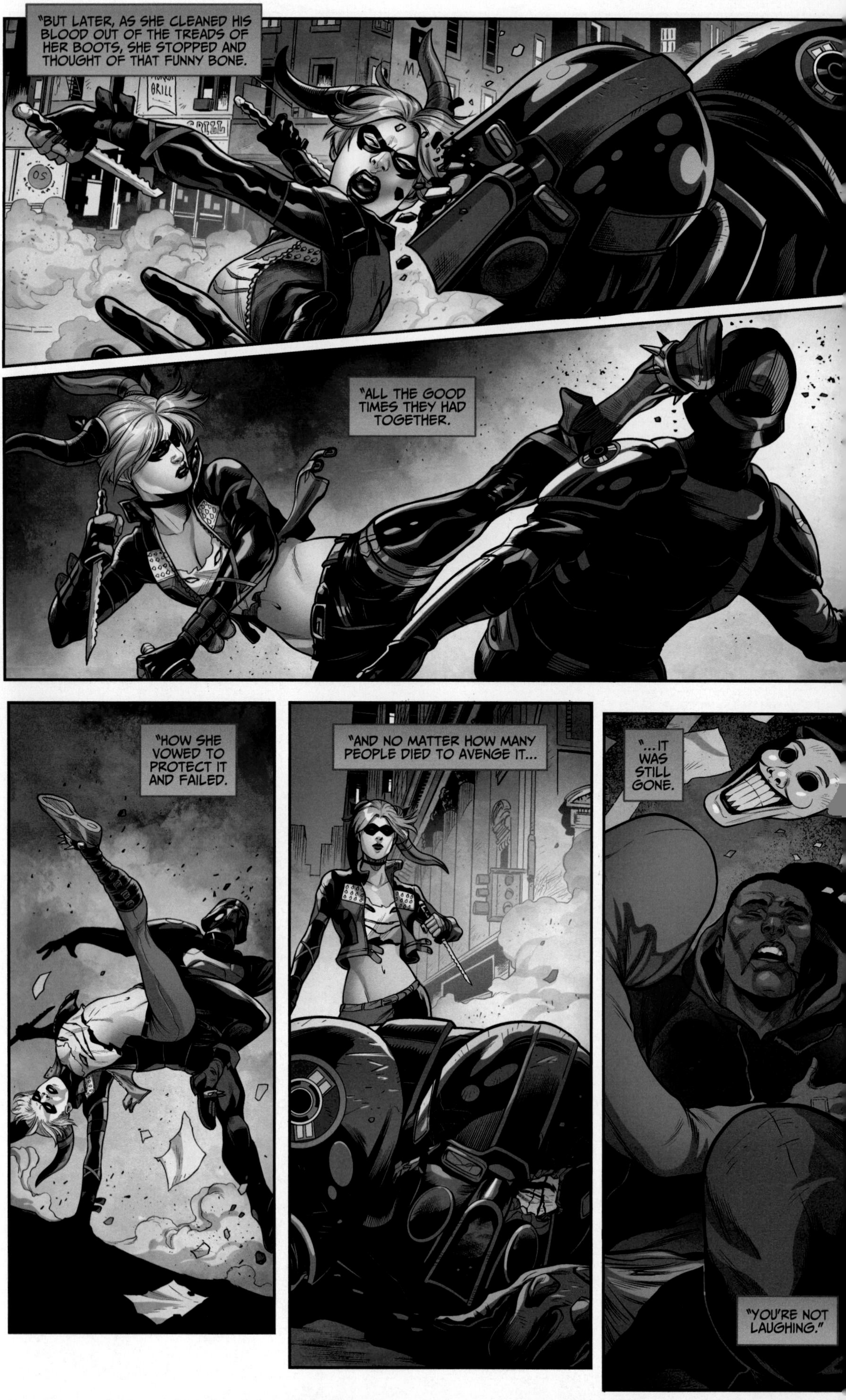
"BUT LATER, AS SHE CLEANED HIS BLOOD OUT OF THE TREADS OF HER BOOTS, SHE STOPPED AND THOUGHT OF THAT FUNNY BONE.
"ALL THE GOOD TIMES THEY HAD TOGETHER.
"HOW SHE VOWED TO PROTECT IT AND FAILED.
"AND NO MATTER HOW MANY PEOPLE DIED TO AVENGE IT...
"...IT WAS STILL GONE.
"YOU'RE NOT LAUGHING."

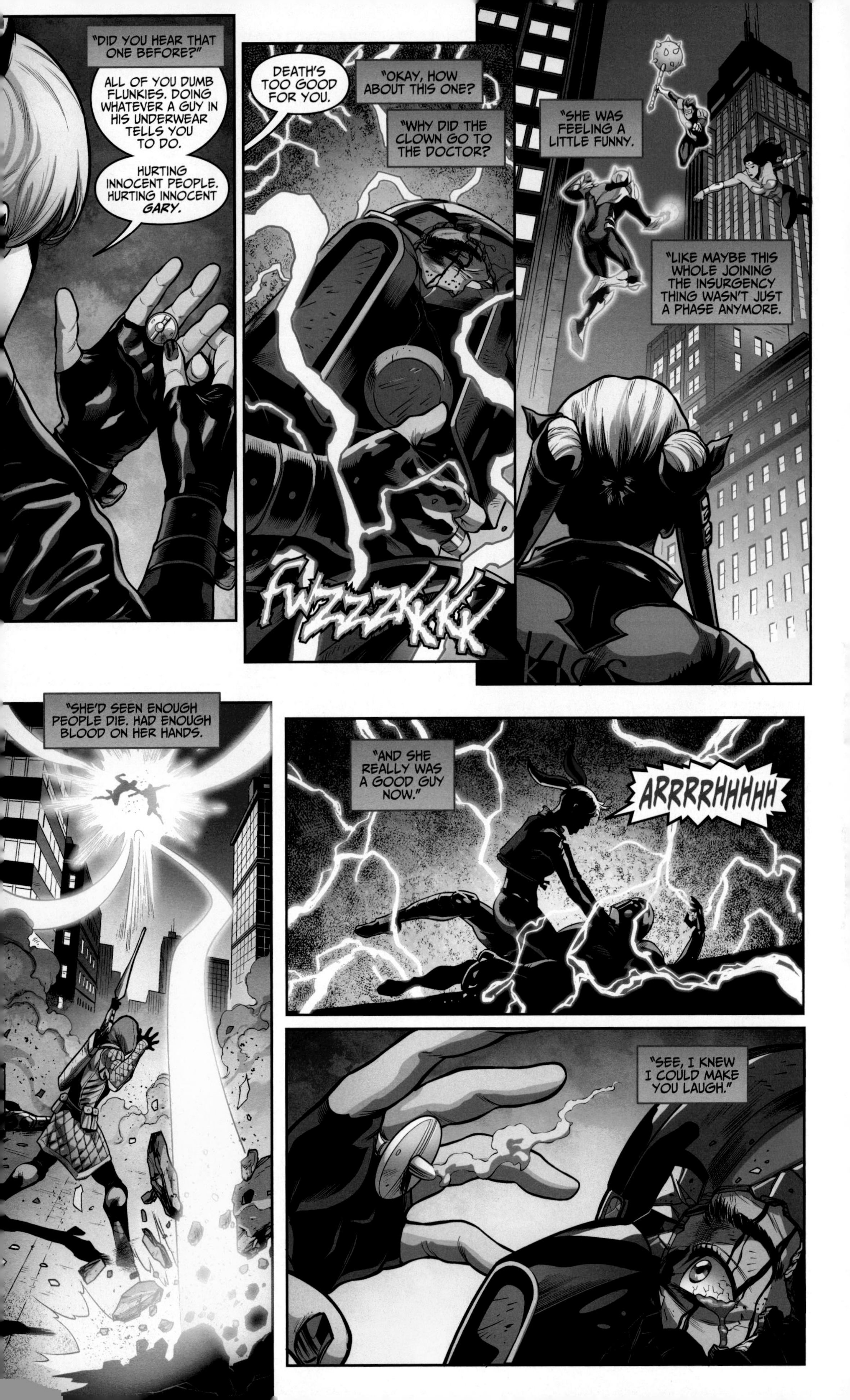
"DID YOU HEAR THAT ONE BEFORE?"
ALL OF YOU DUMB FLUNKIES. DOING WHATEVER A GUY IN HIS UNDERWEAR TELLS YOU TO DO.
HURTING INNOCENT PEOPLE. HURTING INNOCENT GARY.
DEATH'S TOO GOOD FOR YOU.
"OKAY, HOW ABOUT THIS ONE?
"WHY DID THE CLOWN GO TO THE DOCTOR?
FWZZZKKKK
"SHE WAS FEELING A LITTLE FUNNY.
"LIKE MAYBE THIS WHOLE JOINING THE INSURGENCY THING WASN'T JUST A PHASE ANYMORE.
"SHE'D SEEN ENOUGH PEOPLE DIE. HAD ENOUGH BLOOD ON HER HANDS.
"AND SHE REALLY WAS A GOOD GUY NOW."
ARRRRHHHHH
"SEE, I KNEW I COULD MAKE YOU LAUGH."

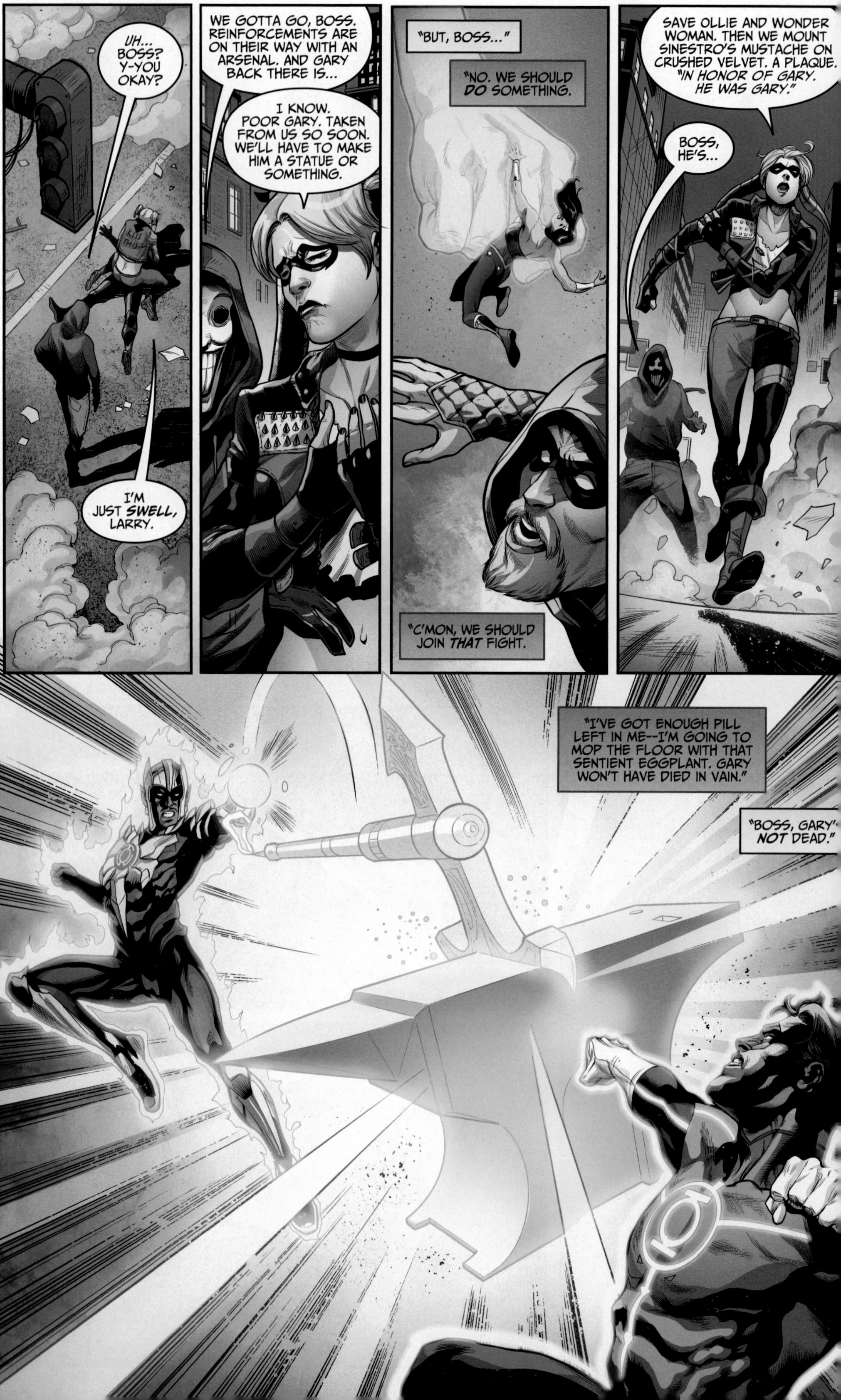
UH... BOSS? Y-YOU OKAY?
I'M JUST SWELL, LARRY.
WE GOTTA GO, BOSS. REINFORCEMENTS ARE ON THEIR WAY WITH AN ARSENAL. AND GARY BACK THERE IS...
I KNOW. POOR GARY. TAKEN FROM US SO SOON. WE'LL HAVE TO MAKE HIM A STATUE OR SOMETHING.
"BUT, BOSS..."
"NO. WE SHOULD DO SOMETHING.
"C'MON, WE SHOULD JOIN THAT FIGHT.
SAVE OLLIE AND WONDER WOMAN. THEN WE MOUNT SINESTRO'S MUSTACHE ON CRUSHED VELVET. A PLAQUE. "IN HONOR OF GARY. HE WAS GARY."
BOSS, HE'S...
"I'VE GOT ENOUGH PILL LEFT IN ME--I'M GOING TO MOP THE FLOOR WITH THAT SENTIENT EGGPLANT. GARY WON'T HAVE DIED IN VAIN."
"BOSS, GARY NOT DEAD."

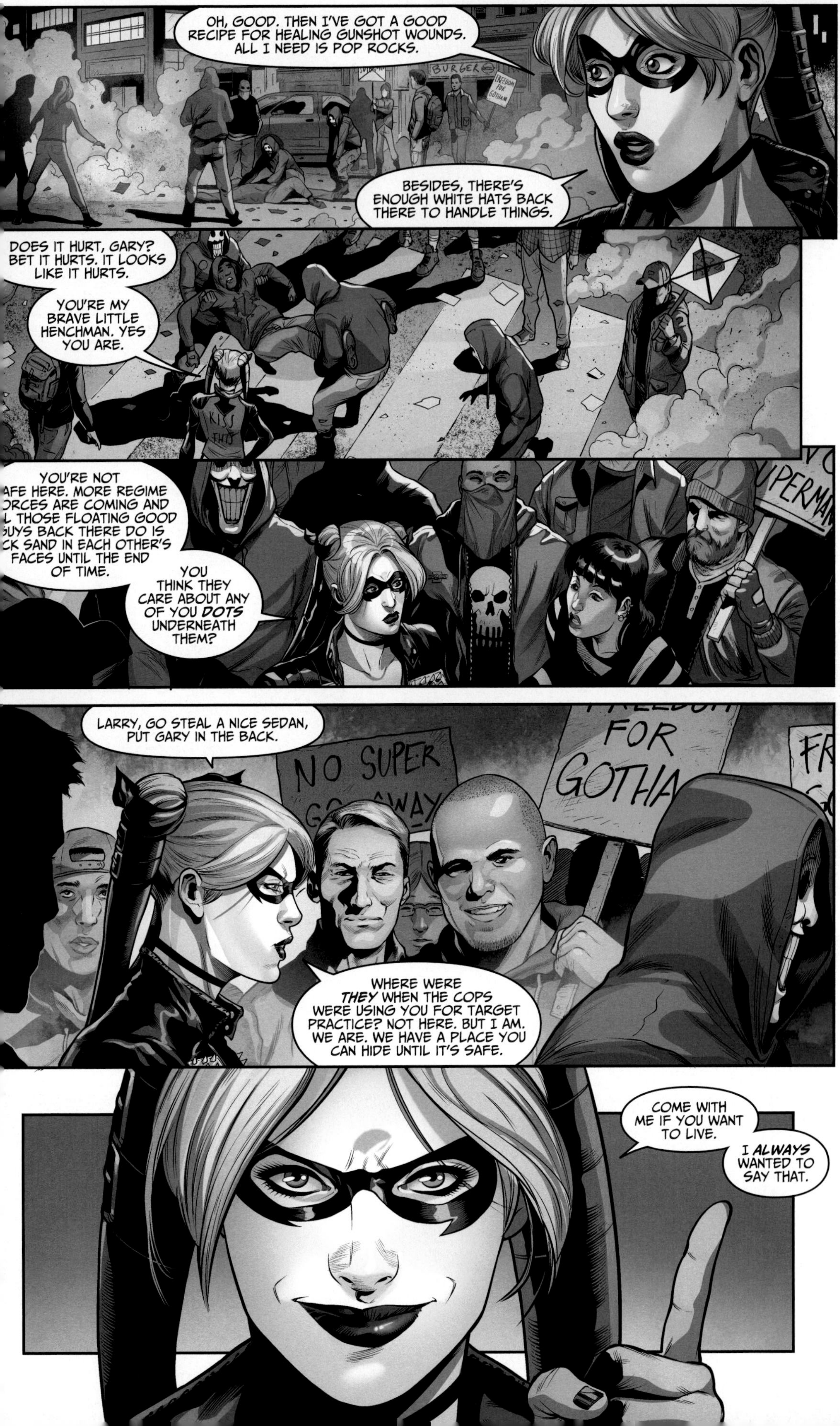
OH, GOOD. THEN I'VE GOT A GOOD RECIPE FOR HEALING GUNSHOT WOUNDS. ALL I NEED IS POP ROCKS.
BURGER
BESIDES, THERE'S ENOUGH WHITE HATS BACK THERE TO HANDLE THINGS.
DOES IT HURT, GARY? BET IT HURTS. IT LOOKS LIKE IT HURTS.
YOU'RE MY BRAVE LITTLE HENCHMAN. YES YOU ARE.
YOU'RE NOT AFE HERE. MORE REGIME ORCES ARE COMING AND L THOSE FLOATING GOOD UYS BACK THERE DO IS CK SAND IN EACH OTHER'S FACES UNTIL THE END OF TIME.
YOU THINK THEY CARE ABOUT ANY OF YOU *DOTS* UNDERNEATH THEM?
UPERMAN
LARRY, GO STEAL A NICE SEDAN, PUT GARY IN THE BACK.
NO SUPER
FOR GOTHA
WHERE WERE *THEY* WHEN THE COPS WERE USING YOU FOR TARGET PRACTICE? NOT HERE. BUT I AM. WE ARE. WE HAVE A PLACE YOU CAN HIDE UNTIL IT'S SAFE.
COME WITH ME IF YOU WANT TO LIVE.
I *ALWAYS* WANTED TO SAY THAT.

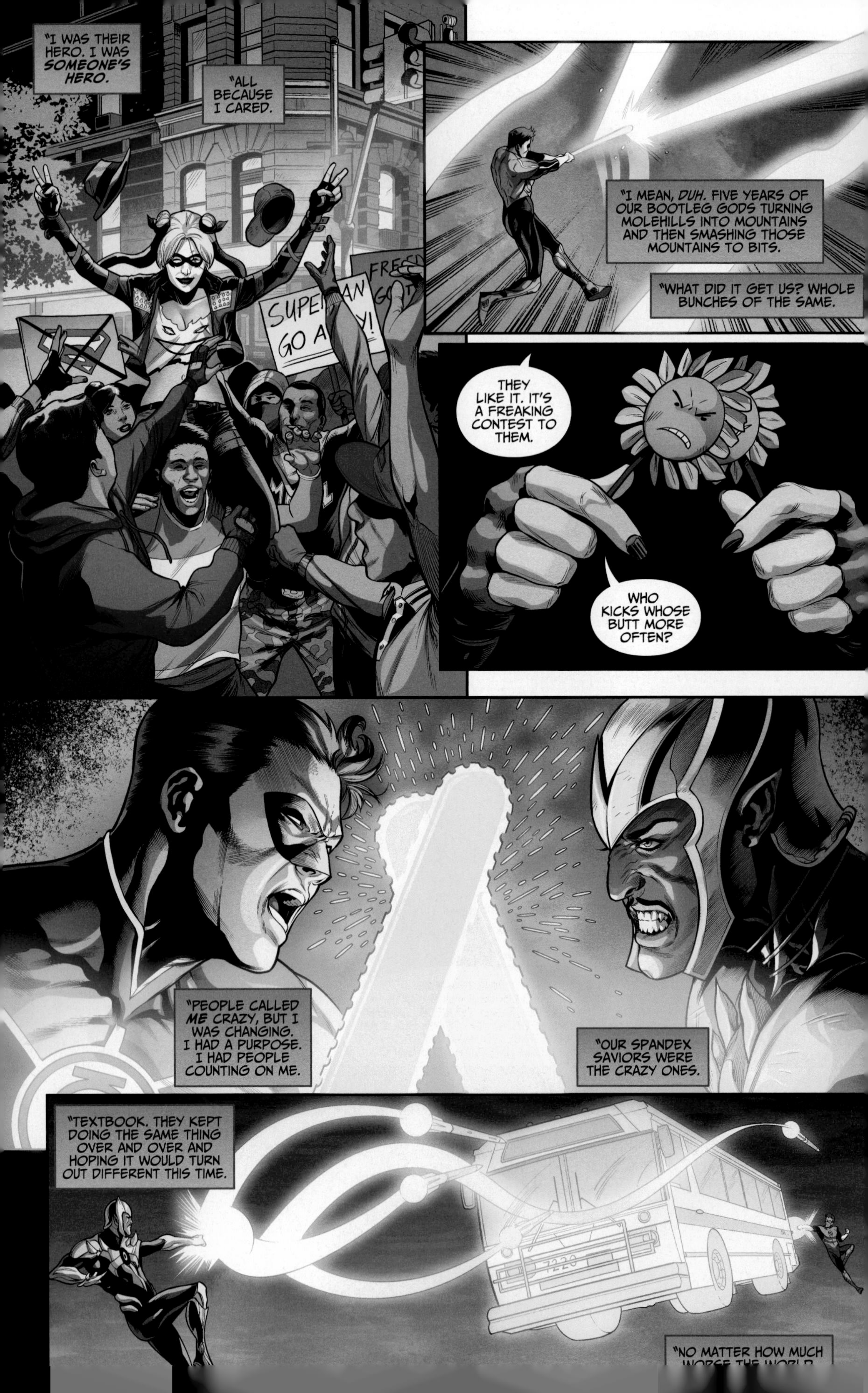
"I WAS THEIR HERO. I WAS SOMEONE'S HERO.
"ALL BECAUSE I CARED.
"I MEAN, DUH. FIVE YEARS OF OUR BOOTLEG GODS TURNING MOLEHILLS INTO MOUNTAINS AND THEN SMASHING THOSE MOUNTAINS TO BITS.
"WHAT DID IT GET US? WHOLE BUNCHES OF THE SAME.
THEY LIKE IT. IT'S A FREAKING CONTEST TO THEM.
WHO KICKS WHOSE BUTT MORE OFTEN?
"PEOPLE CALLED ME CRAZY, BUT I WAS CHANGING. I HAD A PURPOSE. I HAD PEOPLE COUNTING ON ME.
"OUR SPANDEX SAVIORS WERE THE CRAZY ONES.
"TEXTBOOK. THEY KEPT DOING THE SAME THING OVER AND OVER AND HOPING IT WOULD TURN OUT DIFFERENT THIS TIME.
"NO MATTER HOW MUCH

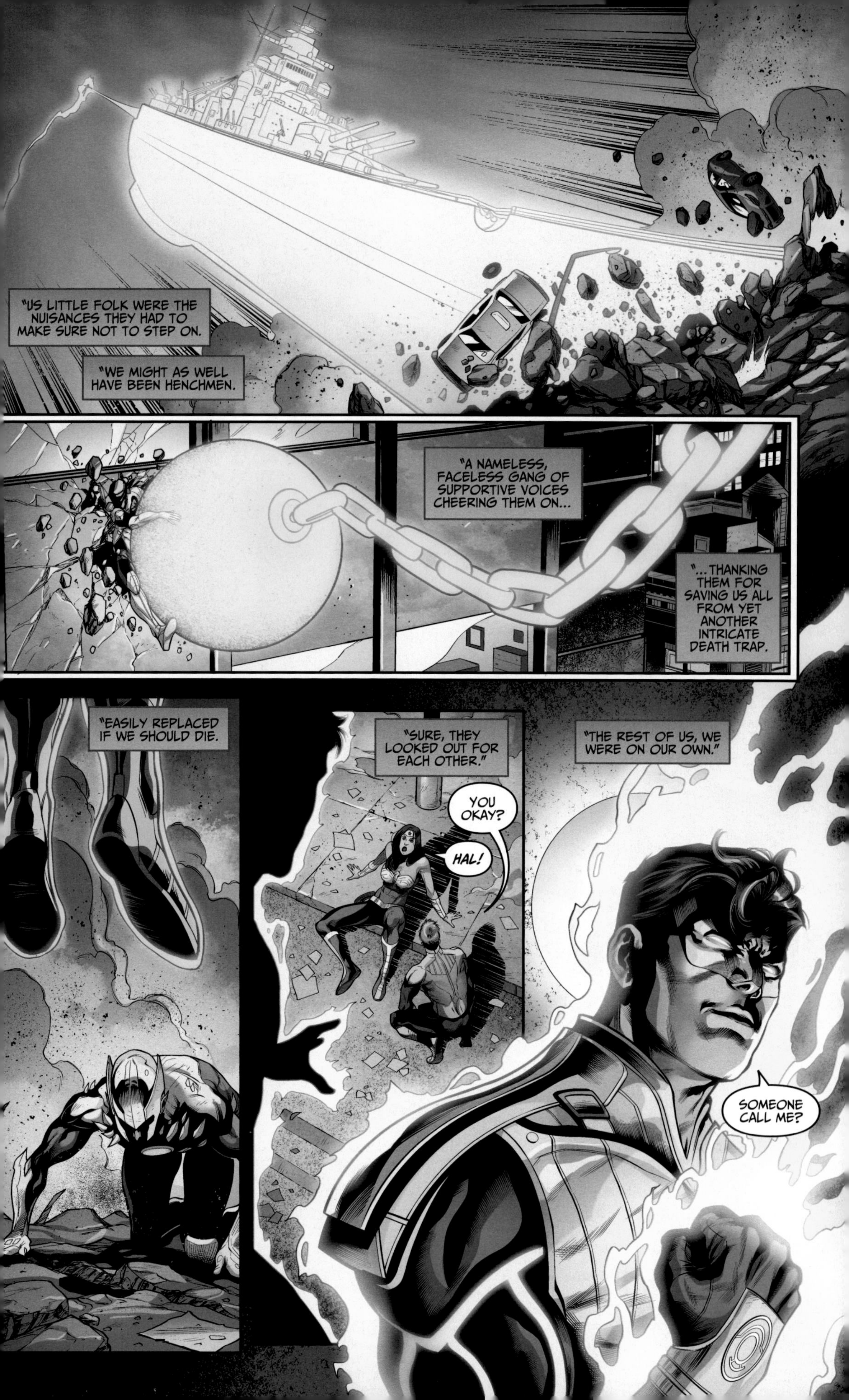
"US LITTLE FOLK WERE THE NUISANCES THEY HAD TO MAKE SURE NOT TO STEP ON.
"WE MIGHT AS WELL HAVE BEEN HENCHMEN.
"A NAMELESS, FACELESS GANG OF SUPPORTIVE VOICES CHEERING THEM ON...
"...THANKING THEM FOR SAVING US ALL FROM YET ANOTHER INTRICATE DEATH TRAP.
"EASILY REPLACED IF WE SHOULD DIE.
"SURE, THEY LOOKED OUT FOR EACH OTHER."
YOU OKAY?
HAL!
"THE REST OF US, WE WERE ON OUR OWN."
SOMEONE CALL ME?

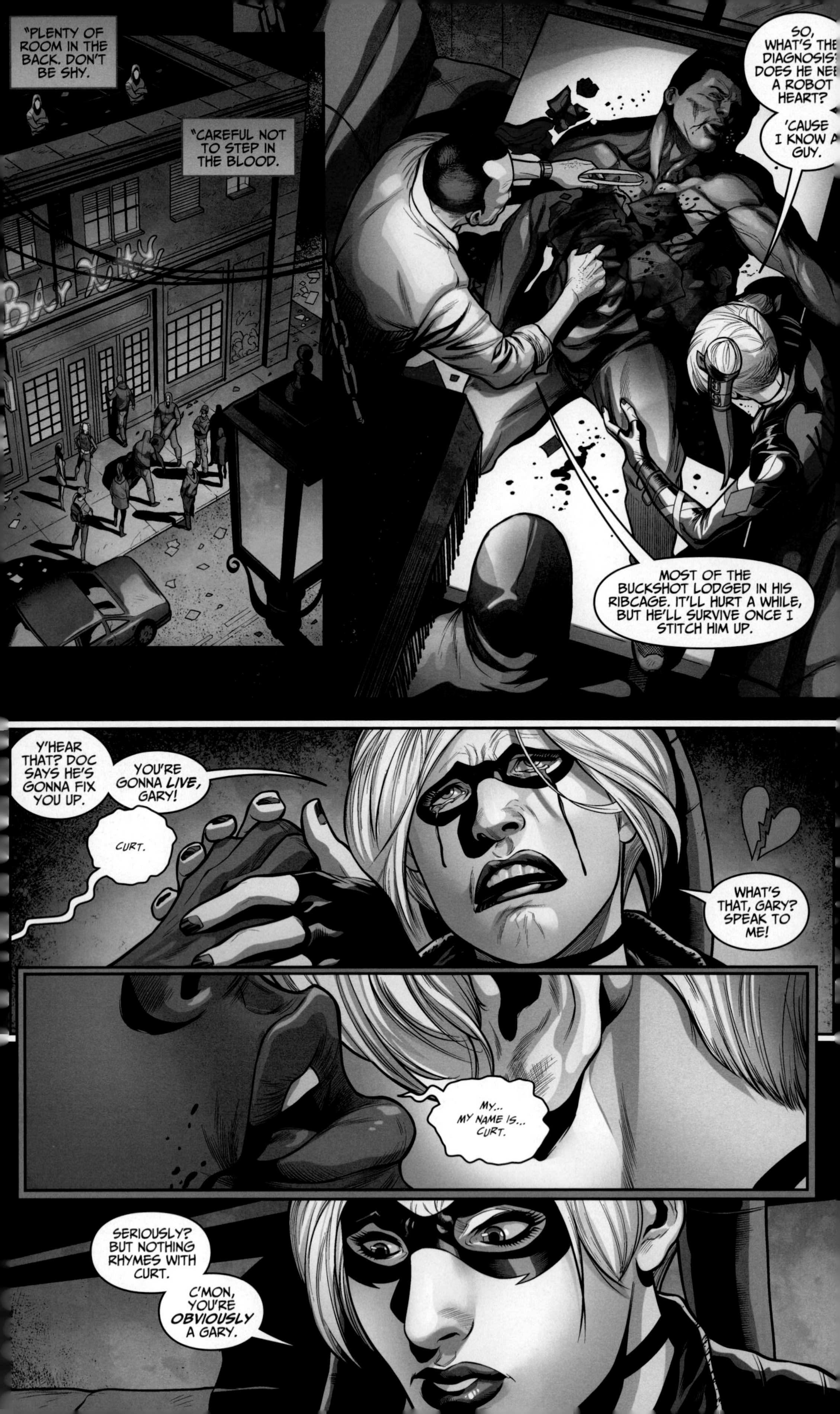
"PLENTY OF ROOM IN THE BACK. DON'T BE SHY.
"CAREFUL NOT TO STEP IN THE BLOOD.
SO, WHAT'S THE DIAGNOSIS? DOES HE NEED A ROBOT HEART?
'CAUSE I KNOW A GUY.
MOST OF THE BUCKSHOT LODGED IN HIS RIBCAGE. IT'LL HURT A WHILE, BUT HE'LL SURVIVE ONCE I STITCH HIM UP.
Y'HEAR THAT? DOC SAYS HE'S GONNA FIX YOU UP.
YOU'RE GONNA LIVE, GARY!
CURT.
WHAT'S THAT, GARY? SPEAK TO ME!
MY... MY NAME IS... CURT.
SERIOUSLY? BUT NOTHING RHYMES WITH CURT.
C'MON, YOU'RE OBVIOUSLY A GARY.

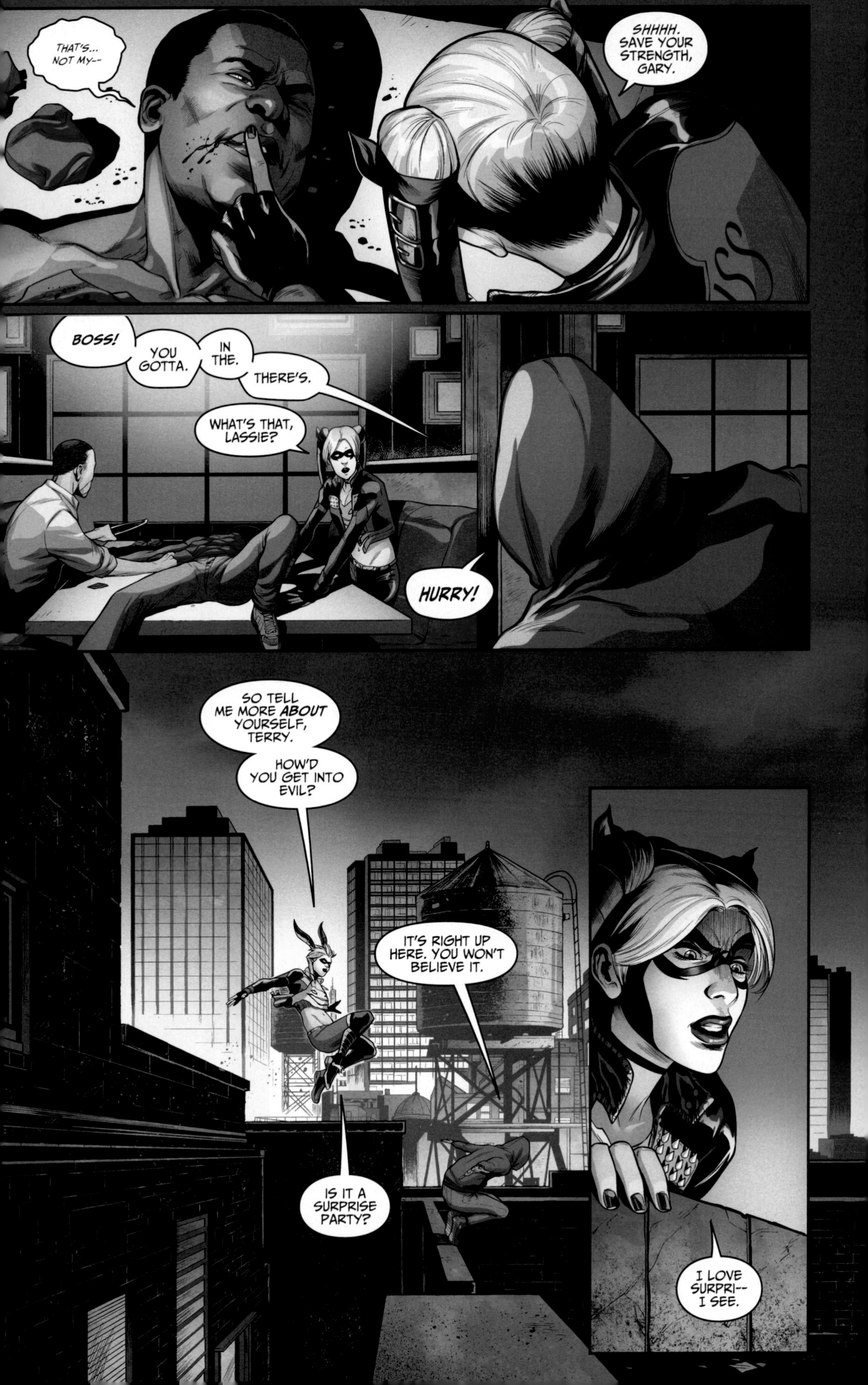
THAT'S... NOT MY--
SHHHH. SAVE YOUR STRENGTH, GARY.
BOSS!
YOU GOTTA.
IN THE.
THERE'S.
WHAT'S THAT, LASSIE?
HURRY!
SO TELL ME MORE ABOUT YOURSELF, TERRY.
HOW'D YOU GET INTO EVIL?
IT'S RIGHT UP HERE. YOU WON'T BELIEVE IT.
IS IT A SURPRISE PARTY?
I LOVE SURPRI-- I SEE.

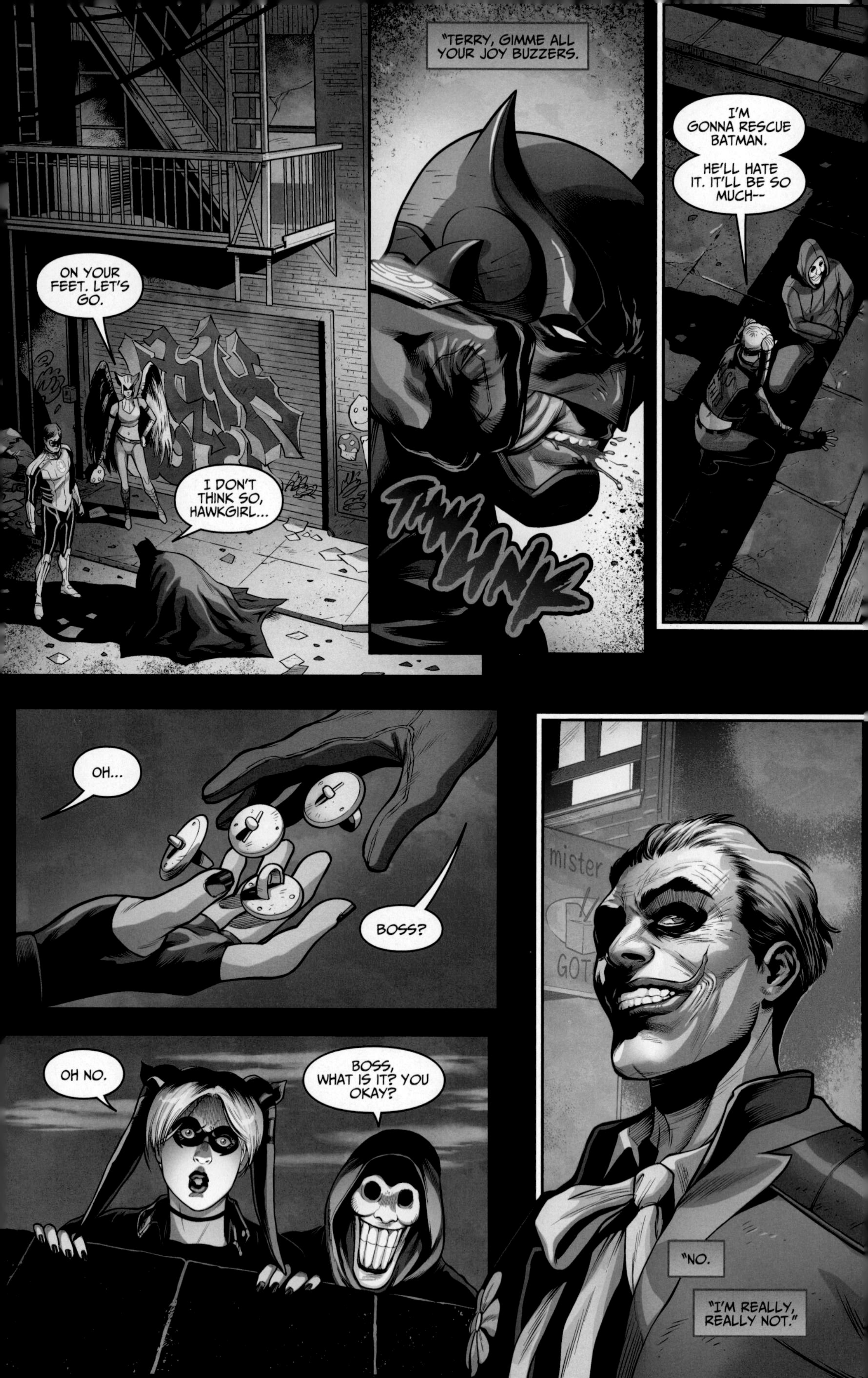
ON YOUR FEET. LET'S GO.
I DON'T THINK SO, HAWKGIRL...
"TERRY, GIMME ALL YOUR JOY BUZZERS.
THWUNK
I'M GONNA RESCUE BATMAN.
HE'LL HATE IT. IT'LL BE SO MUCH--
OH...
BOSS?
OH NO.
BOSS, WHAT IS IT? YOU OKAY?
mister
GOT
"NO.
"I'M REALLY, REALLY NOT."

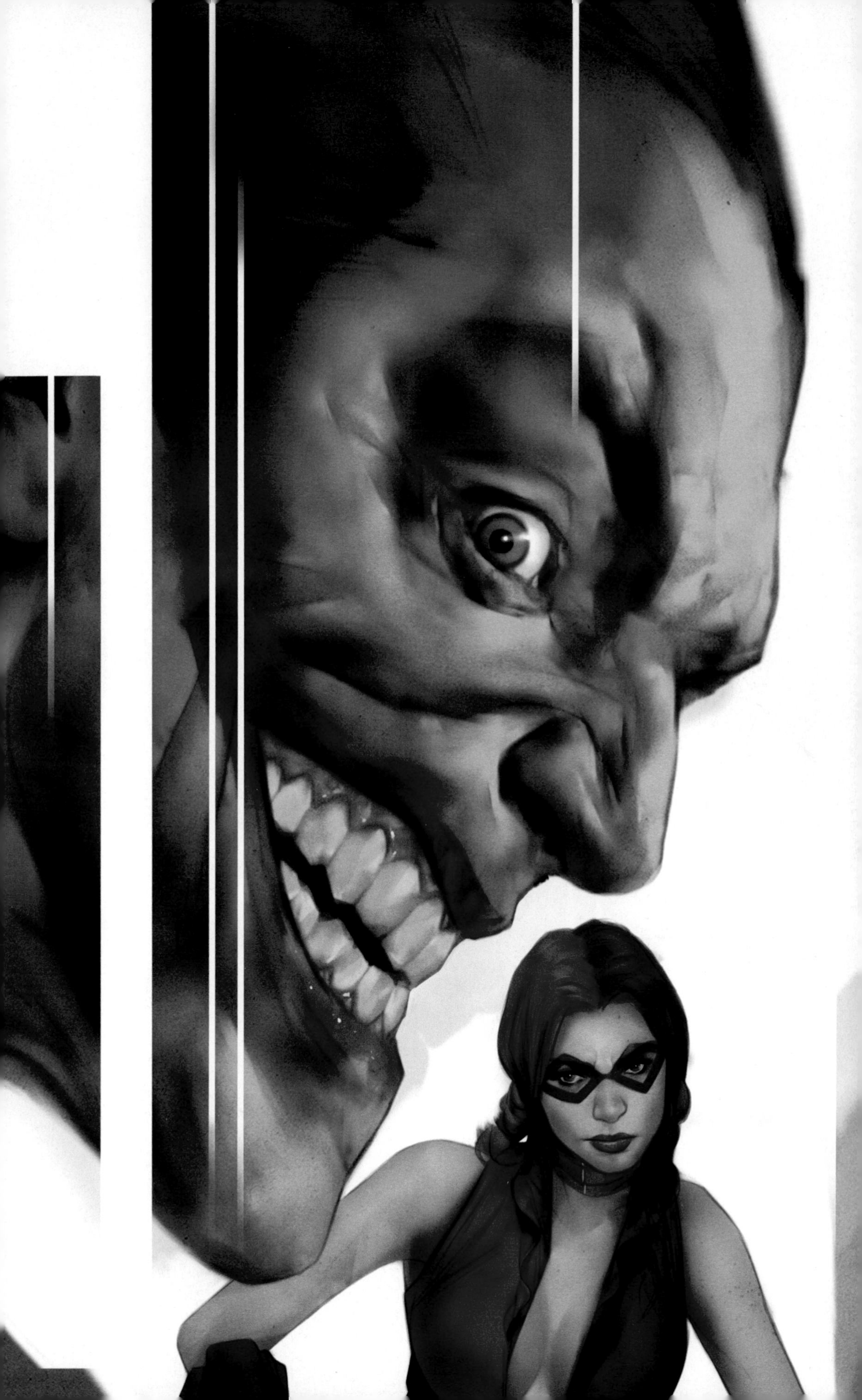

"The Joke's On Harley: Part 1" **Pop Mhan** Artist **J. Nanjan** Colorist
"The Joke's On Harley: Part 2" **Marco Santucci** Artist **J. Nanjan** Colorist

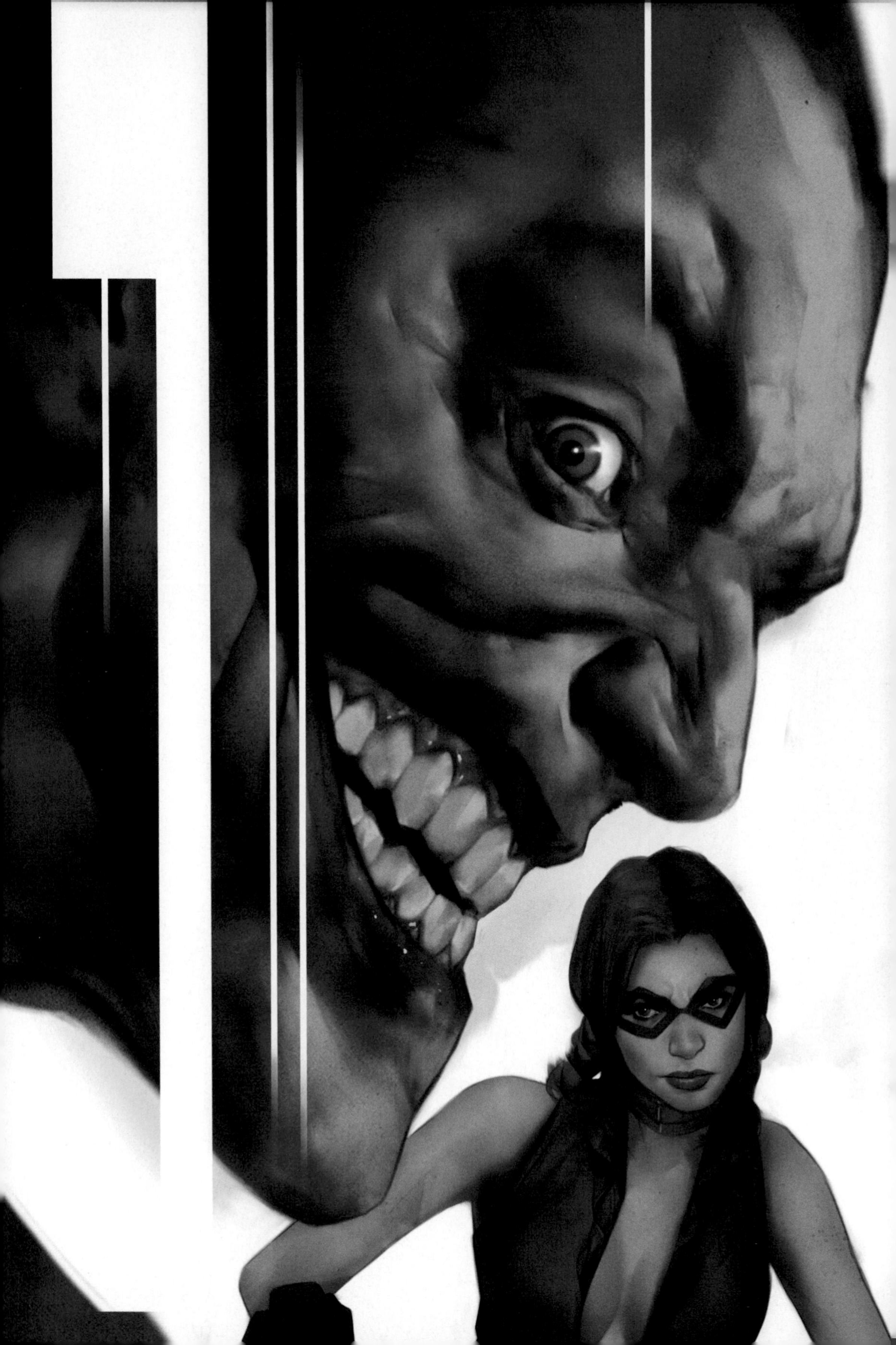

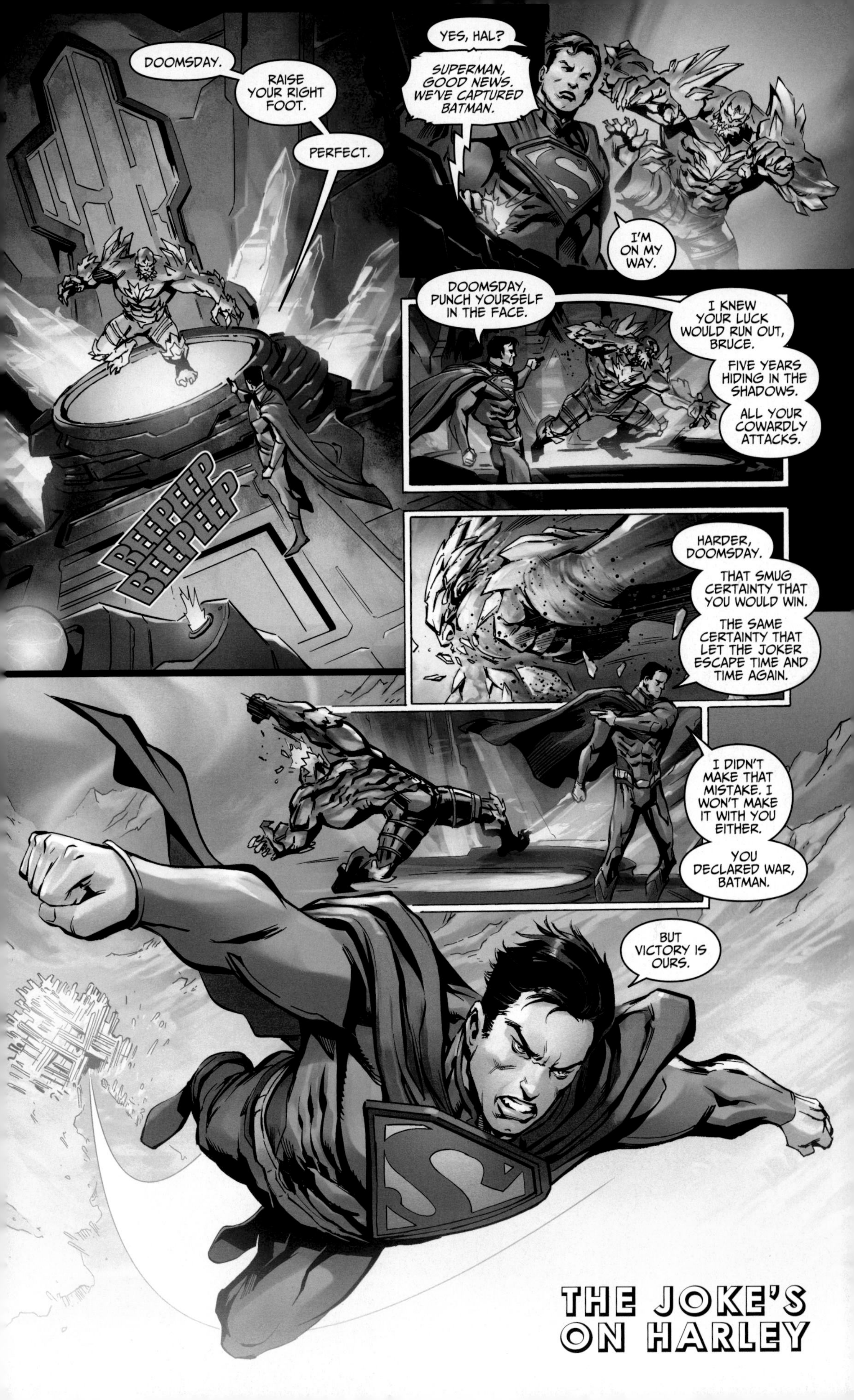
DOOMSDAY.
RAISE YOUR RIGHT FOOT.
PERFECT.
BEEPEEP BEEPEEP
YES, HAL?
SUPERMAN, GOOD NEWS. WE'VE CAPTURED BATMAN.
I'M ON MY WAY.
DOOMSDAY, PUNCH YOURSELF IN THE FACE.
I KNEW YOUR LUCK WOULD RUN OUT, BRUCE.
FIVE YEARS HIDING IN THE SHADOWS.
ALL YOUR COWARDLY ATTACKS.
HARDER, DOOMSDAY.
THAT SMUG CERTAINTY THAT YOU WOULD WIN.
THE SAME CERTAINTY THAT LET THE JOKER ESCAPE TIME AND TIME AGAIN.
I DIDN'T MAKE THAT MISTAKE. I WON'T MAKE IT WITH YOU EITHER.
YOU DECLARED WAR, BATMAN.
BUT VICTORY IS OURS.
THE JOKE'S ON HARLEY

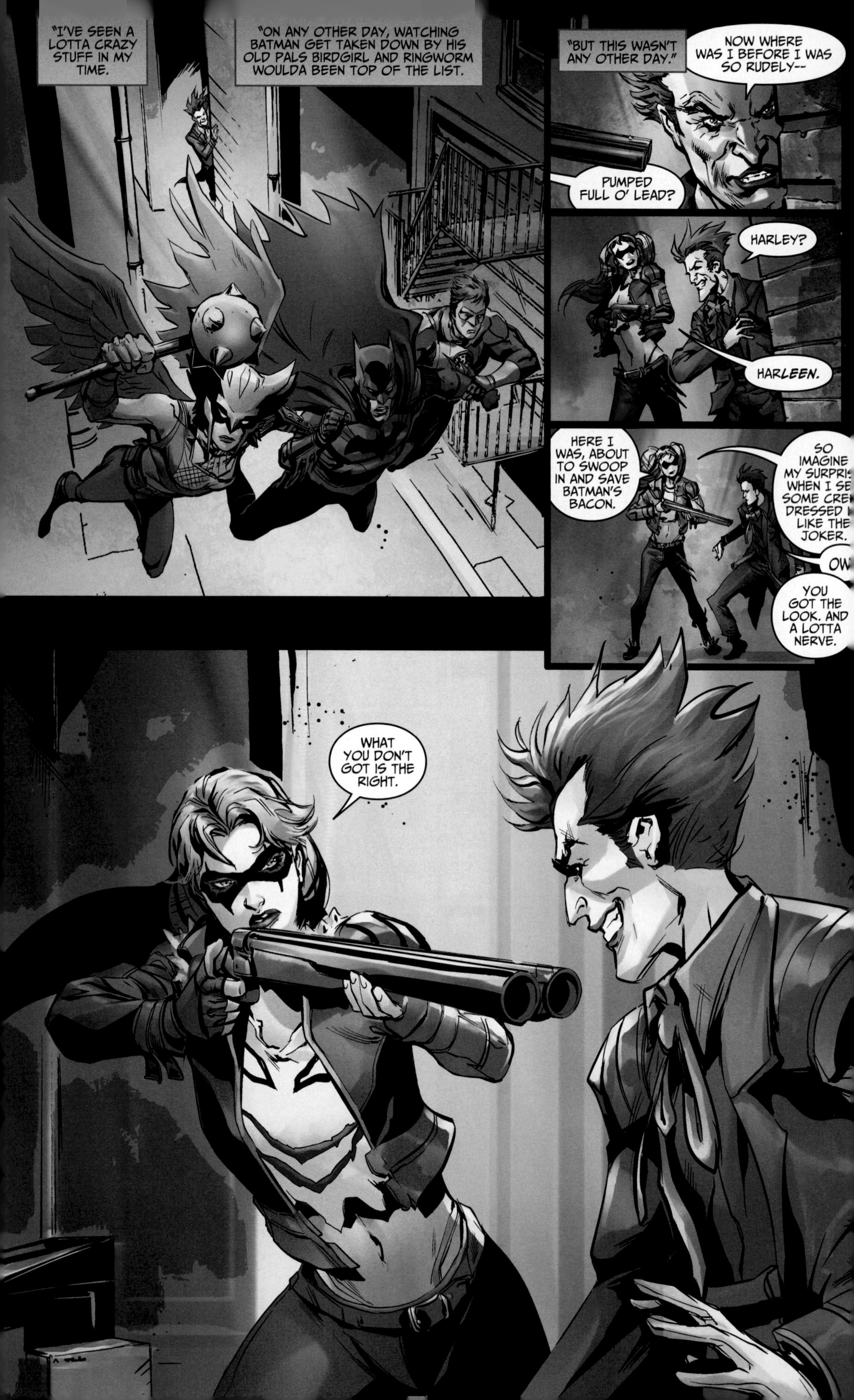
"I'VE SEEN A LOTTA CRAZY STUFF IN MY TIME.
"ON ANY OTHER DAY, WATCHING BATMAN GET TAKEN DOWN BY HIS OLD PALS BIRDGIRL AND RINGWORM WOULDA BEEN TOP OF THE LIST.
"BUT THIS WASN'T ANY OTHER DAY."
NOW WHERE WAS I BEFORE I WAS SO RUDELY--
PUMPED FULL O' LEAD?
HARLEY?
HARLEEN.
HERE I WAS, ABOUT TO SWOOP IN AND SAVE BATMAN'S BACON.
SO IMAGINE MY SURPRIS WHEN I SE SOME CRE DRESSED LIKE THE JOKER.
OW
YOU GOT THE LOOK. AND A LOTTA NERVE.
WHAT YOU DON'T GOT IS THE RIGHT.

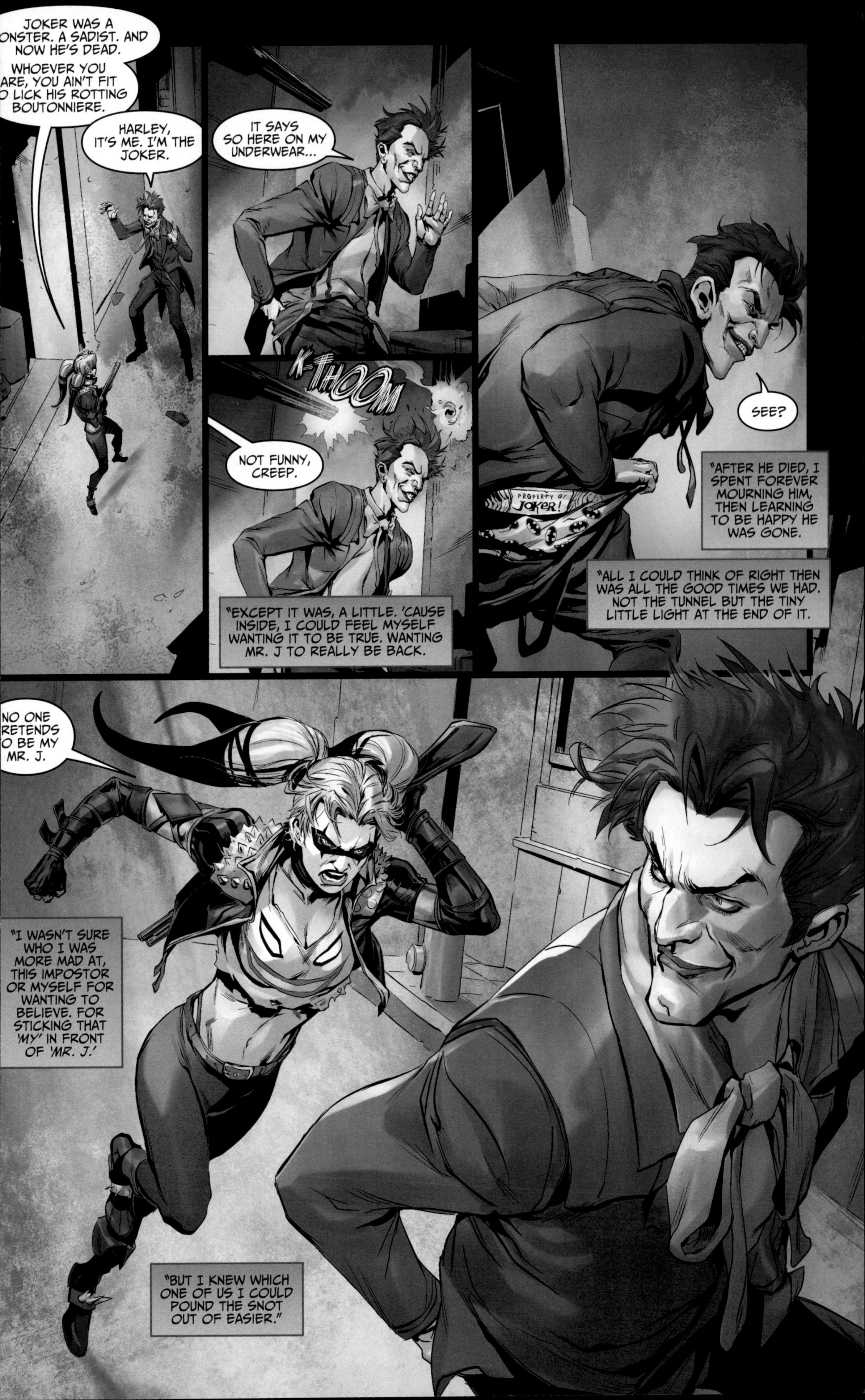

JOKER WAS A ONSTER. A SADIST. AND NOW HE'S DEAD.
WHOEVER YOU ARE, YOU AIN'T FIT O LICK HIS ROTTING BOUTONNIERE.
HARLEY, IT'S ME. I'M THE JOKER.
IT SAYS SO HERE ON MY UNDERWEAR...
K-THOOM
NOT FUNNY, CREEP.
"EXCEPT IT WAS, A LITTLE. 'CAUSE INSIDE, I COULD FEEL MYSELF WANTING IT TO BE TRUE. WANTING MR. J TO REALLY BE BACK.
PROPERTY OF JOKER!
SEE?
"AFTER HE DIED, I SPENT FOREVER MOURNING HIM, THEN LEARNING TO BE HAPPY HE WAS GONE.
"ALL I COULD THINK OF RIGHT THEN WAS ALL THE GOOD TIMES WE HAD. NOT THE TUNNEL BUT THE TINY LITTLE LIGHT AT THE END OF IT.
NO ONE RETENDS O BE MY MR. J.
"I WASN'T SURE WHO I WAS MORE MAD AT, THIS IMPOSTOR OR MYSELF FOR WANTING TO BELIEVE. FOR STICKING THAT 'MY' IN FRONT OF 'MR. J.'
"BUT I KNEW WHICH ONE OF US I COULD POUND THE SNOT OUT OF EASIER."

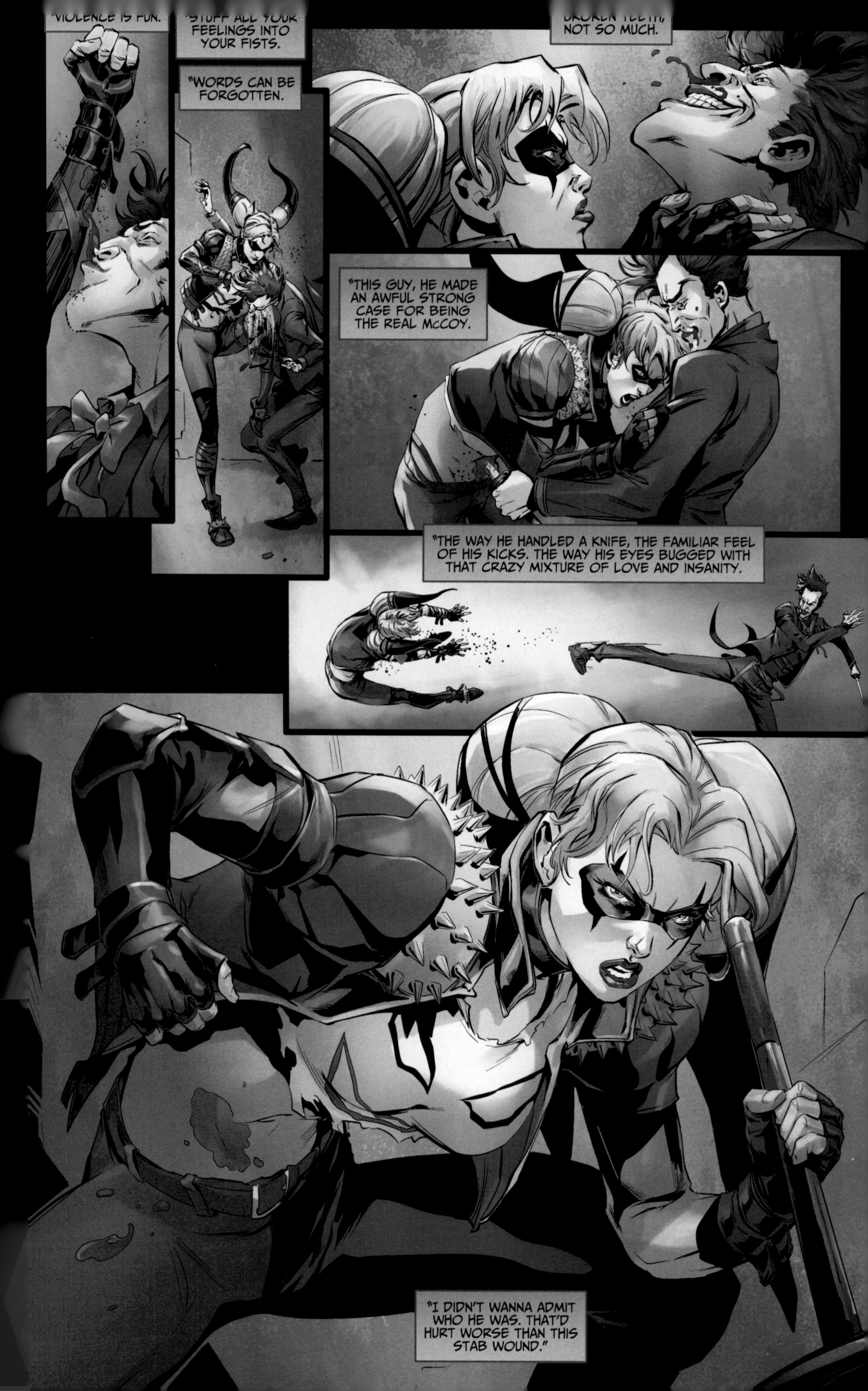
"VIOLENCE IS FUN.
"STUFF ALL YOUR FEELINGS INTO YOUR FISTS.
"WORDS CAN BE FORGOTTEN.
BROKEN TEETH, NOT SO MUCH.
"THIS GUY, HE MADE AN AWFUL STRONG CASE FOR BEING THE REAL McCOY.
"THE WAY HE HANDLED A KNIFE, THE FAMILIAR FEEL OF HIS KICKS. THE WAY HIS EYES BUGGED WITH THAT CRAZY MIXTURE OF LOVE AND INSANITY.
"I DIDN'T WANNA ADMIT WHO HE WAS. THAT'D HURT WORSE THAN THIS STAB WOUND."

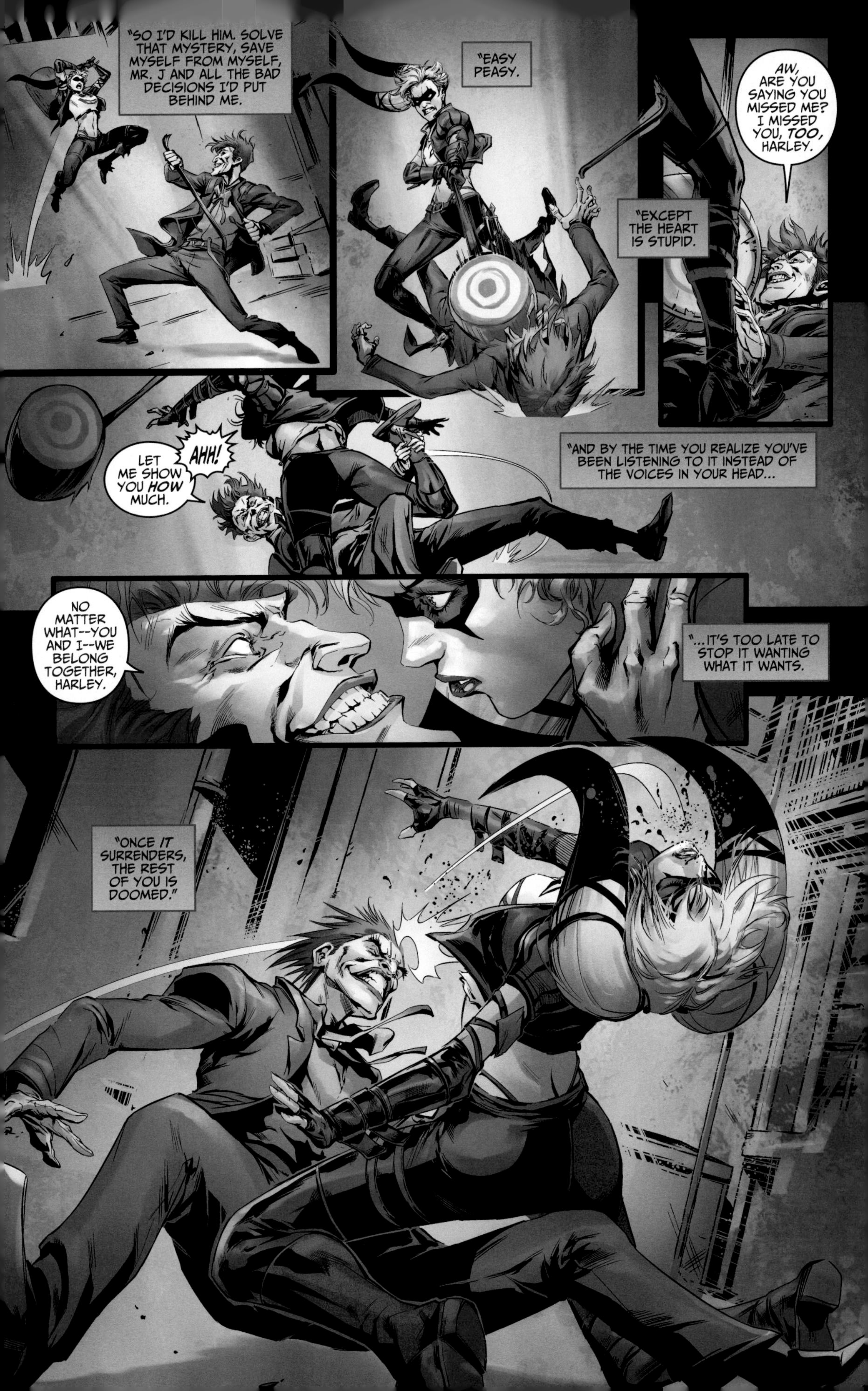
"SO I'D KILL HIM. SOLVE THAT MYSTERY, SAVE MYSELF FROM MYSELF, MR. J AND ALL THE BAD DECISIONS I'D PUT BEHIND ME.
"EASY PEASY.
"EXCEPT THE HEART IS STUPID.
AW, ARE YOU SAYING YOU MISSED ME? I MISSED YOU, TOO, HARLEY.
LET ME SHOW YOU HOW MUCH.
AHH!
"AND BY THE TIME YOU REALIZE YOU'VE BEEN LISTENING TO IT INSTEAD OF THE VOICES IN YOUR HEAD...
NO MATTER WHAT--YOU AND I--WE BELONG TOGETHER, HARLEY.
"...IT'S TOO LATE TO STOP IT WANTING WHAT IT WANTS.
"ONCE IT SURRENDERS, THE REST OF YOU IS DOOMED."

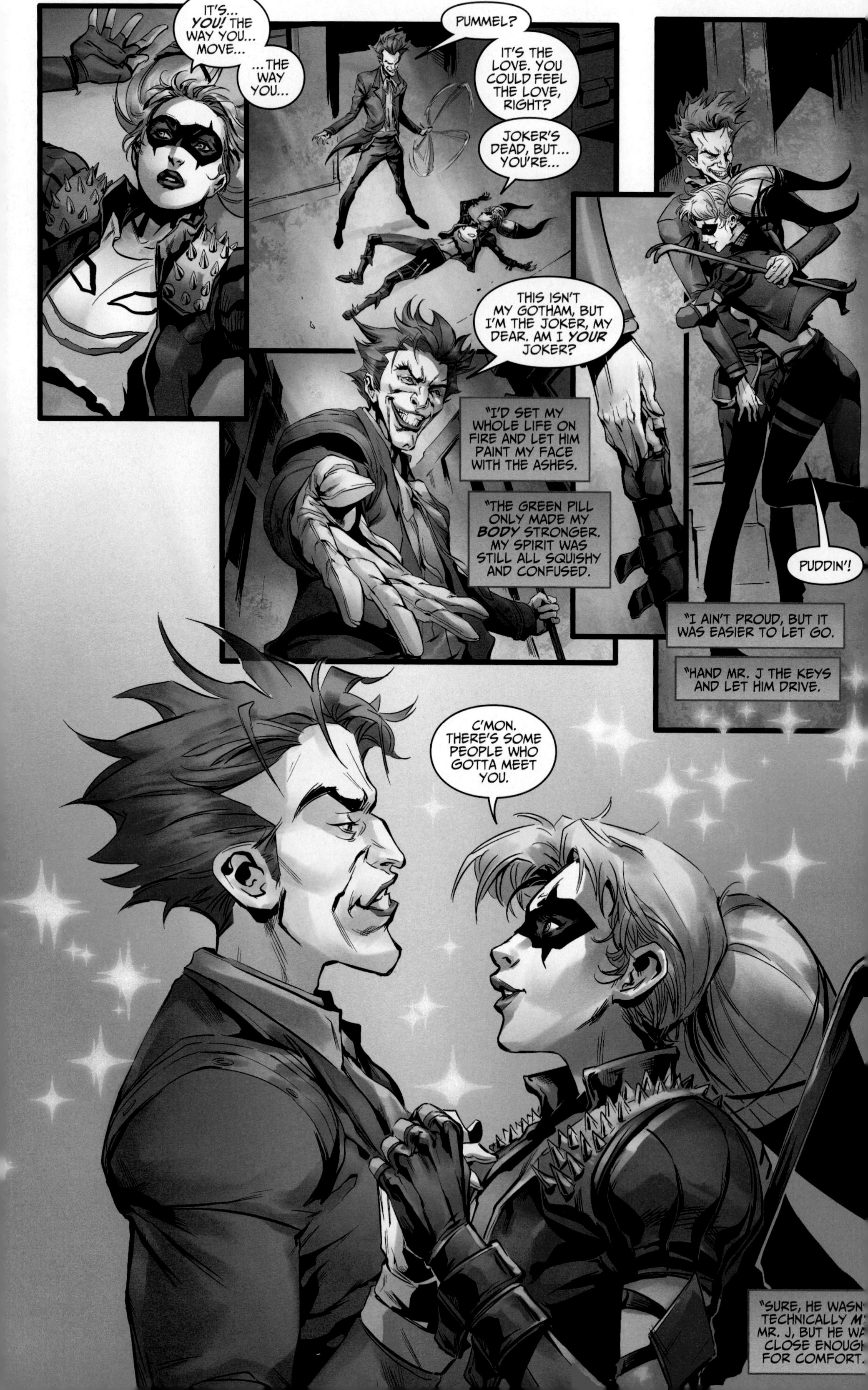
IT'S... YOU! THE WAY YOU... MOVE...
...THE WAY YOU...
PUMMEL?
IT'S THE LOVE. YOU COULD FEEL THE LOVE, RIGHT?
JOKER'S DEAD, BUT... YOU'RE...
THIS ISN'T MY GOTHAM, BUT I'M THE JOKER, MY DEAR. AM I YOUR JOKER?
"I'D SET MY WHOLE LIFE ON FIRE AND LET HIM PAINT MY FACE WITH THE ASHES.
"THE GREEN PILL ONLY MADE MY BODY STRONGER. MY SPIRIT WAS STILL ALL SQUISHY AND CONFUSED.
PUDDIN'!
"I AIN'T PROUD, BUT IT WAS EASIER TO LET GO.
"HAND MR. J THE KEYS AND LET HIM DRIVE.
C'MON. THERE'S SOME PEOPLE WHO GOTTA MEET YOU.
"SURE, HE WASN' TECHNICALLY M MR. J, BUT HE WA CLOSE ENOUG FOR COMFORT.

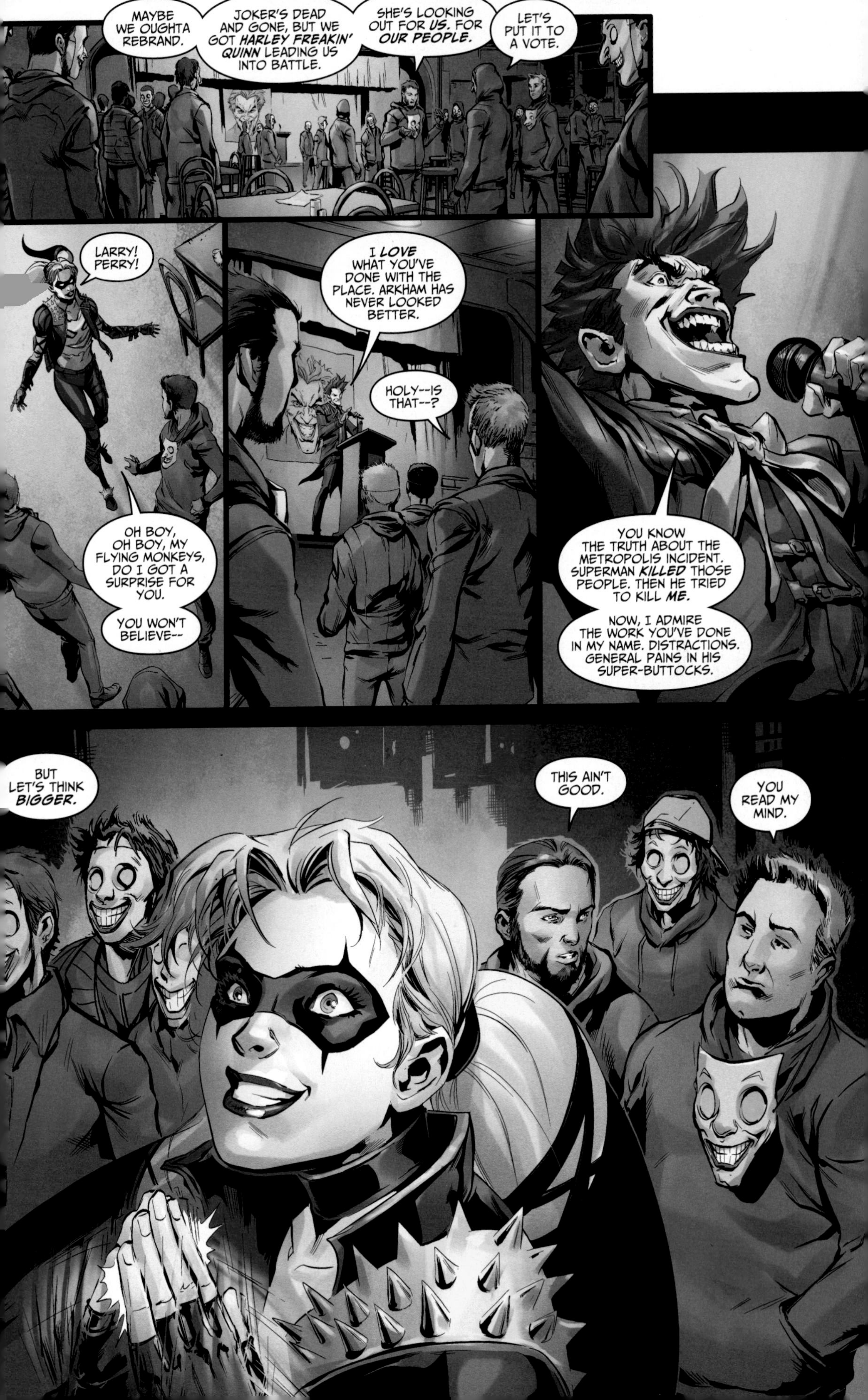
MAYBE WE OUGHTA REBRAND.
JOKER'S DEAD AND GONE, BUT WE GOT HARLEY FREAKIN' QUINN LEADING US INTO BATTLE.
SHE'S LOOKING OUT FOR US. FOR OUR PEOPLE.
LET'S PUT IT TO A VOTE.
LARRY! PERRY!
OH BOY, OH BOY, MY FLYING MONKEYS, DO I GOT A SURPRISE FOR YOU.
YOU WON'T BELIEVE--
I LOVE WHAT YOU'VE DONE WITH THE PLACE. ARKHAM HAS NEVER LOOKED BETTER.
HOLY--IS THAT--?
YOU KNOW THE TRUTH ABOUT THE METROPOLIS INCIDENT. SUPERMAN KILLED THOSE PEOPLE. THEN HE TRIED TO KILL ME.
NOW, I ADMIRE THE WORK YOU'VE DONE IN MY NAME. DISTRACTIONS. GENERAL PAINS IN HIS SUPER-BUTTOCKS.
BUT LET'S THINK BIGGER.
THIS AIN'T GOOD.
YOU READ MY MIND.

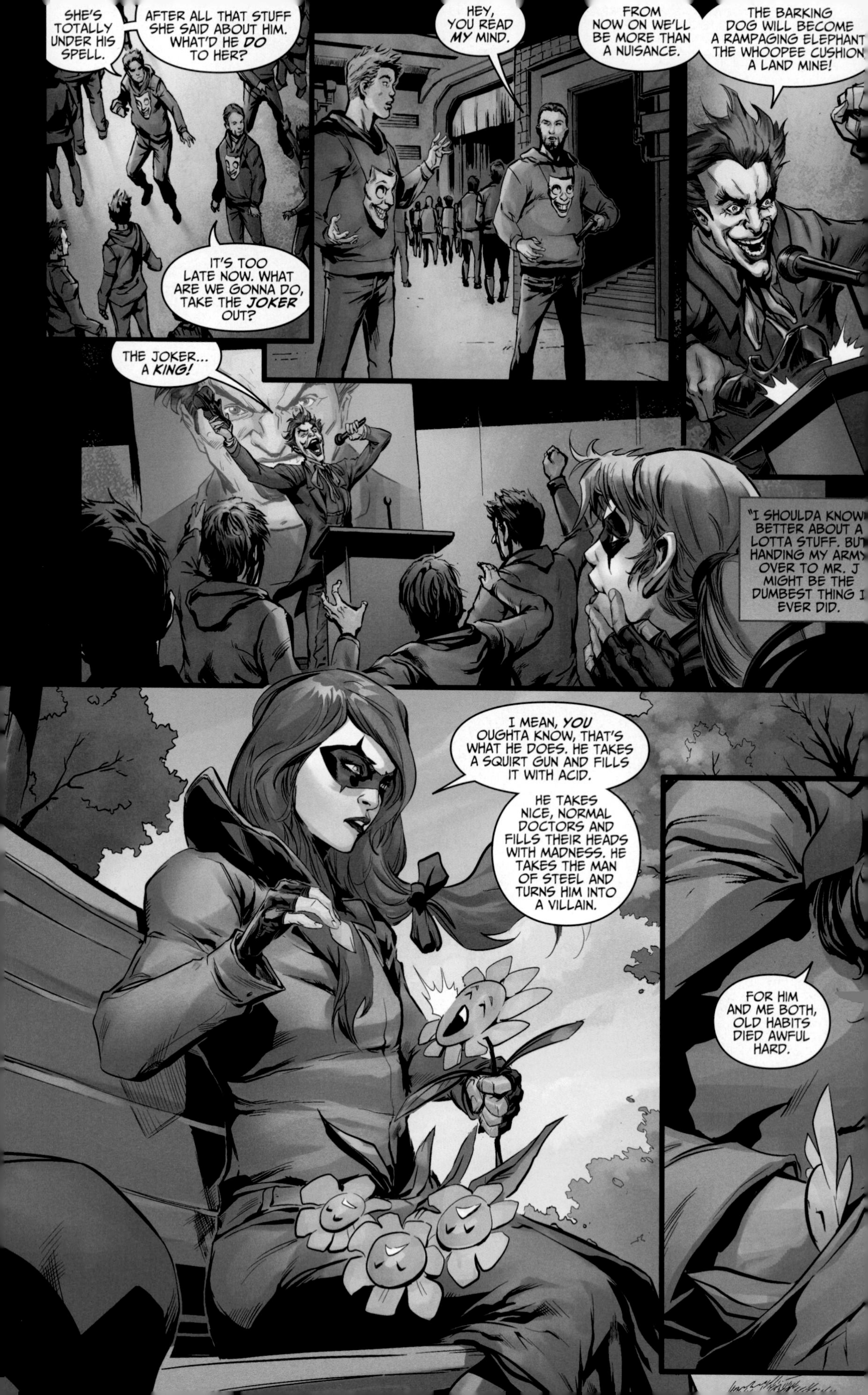
SHE'S TOTALLY UNDER HIS SPELL.
AFTER ALL THAT STUFF SHE SAID ABOUT HIM. WHAT'D HE DO TO HER?
IT'S TOO LATE NOW. WHAT ARE WE GONNA DO, TAKE THE JOKER OUT?
HEY, YOU READ MY MIND.
FROM NOW ON WE'LL BE MORE THAN A NUISANCE.
THE BARKING DOG WILL BECOME A RAMPAGING ELEPHANT THE WHOOPEE CUSHION A LAND MINE!
THE JOKER... A KING!
"I SHOULDA KNOW BETTER ABOUT A LOTTA STUFF. BUT HANDING MY ARMY OVER TO MR. J MIGHT BE THE DUMBEST THING I EVER DID.
I MEAN, YOU OUGHTA KNOW, THAT'S WHAT HE DOES. HE TAKES A SQUIRT GUN AND FILLS IT WITH ACID.
HE TAKES NICE, NORMAL DOCTORS AND FILLS THEIR HEADS WITH MADNESS. HE TAKES THE MAN OF STEEL AND TURNS HIM INTO A VILLAIN.
FOR HIM AND ME BOTH, OLD HABITS DIED AWFUL HARD.

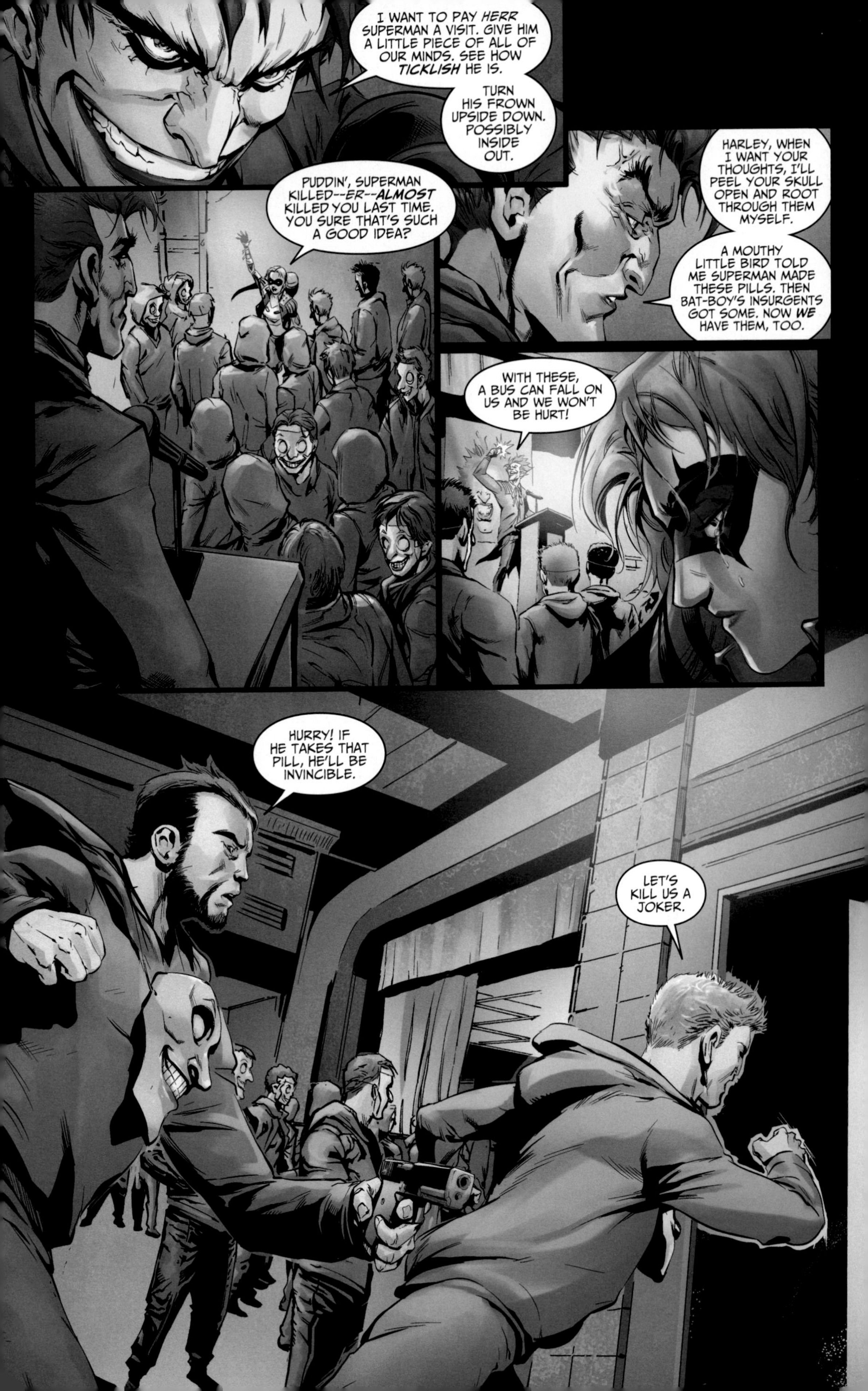

I WANT TO PAY *HERR* SUPERMAN A VISIT. GIVE HIM A LITTLE PIECE OF ALL OF OUR MINDS. SEE HOW *TICKLISH* HE IS.
TURN HIS FROWN UPSIDE DOWN. POSSIBLY INSIDE OUT.
PUDDIN', SUPERMAN KILLED--*ER*--*ALMOST* KILLED YOU LAST TIME. YOU SURE THAT'S SUCH A GOOD IDEA?
HARLEY, WHEN I WANT YOUR THOUGHTS, I'LL PEEL YOUR SKULL OPEN AND ROOT THROUGH THEM MYSELF.
A MOUTHY LITTLE BIRD TOLD ME SUPERMAN MADE THESE PILLS. THEN BAT-BOY'S INSURGENTS GOT SOME. NOW *WE* HAVE THEM, TOO.
WITH THESE, A BUS CAN FALL ON US AND WE WON'T BE HURT!
HURRY! IF HE TAKES THAT PILL, HE'LL BE INVINCIBLE.
LET'S KILL US A JOKER.

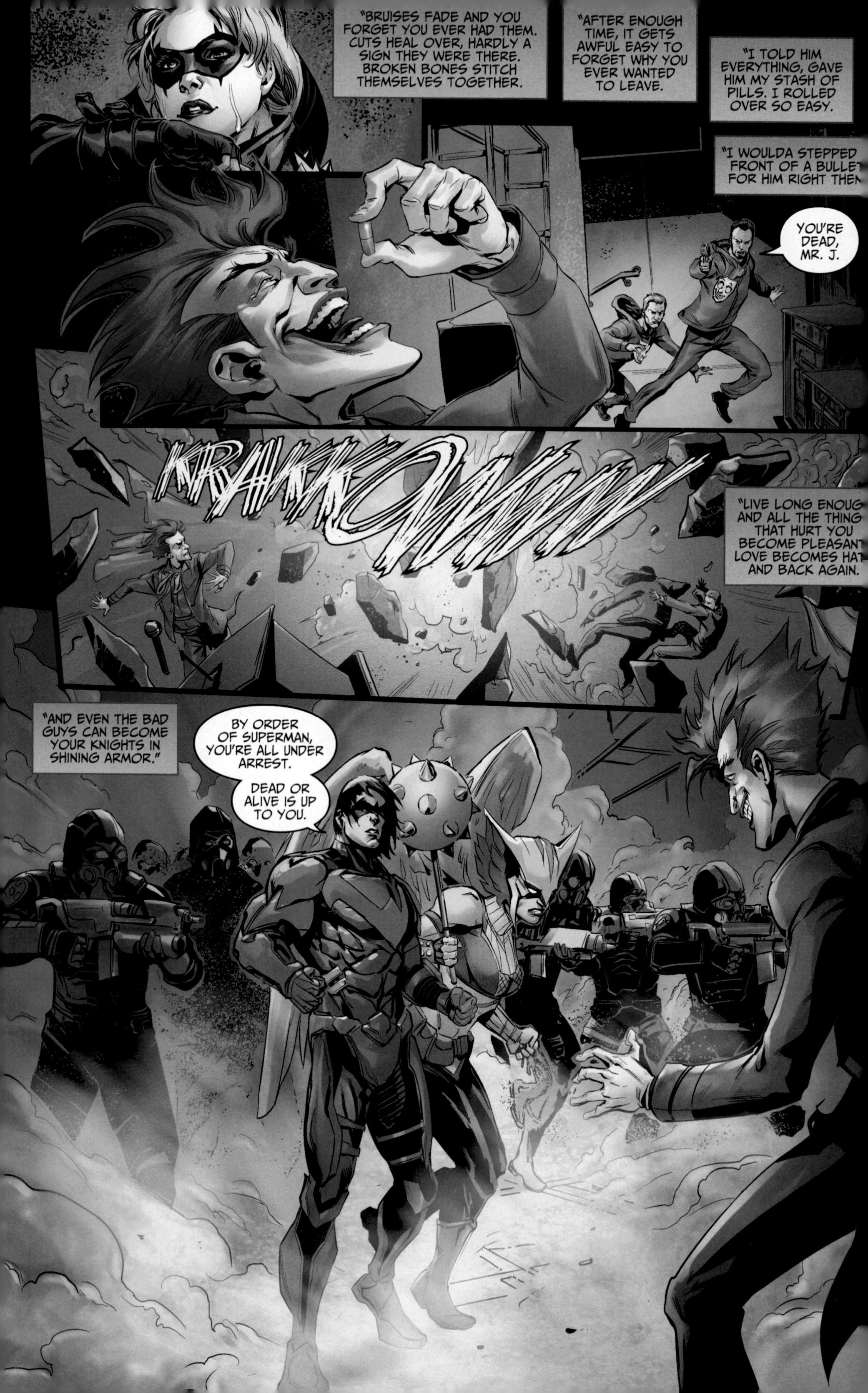
"BRUISES FADE AND YOU FORGET YOU EVER HAD THEM. CUTS HEAL OVER, HARDLY A SIGN THEY WERE THERE. BROKEN BONES STITCH THEMSELVES TOGETHER.
"AFTER ENOUGH TIME, IT GETS AWFUL EASY TO FORGET WHY YOU EVER WANTED TO LEAVE.
"I TOLD HIM EVERYTHING, GAVE HIM MY STASH OF PILLS. I ROLLED OVER SO EASY.
"I WOULDA STEPPED FRONT OF A BULLET FOR HIM RIGHT THEN
YOU'RE DEAD, MR. J.
KRAKKOWWW
"LIVE LONG ENOUG AND ALL THE THING THAT HURT YOU BECOME PLEASANT LOVE BECOMES HAT AND BACK AGAIN.
"AND EVEN THE BAD GUYS CAN BECOME YOUR KNIGHTS IN SHINING ARMOR."
BY ORDER OF SUPERMAN, YOU'RE ALL UNDER ARREST.
DEAD OR ALIVE IS UP TO YOU.

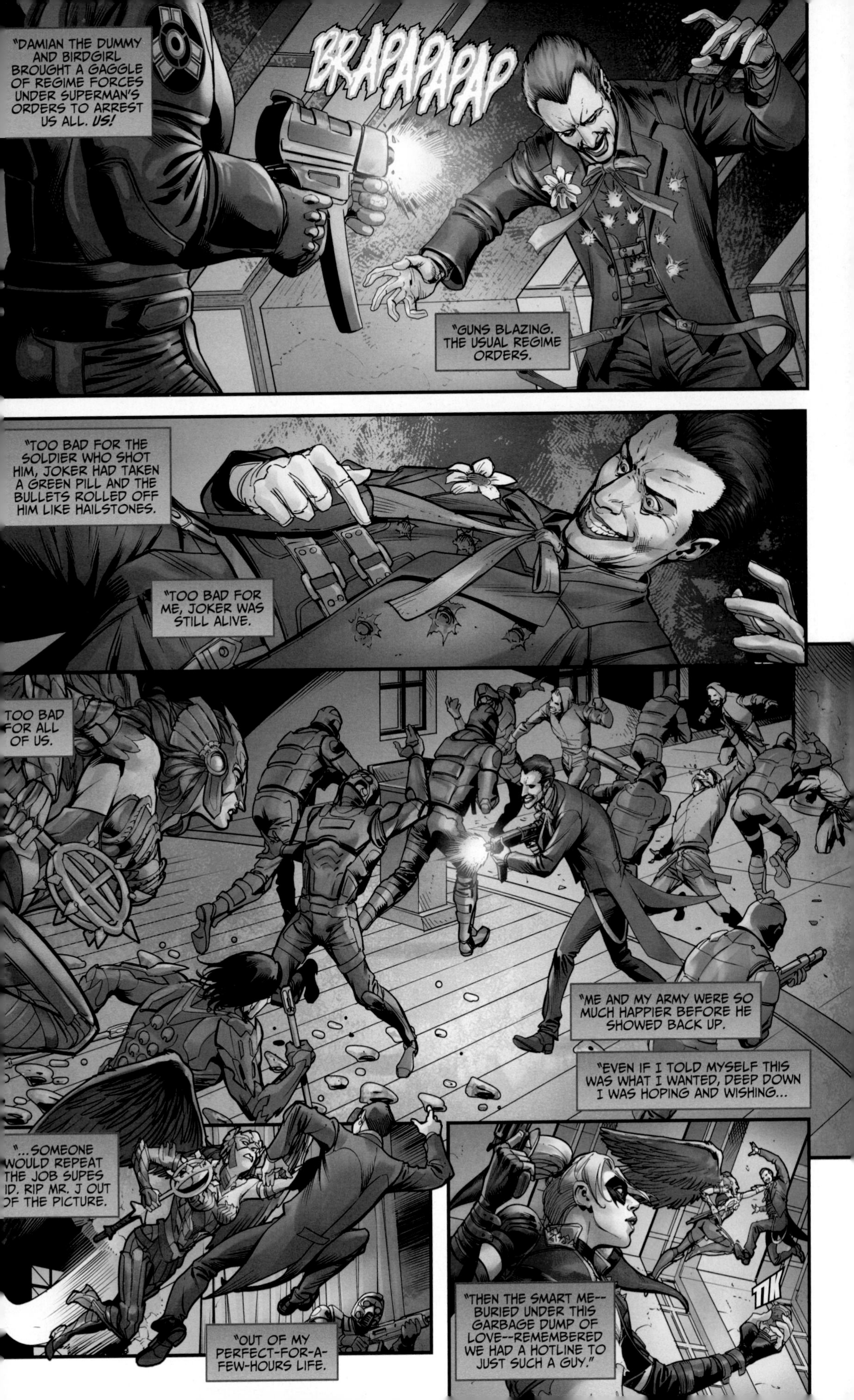
"DAMIAN THE DUMMY AND BIRDGIRL BROUGHT A GAGGLE OF REGIME FORCES UNDER SUPERMAN'S ORDERS TO ARREST US ALL. US!
BRAPAPAPAP
"GUNS BLAZING. THE USUAL REGIME ORDERS.
"TOO BAD FOR THE SOLDIER WHO SHOT HIM, JOKER HAD TAKEN A GREEN PILL AND THE BULLETS ROLLED OFF HIM LIKE HAILSTONES.
"TOO BAD FOR ME, JOKER WAS STILL ALIVE.
TOO BAD FOR ALL OF US.
"ME AND MY ARMY WERE SO MUCH HAPPIER BEFORE HE SHOWED BACK UP.
"EVEN IF I TOLD MYSELF THIS WAS WHAT I WANTED, DEEP DOWN I WAS HOPING AND WISHING...
"...SOMEONE WOULD REPEAT THE JOB SUPES DID. RIP MR. J OUT OF THE PICTURE.
"OUT OF MY PERFECT-FOR-A-FEW-HOURS LIFE.
"THEN THE SMART ME--BURIED UNDER THIS GARBAGE DUMP OF LOVE--REMEMBERED WE HAD A HOTLINE TO JUST SUCH A GUY."
TIK

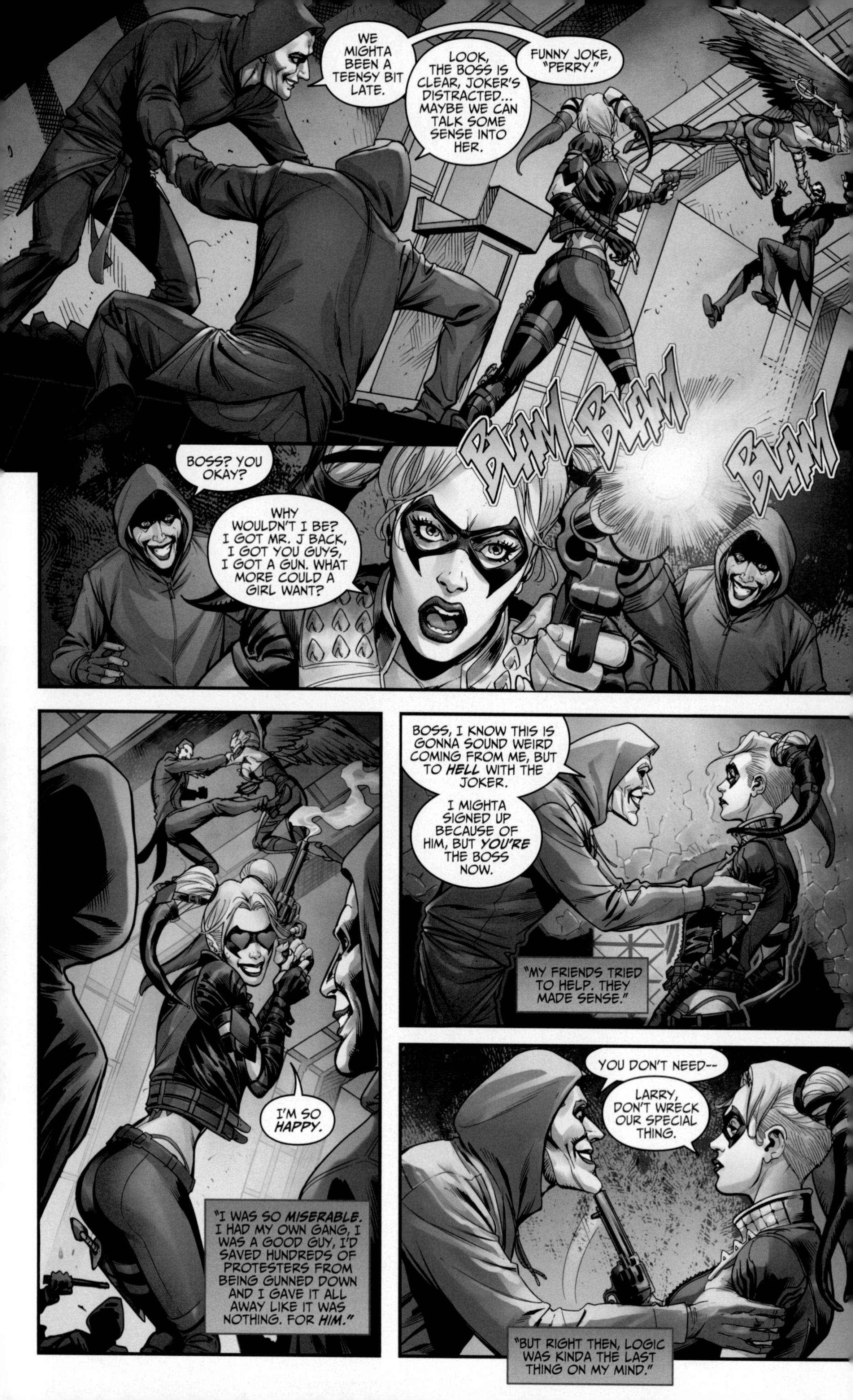
WE MIGHTA BEEN A TEENSY BIT LATE.
LOOK, THE BOSS IS CLEAR, JOKER'S DISTRACTED... MAYBE WE CAN TALK SOME SENSE INTO HER.
FUNNY JOKE, "PERRY."
BLAM BLAM
BLAM
BOSS? YOU OKAY?
WHY WOULDN'T I BE? I GOT MR. J BACK, I GOT YOU GUYS, I GOT A GUN. WHAT MORE COULD A GIRL WANT?
I'M SO HAPPY.
"I WAS SO MISERABLE. I HAD MY OWN GANG, I WAS A GOOD GUY, I'D SAVED HUNDREDS OF PROTESTERS FROM BEING GUNNED DOWN AND I GAVE IT ALL AWAY LIKE IT WAS NOTHING. FOR HIM."
BOSS, I KNOW THIS IS GONNA SOUND WEIRD COMING FROM ME, BUT TO HELL WITH THE JOKER.
I MIGHTA SIGNED UP BECAUSE OF HIM, BUT YOU'RE THE BOSS NOW.
"MY FRIENDS TRIED TO HELP. THEY MADE SENSE."
YOU DON'T NEED--
LARRY, DON'T WRECK OUR SPECIAL THING.
"BUT RIGHT THEN, LOGIC WAS KINDA THE LAST THING ON MY MIND."

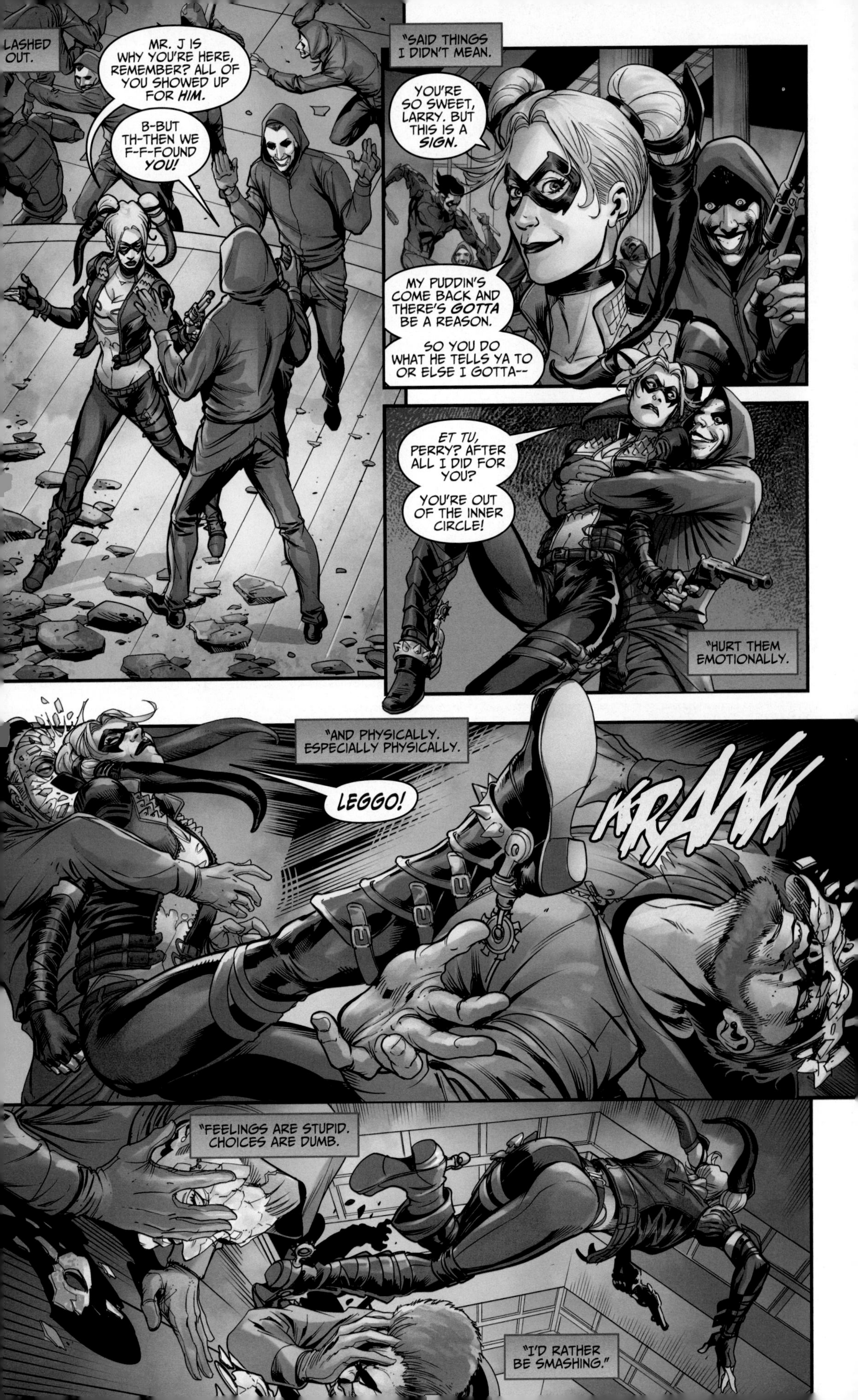
LASHED OUT.
MR. J IS WHY YOU'RE HERE, REMEMBER? ALL OF YOU SHOWED UP FOR HIM.
B-BUT TH-THEN WE F-F-FOUND YOU!
"SAID THINGS I DIDN'T MEAN.
YOU'RE SO SWEET, LARRY. BUT THIS IS A SIGN.
MY PUDDIN'S COME BACK AND THERE'S GOTTA BE A REASON.
SO YOU DO WHAT HE TELLS YA TO OR ELSE I GOTTA--
ET TU, PERRY? AFTER ALL I DID FOR YOU?
YOU'RE OUT OF THE INNER CIRCLE!
"HURT THEM EMOTIONALLY.
"AND PHYSICALLY. ESPECIALLY PHYSICALLY.
LEGGO!
KRAKK
"FEELINGS ARE STUPID. CHOICES ARE DUMB.
"I'D RATHER BE SMASHING."

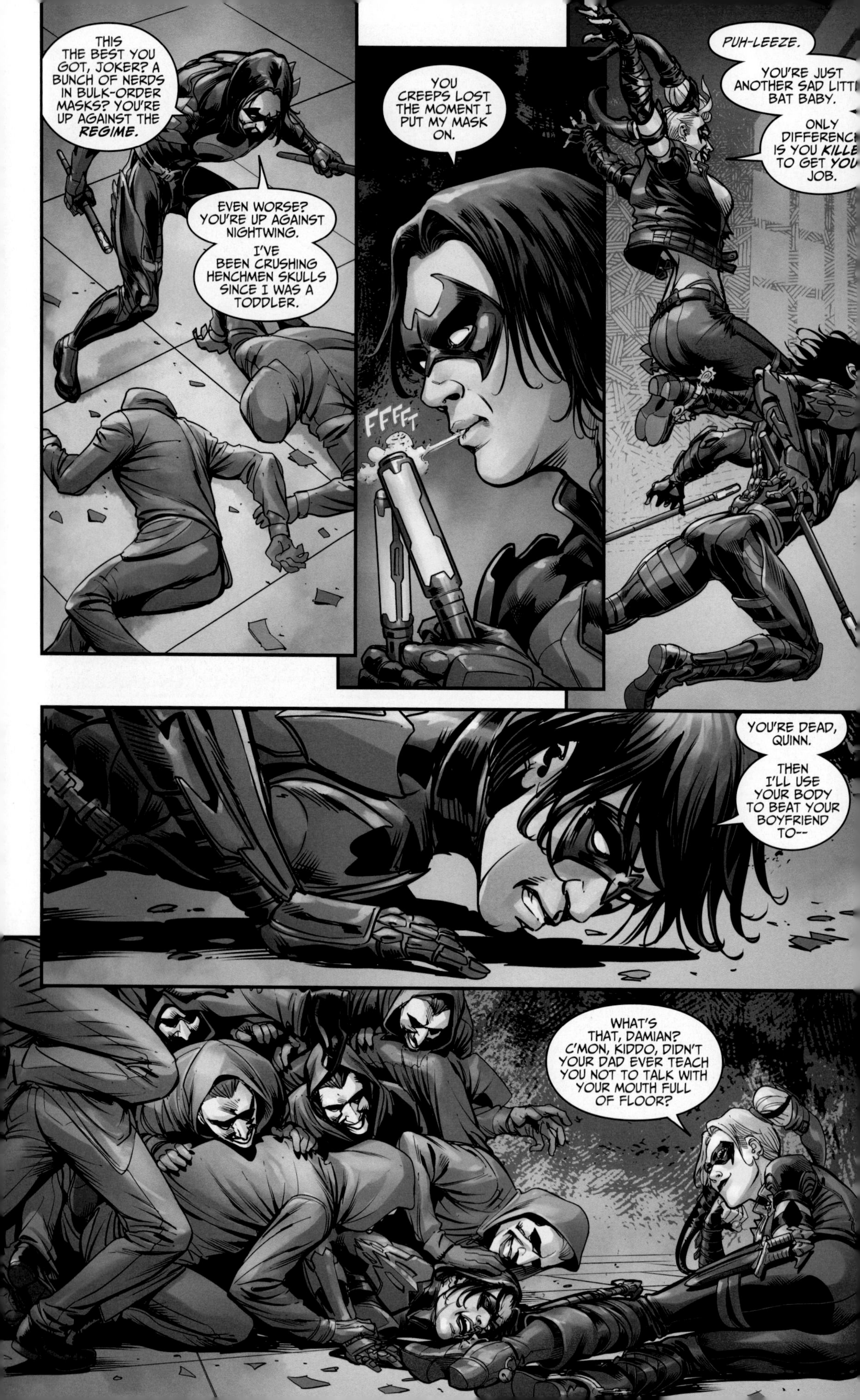
THIS THE BEST YOU GOT, JOKER? A BUNCH OF NERDS IN BULK-ORDER MASKS? YOU'RE UP AGAINST THE *REGIME.*
EVEN WORSE? YOU'RE UP AGAINST NIGHTWING.
I'VE BEEN CRUSHING HENCHMEN SKULLS SINCE I WAS A TODDLER.
YOU CREEPS LOST THE MOMENT I PUT MY MASK ON.
FFFFT
PUH-LEEZE.
YOU'RE JUST ANOTHER SAD LITTL BAT BABY.
ONLY DIFFERENC IS YOU *KILLE* TO GET *YOU* JOB.
YOU'RE DEAD, QUINN.
THEN I'LL USE YOUR BODY TO BEAT YOUR BOYFRIEND TO--
WHAT'S THAT, DAMIAN? C'MON, KIDDO, DIDN'T YOUR DAD EVER TEACH YOU NOT TO TALK WITH YOUR MOUTH FULL OF FLOOR?

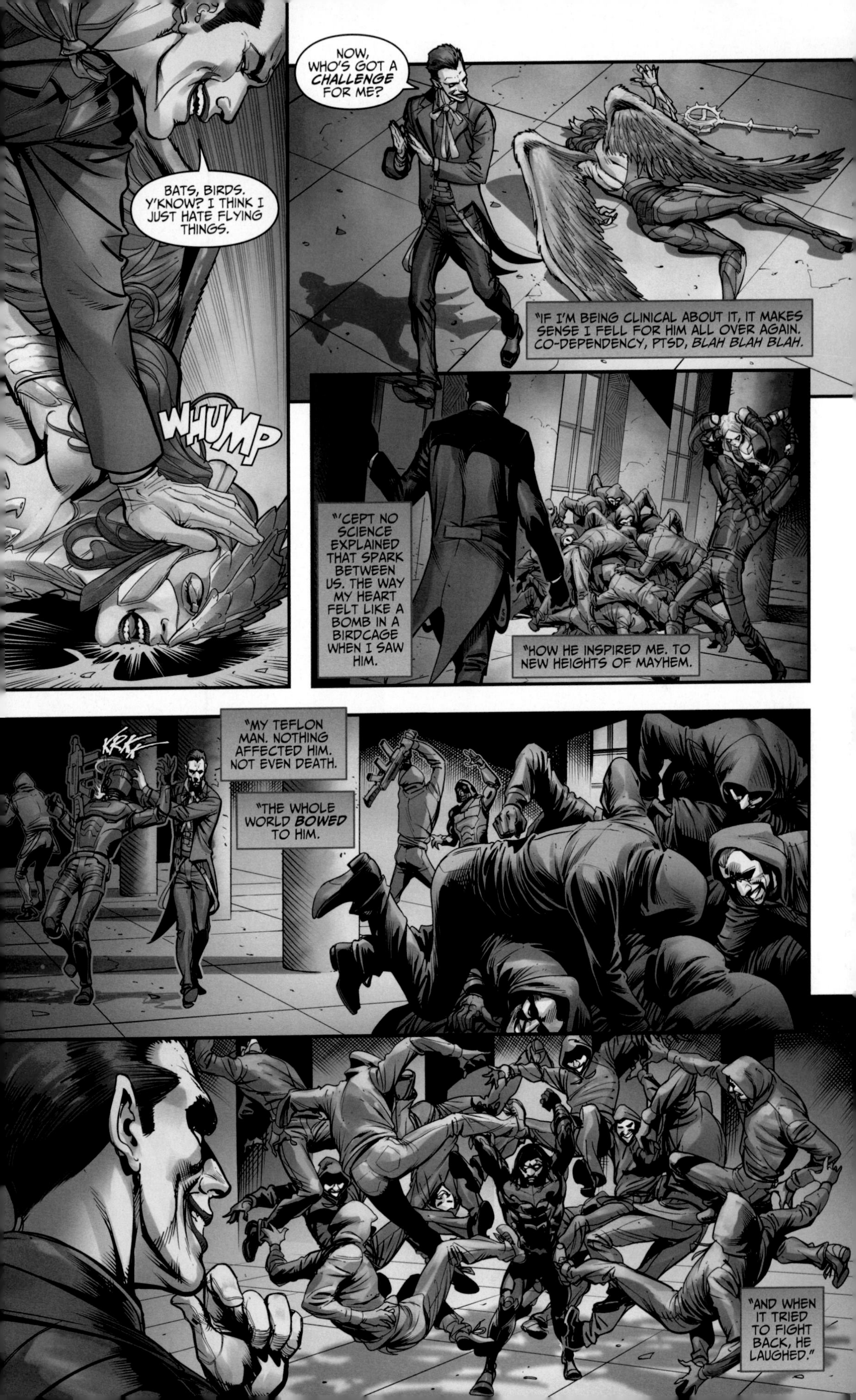
BATS, BIRDS. Y'KNOW? I THINK I JUST HATE FLYING THINGS.
WHUMP
NOW, WHO'S GOT A CHALLENGE FOR ME?
"IF I'M BEING CLINICAL ABOUT IT, IT MAKES SENSE I FELL FOR HIM ALL OVER AGAIN. CO-DEPENDENCY, PTSD, BLAH BLAH BLAH.
"'CEPT NO SCIENCE EXPLAINED THAT SPARK BETWEEN US. THE WAY MY HEART FELT LIKE A BOMB IN A BIRDCAGE WHEN I SAW HIM.
"HOW HE INSPIRED ME. TO NEW HEIGHTS OF MAYHEM.
KRKK
"MY TEFLON MAN. NOTHING AFFECTED HIM. NOT EVEN DEATH.
"THE WHOLE WORLD BOWED TO HIM.
"AND WHEN IT TRIED TO FIGHT BACK, HE LAUGHED."

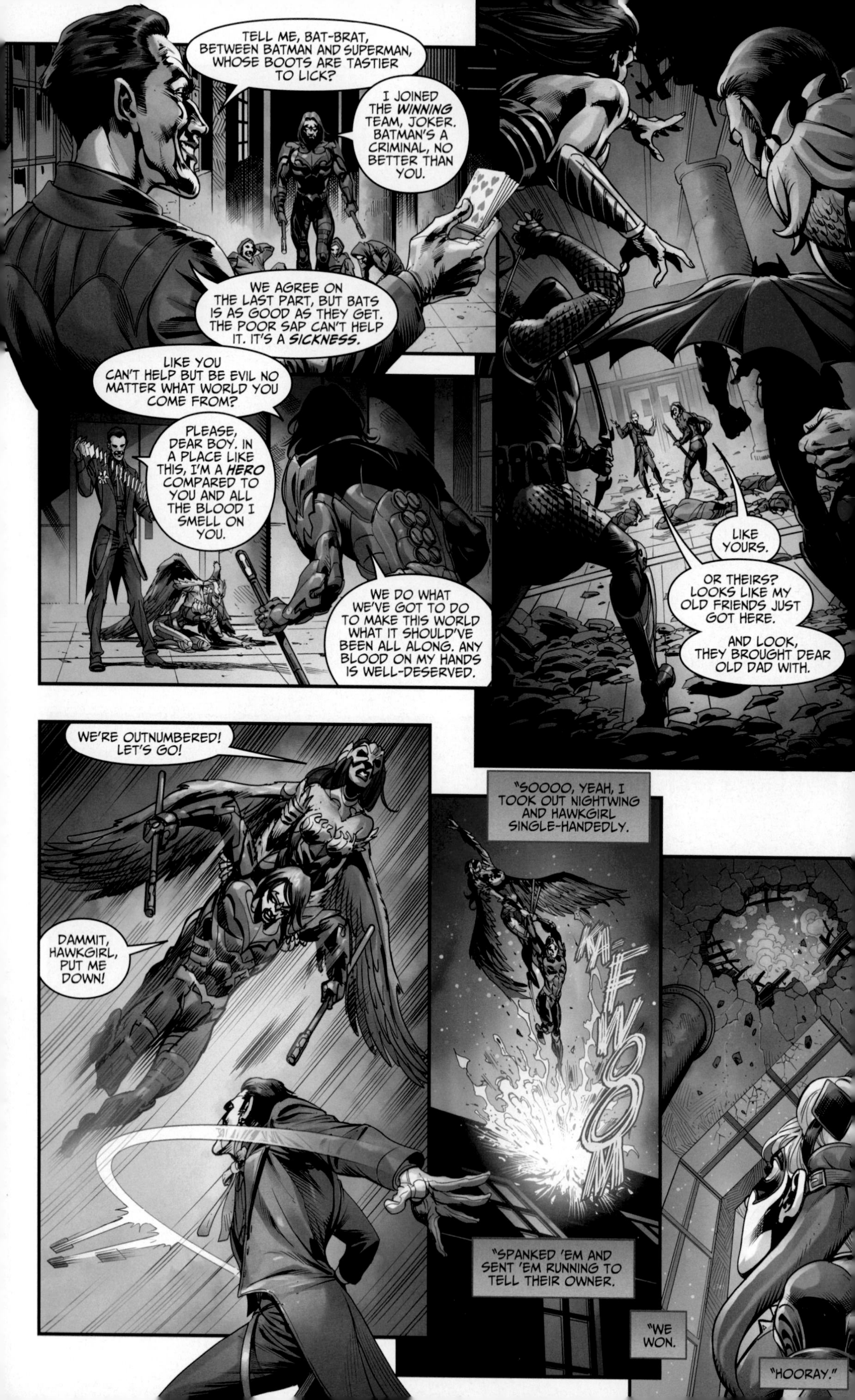
TELL ME, BAT-BRAT, BETWEEN BATMAN AND SUPERMAN, WHOSE BOOTS ARE TASTIER TO LICK?
I JOINED THE WINNING TEAM, JOKER. BATMAN'S A CRIMINAL, NO BETTER THAN YOU.
WE AGREE ON THE LAST PART, BUT BATS IS AS GOOD AS THEY GET. THE POOR SAP CAN'T HELP IT. IT'S A SICKNESS.
LIKE YOU CAN'T HELP BUT BE EVIL NO MATTER WHAT WORLD YOU COME FROM?
PLEASE, DEAR BOY. IN A PLACE LIKE THIS, I'M A HERO COMPARED TO YOU AND ALL THE BLOOD I SMELL ON YOU.
WE DO WHAT WE'VE GOT TO DO TO MAKE THIS WORLD WHAT IT SHOULD'VE BEEN ALL ALONG. ANY BLOOD ON MY HANDS IS WELL-DESERVED.
LIKE YOURS.
OR THEIRS? LOOKS LIKE MY OLD FRIENDS JUST GOT HERE.
AND LOOK, THEY BROUGHT DEAR OLD DAD WITH.
WE'RE OUTNUMBERED! LET'S GO!
DAMMIT, HAWKGIRL, PUT ME DOWN!
"SOOOO, YEAH, I TOOK OUT NIGHTWING AND HAWKGIRL SINGLE-HANDEDLY.
"SPANKED 'EM AND SENT 'EM RUNNING TO TELL THEIR OWNER.
"WE WON.
"HOORAY."

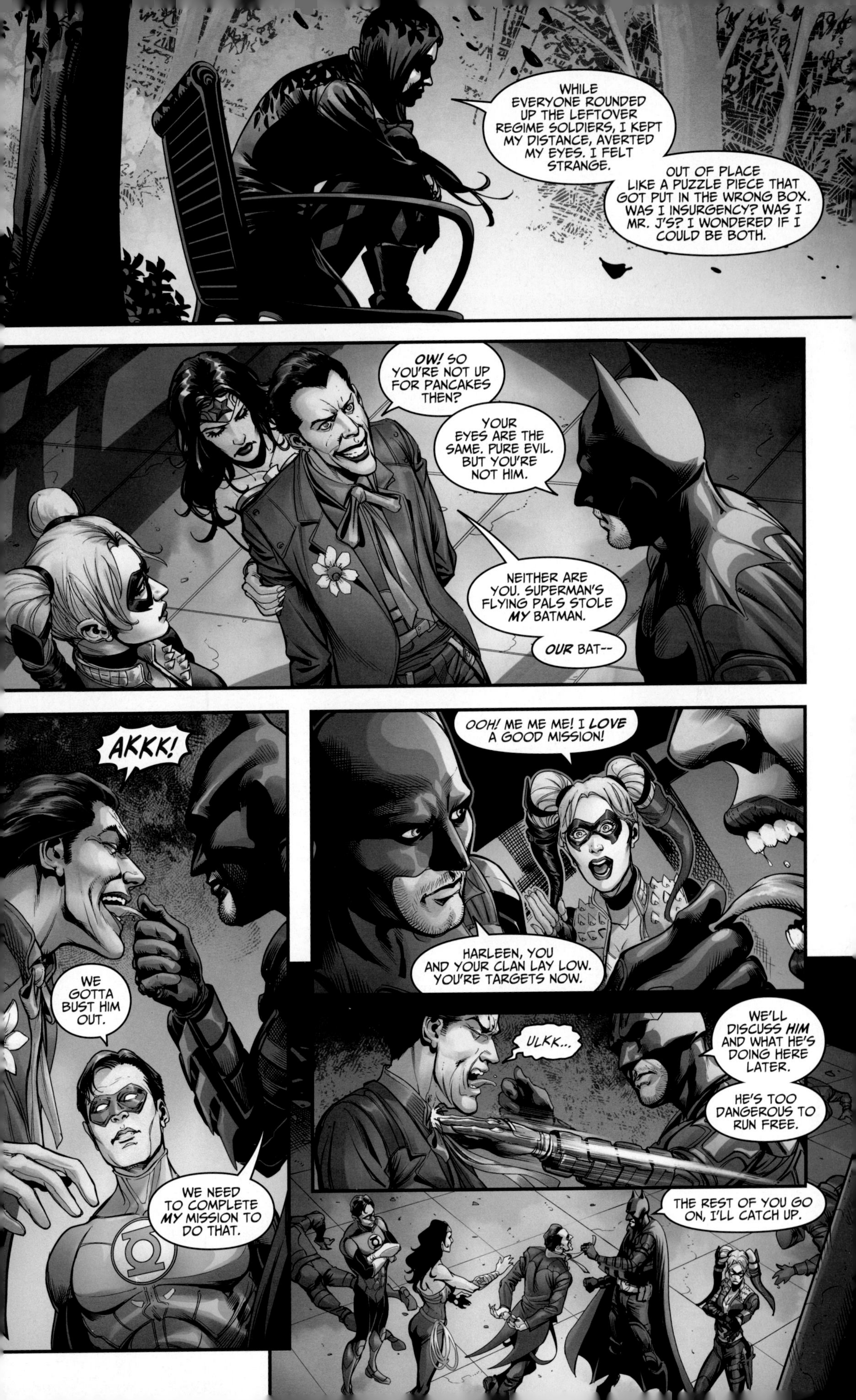
WHILE EVERYONE ROUNDED UP THE LEFTOVER REGIME SOLDIERS, I KEPT MY DISTANCE, AVERTED MY EYES. I FELT STRANGE.
OUT OF PLACE LIKE A PUZZLE PIECE THAT GOT PUT IN THE WRONG BOX. WAS I INSURGENCY? WAS I MR. J'S? I WONDERED IF I COULD BE BOTH.
OW! SO YOU'RE NOT UP FOR PANCAKES THEN?
YOUR EYES ARE THE SAME. PURE EVIL. BUT YOU'RE NOT HIM.
NEITHER ARE YOU. SUPERMAN'S FLYING PALS STOLE MY BATMAN.
OUR BAT--
AKKK!
WE GOTTA BUST HIM OUT.
WE NEED TO COMPLETE MY MISSION TO DO THAT.
OOH! ME ME ME! I LOVE A GOOD MISSION!
HARLEEN, YOU AND YOUR CLAN LAY LOW. YOU'RE TARGETS NOW.
ULKK...
WE'LL DISCUSS HIM AND WHAT HE'S DOING HERE LATER.
HE'S TOO DANGEROUS TO RUN FREE.
THE REST OF YOU GO ON, I'LL CATCH UP.

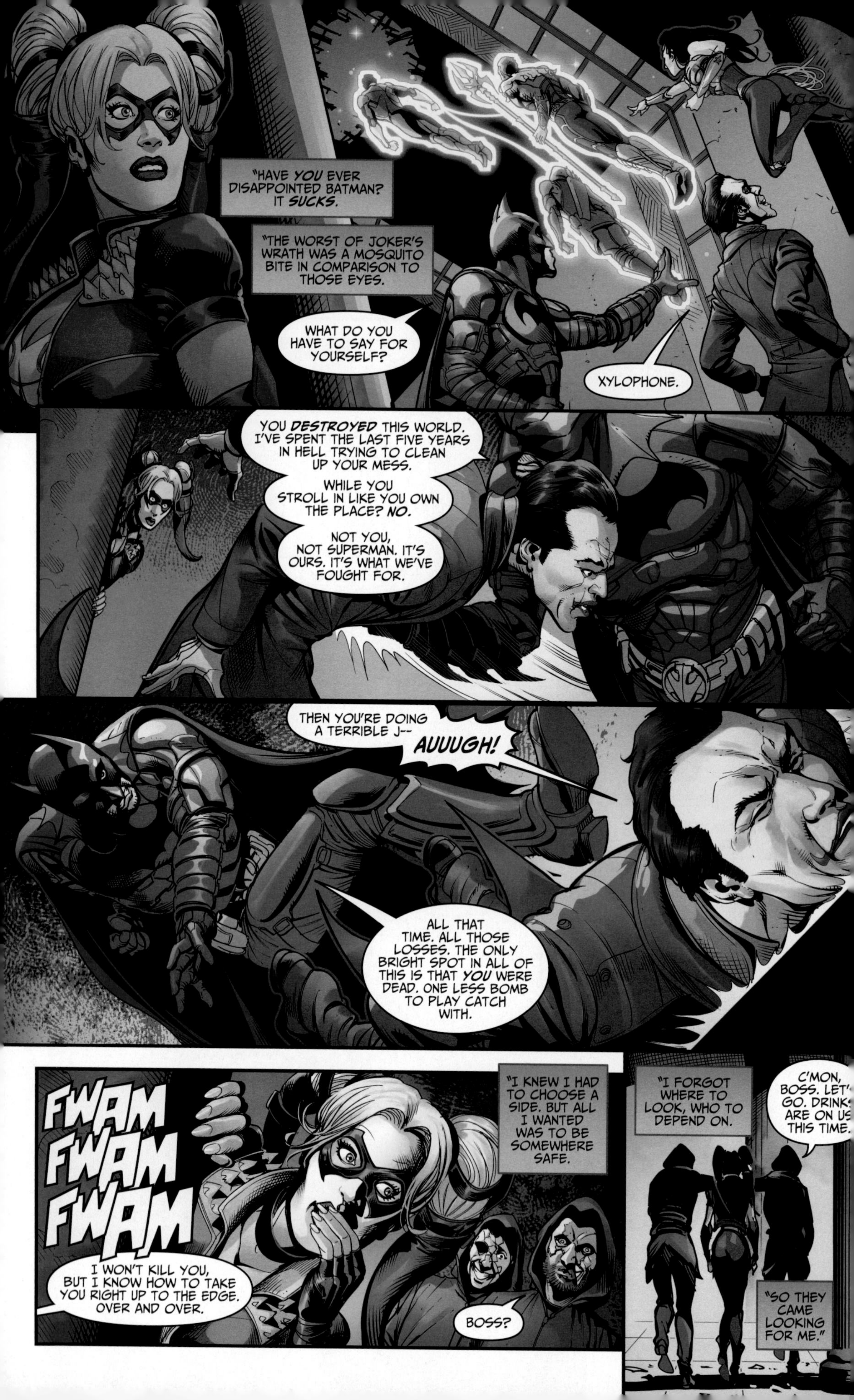
"HAVE YOU EVER DISAPPOINTED BATMAN? IT SUCKS.
"THE WORST OF JOKER'S WRATH WAS A MOSQUITO BITE IN COMPARISON TO THOSE EYES.
WHAT DO YOU HAVE TO SAY FOR YOURSELF?
XYLOPHONE.
YOU DESTROYED THIS WORLD. I'VE SPENT THE LAST FIVE YEARS IN HELL TRYING TO CLEAN UP YOUR MESS.
WHILE YOU STROLL IN LIKE YOU OWN THE PLACE? NO.
NOT YOU, NOT SUPERMAN. IT'S OURS. IT'S WHAT WE'VE FOUGHT FOR.
THEN YOU'RE DOING A TERRIBLE J--
AUUUGH!
ALL THAT TIME. ALL THOSE LOSSES. THE ONLY BRIGHT SPOT IN ALL OF THIS IS THAT YOU WERE DEAD. ONE LESS BOMB TO PLAY CATCH WITH.
FWAM FWAM FWAM
I WON'T KILL YOU, BUT I KNOW HOW TO TAKE YOU RIGHT UP TO THE EDGE. OVER AND OVER.
"I KNEW I HAD TO CHOOSE A SIDE. BUT ALL I WANTED WAS TO BE SOMEWHERE SAFE.
BOSS?
"I FORGOT WHERE TO LOOK, WHO TO DEPEND ON.
C'MON, BOSS. LET'S GO. DRINKS ARE ON US THIS TIME.
"SO THEY CAME LOOKING FOR ME."

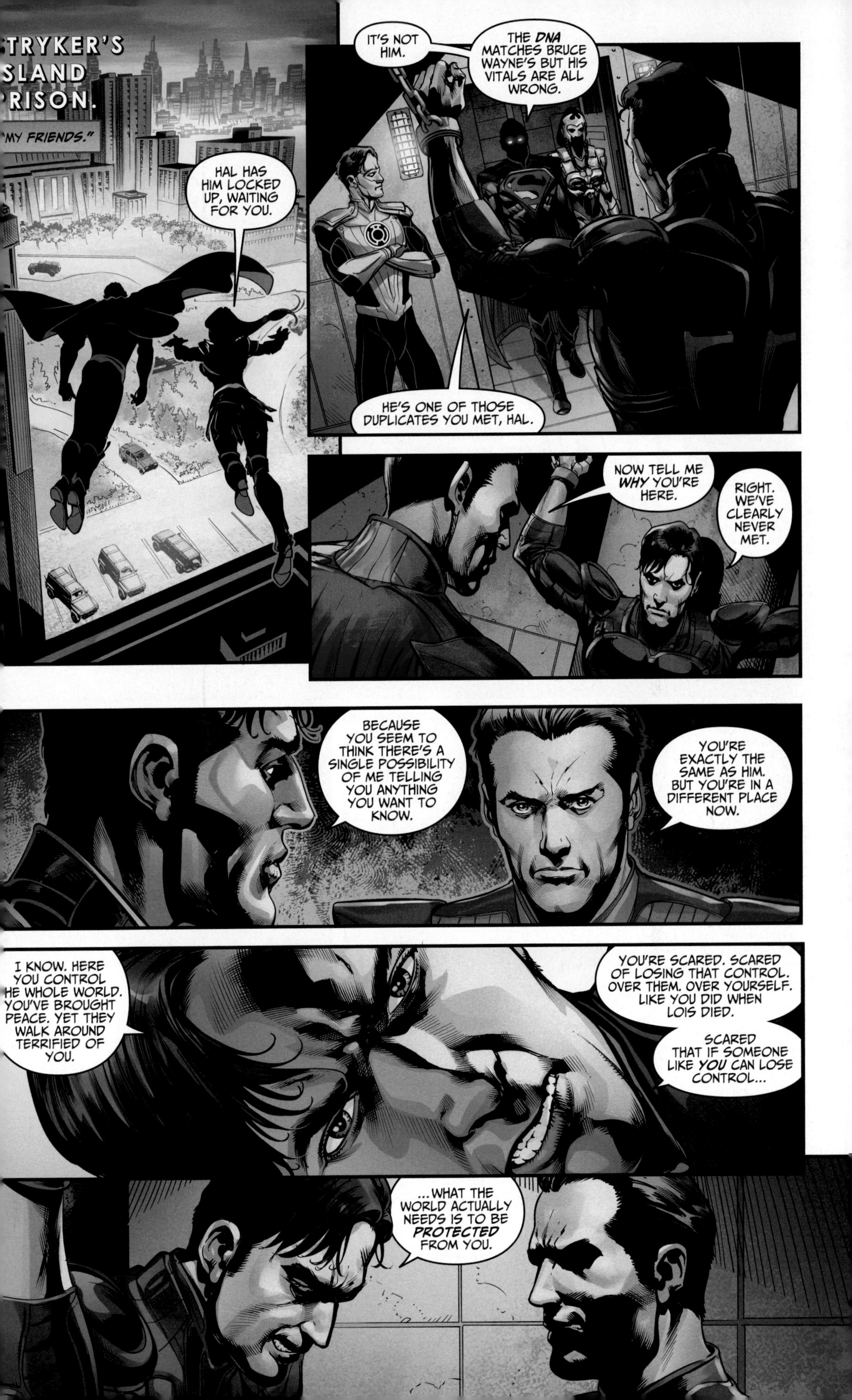
TRYKER'S SLAND RISON.
"MY FRIENDS."
HAL HAS HIM LOCKED UP, WAITING FOR YOU.
IT'S NOT HIM.
THE DNA MATCHES BRUCE WAYNE'S BUT HIS VITALS ARE ALL WRONG.
HE'S ONE OF THOSE DUPLICATES YOU MET, HAL.
NOW TELL ME WHY YOU'RE HERE.
RIGHT. WE'VE CLEARLY NEVER MET.
BECAUSE YOU SEEM TO THINK THERE'S A SINGLE POSSIBILITY OF ME TELLING YOU ANYTHING YOU WANT TO KNOW.
YOU'RE EXACTLY THE SAME AS HIM. BUT YOU'RE IN A DIFFERENT PLACE NOW.
I KNOW. HERE YOU CONTROL HE WHOLE WORLD. YOU'VE BROUGHT PEACE. YET THEY WALK AROUND TERRIFIED OF YOU.
YOU'RE SCARED. SCARED OF LOSING THAT CONTROL. OVER THEM. OVER YOURSELF. LIKE YOU DID WHEN LOIS DIED.
SCARED THAT IF SOMEONE LIKE YOU CAN LOSE CONTROL...
...WHAT THE WORLD ACTUALLY NEEDS IS TO BE PROTECTED FROM YOU.

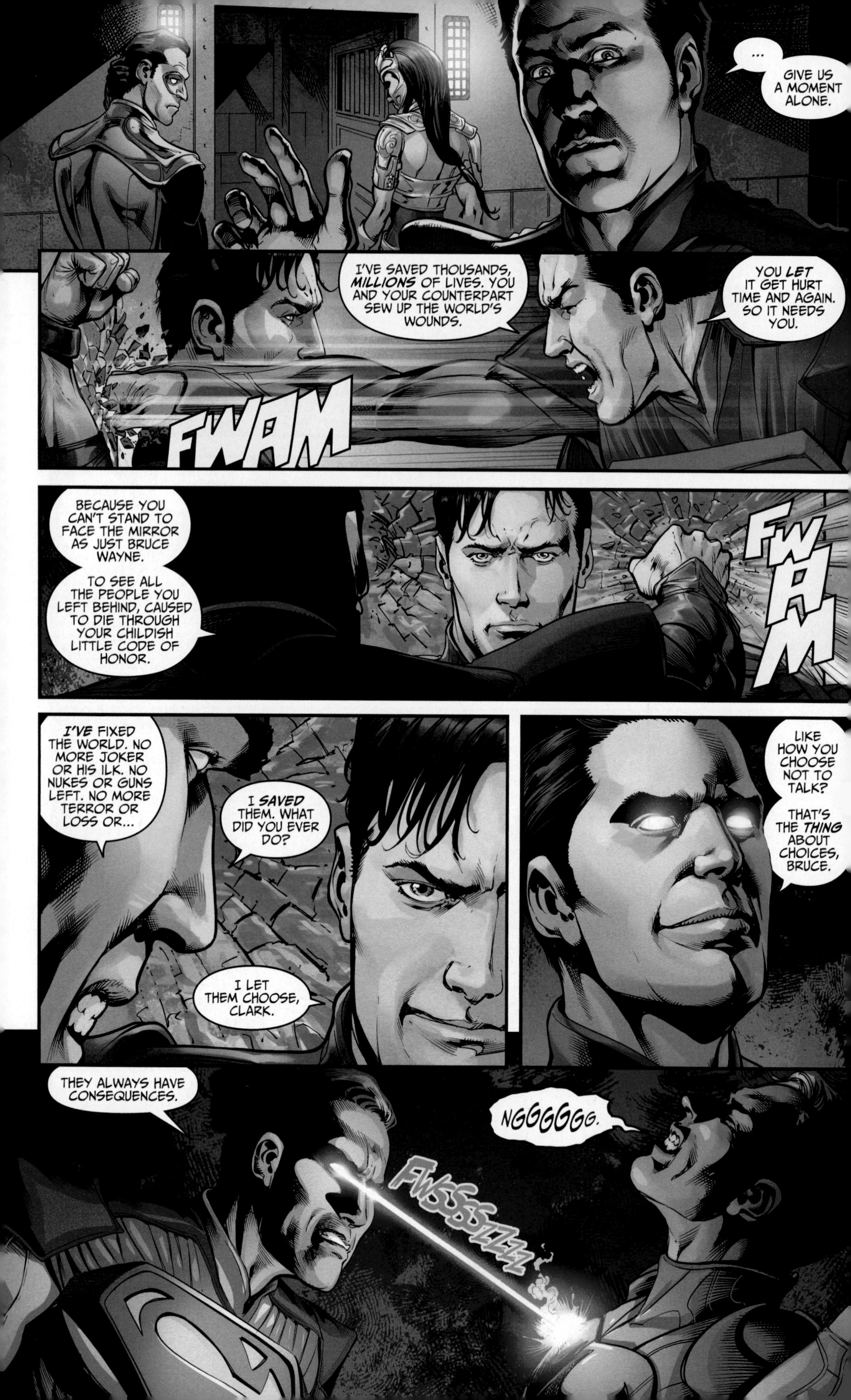
...
GIVE US A MOMENT ALONE.
I'VE SAVED THOUSANDS, MILLIONS OF LIVES. YOU AND YOUR COUNTERPART SEW UP THE WORLD'S WOUNDS.
YOU LET IT GET HURT TIME AND AGAIN. SO IT NEEDS YOU.
FWAM
BECAUSE YOU CAN'T STAND TO FACE THE MIRROR AS JUST BRUCE WAYNE.
TO SEE ALL THE PEOPLE YOU LEFT BEHIND, CAUSED TO DIE THROUGH YOUR CHILDISH LITTLE CODE OF HONOR.
FWAM
I'VE FIXED THE WORLD. NO MORE JOKER OR HIS ILK. NO NUKES OR GUNS LEFT. NO MORE TERROR OR LOSS OR...
I SAVED THEM. WHAT DID YOU EVER DO?
I LET THEM CHOOSE, CLARK.
LIKE HOW YOU CHOOSE NOT TO TALK?
THAT'S THE THING ABOUT CHOICES, BRUCE.
THEY ALWAYS HAVE CONSEQUENCES.
NGGGGGG.
FWSSSSZZZZ

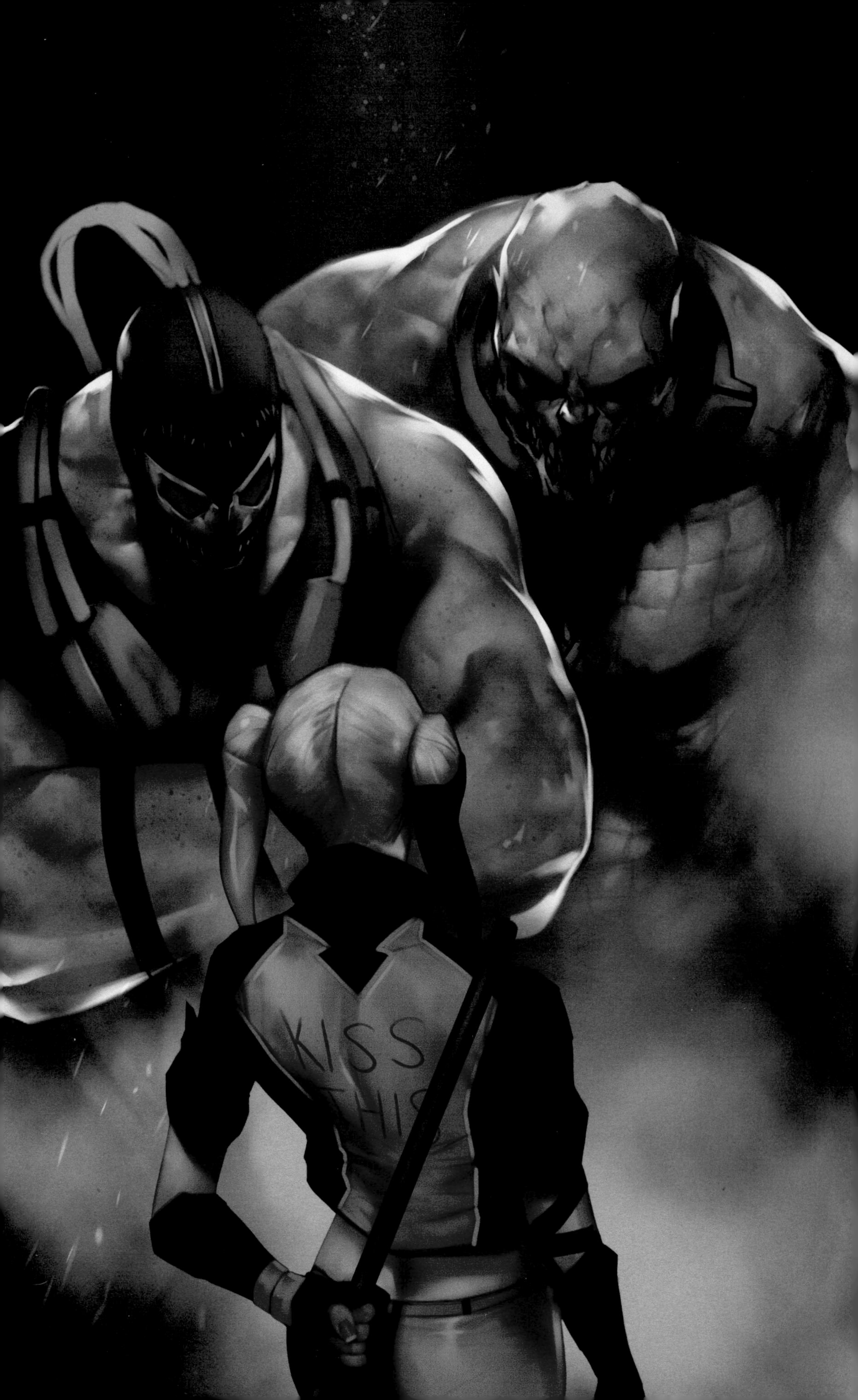
KISS
THIS

"Recruitment: Part 1" **Daniel Sampere** Penciller **Juan Albarran** Inker **J. Nanjan** Colorist
"Recruitment: Part 2" **Pop Mhan** Artist **Mark Roberts** Colorist

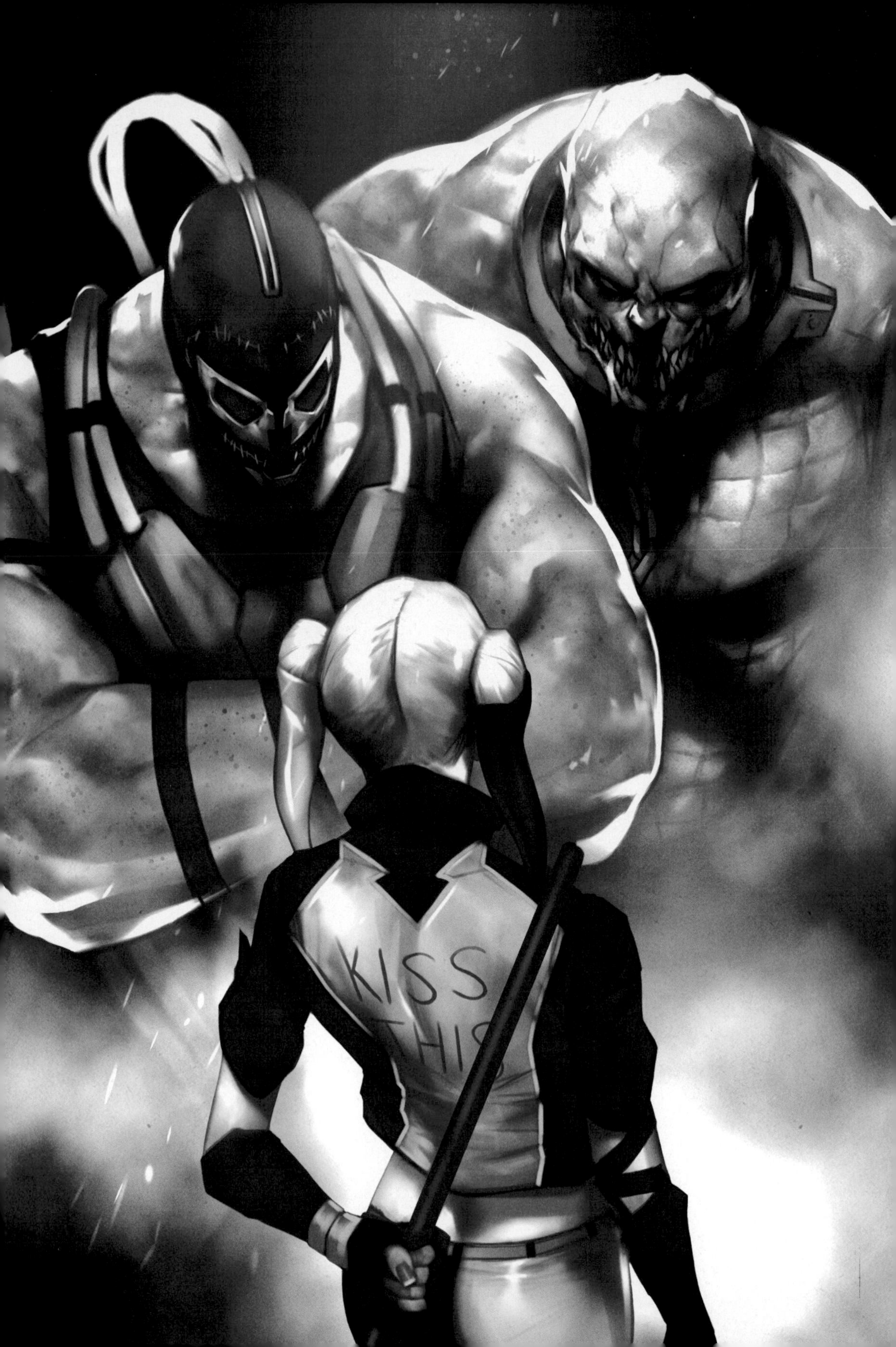
KISS THIS

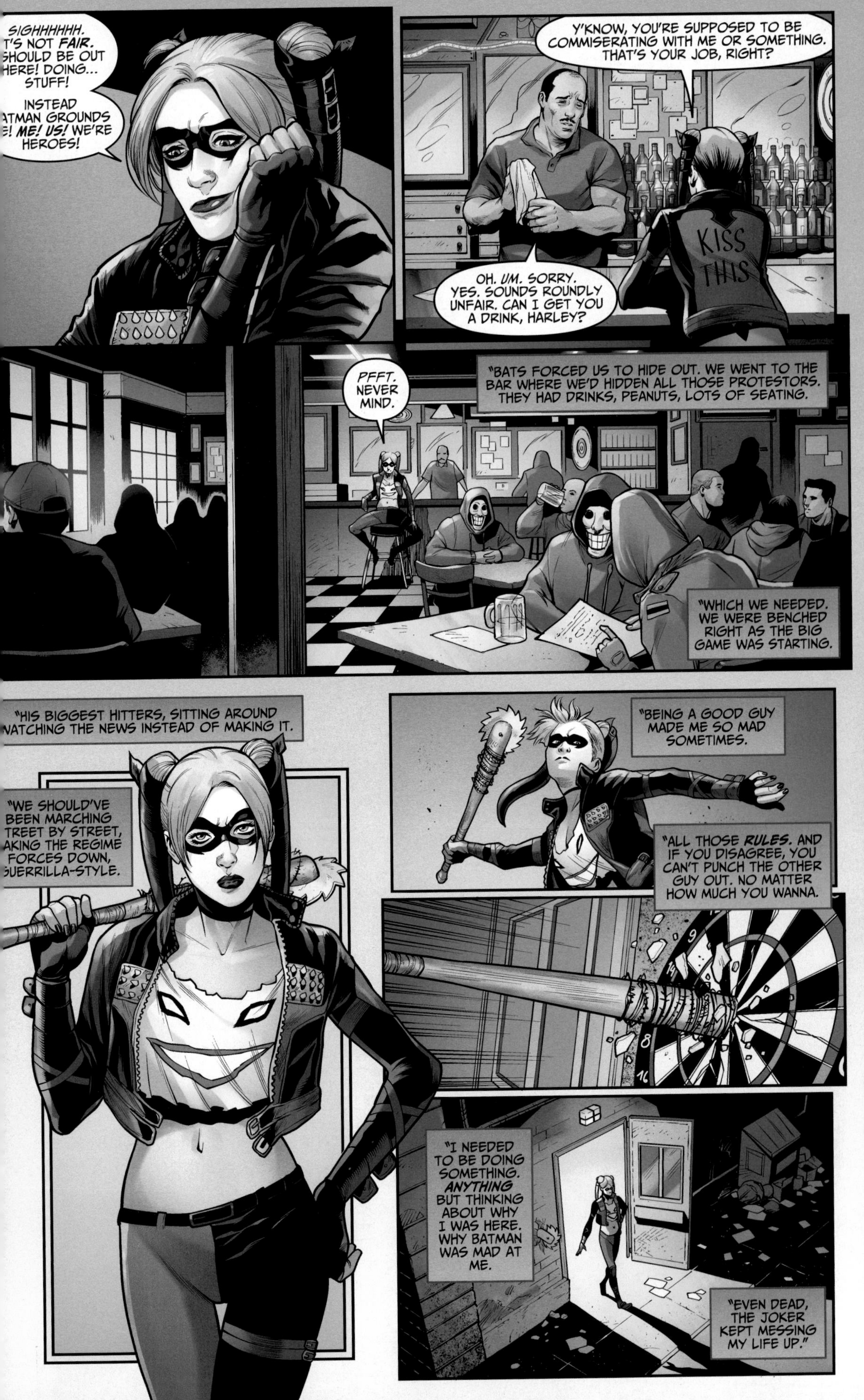
SIGHHHHHH.
T'S NOT FAIR.
SHOULD BE OUT
HERE! DOING...
STUFF!
INSTEAD
ATMAN GROUNDS
E! ME! US! WE'RE
HEROES!
Y'KNOW, YOU'RE SUPPOSED TO BE COMMISERATING WITH ME OR SOMETHING. THAT'S YOUR JOB, RIGHT?
KISS THIS
OH. UM. SORRY. YES. SOUNDS ROUNDLY UNFAIR. CAN I GET YOU A DRINK, HARLEY?
PFFT. NEVER MIND.
"BATS FORCED US TO HIDE OUT. WE WENT TO THE BAR WHERE WE'D HIDDEN ALL THOSE PROTESTORS. THEY HAD DRINKS, PEANUTS, LOTS OF SEATING.
"WHICH WE NEEDED. WE WERE BENCHED RIGHT AS THE BIG GAME WAS STARTING.
"HIS BIGGEST HITTERS, SITTING AROUND
WATCHING THE NEWS INSTEAD OF MAKING IT.
"WE SHOULD'VE
BEEN MARCHING
TREET BY STREET,
AKING THE REGIME
FORCES DOWN,
GUERRILLA-STYLE.
"BEING A GOOD GUY MADE ME SO MAD SOMETIMES.
"ALL THOSE RULES. AND IF YOU DISAGREE, YOU CAN'T PUNCH THE OTHER GUY OUT. NO MATTER HOW MUCH YOU WANNA.
"I NEEDED TO BE DOING SOMETHING. ANYTHING BUT THINKING ABOUT WHY I WAS HERE. WHY BATMAN WAS MAD AT ME.
"EVEN DEAD, THE JOKER KEPT MESSING MY LIFE UP."

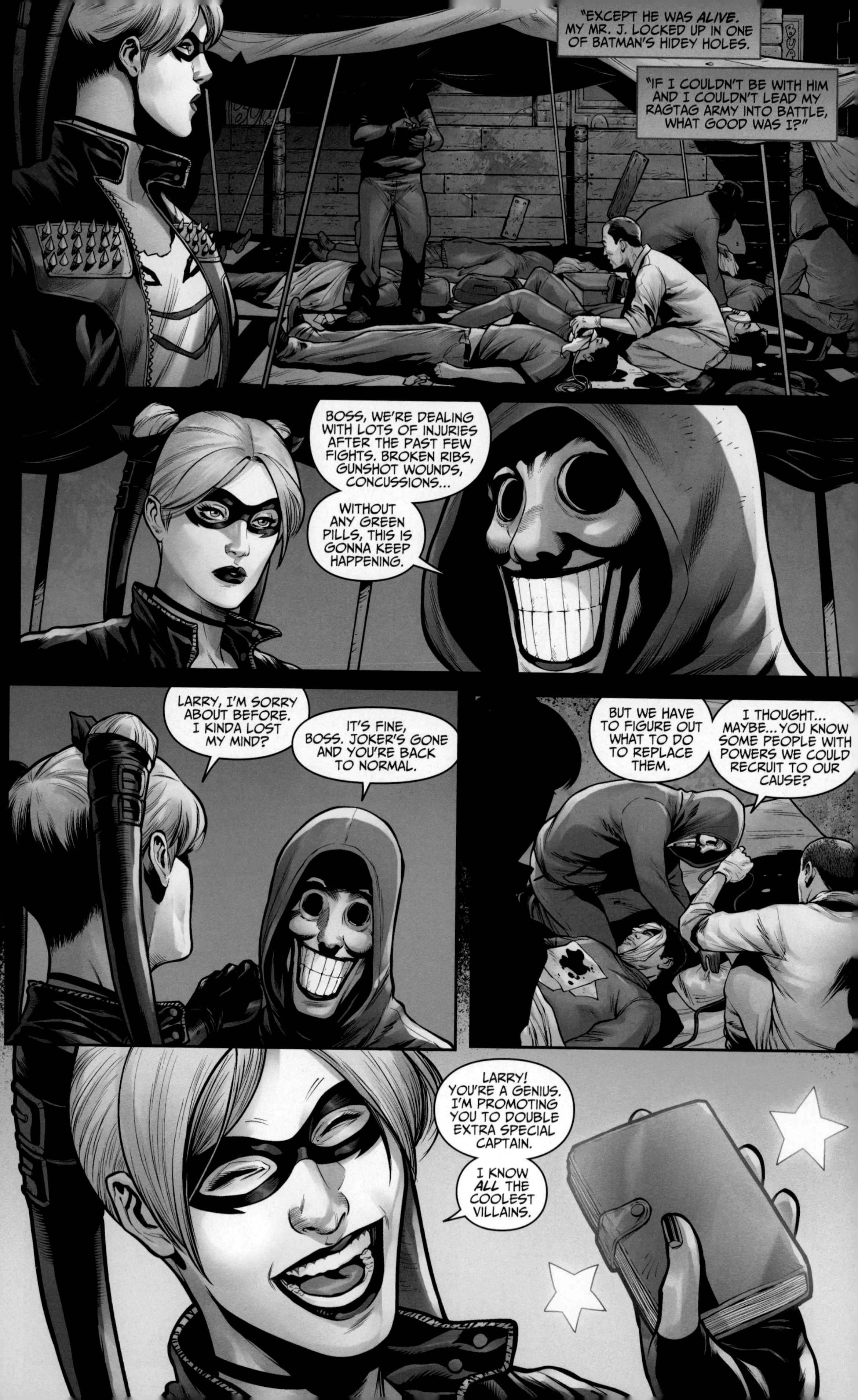
"EXCEPT HE WAS ALIVE. MY MR. J. LOCKED UP IN ONE OF BATMAN'S HIDEY HOLES.
"IF I COULDN'T BE WITH HIM AND I COULDN'T LEAD MY RAGTAG ARMY INTO BATTLE, WHAT GOOD WAS I?"
BOSS, WE'RE DEALING WITH LOTS OF INJURIES AFTER THE PAST FEW FIGHTS. BROKEN RIBS, GUNSHOT WOUNDS, CONCUSSIONS...
WITHOUT ANY GREEN PILLS, THIS IS GONNA KEEP HAPPENING.
LARRY, I'M SORRY ABOUT BEFORE. I KINDA LOST MY MIND?
IT'S FINE, BOSS. JOKER'S GONE AND YOU'RE BACK TO NORMAL.
BUT WE HAVE TO FIGURE OUT WHAT TO DO TO REPLACE THEM.
I THOUGHT... MAYBE...YOU KNOW SOME PEOPLE WITH POWERS WE COULD RECRUIT TO OUR CAUSE?
LARRY! YOU'RE A GENIUS. I'M PROMOTING YOU TO DOUBLE EXTRA SPECIAL CAPTAIN.
I KNOW ALL THE COOLEST VILLAINS.

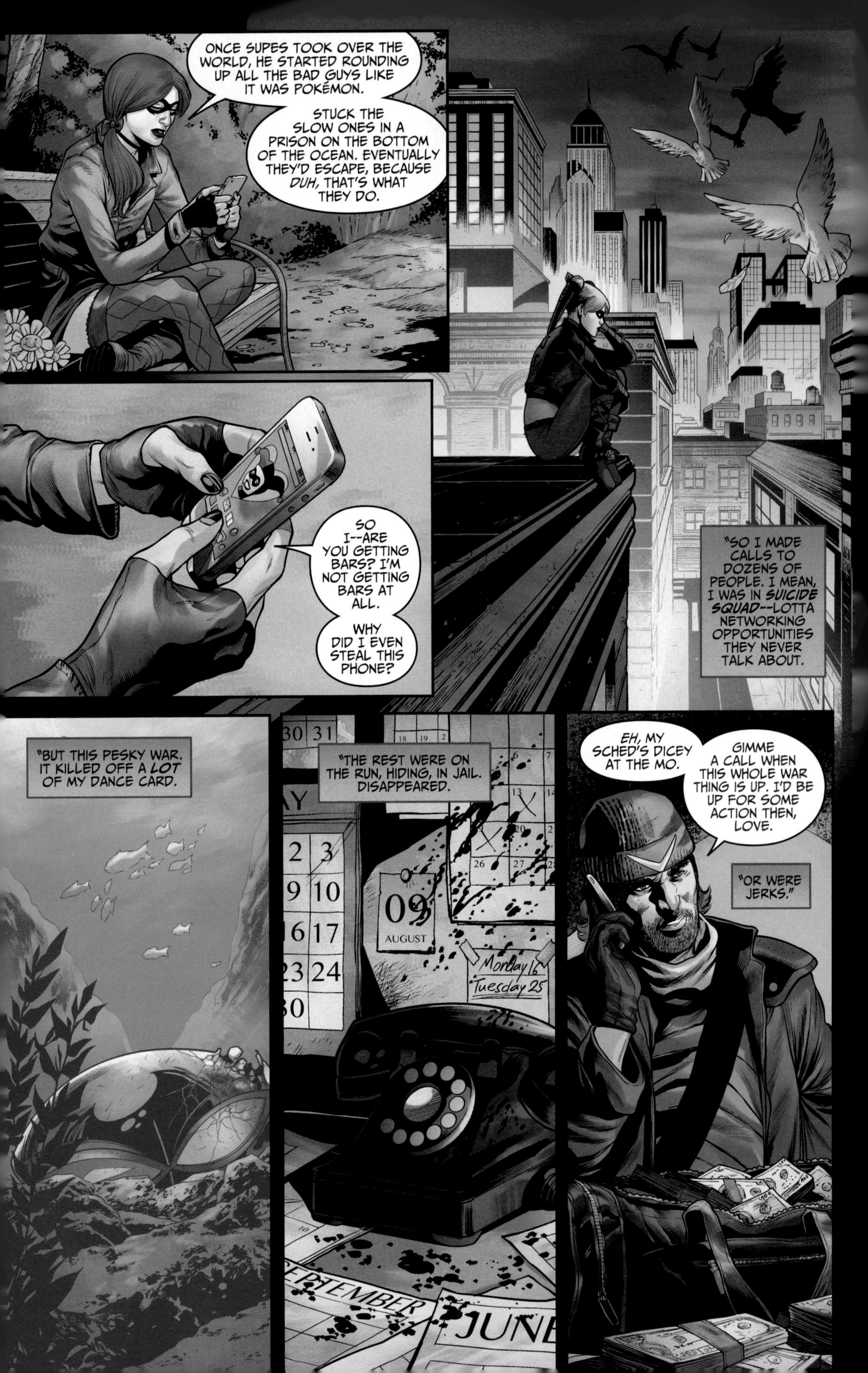

ONCE SUPES TOOK OVER THE WORLD, HE STARTED ROUNDING UP ALL THE BAD GUYS LIKE IT WAS POKÉMON.
STUCK THE SLOW ONES IN A PRISON ON THE BOTTOM OF THE OCEAN. EVENTUALLY THEY'D ESCAPE, BECAUSE *DUH*, THAT'S WHAT THEY DO.
SO I--ARE YOU GETTING BARS? I'M NOT GETTING BARS AT ALL.
WHY DID I EVEN STEAL THIS PHONE?
"SO I MADE CALLS TO DOZENS OF PEOPLE. I MEAN, I WAS IN **SUICIDE SQUAD**--LOTTA NETWORKING OPPORTUNITIES THEY NEVER TALK ABOUT.
"BUT THIS PESKY WAR. IT KILLED OFF A ***LOT*** OF MY DANCE CARD.
"THE REST WERE ON THE RUN, HIDING, IN JAIL. DISAPPEARED.
09
AUGUST
Monday 16
Tuesday 25
SEPTEMBER
JUNE
EH, MY SCHED'S DICEY AT THE MO.
GIMME A CALL WHEN THIS WHOLE WAR THING IS UP. I'D BE UP FOR SOME ACTION THEN, LOVE.
"OR WERE JERKS."

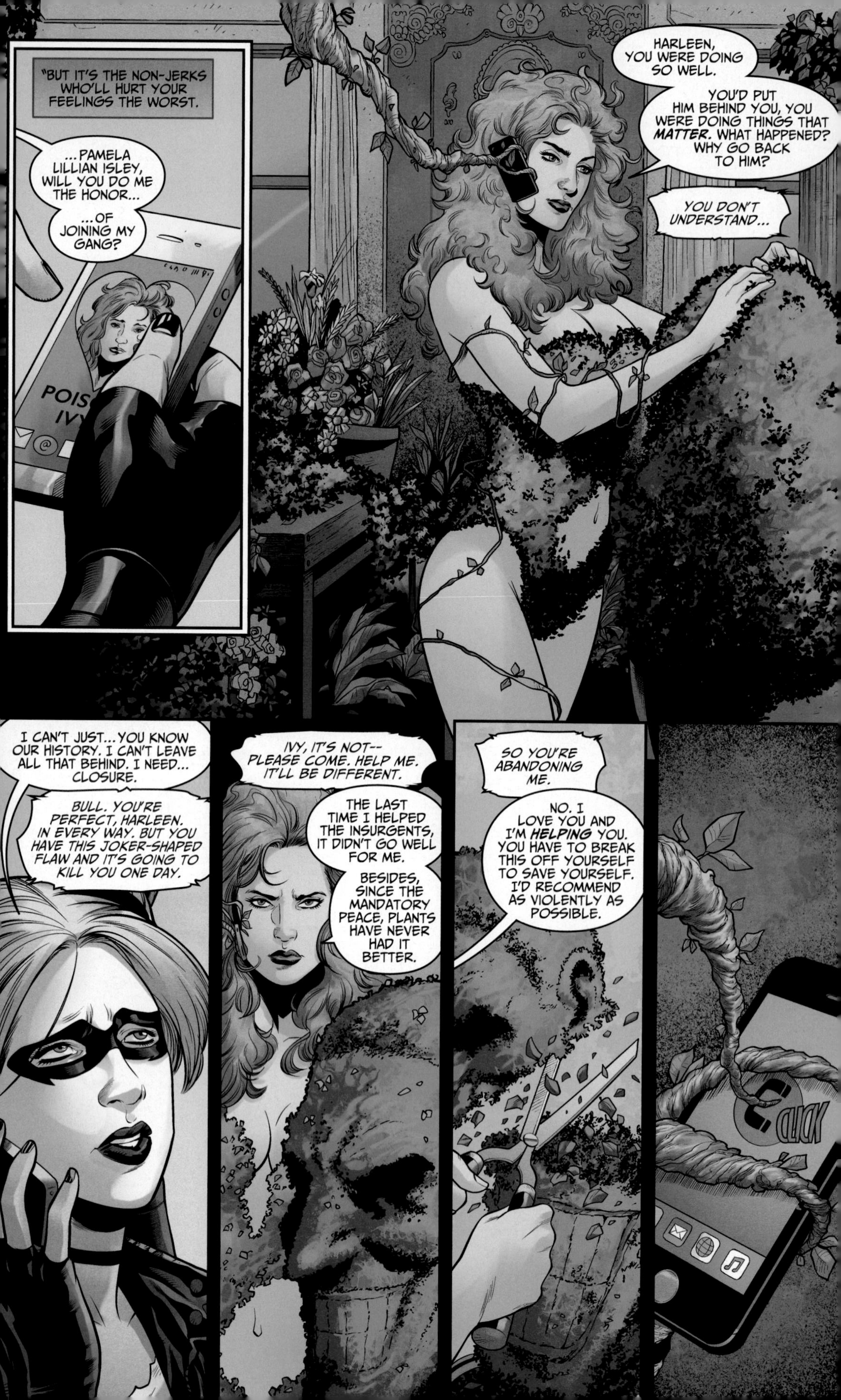
"BUT IT'S THE NON-JERKS WHO'LL HURT YOUR FEELINGS THE WORST.
...PAMELA LILLIAN ISLEY, WILL YOU DO ME THE HONOR...
...OF JOINING MY GANG?
HARLEEN, YOU WERE DOING SO WELL.
YOU'D PUT HIM BEHIND YOU, YOU WERE DOING THINGS THAT MATTER. WHAT HAPPENED? WHY GO BACK TO HIM?
YOU DON'T UNDERSTAND...
I CAN'T JUST...YOU KNOW OUR HISTORY. I CAN'T LEAVE ALL THAT BEHIND. I NEED... CLOSURE.
BULL. YOU'RE PERFECT, HARLEEN. IN EVERY WAY. BUT YOU HAVE THIS JOKER-SHAPED FLAW AND IT'S GOING TO KILL YOU ONE DAY.
IVY, IT'S NOT-- PLEASE COME. HELP ME. IT'LL BE DIFFERENT.
THE LAST TIME I HELPED THE INSURGENTS, IT DIDN'T GO WELL FOR ME.
BESIDES, SINCE THE MANDATORY PEACE, PLANTS HAVE NEVER HAD IT BETTER.
SO YOU'RE ABANDONING ME.
NO. I LOVE YOU AND I'M HELPING YOU. YOU HAVE TO BREAK THIS OFF YOURSELF TO SAVE YOURSELF. I'D RECOMMEND AS VIOLENTLY AS POSSIBLE.
CLICK

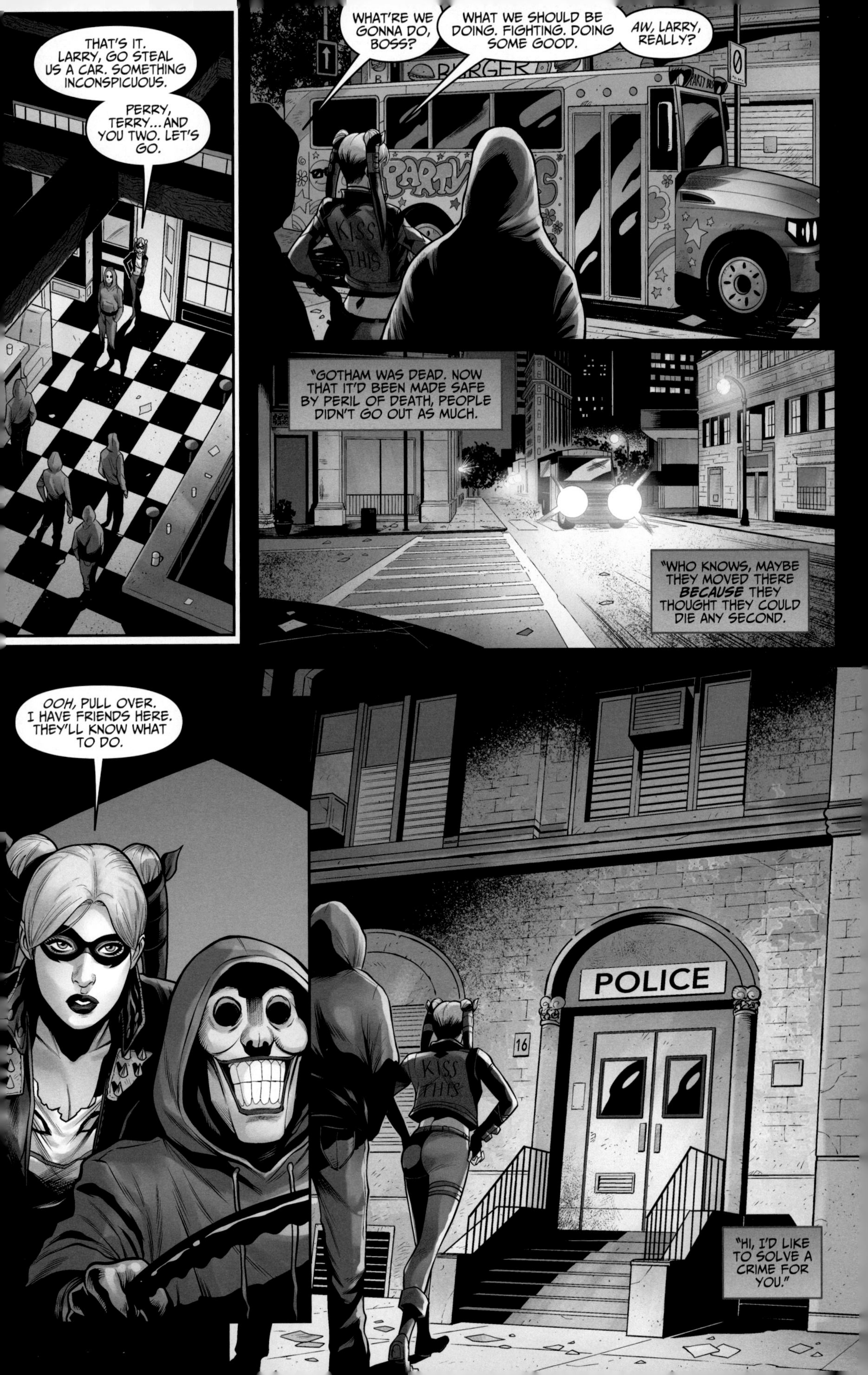
THAT'S IT. LARRY, GO STEAL US A CAR. SOMETHING INCONSPICUOUS.
PERRY, TERRY... AND YOU TWO. LET'S GO.
WHAT'RE WE GONNA DO, BOSS?
WHAT WE SHOULD BE DOING. FIGHTING. DOING SOME GOOD.
AW, LARRY, REALLY?
BURGER
PARTY
"GOTHAM WAS DEAD. NOW THAT IT'D BEEN MADE SAFE BY PERIL OF DEATH, PEOPLE DIDN'T GO OUT AS MUCH.
"WHO KNOWS, MAYBE THEY MOVED THERE BECAUSE THEY THOUGHT THEY COULD DIE ANY SECOND.
OOH, PULL OVER. I HAVE FRIENDS HERE. THEY'LL KNOW WHAT TO DO.
POLICE
16
"HI, I'D LIKE TO SOLVE A CRIME FOR YOU."

YEAH, WE DON'T HANDLE THAT NO MORE. I DUNNO, ASK SUPERMAN TO HELP.

OFFICER RENNER!

Y-Y-YOU'RE...

EASY, MARTINEZ. ME AND HARLEY GO BACK. I'VE LOCKED HER UP A DOZEN TIMES.

AND I ESCAPED EVERY SINGLE TIME.

SOOOO WHAT'S NEW?

SQUAT. THANKS TO MARTIAL LAW, ALL OUR SELLOUT BUDDIES ARE WEARING REGIME SUITS, DOING OUR JOBS.

WE SHOW UP, TAKE CALLS, GO HELP SOMEONE FIND THEIR MISSING KITTIES.

THAT SOUNDS FUN. DO YOU KNOW OF ANY CRIMES I CAN SOLVE?

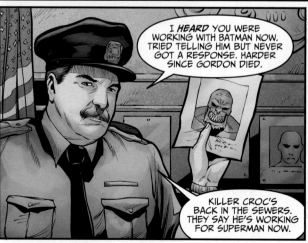

I HEARD YOU WERE WORKING WITH BATMAN NOW. TRIED TELLING HIM BUT NEVER GOT A RESPONSE. HARDER SINCE GORDON DIED.

KILLER CROC'S BACK IN THE SEWERS. THEY SAY HE'S WORKING FOR SUPERMAN NOW.

I'M SO ON IT! I'LL MAKE YOU PROUD, RENNER!

UH-HUH. HAVE FUN STORMING THE SEWER.

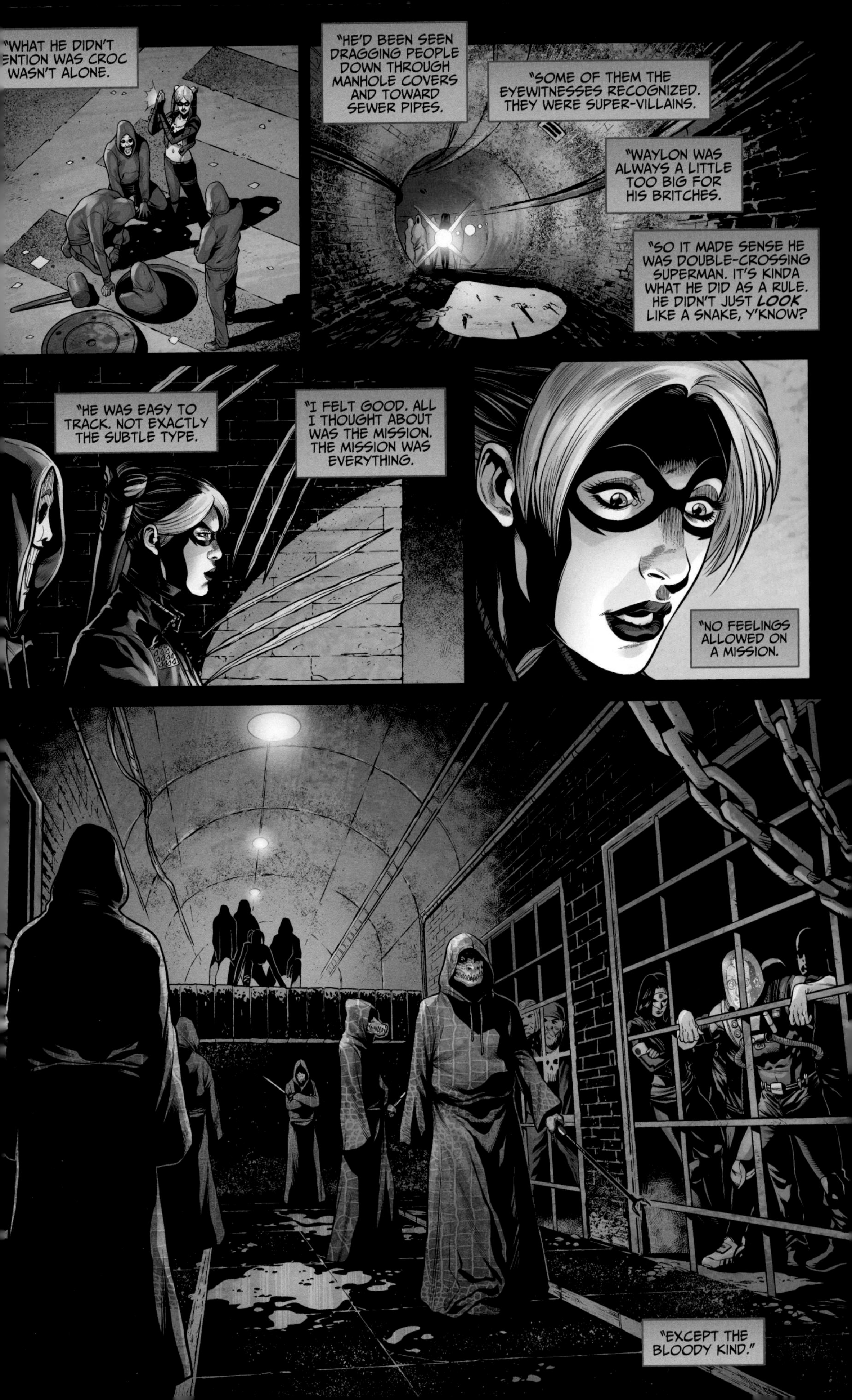
"WHAT HE DIDN'T
ENTION WAS CROC WASN'T ALONE.
"HE'D BEEN SEEN DRAGGING PEOPLE DOWN THROUGH MANHOLE COVERS AND TOWARD SEWER PIPES.
"SOME OF THEM THE EYEWITNESSES RECOGNIZED. THEY WERE SUPER-VILLAINS.
"WAYLON WAS ALWAYS A LITTLE TOO BIG FOR HIS BRITCHES.
"SO IT MADE SENSE HE WAS DOUBLE-CROSSING SUPERMAN. IT'S KINDA WHAT HE DID AS A RULE. HE DIDN'T JUST LOOK LIKE A SNAKE, Y'KNOW?
"HE WAS EASY TO TRACK. NOT EXACTLY THE SUBTLE TYPE.
"I FELT GOOD. ALL I THOUGHT ABOUT WAS THE MISSION. THE MISSION WAS EVERYTHING.
"NO FEELINGS ALLOWED ON A MISSION.
"EXCEPT THE BLOODY KIND."

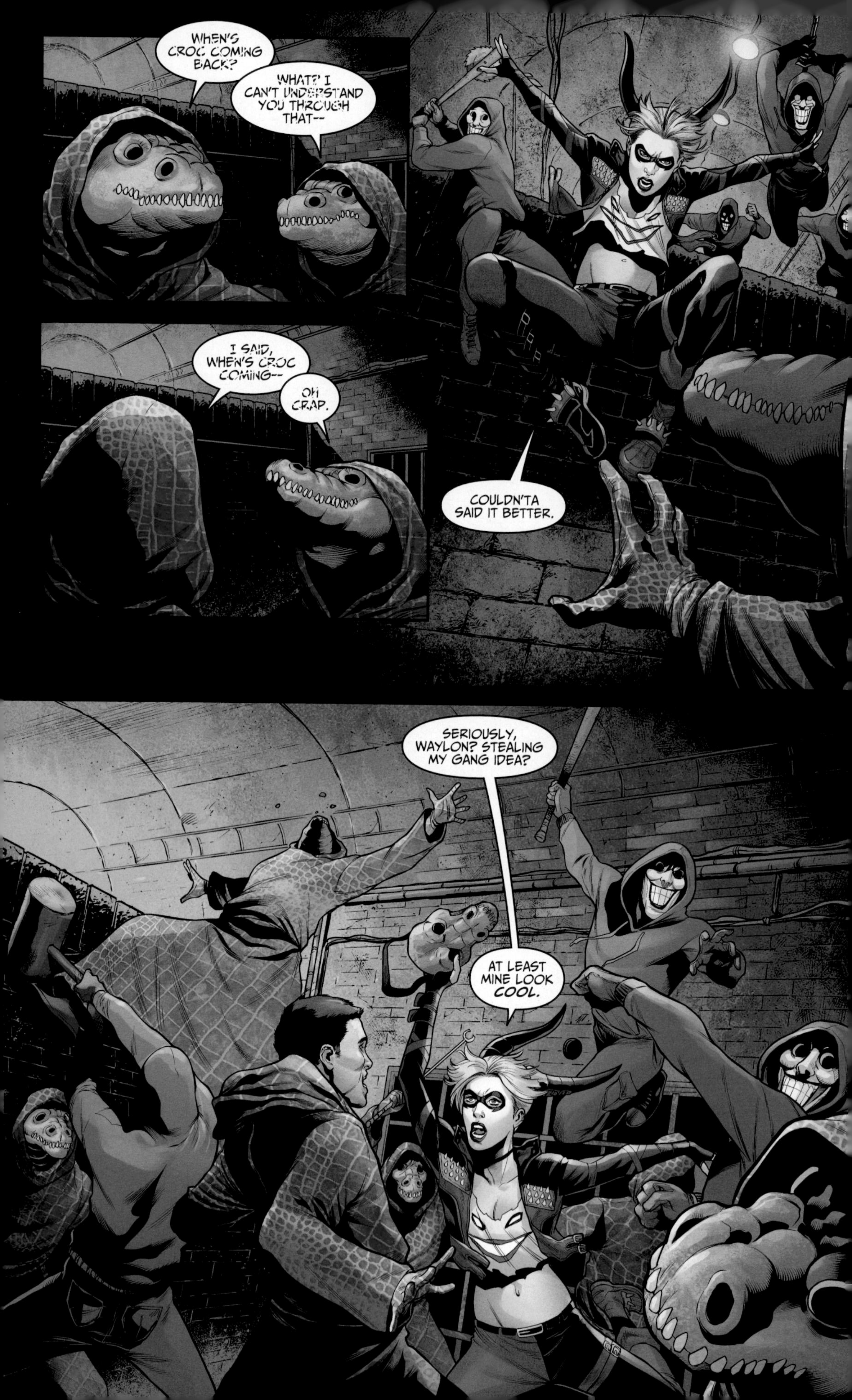
WHEN'S CROC COMING BACK?
WHAT? I CAN'T UNDERSTAND YOU THROUGH THAT--
I SAID, WHEN'S CROC COMING--
OH CRAP.
COULDN'TA SAID IT BETTER.
SERIOUSLY, WAYLON? STEALING MY GANG IDEA?
AT LEAST MINE LOOK COOL.

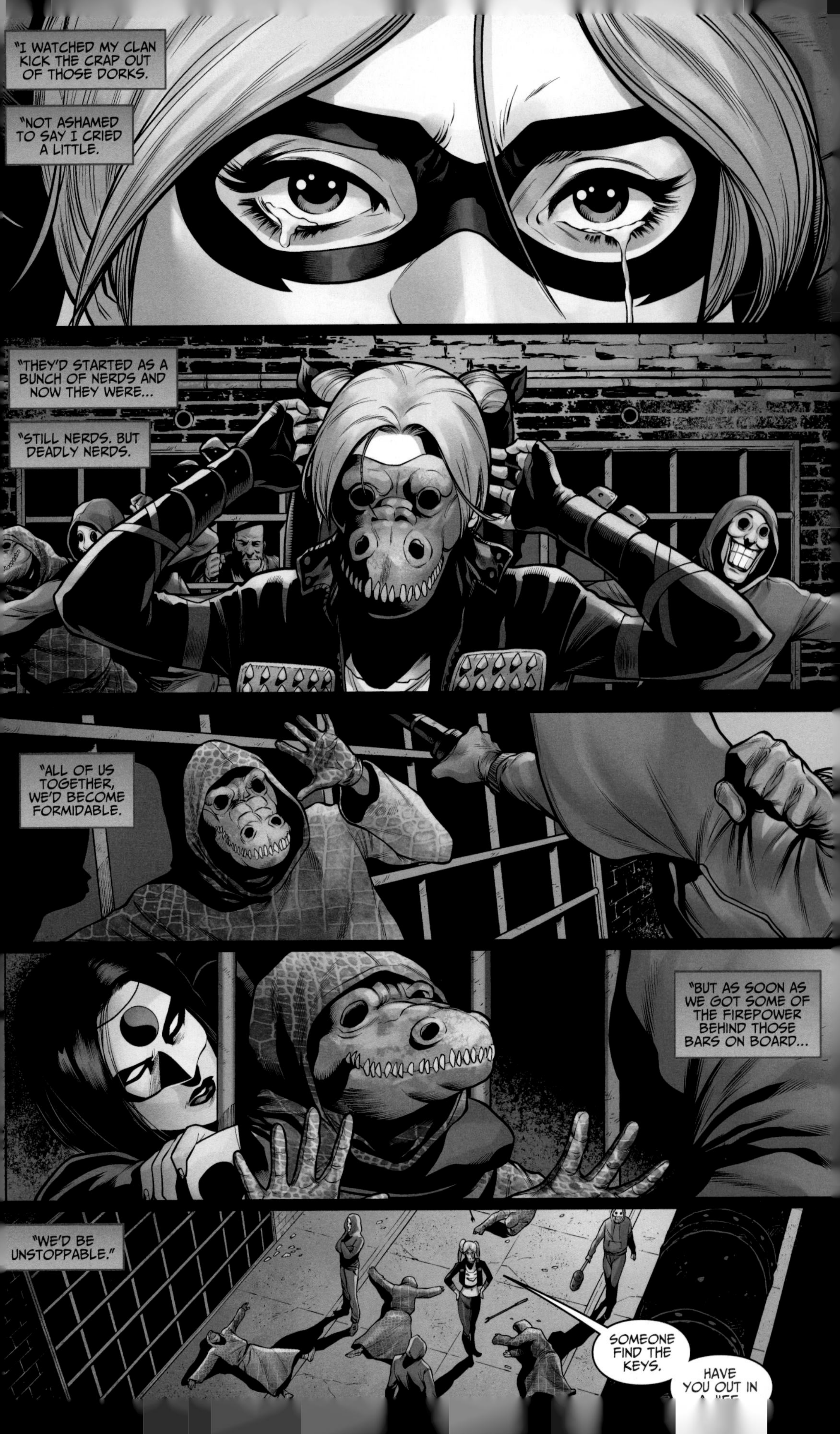
"I WATCHED MY CLAN KICK THE CRAP OUT OF THOSE DORKS.
"NOT ASHAMED TO SAY I CRIED A LITTLE.
"THEY'D STARTED AS A BUNCH OF NERDS AND NOW THEY WERE...
"STILL NERDS. BUT DEADLY NERDS.
"ALL OF US TOGETHER, WE'D BECOME FORMIDABLE.
"BUT AS SOON AS WE GOT SOME OF THE FIREPOWER BEHIND THOSE BARS ON BOARD...
"WE'D BE UNSTOPPABLE."
SOMEONE FIND THE KEYS.
HAVE YOU OUT IN

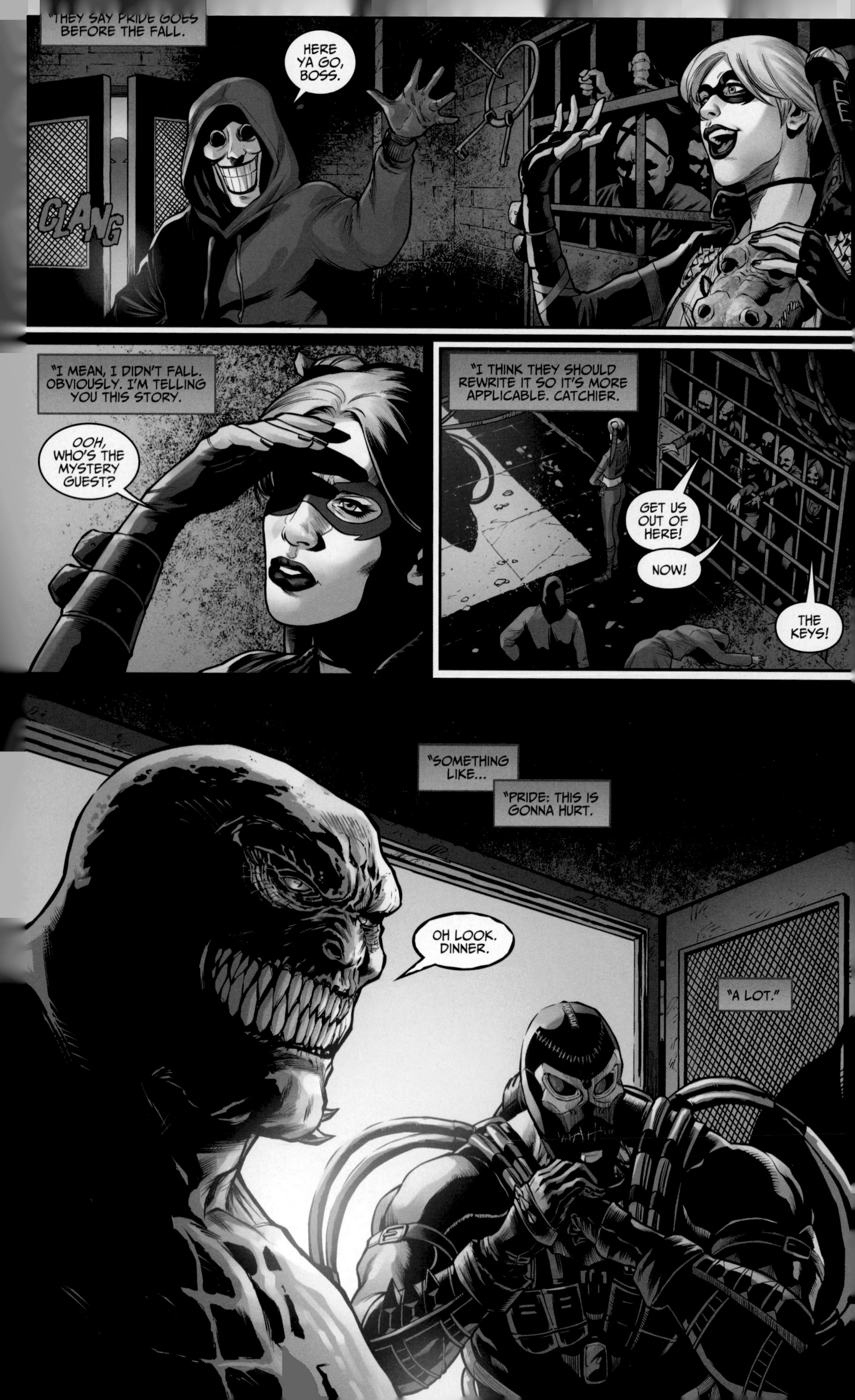
"THEY SAY PRIDE GOES BEFORE THE FALL.
HERE YA GO, BOSS.
CLANG
"I MEAN, I DIDN'T FALL. OBVIOUSLY. I'M TELLING YOU THIS STORY.
OOH, WHO'S THE MYSTERY GUEST?
"I THINK THEY SHOULD REWRITE IT SO IT'S MORE APPLICABLE. CATCHIER.
GET US OUT OF HERE!
NOW!
THE KEYS!
"SOMETHING LIKE...
"PRIDE: THIS IS GONNA HURT.
OH LOOK. DINNER.
"A LOT."

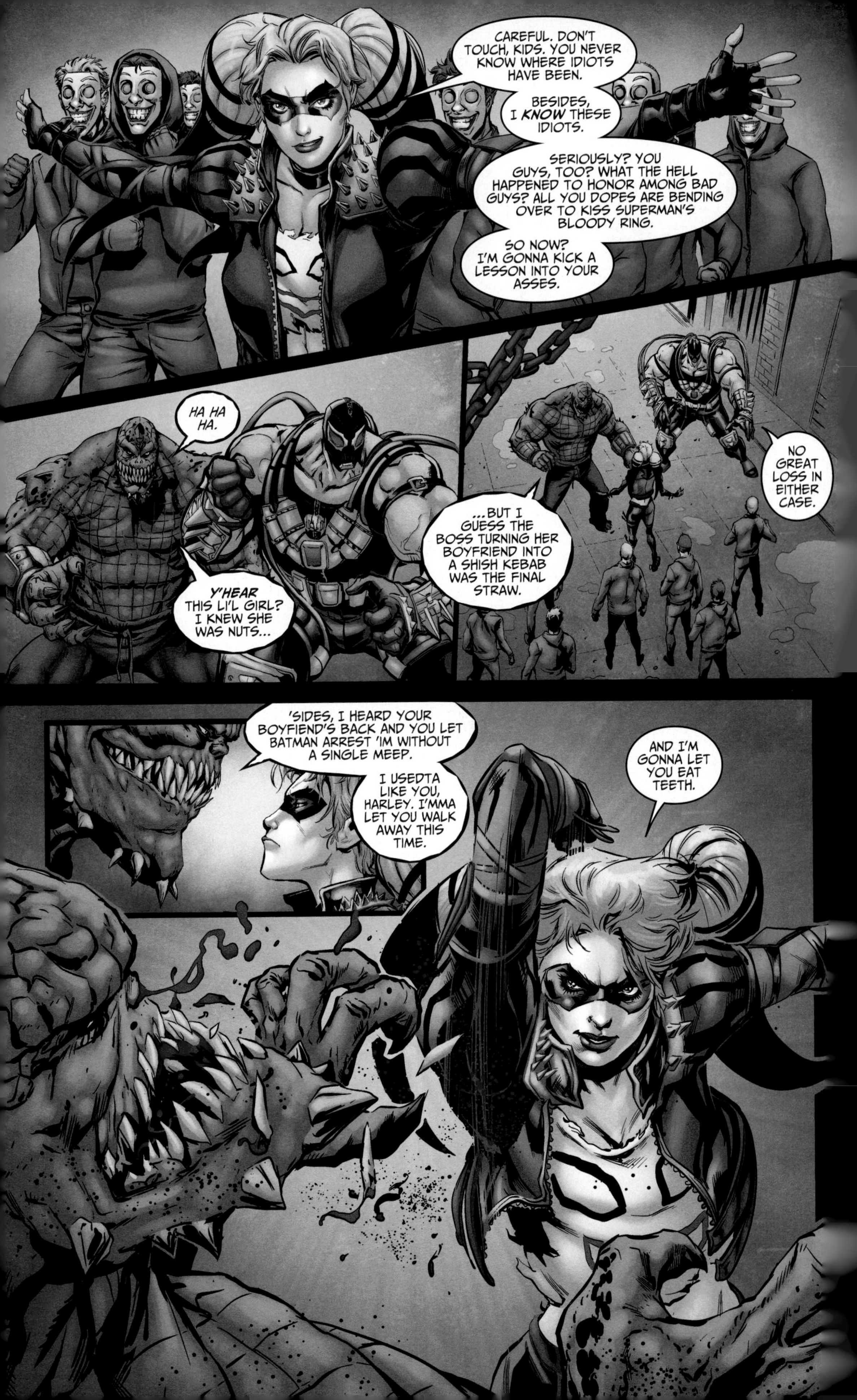
CAREFUL. DON'T TOUCH, KIDS. YOU NEVER KNOW WHERE IDIOTS HAVE BEEN.
BESIDES, I KNOW THESE IDIOTS.
SERIOUSLY? YOU GUYS, TOO? WHAT THE HELL HAPPENED TO HONOR AMONG BAD GUYS? ALL YOU DOPES ARE BENDING OVER TO KISS SUPERMAN'S BLOODY RING.
SO NOW? I'M GONNA KICK A LESSON INTO YOUR ASSES.
HA HA HA.
Y'HEAR THIS LI'L GIRL? I KNEW SHE WAS NUTS...
...BUT I GUESS THE BOSS TURNING HER BOYFRIEND INTO A SHISH KEBAB WAS THE FINAL STRAW.
NO GREAT LOSS IN EITHER CASE.
'SIDES, I HEARD YOUR BOYFRIEND'S BACK AND YOU LET BATMAN ARREST 'IM WITHOUT A SINGLE MEEP.
I USEDTA LIKE YOU, HARLEY. I'MMA LET YOU WALK AWAY THIS TIME.
AND I'M GONNA LET YOU EAT TEETH.

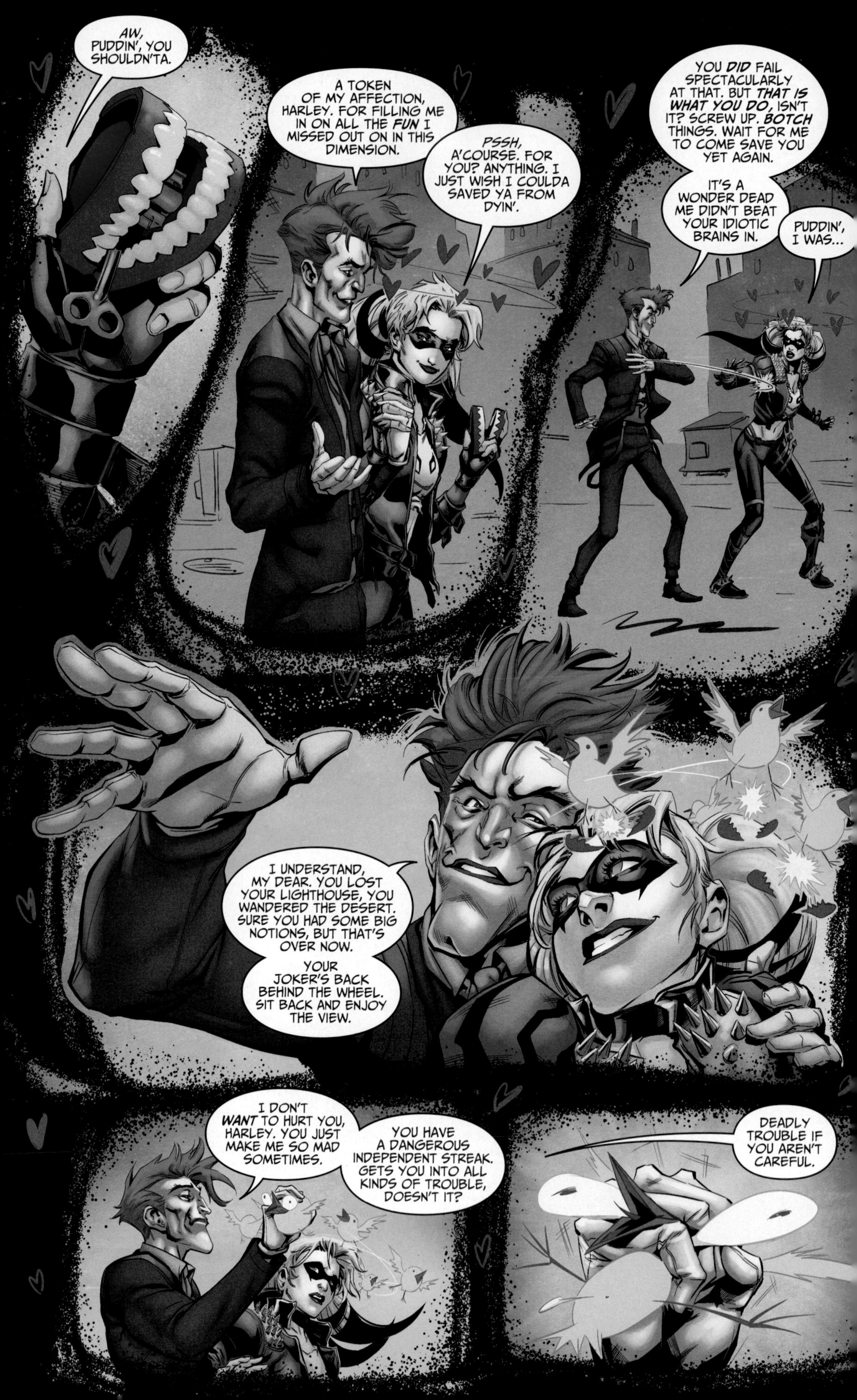
AW, PUDDIN', YOU SHOULDN'TA.
A TOKEN OF MY AFFECTION, HARLEY. FOR FILLING ME IN ON ALL THE *FUN* I MISSED OUT ON IN THIS DIMENSION.
PSSH, A'COURSE. FOR YOU? ANYTHING. I JUST WISH I COULDA SAVED YA FROM DYIN'.
YOU *DID* FAIL SPECTACULARLY AT THAT. BUT *THAT IS WHAT YOU DO,* ISN'T IT? SCREW UP. *BOTCH* THINGS. WAIT FOR ME TO COME SAVE YOU YET AGAIN.
IT'S A WONDER DEAD ME DIDN'T BEAT YOUR IDIOTIC BRAINS IN.
PUDDIN', I WAS...
I UNDERSTAND, MY DEAR. YOU LOST YOUR LIGHTHOUSE, YOU WANDERED THE DESERT. SURE YOU HAD SOME BIG NOTIONS, BUT THAT'S OVER NOW.
YOUR JOKER'S BACK BEHIND THE WHEEL. SIT BACK AND ENJOY THE VIEW.
I DON'T *WANT* TO HURT YOU, HARLEY. YOU JUST MAKE ME SO MAD SOMETIMES.
YOU HAVE A DANGEROUS INDEPENDENT STREAK. GETS YOU INTO ALL KINDS OF TROUBLE, DOESN'T IT?
DEADLY TROUBLE IF YOU AREN'T CAREFUL.

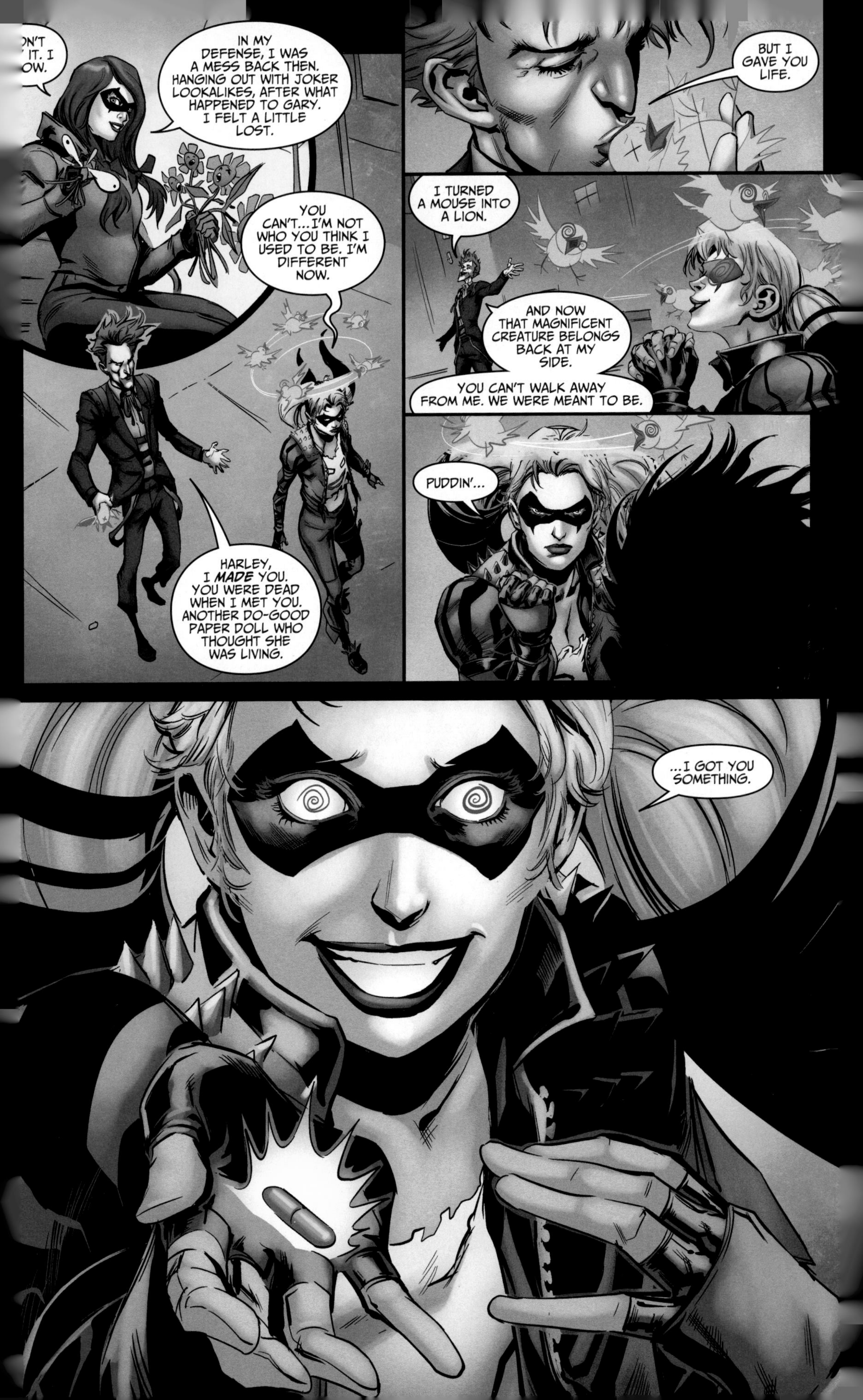
IN MY DEFENSE, I WAS A MESS BACK THEN. HANGING OUT WITH JOKER LOOKALIKES, AFTER WHAT HAPPENED TO GARY. I FELT A LITTLE LOST.
YOU CAN'T... I'M NOT WHO YOU THINK I USED TO BE. I'M DIFFERENT NOW.
HARLEY, I *MADE* YOU. YOU WERE DEAD WHEN I MET YOU. ANOTHER DO-GOOD PAPER DOLL WHO THOUGHT SHE WAS LIVING.
BUT I GAVE YOU LIFE.
I TURNED A MOUSE INTO A LION.
AND NOW THAT MAGNIFICENT CREATURE BELONGS BACK AT MY SIDE.
YOU CAN'T WALK AWAY FROM ME. WE WERE MEANT TO BE.
PUDDIN'...
...I GOT YOU SOMETHING.

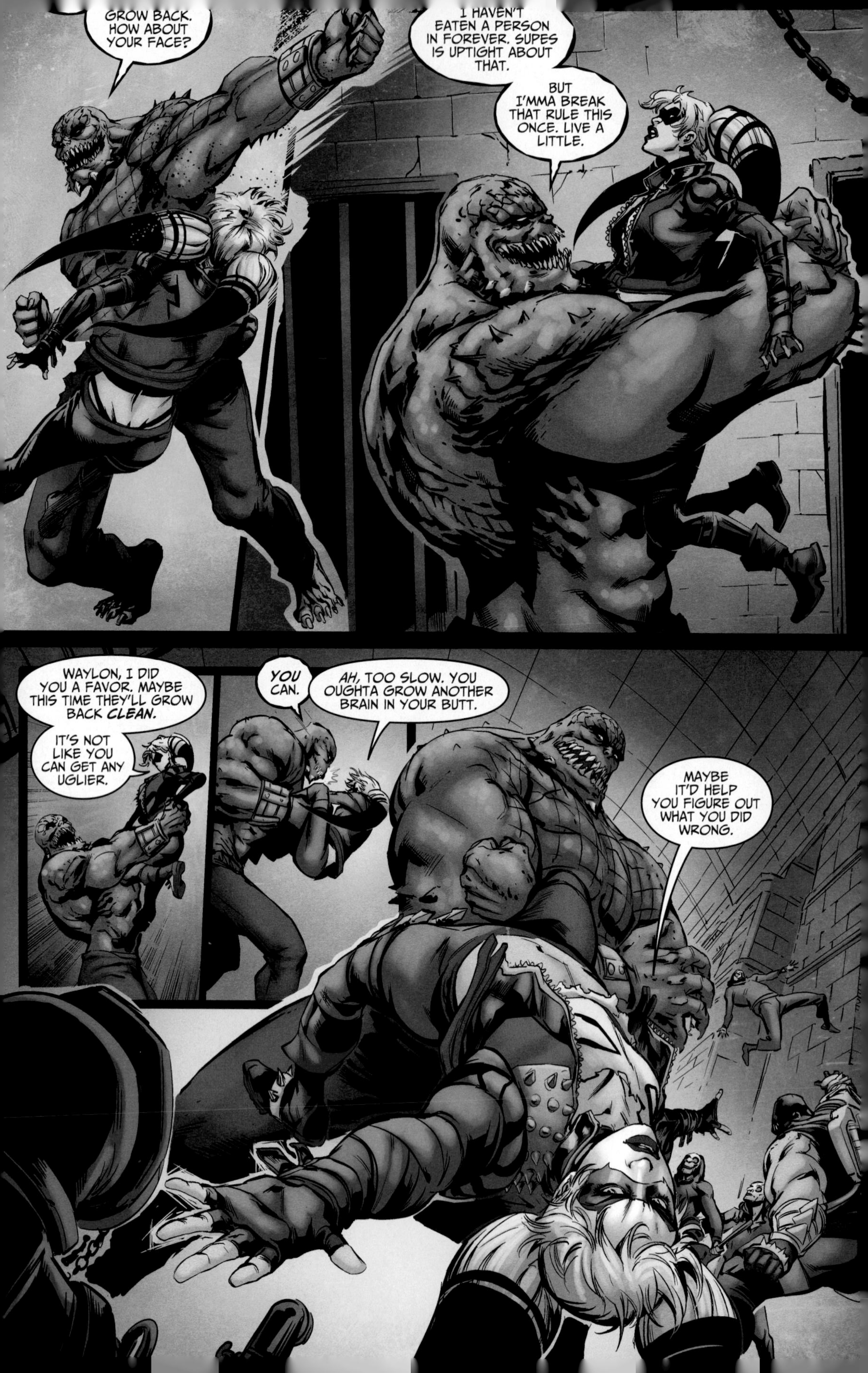
GROW BACK. HOW ABOUT YOUR FACE?
I HAVEN'T EATEN A PERSON IN FOREVER. SUPES IS UPTIGHT ABOUT THAT.
BUT I'MMA BREAK THAT RULE THIS ONCE. LIVE A LITTLE.
WAYLON, I DID YOU A FAVOR. MAYBE THIS TIME THEY'LL GROW BACK CLEAN.
IT'S NOT LIKE YOU CAN GET ANY UGLIER.
YOU CAN.
AH, TOO SLOW. YOU OUGHTA GROW ANOTHER BRAIN IN YOUR BUTT.
MAYBE IT'D HELP YOU FIGURE OUT WHAT YOU DID WRONG.

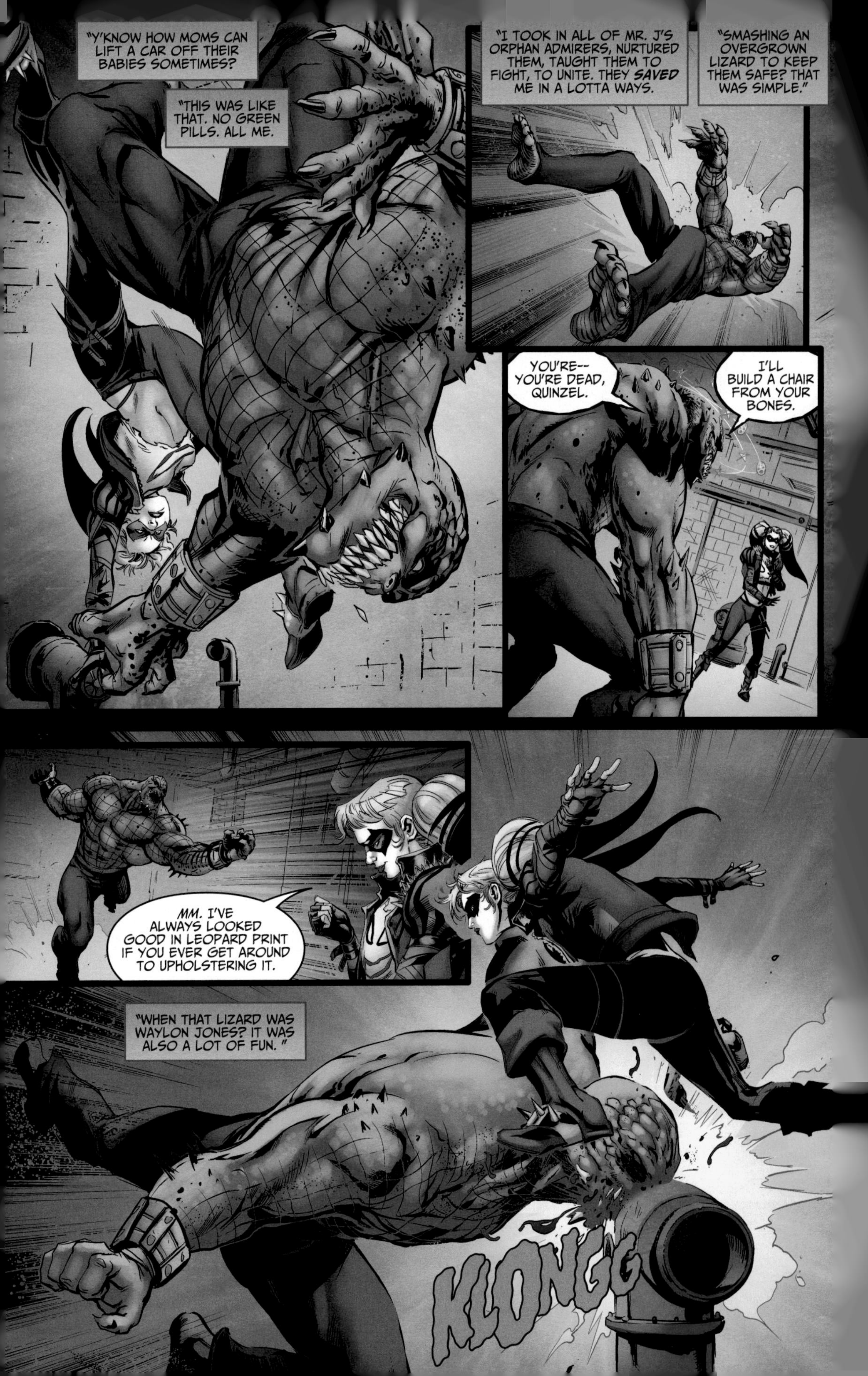
"Y'KNOW HOW MOMS CAN LIFT A CAR OFF THEIR BABIES SOMETIMES?
"THIS WAS LIKE THAT. NO GREEN PILLS. ALL ME.
"I TOOK IN ALL OF MR. J'S ORPHAN ADMIRERS, NURTURED THEM, TAUGHT THEM TO FIGHT, TO UNITE. THEY *SAVED* ME IN A LOTTA WAYS.
"SMASHING AN OVERGROWN LIZARD TO KEEP THEM SAFE? THAT WAS SIMPLE."
YOU'RE-- YOU'RE DEAD, QUINZEL.
I'LL BUILD A CHAIR FROM YOUR BONES.
MM. I'VE ALWAYS LOOKED GOOD IN LEOPARD PRINT IF YOU EVER GET AROUND TO UPHOLSTERING IT.
"WHEN THAT LIZARD WAS WAYLON JONES? IT WAS ALSO A LOT OF FUN."
KLONGG

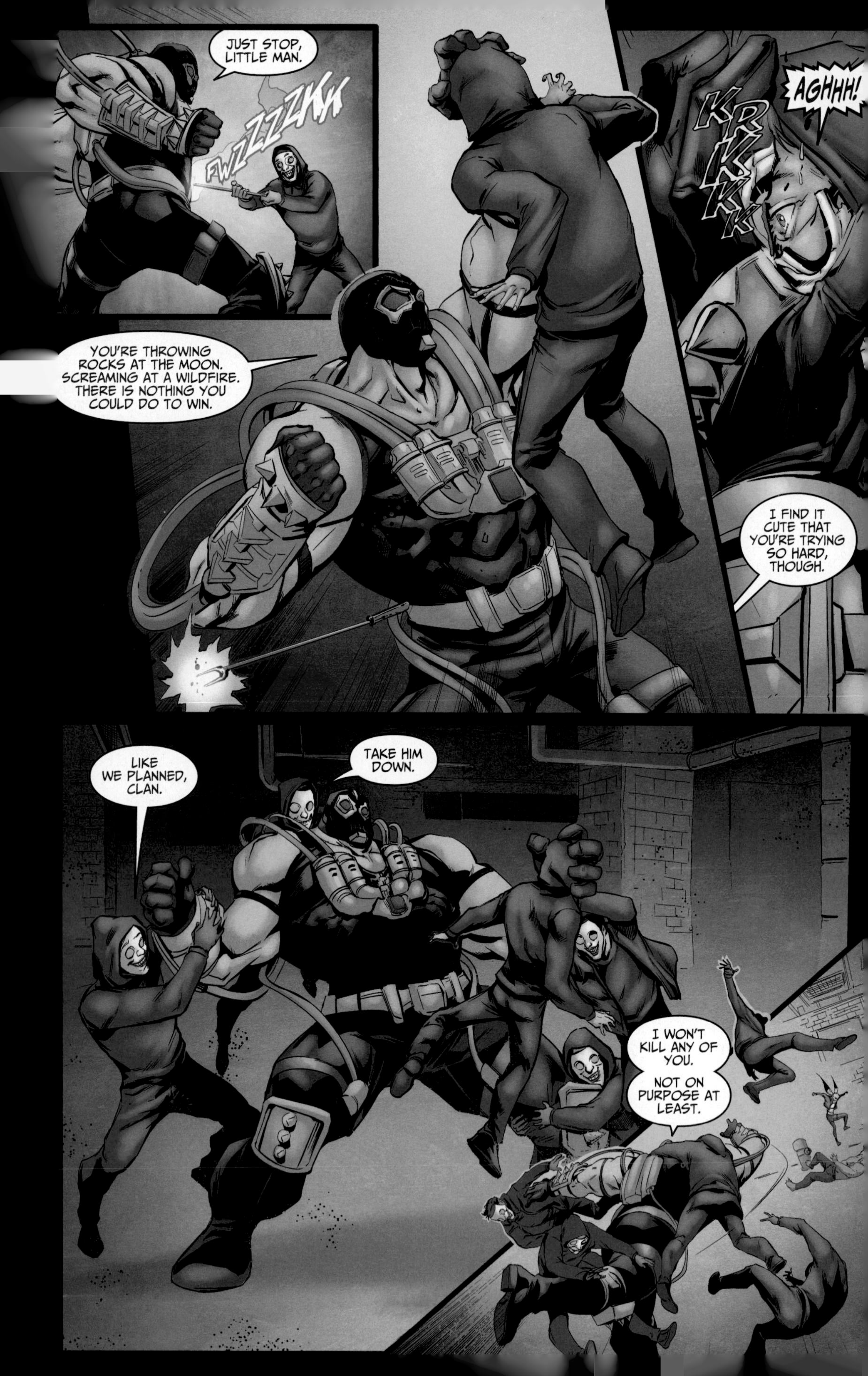
JUST STOP, LITTLE MAN.
FWZZZZKK
KRKKKK
AGHHH!
YOU'RE THROWING ROCKS AT THE MOON. SCREAMING AT A WILDFIRE. THERE IS NOTHING YOU COULD DO TO WIN.
I FIND IT CUTE THAT YOU'RE TRYING SO HARD, THOUGH.
LIKE WE PLANNED, CLAN.
TAKE HIM DOWN.
I WON'T KILL ANY OF YOU.
NOT ON PURPOSE AT LEAST.

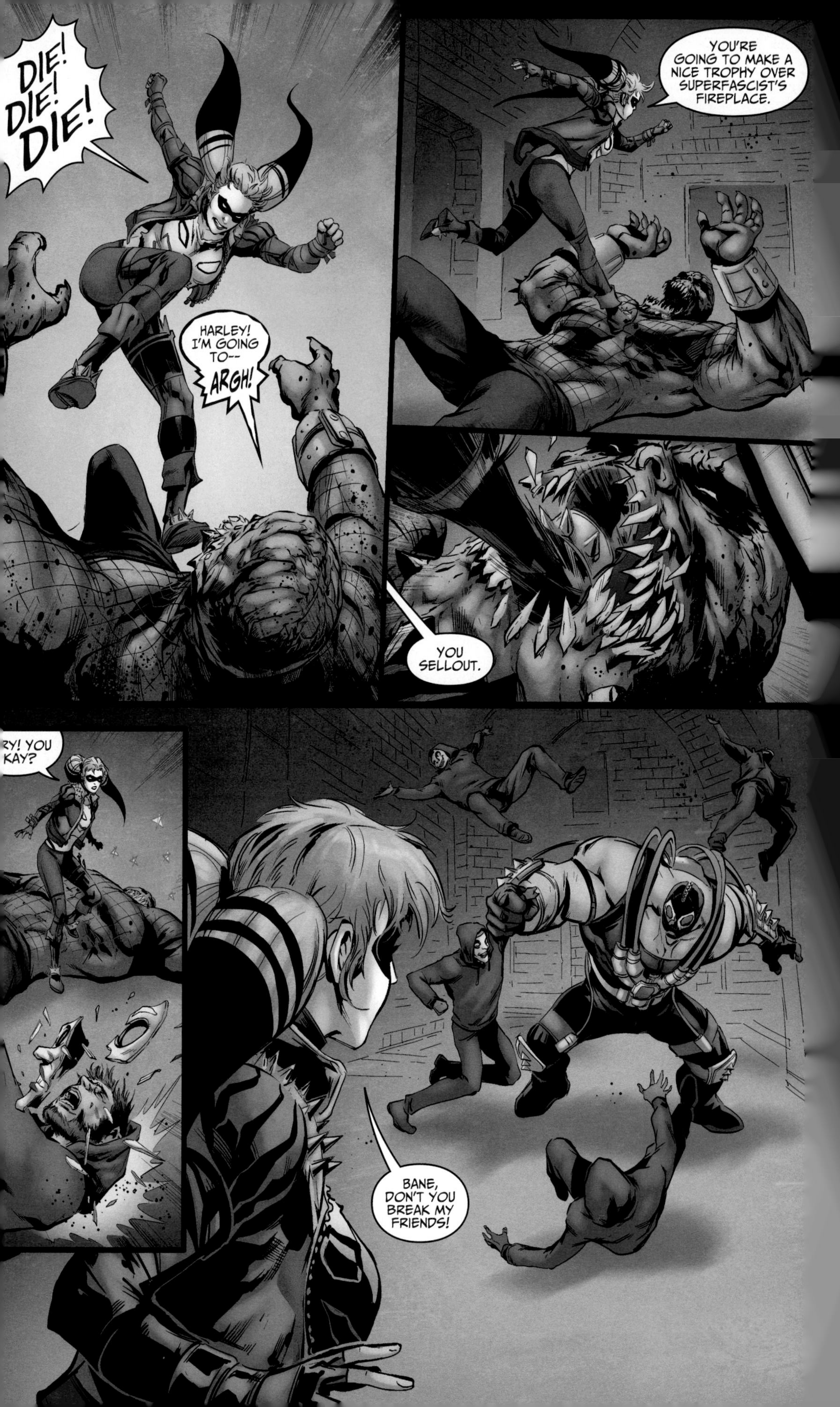
DIE! DIE! DIE!
YOU'RE GOING TO MAKE A NICE TROPHY OVER SUPERFASCIST'S FIREPLACE.
HARLEY! I'M GOING TO-- ARGH!
YOU SELLOUT.
RY! YOU KAY?
BANE, DON'T YOU BREAK MY FRIENDS!

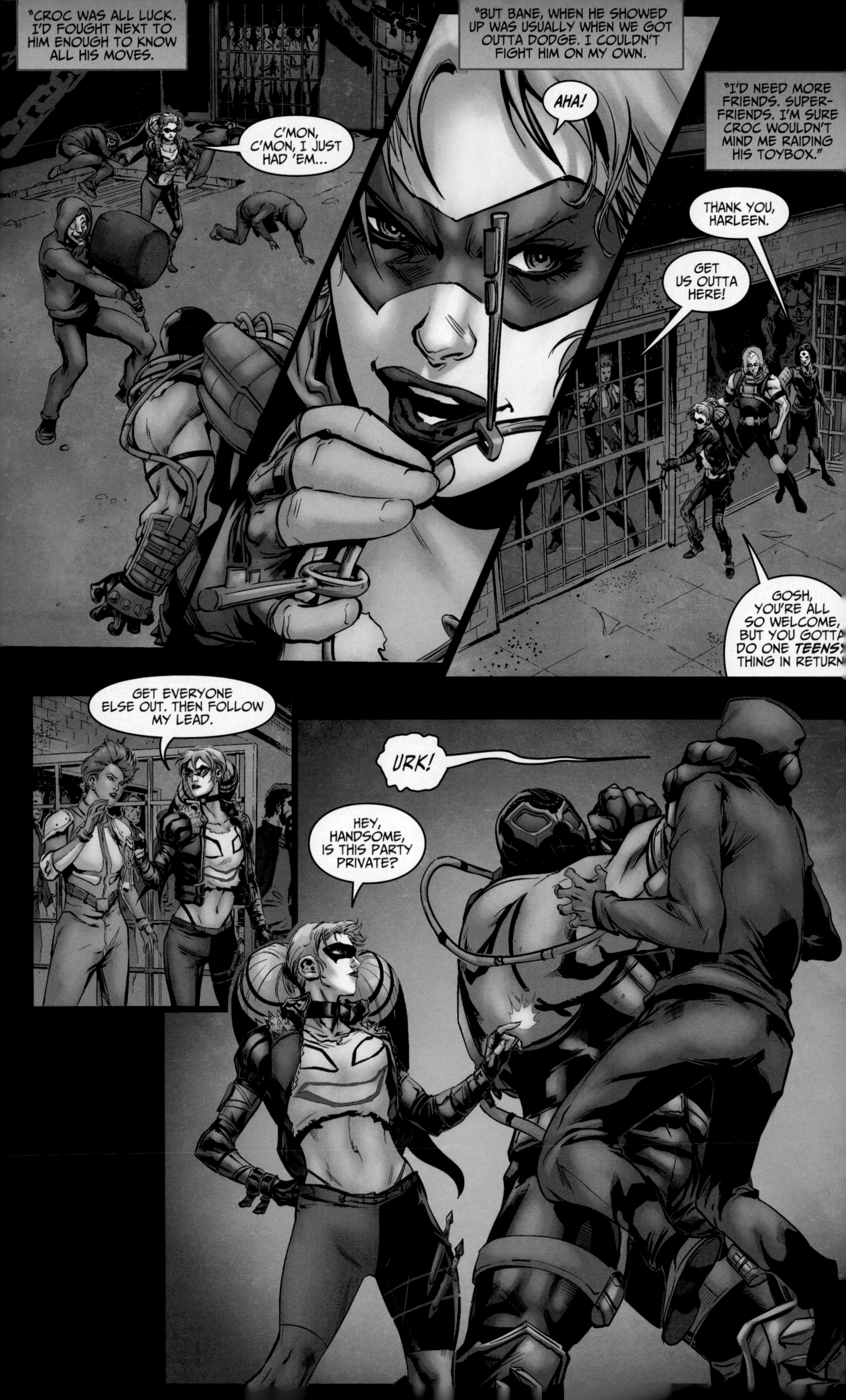
"CROC WAS ALL LUCK. I'D FOUGHT NEXT TO HIM ENOUGH TO KNOW ALL HIS MOVES.
C'MON, C'MON, I JUST HAD 'EM...
"BUT BANE, WHEN HE SHOWED UP WAS USUALLY WHEN WE GOT OUTTA DODGE. I COULDN'T FIGHT HIM ON MY OWN.
AHA!
"I'D NEED MORE FRIENDS. SUPER-FRIENDS. I'M SURE CROC WOULDN'T MIND ME RAIDING HIS TOYBOX."
THANK YOU, HARLEEN.
GET US OUTTA HERE!
GOSH, YOU'RE ALL SO WELCOME, BUT YOU GOTTA DO ONE TEENS THING IN RETURN
GET EVERYONE ELSE OUT. THEN FOLLOW MY LEAD.
URK!
HEY, HANDSOME, IS THIS PARTY PRIVATE?

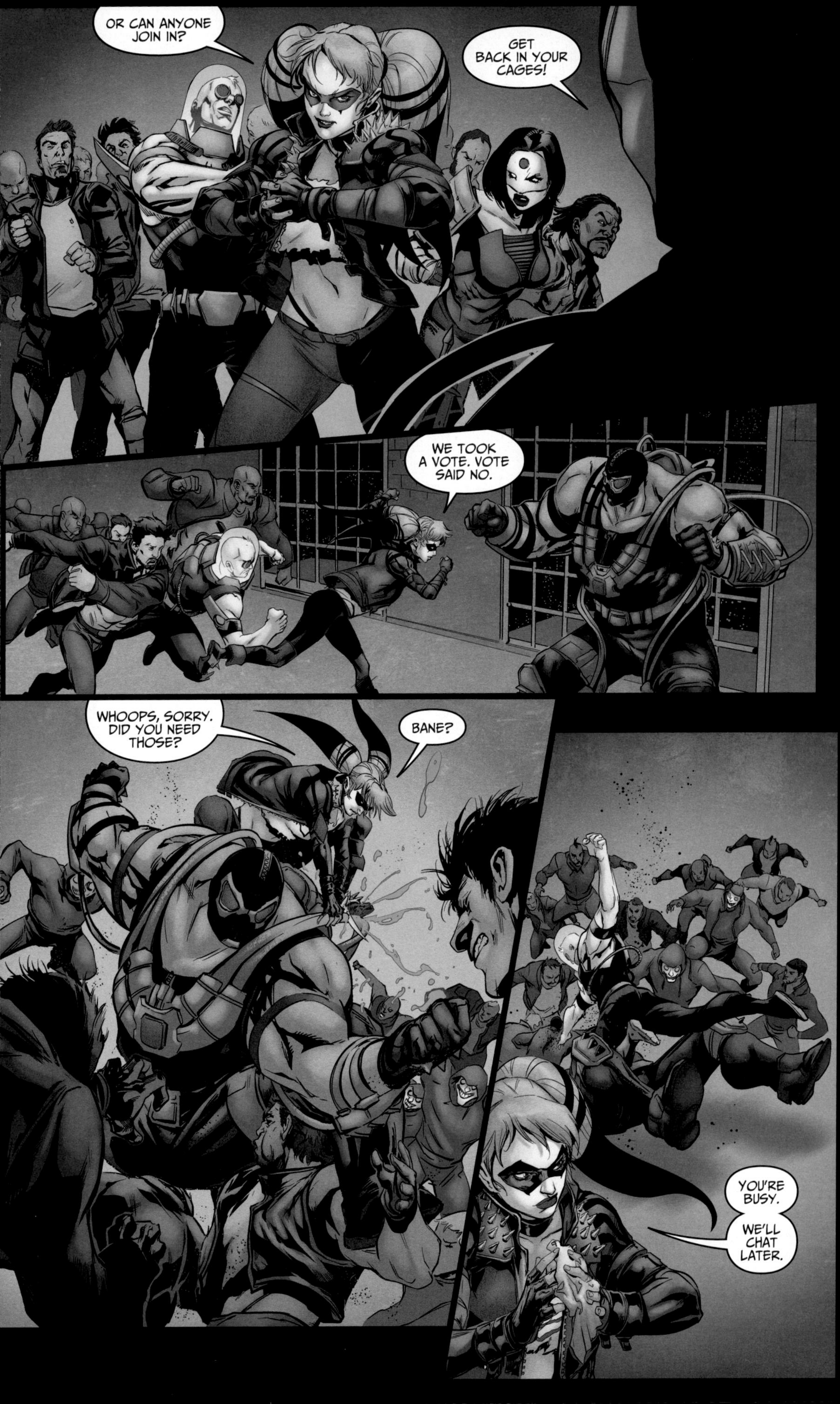
OR CAN ANYONE JOIN IN?
GET BACK IN YOUR CAGES!
WE TOOK A VOTE. VOTE SAID NO.
WHOOPS, SORRY. DID YOU NEED THOSE?
BANE?
YOU'RE BUSY.
WE'LL CHAT LATER.

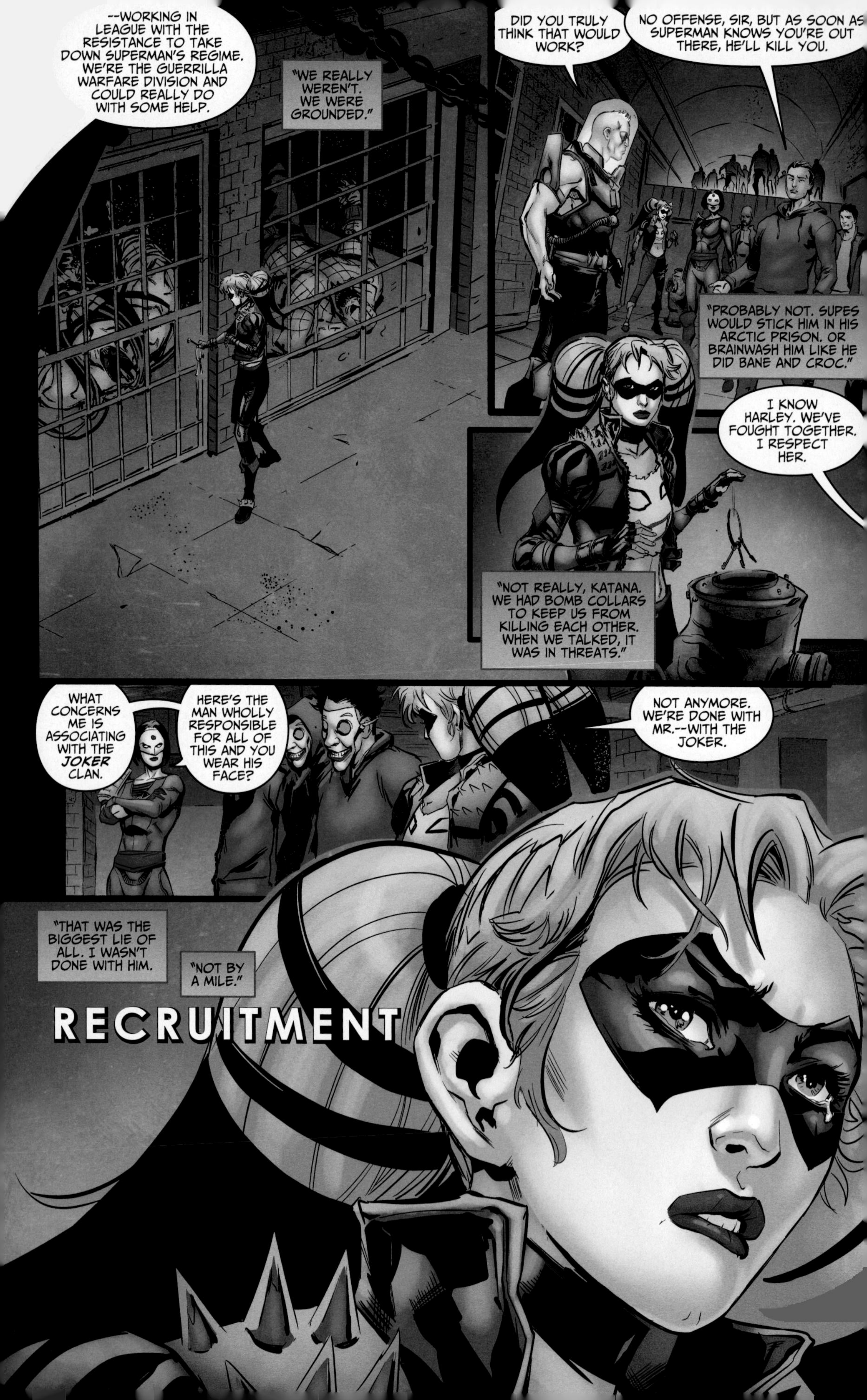
--WORKING IN LEAGUE WITH THE RESISTANCE TO TAKE DOWN SUPERMAN'S REGIME. WE'RE THE GUERRILLA WARFARE DIVISION AND COULD REALLY DO WITH SOME HELP.
"WE REALLY WEREN'T. WE WERE GROUNDED."
DID YOU TRULY THINK THAT WOULD WORK?
NO OFFENSE, SIR, BUT AS SOON AS SUPERMAN KNOWS YOU'RE OUT THERE, HE'LL KILL YOU.
"PROBABLY NOT. SUPES WOULD STICK HIM IN HIS ARCTIC PRISON. OR BRAINWASH HIM LIKE HE DID BANE AND CROC."
I KNOW HARLEY. WE'VE FOUGHT TOGETHER. I RESPECT HER.
"NOT REALLY, KATANA. WE HAD BOMB COLLARS TO KEEP US FROM KILLING EACH OTHER. WHEN WE TALKED, IT WAS IN THREATS."
WHAT CONCERNS ME IS ASSOCIATING WITH THE JOKER CLAN.
HERE'S THE MAN WHOLLY RESPONSIBLE FOR ALL OF THIS AND YOU WEAR HIS FACE?
NOT ANYMORE. WE'RE DONE WITH MR.--WITH THE JOKER.
"THAT WAS THE BIGGEST LIE OF ALL. I WASN'T DONE WITH HIM.
"NOT BY A MILE."
RECRUITMENT

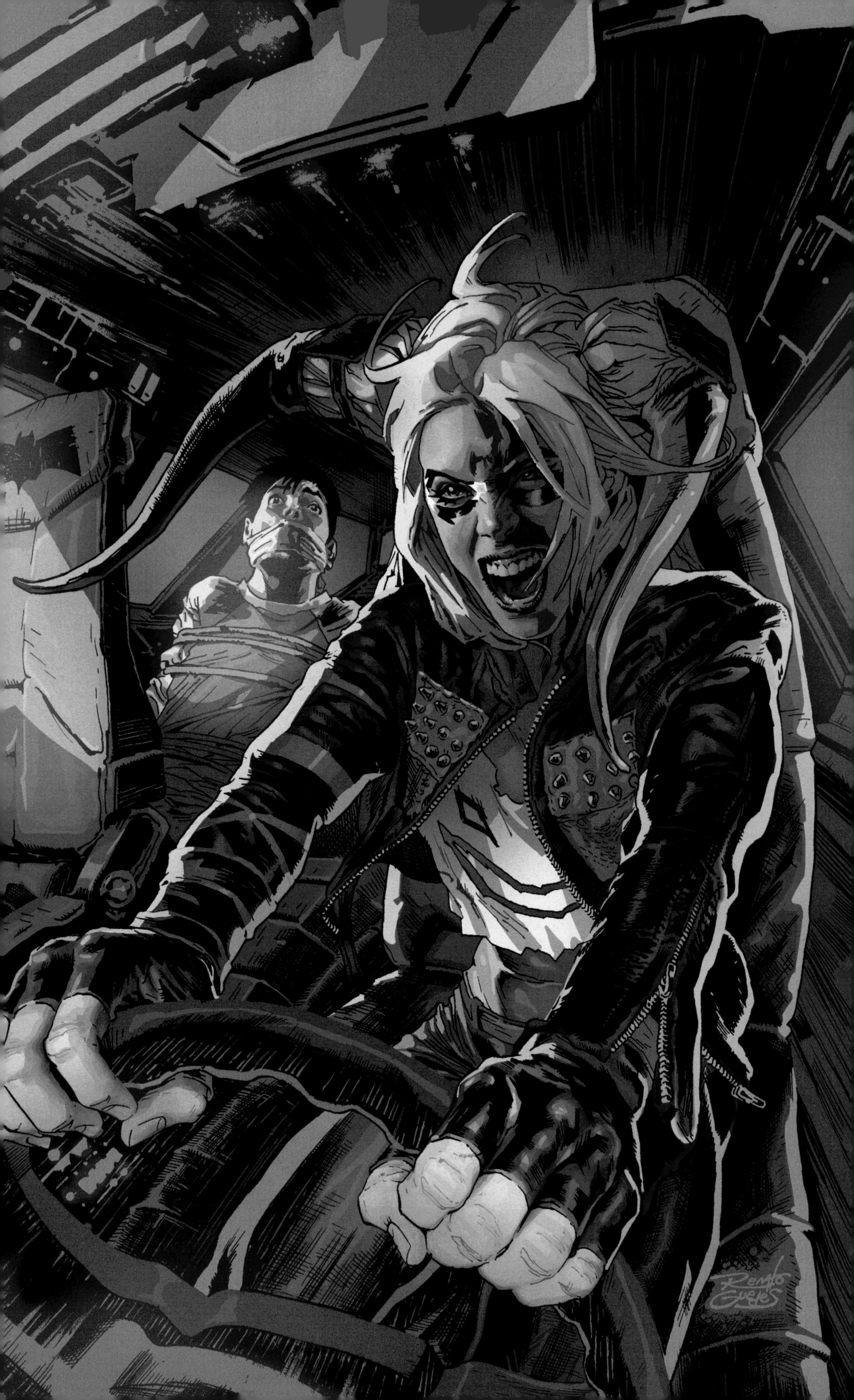

"Muscle Car: Part 1" **Tom Derenick** Artist **J. Nanjan** Colorist
"Muscle Car: Part 2" **Jheremy Raapack** Artist **J. Nanjan** Colorist

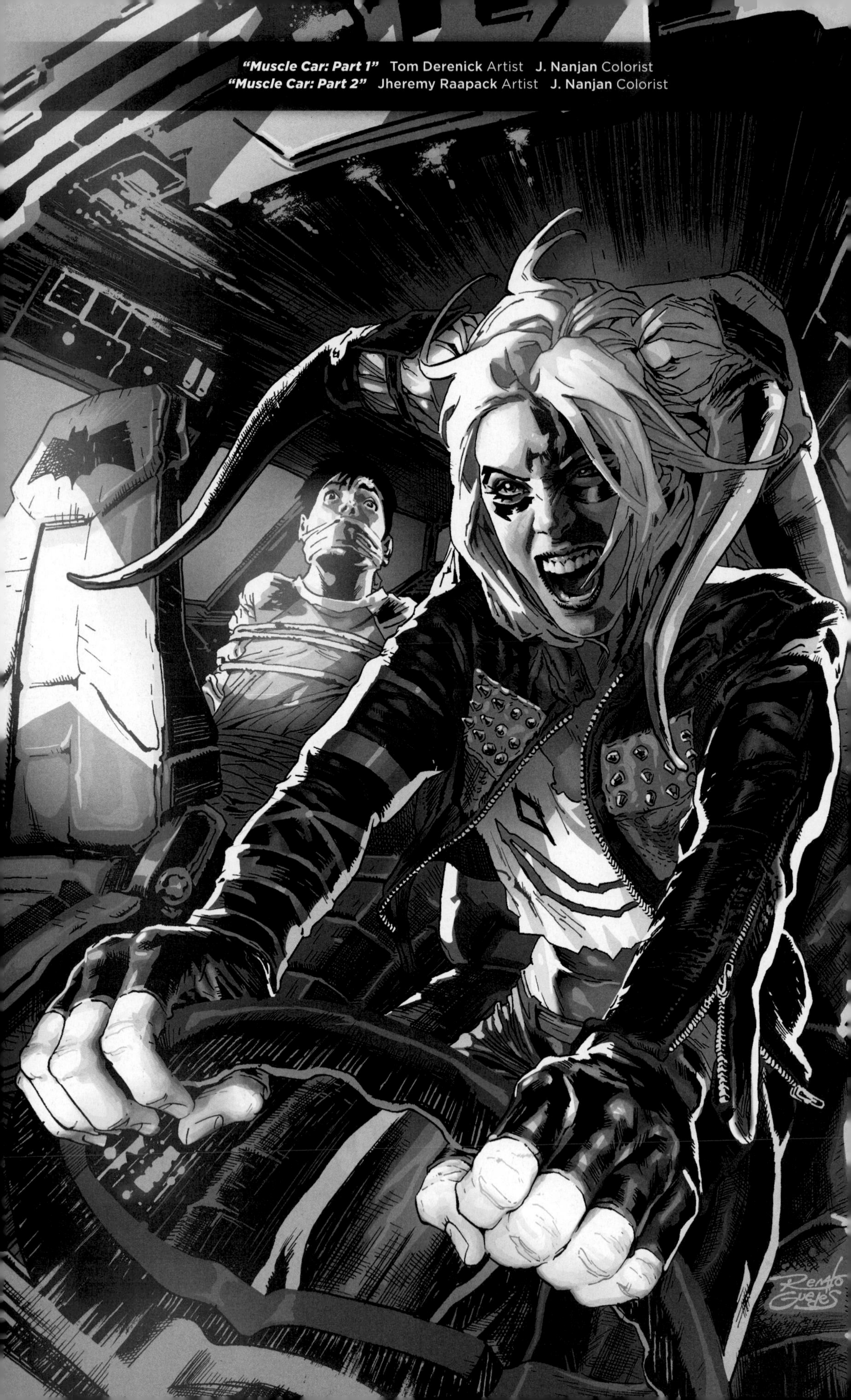

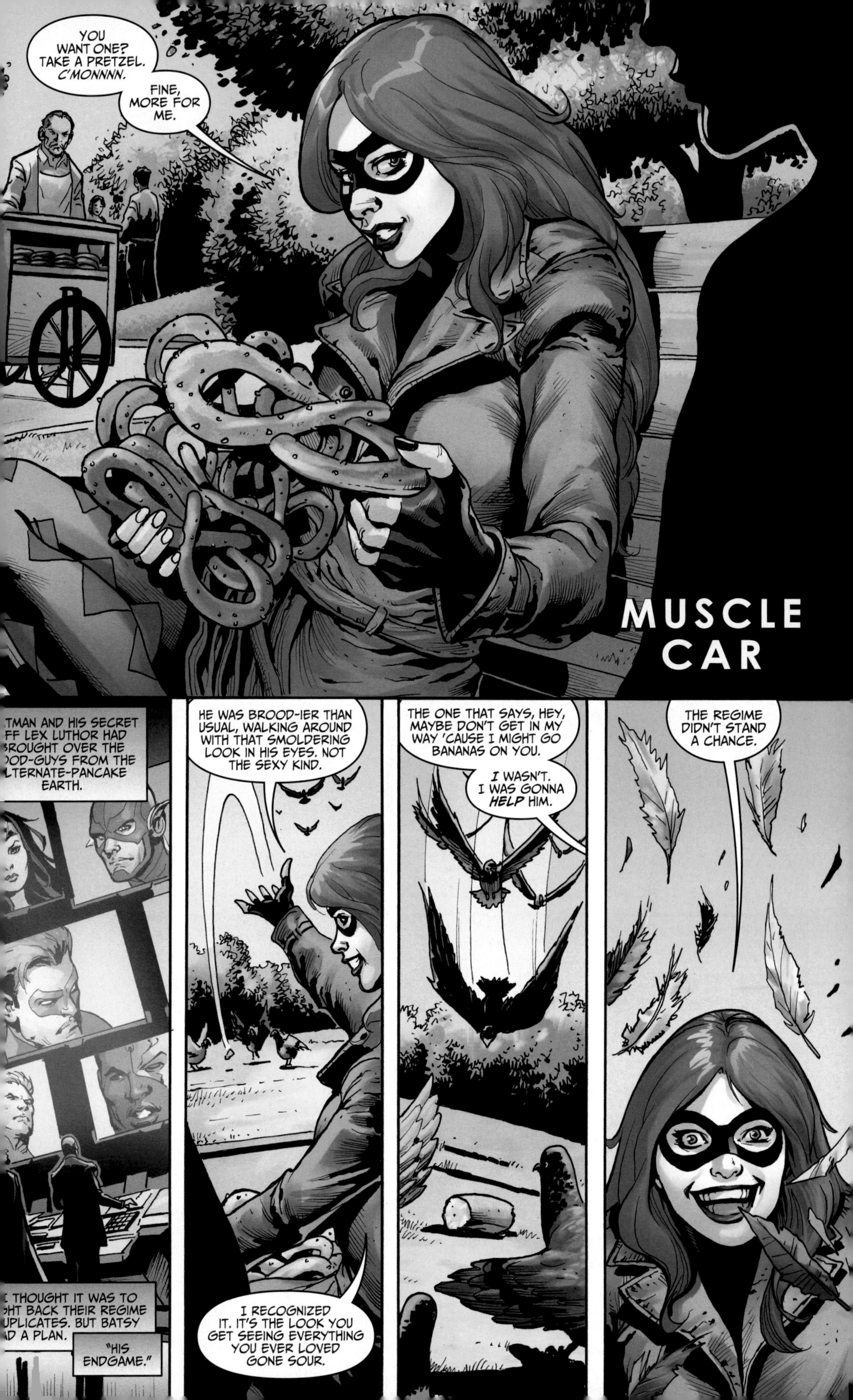
YOU WANT ONE? TAKE A PRETZEL. C'MONNNN.
FINE, MORE FOR ME.
MUSCLE CAR
TMAN AND HIS SECRET FF LEX LUTHOR HAD BROUGHT OVER THE OOD-GUYS FROM THE LTERNATE-PANCAKE EARTH.
THOUGHT IT WAS TO GHT BACK THEIR REGIME UPLICATES. BUT BATSY D A PLAN.
"HIS ENDGAME."
HE WAS BROOD-IER THAN USUAL, WALKING AROUND WITH THAT SMOLDERING LOOK IN HIS EYES. NOT THE SEXY KIND.
I RECOGNIZED IT. IT'S THE LOOK YOU GET SEEING EVERYTHING YOU EVER LOVED GONE SOUR.
THE ONE THAT SAYS, HEY, MAYBE DON'T GET IN MY WAY 'CAUSE I MIGHT GO BANANAS ON YOU.
I WASN'T. I WAS GONNA HELP HIM.
THE REGIME DIDN'T STAND A CHANCE.

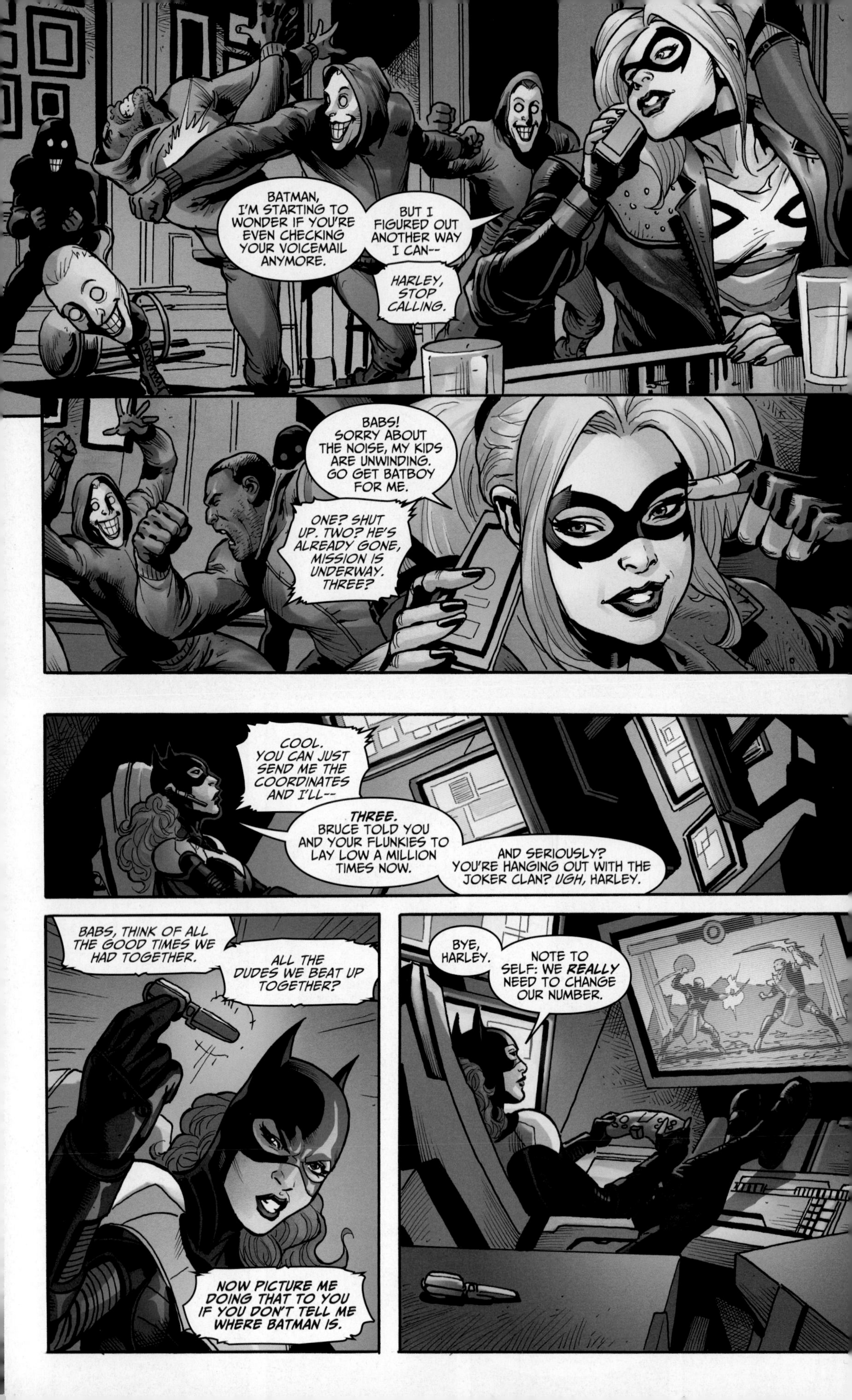
BATMAN, I'M STARTING TO WONDER IF YOU'RE EVEN CHECKING YOUR VOICEMAIL ANYMORE.
BUT I FIGURED OUT ANOTHER WAY I CAN--
HARLEY, STOP CALLING.
BABS! SORRY ABOUT THE NOISE, MY KIDS ARE UNWINDING. GO GET BATBOY FOR ME.
ONE? SHUT UP. TWO? HE'S ALREADY GONE, MISSION IS UNDERWAY. THREE?
COOL. YOU CAN JUST SEND ME THE COORDINATES AND I'LL--
THREE. BRUCE TOLD YOU AND YOUR FLUNKIES TO LAY LOW A MILLION TIMES NOW.
AND SERIOUSLY? YOU'RE HANGING OUT WITH THE JOKER CLAN? UGH, HARLEY.
BABS, THINK OF ALL THE GOOD TIMES WE HAD TOGETHER.
ALL THE DUDES WE BEAT UP TOGETHER?
NOW PICTURE ME DOING THAT TO YOU IF YOU DON'T TELL ME WHERE BATMAN IS.
BYE, HARLEY.
NOTE TO SELF: WE REALLY NEED TO CHANGE OUR NUMBER.

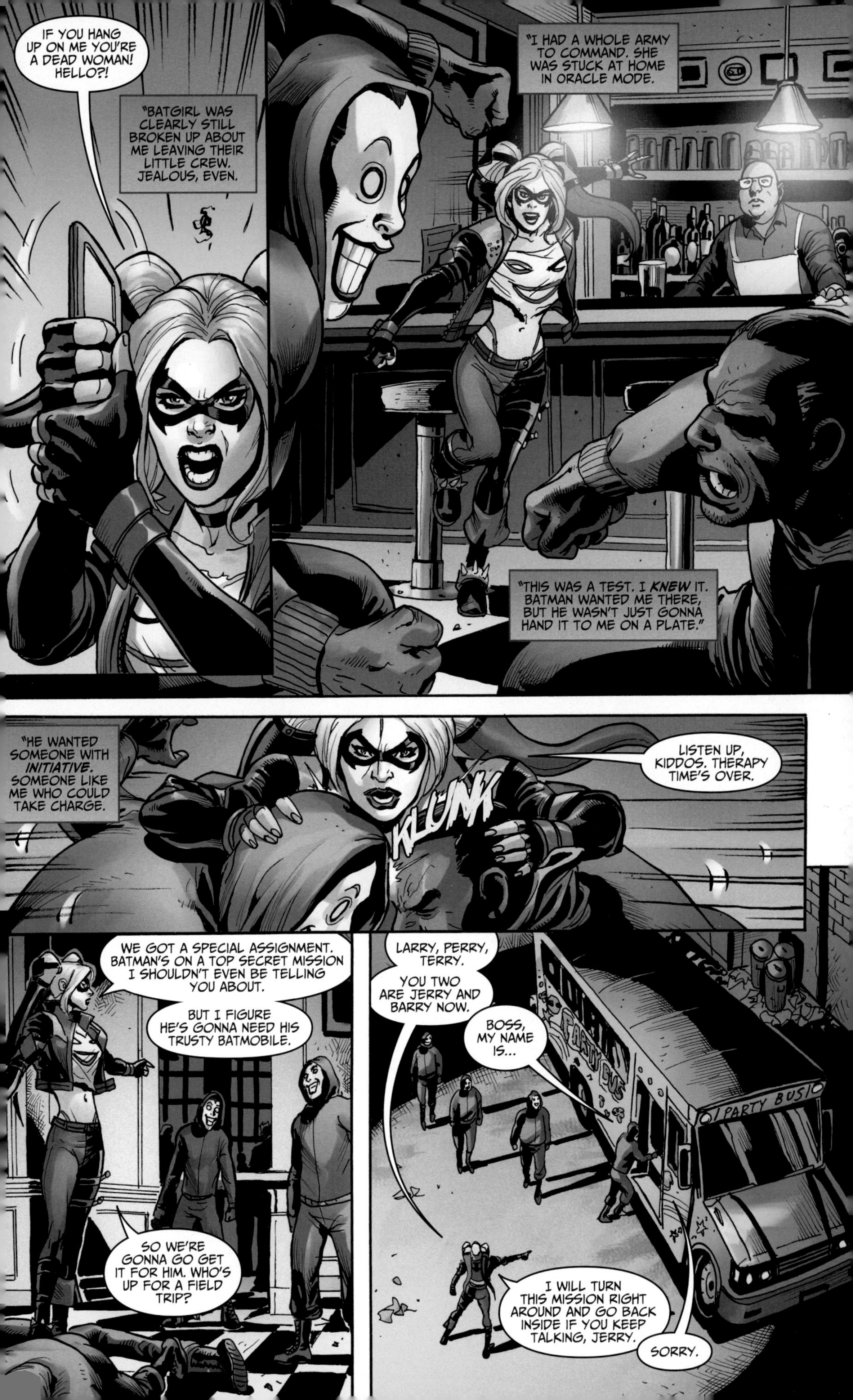
IF YOU HANG UP ON ME YOU'RE A DEAD WOMAN! HELLO?!
"BATGIRL WAS CLEARLY STILL BROKEN UP ABOUT ME LEAVING THEIR LITTLE CREW. JEALOUS, EVEN.
"I HAD A WHOLE ARMY TO COMMAND. SHE WAS STUCK AT HOME IN ORACLE MODE.
"THIS WAS A TEST. I KNEW IT. BATMAN WANTED ME THERE, BUT HE WASN'T JUST GONNA HAND IT TO ME ON A PLATE."
"HE WANTED SOMEONE WITH INITIATIVE. SOMEONE LIKE ME WHO COULD TAKE CHARGE.
LISTEN UP, KIDDOS. THERAPY TIME'S OVER.
KLUNK
WE GOT A SPECIAL ASSIGNMENT. BATMAN'S ON A TOP SECRET MISSION I SHOULDN'T EVEN BE TELLING YOU ABOUT.
BUT I FIGURE HE'S GONNA NEED HIS TRUSTY BATMOBILE.
SO WE'RE GONNA GO GET IT FOR HIM. WHO'S UP FOR A FIELD TRIP?
LARRY, PERRY, TERRY.
YOU TWO ARE JERRY AND BARRY NOW.
BOSS, MY NAME IS...
PARTY BUS
I WILL TURN THIS MISSION RIGHT AROUND AND GO BACK INSIDE IF YOU KEEP TALKING, JERRY.
SORRY.

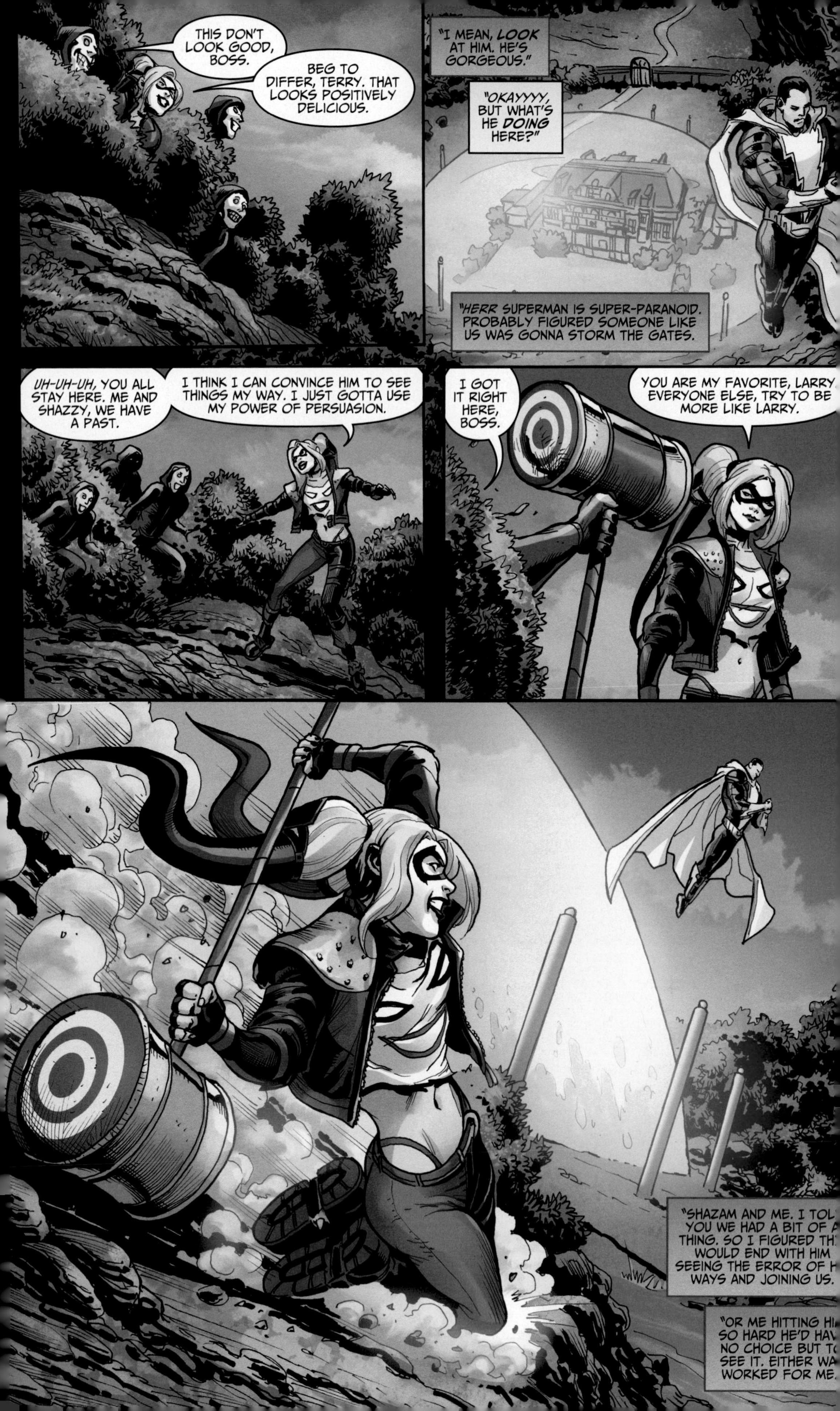
THIS DON'T LOOK GOOD, BOSS.
BEG TO DIFFER, TERRY. THAT LOOKS POSITIVELY DELICIOUS.
"I MEAN, *LOOK* AT HIM. HE'S GORGEOUS."
"OKAYYYY, BUT WHAT'S HE *DOING* HERE?"
"*HERR* SUPERMAN IS SUPER-PARANOID. PROBABLY FIGURED SOMEONE LIKE US WAS GONNA STORM THE GATES.
UH-UH-UH, YOU ALL STAY HERE. ME AND SHAZZY, WE HAVE A PAST.
I THINK I CAN CONVINCE HIM TO SEE THINGS MY WAY. I JUST GOTTA USE MY POWER OF PERSUASION.
I GOT IT RIGHT HERE, BOSS.
YOU ARE MY FAVORITE, LARRY. EVERYONE ELSE, TRY TO BE MORE LIKE LARRY.
"SHAZAM AND ME. I TOL YOU WE HAD A BIT OF A THING. SO I FIGURED TH WOULD END WITH HIM SEEING THE ERROR OF H WAYS AND JOINING US.
"OR ME HITTING HI SO HARD HE'D HAV NO CHOICE BUT T SEE IT. EITHER WA WORKED FOR ME.

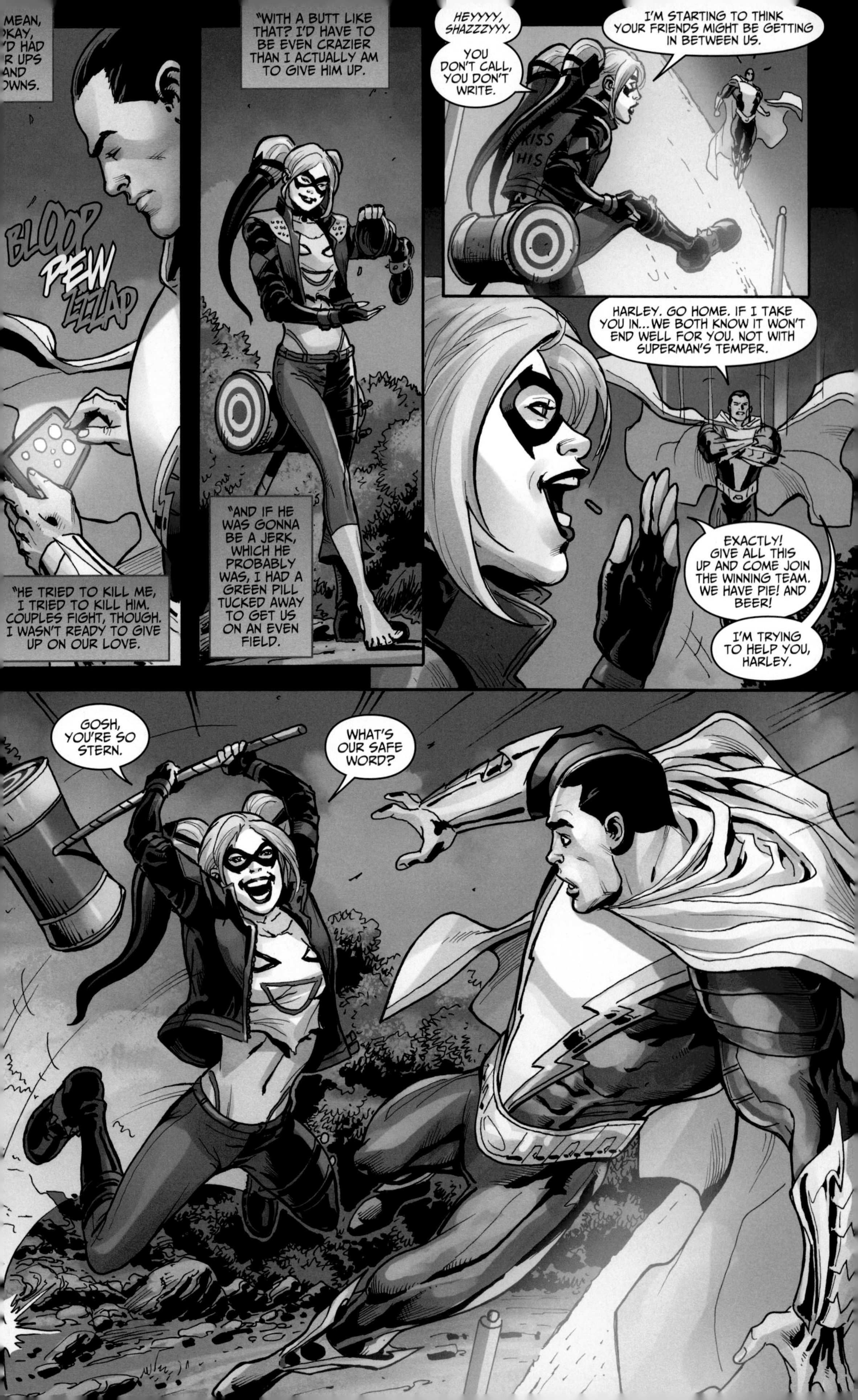
MEAN, KAY, 'D HAD R UPS AND OWNS.
BLOOP
PEW
ZZZAP
"HE TRIED TO KILL ME, I TRIED TO KILL HIM. COUPLES FIGHT, THOUGH. I WASN'T READY TO GIVE UP ON OUR LOVE.
"WITH A BUTT LIKE THAT? I'D HAVE TO BE EVEN CRAZIER THAN I ACTUALLY AM TO GIVE HIM UP.
"AND IF HE WAS GONNA BE A JERK, WHICH HE PROBABLY WAS, I HAD A GREEN PILL TUCKED AWAY TO GET US ON AN EVEN FIELD.
HEYYYY, SHAZZZYYY.
YOU DON'T CALL, YOU DON'T WRITE.
I'M STARTING TO THINK YOUR FRIENDS MIGHT BE GETTING IN BETWEEN US.
KISS HIS
HARLEY. GO HOME. IF I TAKE YOU IN... WE BOTH KNOW IT WON'T END WELL FOR YOU. NOT WITH SUPERMAN'S TEMPER.
EXACTLY! GIVE ALL THIS UP AND COME JOIN THE WINNING TEAM. WE HAVE PIE! AND BEER!
I'M TRYING TO HELP YOU, HARLEY.
GOSH, YOU'RE SO STERN.
WHAT'S OUR SAFE WORD?

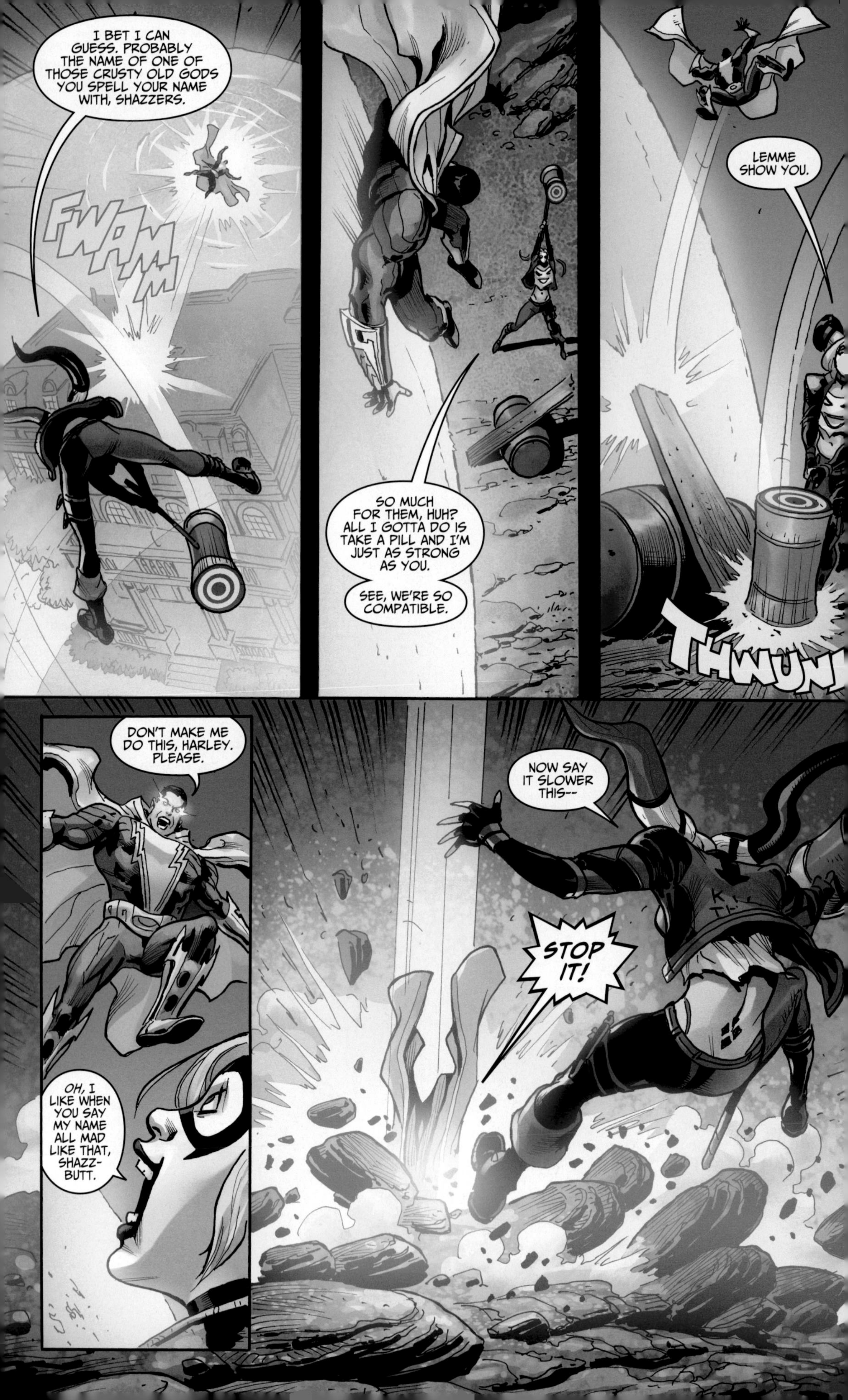
I BET I CAN GUESS. PROBABLY THE NAME OF ONE OF THOSE CRUSTY OLD GODS YOU SPELL YOUR NAME WITH, SHAZZERS.
FWAMM
SO MUCH FOR THEM, HUH? ALL I GOTTA DO IS TAKE A PILL AND I'M JUST AS STRONG AS YOU.
SEE, WE'RE SO COMPATIBLE.
LEMME SHOW YOU.
THWUN
DON'T MAKE ME DO THIS, HARLEY. PLEASE.
OH, I LIKE WHEN YOU SAY MY NAME ALL MAD LIKE THAT, SHAZZ-BUTT.
NOW SAY IT SLOWER THIS--
STOP IT!

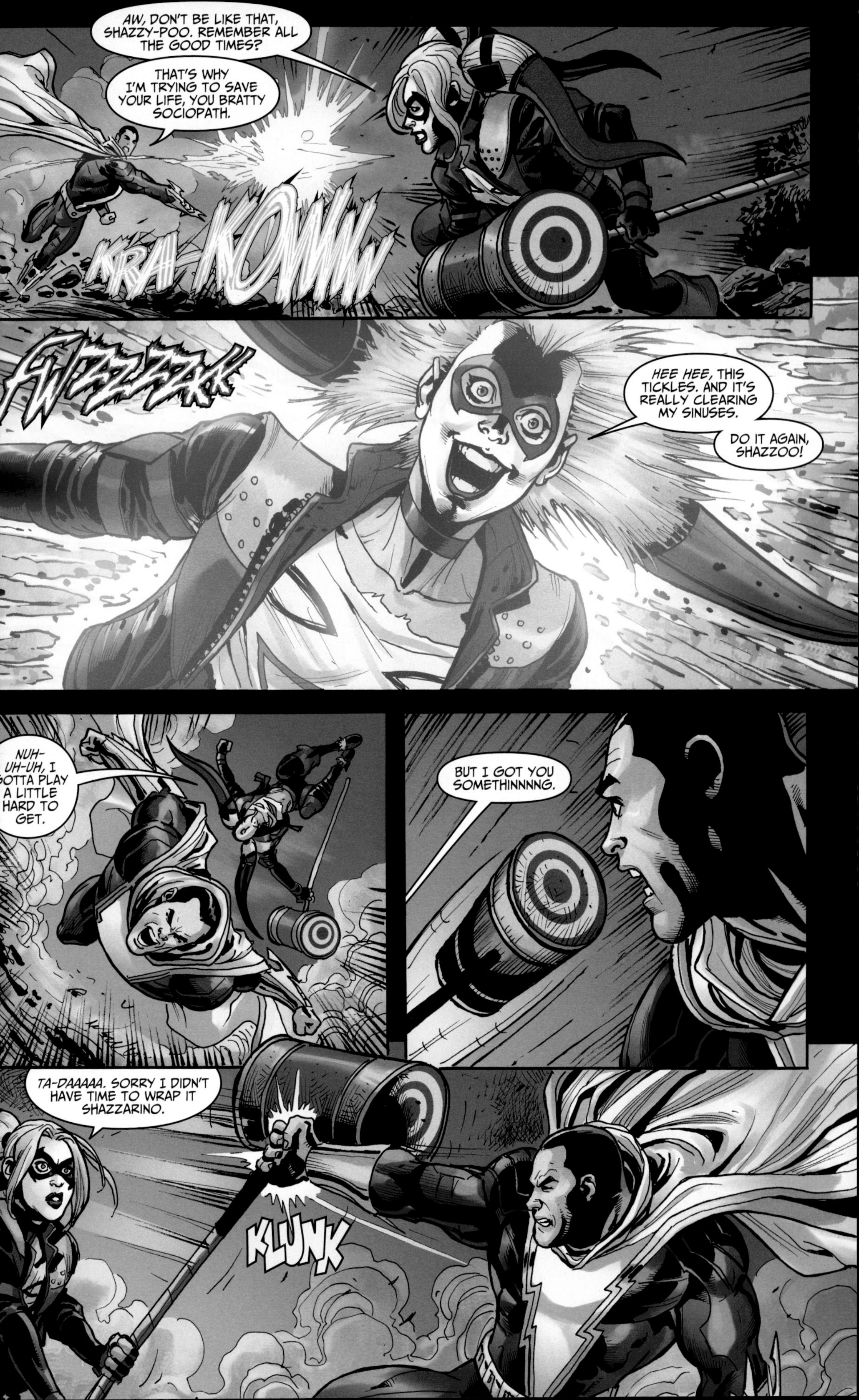
AW, DON'T BE LIKE THAT, SHAZZY-POO. REMEMBER ALL THE GOOD TIMES?
THAT'S WHY I'M TRYING TO SAVE YOUR LIFE, YOU BRATTY SOCIOPATH.
KRA-KOWWW
FWZZZAKK
HEE HEE, THIS TICKLES. AND IT'S REALLY CLEARING MY SINUSES.
DO IT AGAIN, SHAZZOO!
NUH-UH-UH, I GOTTA PLAY A LITTLE HARD TO GET.
BUT I GOT YOU SOMETHINNNNG.
TA-DAAAAA. SORRY I DIDN'T HAVE TIME TO WRAP IT SHAZZARINO.
KLUNK

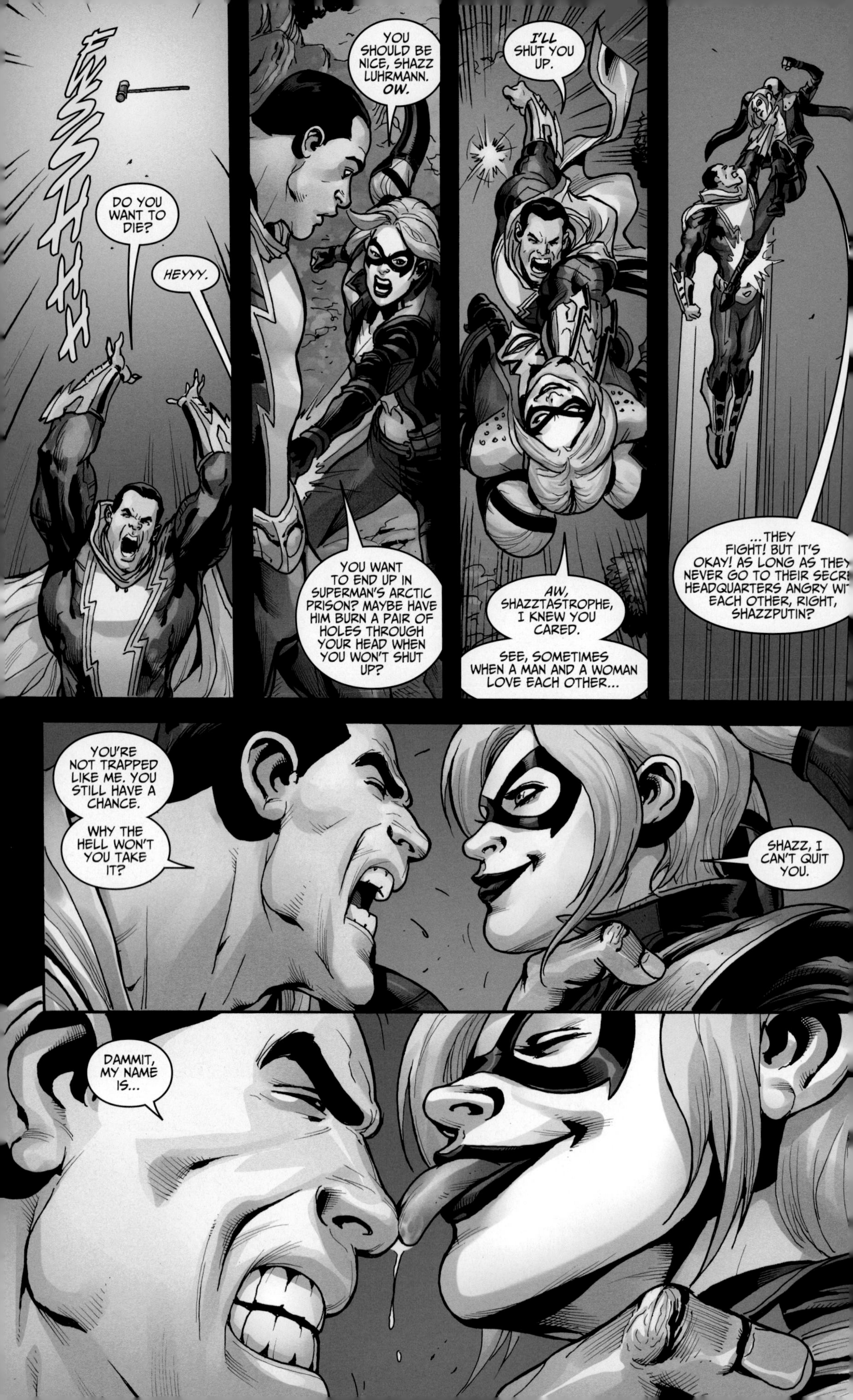
DO YOU WANT TO DIE?
HEYYY.
YOU SHOULD BE NICE, SHAZZ LUHRMANN. OW.
YOU WANT TO END UP IN SUPERMAN'S ARCTIC PRISON? MAYBE HAVE HIM BURN A PAIR OF HOLES THROUGH YOUR HEAD WHEN YOU WON'T SHUT UP?
I'LL SHUT YOU UP.
AW, SHAZZTASTROPHE, I KNEW YOU CARED.
SEE, SOMETIMES WHEN A MAN AND A WOMAN LOVE EACH OTHER...
...THEY FIGHT! BUT IT'S OKAY! AS LONG AS THEY NEVER GO TO THEIR SECR HEADQUARTERS ANGRY WIT EACH OTHER, RIGHT, SHAZZPUTIN?
YOU'RE NOT TRAPPED LIKE ME. YOU STILL HAVE A CHANCE.
WHY THE HELL WON'T YOU TAKE IT?
SHAZZ, I CAN'T QUIT YOU.
DAMMIT, MY NAME IS...

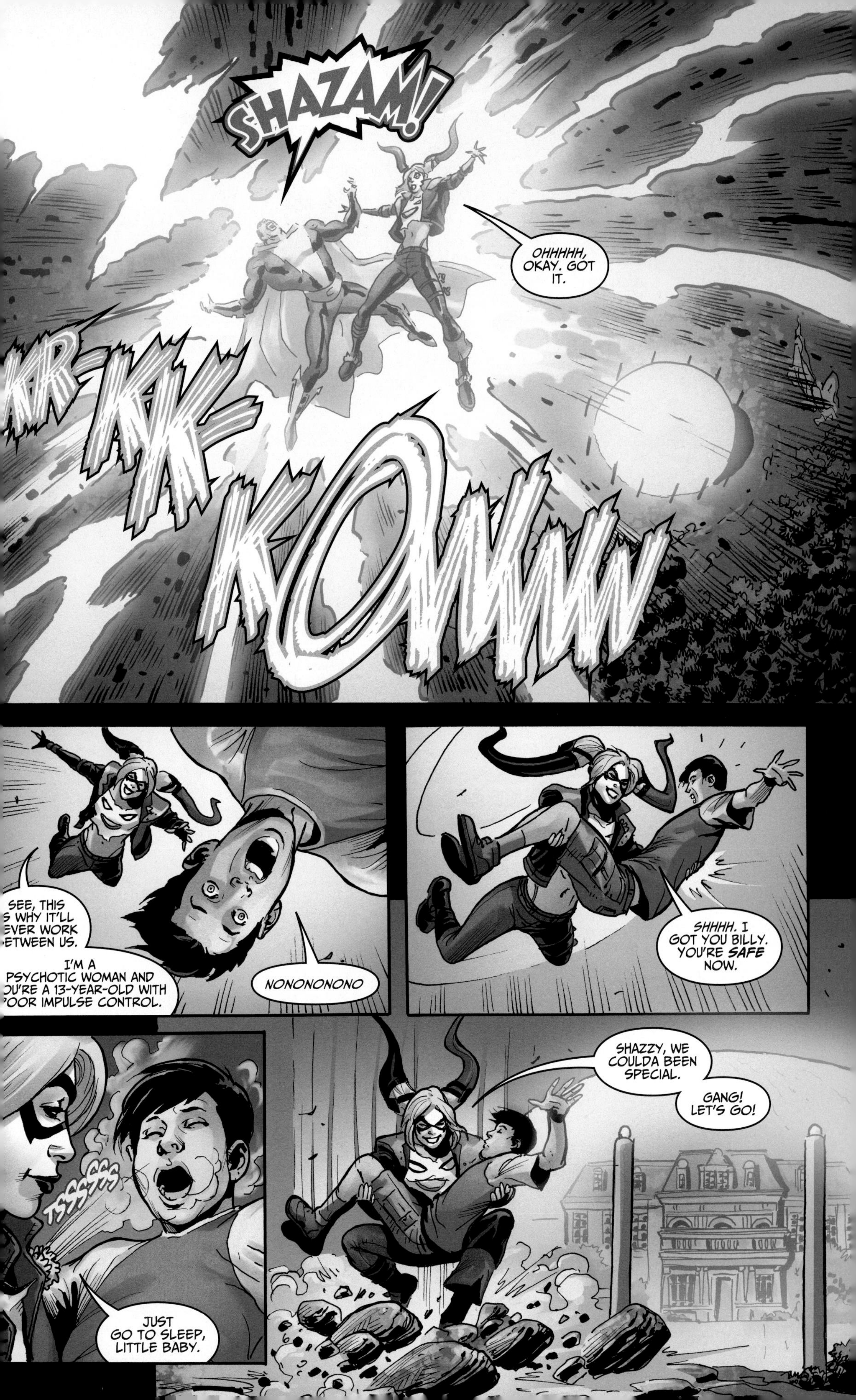
SHAZAM!
OHHHHH, OKAY. GOT IT.
SEE, THIS S WHY IT'LL EVER WORK ETWEEN US.
I'M A PSYCHOTIC WOMAN AND OU'RE A 13-YEAR-OLD WITH POOR IMPULSE CONTROL.
NONONONONO
SHHHH. I GOT YOU BILLY. YOU'RE SAFE NOW.
TSSSSSS
JUST GO TO SLEEP, LITTLE BABY.
SHAZZY, WE COULDA BEEN SPECIAL.
GANG! LET'S GO!

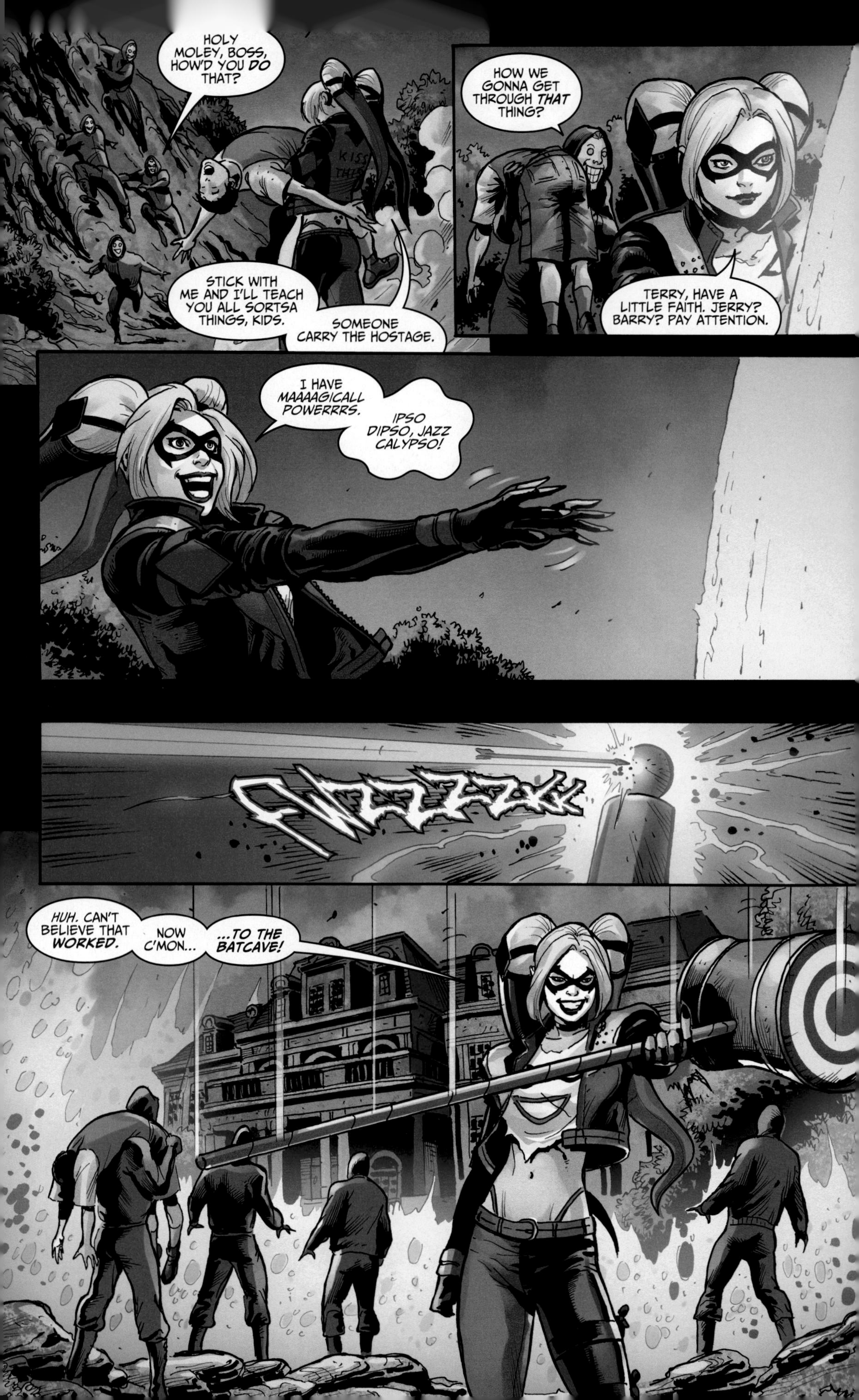
HOLY MOLEY, BOSS, HOW'D YOU *DO* THAT?
STICK WITH ME AND I'LL TEACH YOU ALL SORTSA THINGS, KIDS.
SOMEONE CARRY THE HOSTAGE.
KISS THIS
HOW WE GONNA GET THROUGH *THAT* THING?
TERRY, HAVE A LITTLE FAITH. JERRY? BARRY? PAY ATTENTION.
I HAVE MAAAAGICALL POWERRRS.
IPSO DIPSO, JAZZ CALYPSO!
HUH. CAN'T BELIEVE THAT **WORKED.**
NOW C'MON...
...TO THE **BATCAVE!**

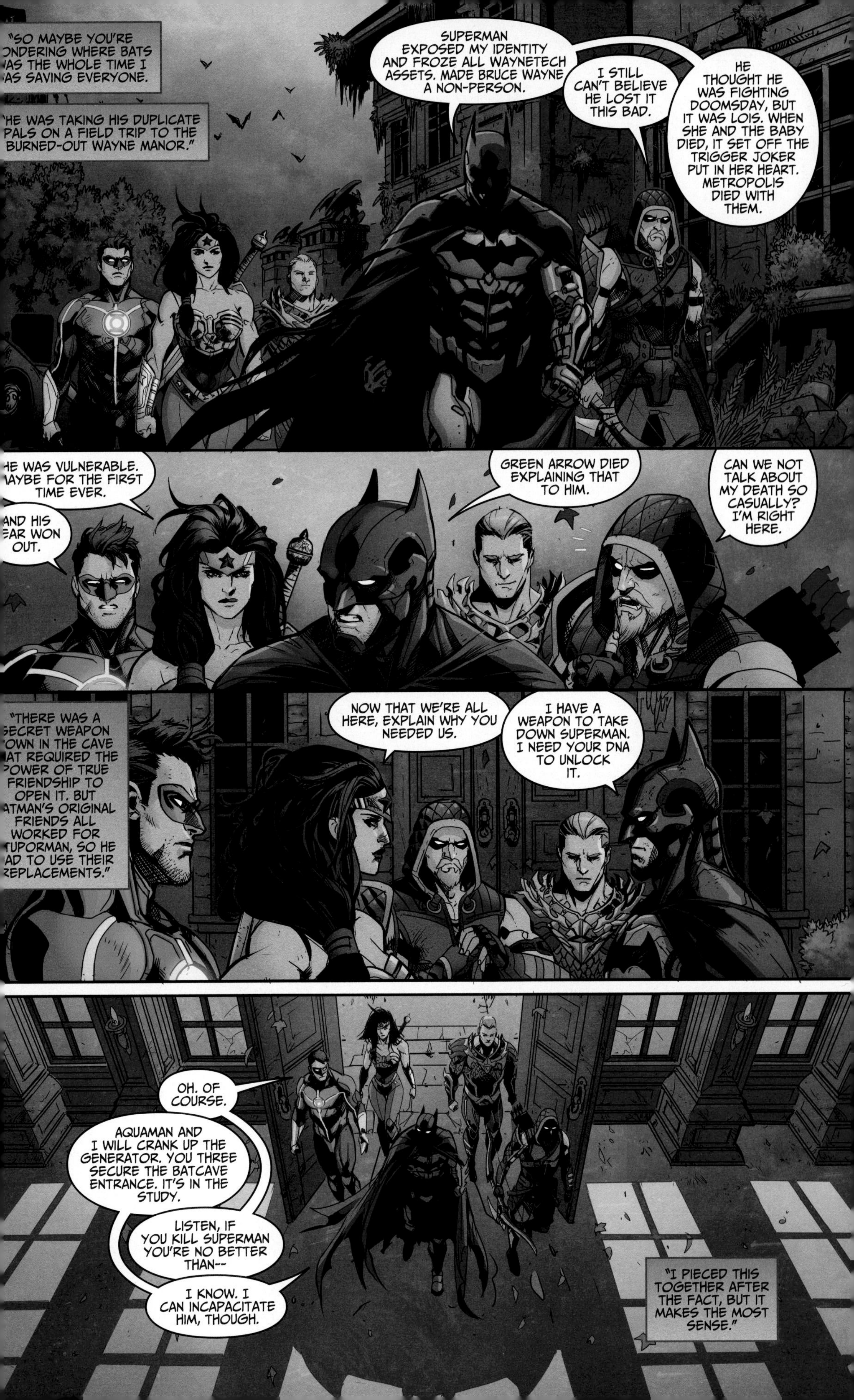
"SO MAYBE YOU'RE ONDERING WHERE BATS AS THE WHOLE TIME I AS SAVING EVERYONE.
HE WAS TAKING HIS DUPLICATE PALS ON A FIELD TRIP TO THE BURNED-OUT WAYNE MANOR."
SUPERMAN EXPOSED MY IDENTITY AND FROZE ALL WAYNETECH ASSETS. MADE BRUCE WAYNE A NON-PERSON.
I STILL CAN'T BELIEVE HE LOST IT THIS BAD.
HE THOUGHT HE WAS FIGHTING DOOMSDAY, BUT IT WAS LOIS. WHEN SHE AND THE BABY DIED, IT SET OFF THE TRIGGER JOKER PUT IN HER HEART. METROPOLIS DIED WITH THEM.
HE WAS VULNERABLE. AYBE FOR THE FIRST TIME EVER.
AND HIS EAR WON OUT.
GREEN ARROW DIED EXPLAINING THAT TO HIM.
CAN WE NOT TALK ABOUT MY DEATH SO CASUALLY? I'M RIGHT HERE.
"THERE WAS A SECRET WEAPON OWN IN THE CAVE AT REQUIRED THE POWER OF TRUE FRIENDSHIP TO OPEN IT. BUT ATMAN'S ORIGINAL FRIENDS ALL WORKED FOR UPERMAN, SO HE AD TO USE THEIR REPLACEMENTS."
NOW THAT WE'RE ALL HERE, EXPLAIN WHY YOU NEEDED US.
I HAVE A WEAPON TO TAKE DOWN SUPERMAN. I NEED YOUR DNA TO UNLOCK IT.
OH. OF COURSE.
AQUAMAN AND I WILL CRANK UP THE GENERATOR. YOU THREE SECURE THE BATCAVE ENTRANCE. IT'S IN THE STUDY.
LISTEN, IF YOU KILL SUPERMAN YOU'RE NO BETTER THAN--
I KNOW. I CAN INCAPACITATE HIM, THOUGH.
"I PIECED THIS TOGETHER AFTER THE FACT, BUT IT MAKES THE MOST SENSE."

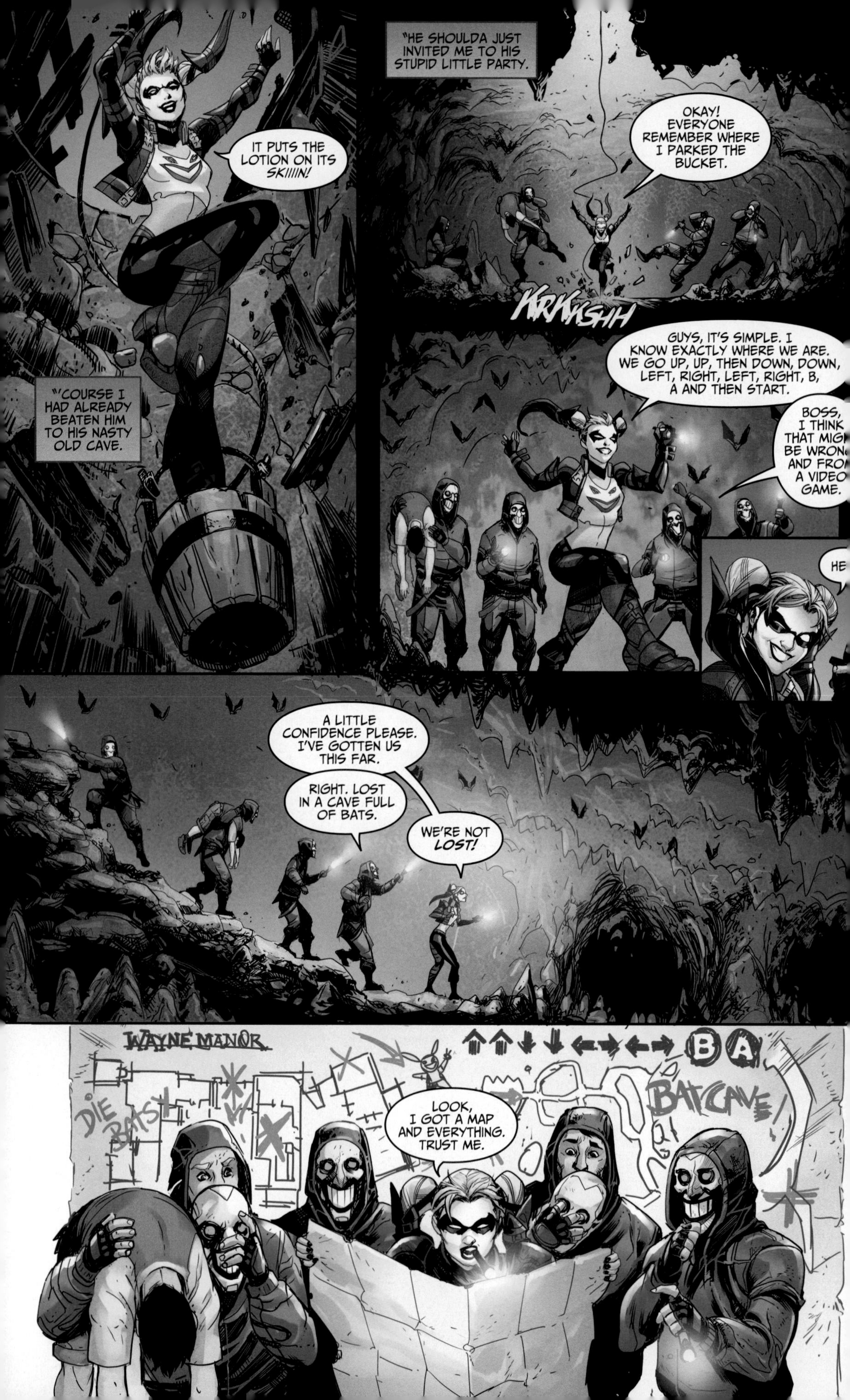
"HE SHOULDA JUST INVITED ME TO HIS STUPID LITTLE PARTY.
IT PUTS THE LOTION ON ITS SKIIIIN!
"'COURSE I HAD ALREADY BEATEN HIM TO HIS NASTY OLD CAVE.
OKAY! EVERYONE REMEMBER WHERE I PARKED THE BUCKET.
KRKKSHH
GUYS, IT'S SIMPLE. I KNOW EXACTLY WHERE WE ARE. WE GO UP, UP, THEN DOWN, DOWN, LEFT, RIGHT, LEFT, RIGHT, B, A AND THEN START.
BOSS, I THINK THAT MIG BE WRON AND FRO A VIDEO GAME.
HE
A LITTLE CONFIDENCE PLEASE. I'VE GOTTEN US THIS FAR.
RIGHT. LOST IN A CAVE FULL OF BATS.
WE'RE NOT LOST!
WAYNE MANOR
B A
DIE BATS
BATCAVE
LOOK, I GOT A MAP AND EVERYTHING. TRUST ME.

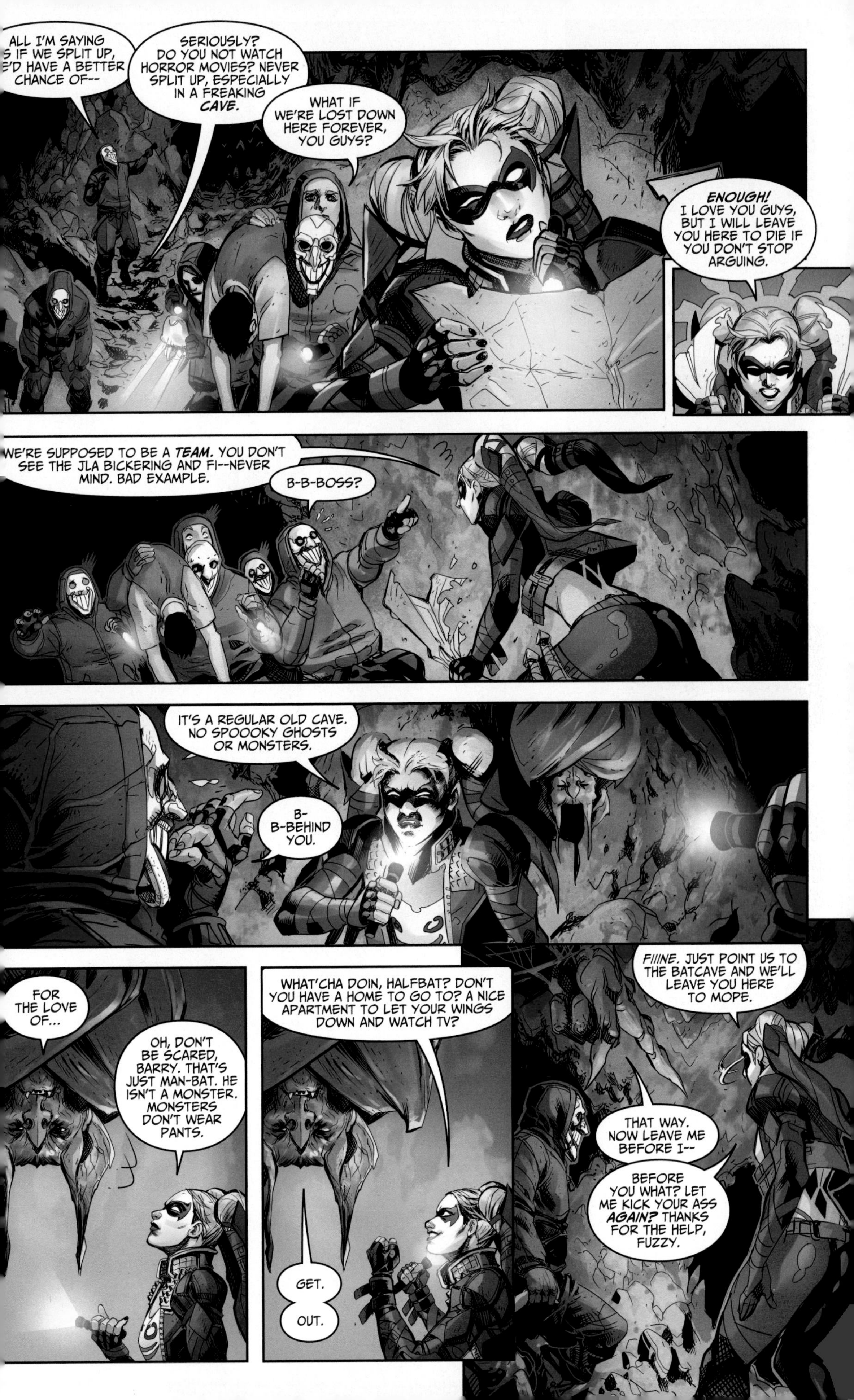
ALL I'M SAYING S IF WE SPLIT UP, E'D HAVE A BETTER CHANCE OF--
SERIOUSLY? DO YOU NOT WATCH HORROR MOVIES? NEVER SPLIT UP, ESPECIALLY IN A FREAKING CAVE.
WHAT IF WE'RE LOST DOWN HERE FOREVER, YOU GUYS?
ENOUGH! I LOVE YOU GUYS, BUT I WILL LEAVE YOU HERE TO DIE IF YOU DON'T STOP ARGUING.
WE'RE SUPPOSED TO BE A TEAM. YOU DON'T SEE THE JLA BICKERING AND FI--NEVER MIND. BAD EXAMPLE.
B-B-BOSS?
IT'S A REGULAR OLD CAVE. NO SPOOOKY GHOSTS OR MONSTERS.
B- B-BEHIND YOU.
FOR THE LOVE OF...
OH, DON'T BE SCARED, BARRY. THAT'S JUST MAN-BAT. HE ISN'T A MONSTER. MONSTERS DON'T WEAR PANTS.
WHAT'CHA DOIN, HALFBAT? DON'T YOU HAVE A HOME TO GO TO? A NICE APARTMENT TO LET YOUR WINGS DOWN AND WATCH TV?
GET.
OUT.
FIIINE. JUST POINT US TO THE BATCAVE AND WE'LL LEAVE YOU HERE TO MOPE.
THAT WAY. NOW LEAVE ME BEFORE I--
BEFORE YOU WHAT? LET ME KICK YOUR ASS AGAIN? THANKS FOR THE HELP, FUZZY.

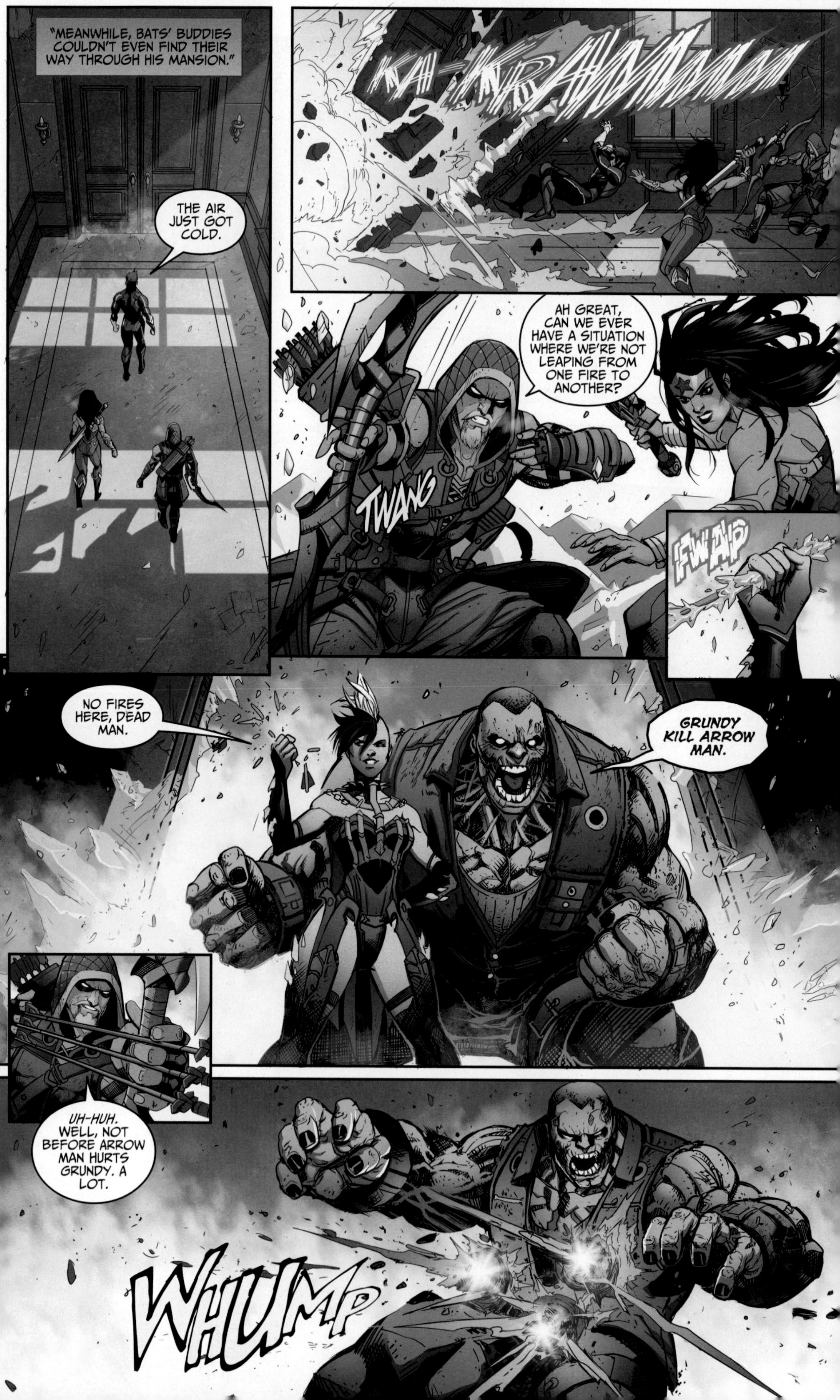
"MEANWHILE, BATS' BUDDIES COULDN'T EVEN FIND THEIR WAY THROUGH HIS MANSION."
THE AIR JUST GOT COLD.
KA-KRAWWWWM
AH GREAT, CAN WE EVER HAVE A SITUATION WHERE WE'RE NOT LEAPING FROM ONE FIRE TO ANOTHER?
TWANG
FWAP
NO FIRES HERE, DEAD MAN.
GRUNDY KILL ARROW MAN.
UH-HUH. WELL, NOT BEFORE ARROW MAN HURTS GRUNDY. A LOT.
WHUMP

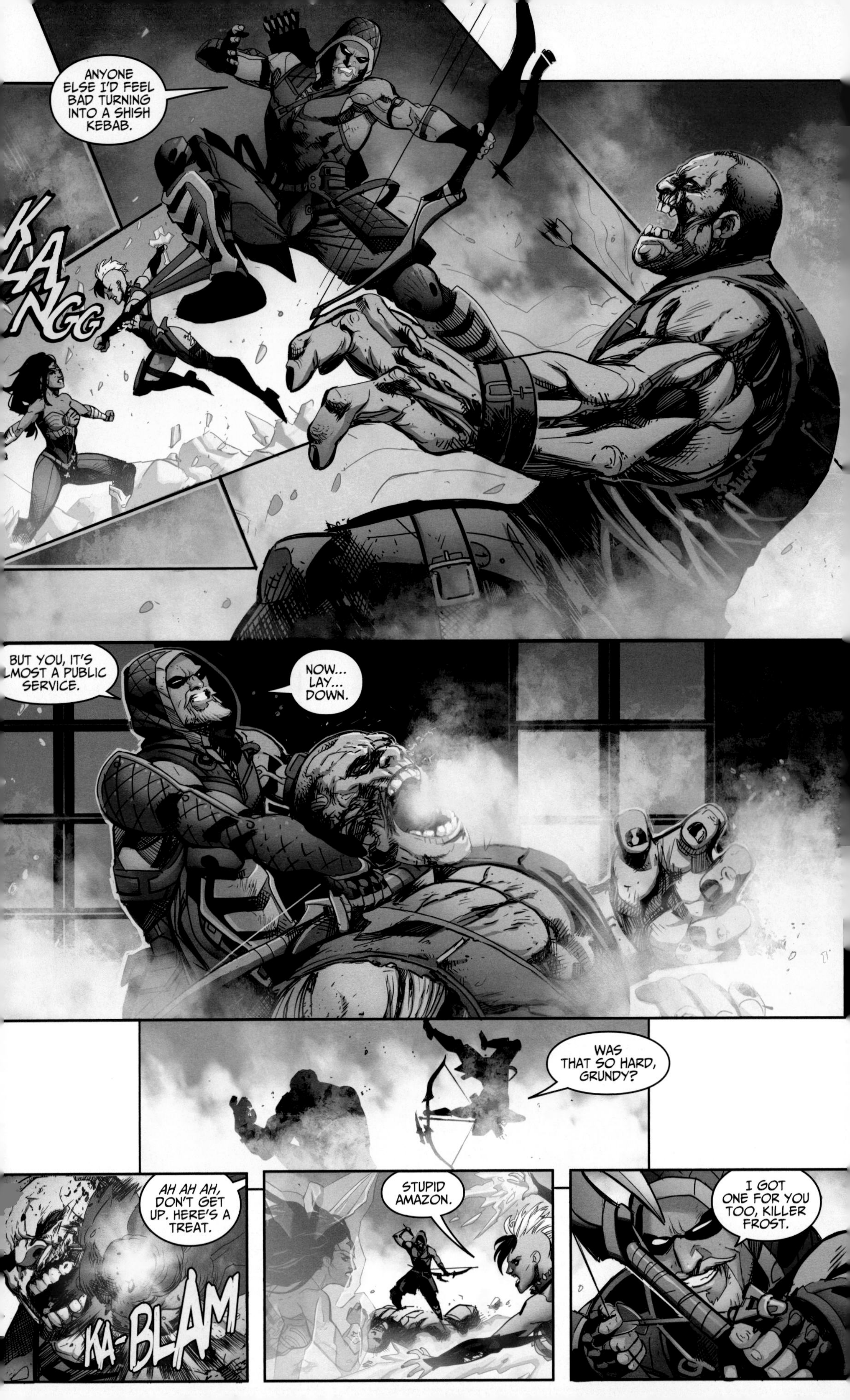
ANYONE ELSE I'D FEEL BAD TURNING INTO A SHISH KEBAB.
KLANGG
BUT YOU, IT'S LMOST A PUBLIC SERVICE.
NOW... LAY... DOWN.
WAS THAT SO HARD, GRUNDY?
AH AH AH, DON'T GET UP. HERE'S A TREAT.
KA-BLAM
STUPID AMAZON.
I GOT ONE FOR YOU TOO, KILLER FROST.

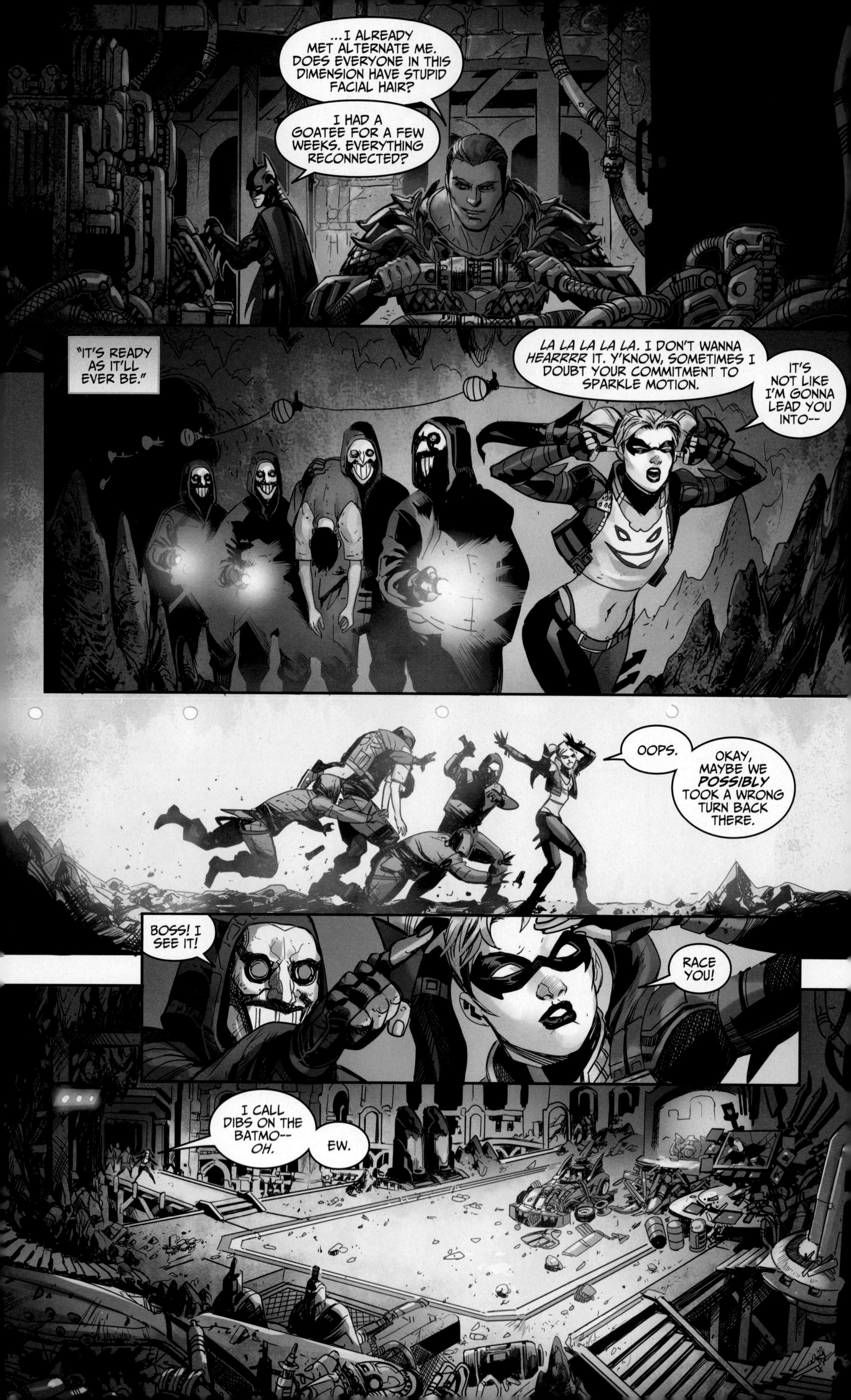
...I ALREADY MET ALTERNATE ME. DOES EVERYONE IN THIS DIMENSION HAVE STUPID FACIAL HAIR?
I HAD A GOATEE FOR A FEW WEEKS. EVERYTHING RECONNECTED?
"IT'S READY AS IT'LL EVER BE."
LA LA LA LA LA. I DON'T WANNA *HEARRRR* IT. Y'KNOW, SOMETIMES I DOUBT YOUR COMMITMENT TO SPARKLE MOTION.
IT'S NOT LIKE I'M GONNA LEAD YOU INTO--
OOPS.
OKAY, MAYBE WE ***POSSIBLY*** TOOK A WRONG TURN BACK THERE.
BOSS! I SEE IT!
RACE YOU!
I CALL DIBS ON THE BATMO-- *OH.*
EW.

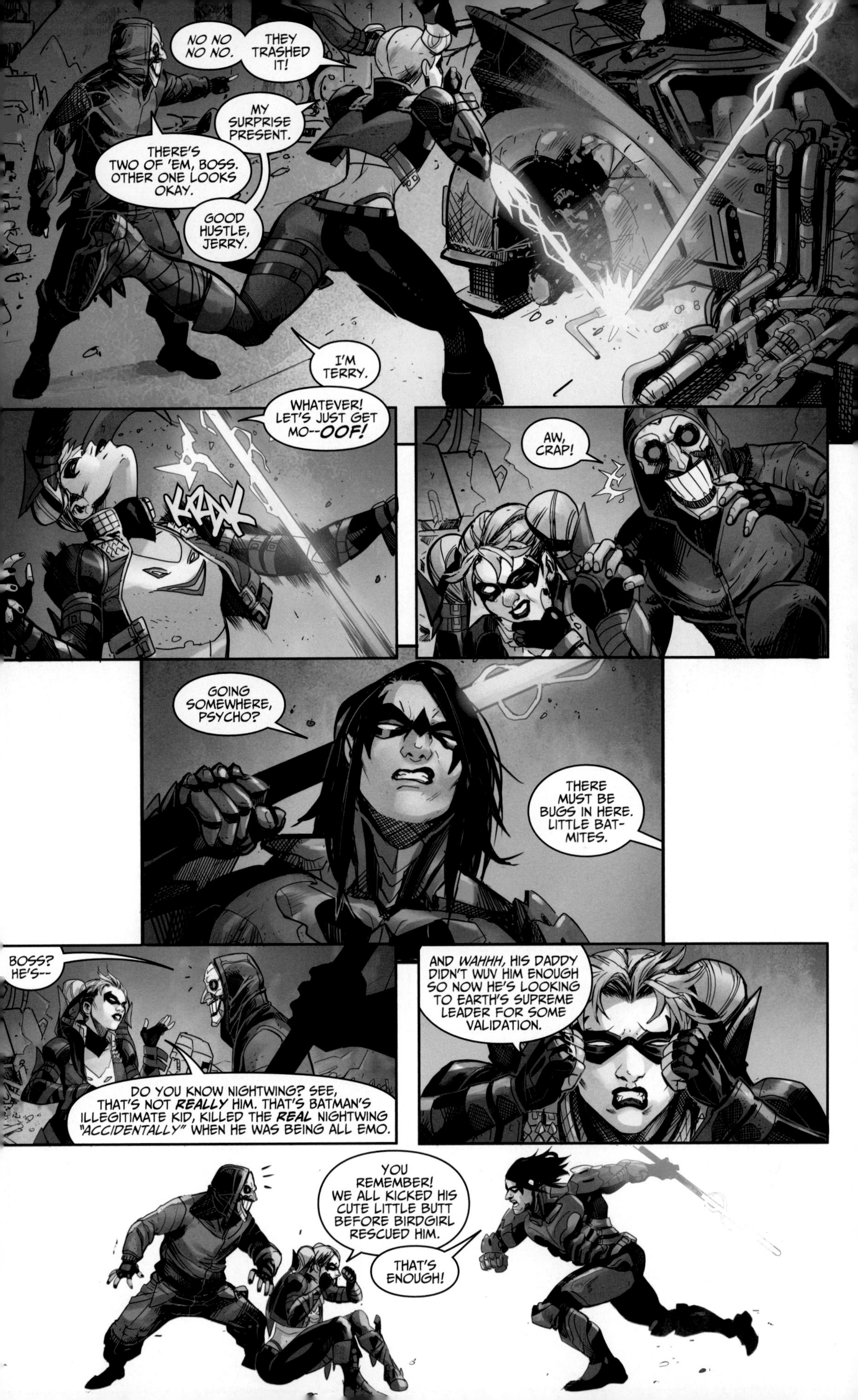
NO NO NO NO.
THEY TRASHED IT!
MY SURPRISE PRESENT.
THERE'S TWO OF 'EM, BOSS. OTHER ONE LOOKS OKAY.
GOOD HUSTLE, JERRY.
I'M TERRY.
WHATEVER! LET'S JUST GET MO--OOF!
KRAK
AW, CRAP!
GOING SOMEWHERE, PSYCHO?
THERE MUST BE BUGS IN HERE. LITTLE BAT-MITES.
BOSS? HE'S--
DO YOU KNOW NIGHTWING? SEE, THAT'S NOT REALLY HIM. THAT'S BATMAN'S ILLEGITIMATE KID, KILLED THE REAL NIGHTWING "ACCIDENTALLY" WHEN HE WAS BEING ALL EMO.
AND WAHHH, HIS DADDY DIDN'T WUV HIM ENOUGH SO NOW HE'S LOOKING TO EARTH'S SUPREME LEADER FOR SOME VALIDATION.
YOU REMEMBER! WE ALL KICKED HIS CUTE LITTLE BUTT BEFORE BIRDGIRL RESCUED HIM.
THAT'S ENOUGH!

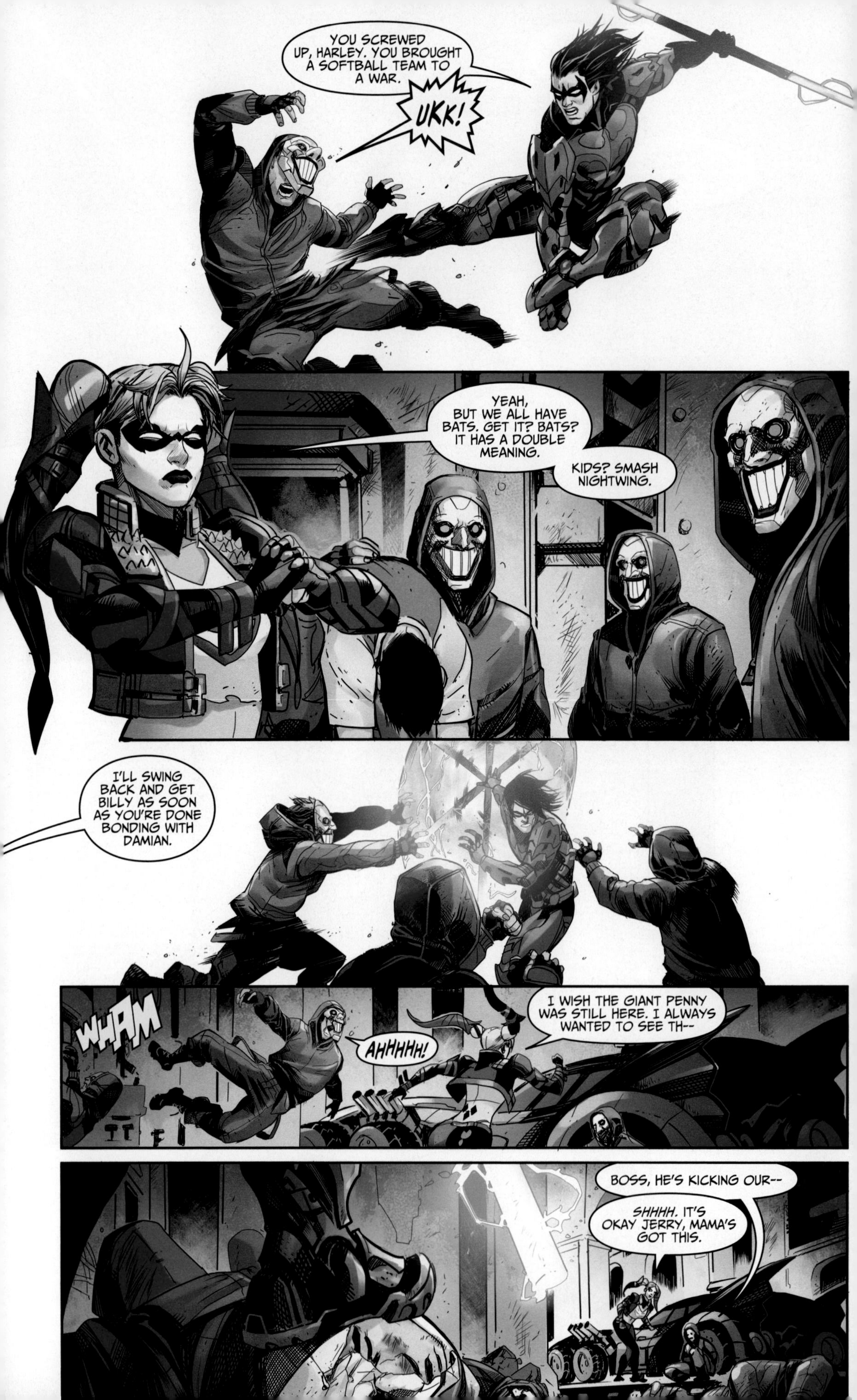
YOU SCREWED UP, HARLEY. YOU BROUGHT A SOFTBALL TEAM TO A WAR.
UKK!
YEAH, BUT WE ALL HAVE BATS. GET IT? BATS? IT HAS A DOUBLE MEANING.
KIDS? SMASH NIGHTWING.
I'LL SWING BACK AND GET BILLY AS SOON AS YOU'RE DONE BONDING WITH DAMIAN.
WHAM
AHHHHH!
I WISH THE GIANT PENNY WAS STILL HERE. I ALWAYS WANTED TO SEE TH--
BOSS, HE'S KICKING OUR--
SHHHH. IT'S OKAY JERRY, MAMA'S GOT THIS.

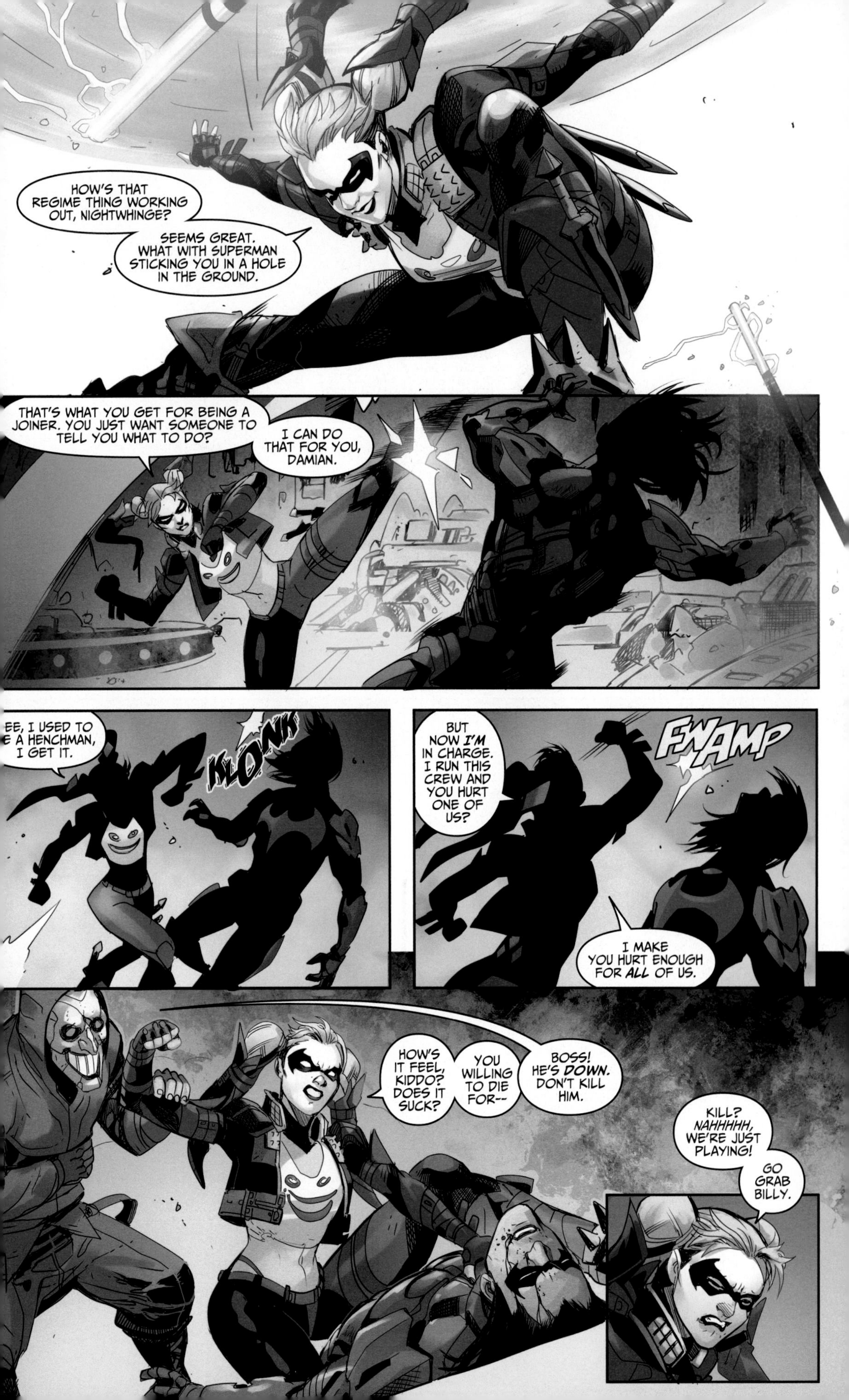
HOW'S THAT REGIME THING WORKING OUT, NIGHTWHINGE?
SEEMS GREAT. WHAT WITH SUPERMAN STICKING YOU IN A HOLE IN THE GROUND.
THAT'S WHAT YOU GET FOR BEING A JOINER. YOU JUST WANT SOMEONE TO TELL YOU WHAT TO DO?
I CAN DO THAT FOR YOU, DAMIAN.
EE, I USED TO E A HENCHMAN, I GET IT.
KLONK
BUT NOW I'M IN CHARGE. I RUN THIS CREW AND YOU HURT ONE OF US?
FWAMP
I MAKE YOU HURT ENOUGH FOR ALL OF US.
HOW'S IT FEEL, KIDDO? DOES IT SUCK?
YOU WILLING TO DIE FOR--
BOSS! HE'S DOWN. DON'T KILL HIM.
KILL? NAHHHHH, WE'RE JUST PLAYING!
GO GRAB BILLY.

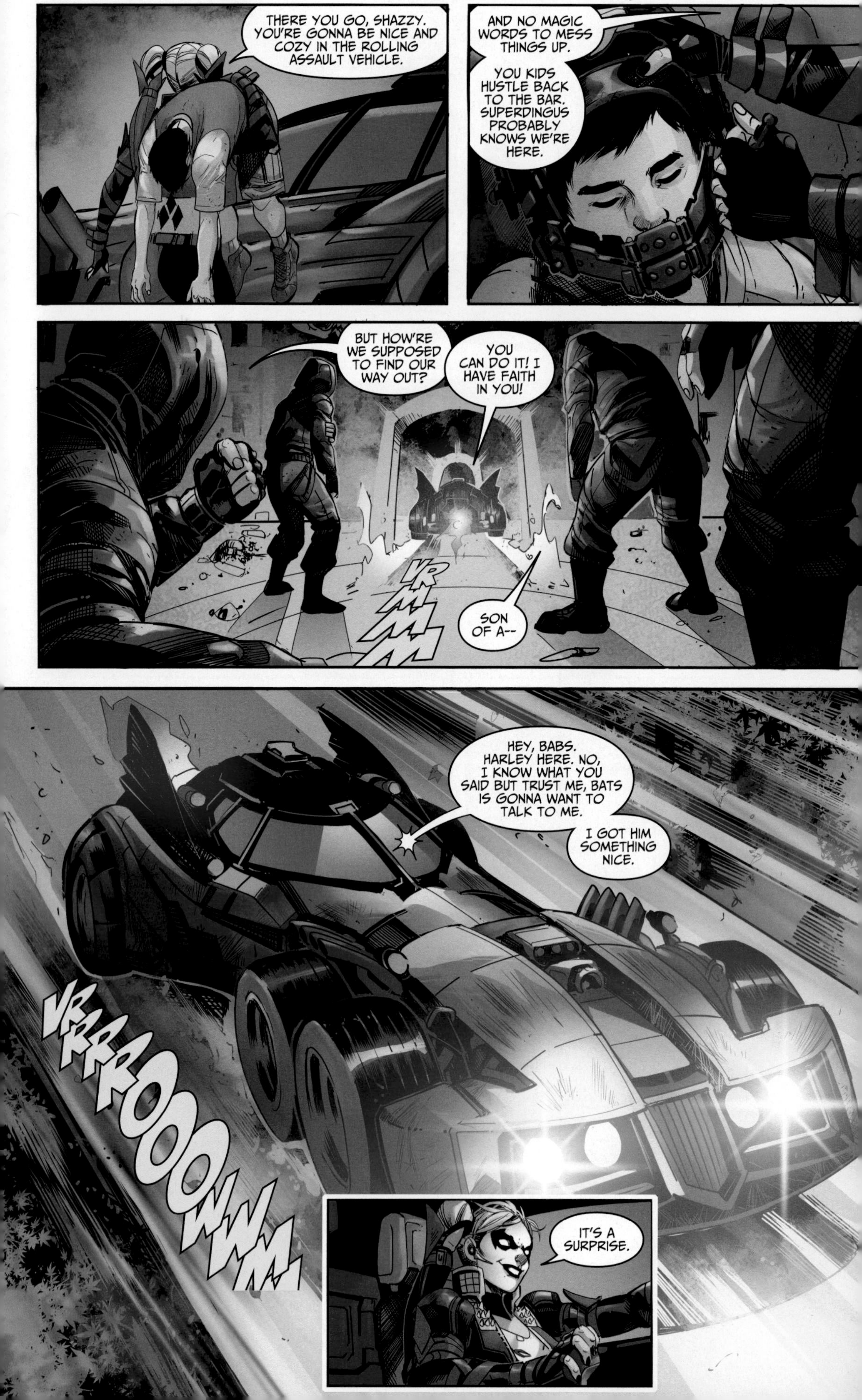
THERE YOU GO, SHAZZY. YOU'RE GONNA BE NICE AND COZY IN THE ROLLING ASSAULT VEHICLE.
AND NO MAGIC WORDS TO MESS THINGS UP.
YOU KIDS HUSTLE BACK TO THE BAR. SUPERDINGUS PROBABLY KNOWS WE'RE HERE.
BUT HOW'RE WE SUPPOSED TO FIND OUR WAY OUT?
YOU CAN DO IT! I HAVE FAITH IN YOU!
VRMMM
SON OF A--
HEY, BABS. HARLEY HERE. NO, I KNOW WHAT YOU SAID BUT TRUST ME, BATS IS GONNA WANT TO TALK TO ME.
I GOT HIM SOMETHING NICE.
VRRRROOOOWWM!
IT'S A SURPRISE.

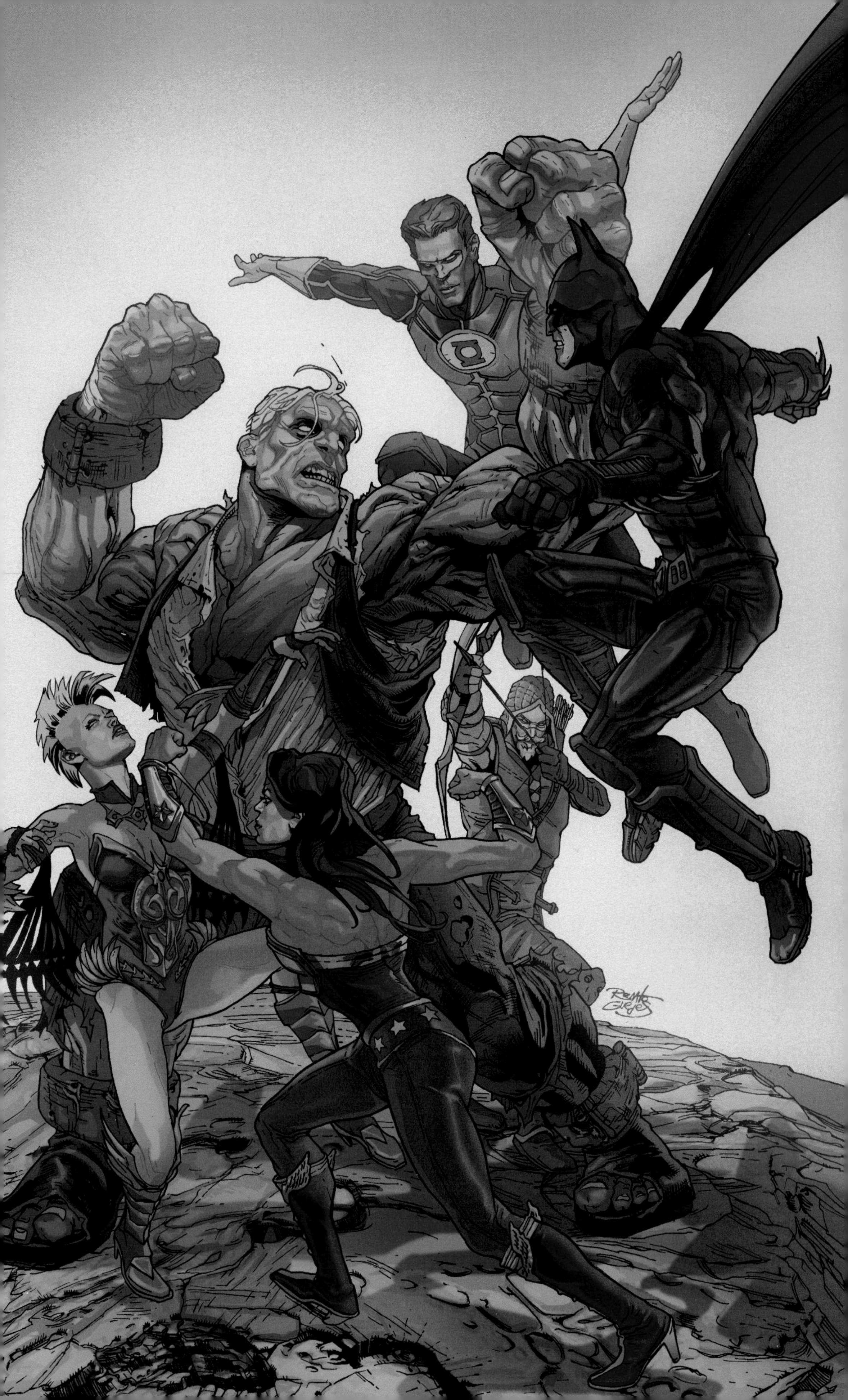

"Black Hearts: Part 1" **Marco Santucci** Artist **J. Nanjan** Colorist
"Black Hearts: Part 2" **Daniel Sampere** Penciller **Juan Albarran** Inker **J. Nanjan** Colorist

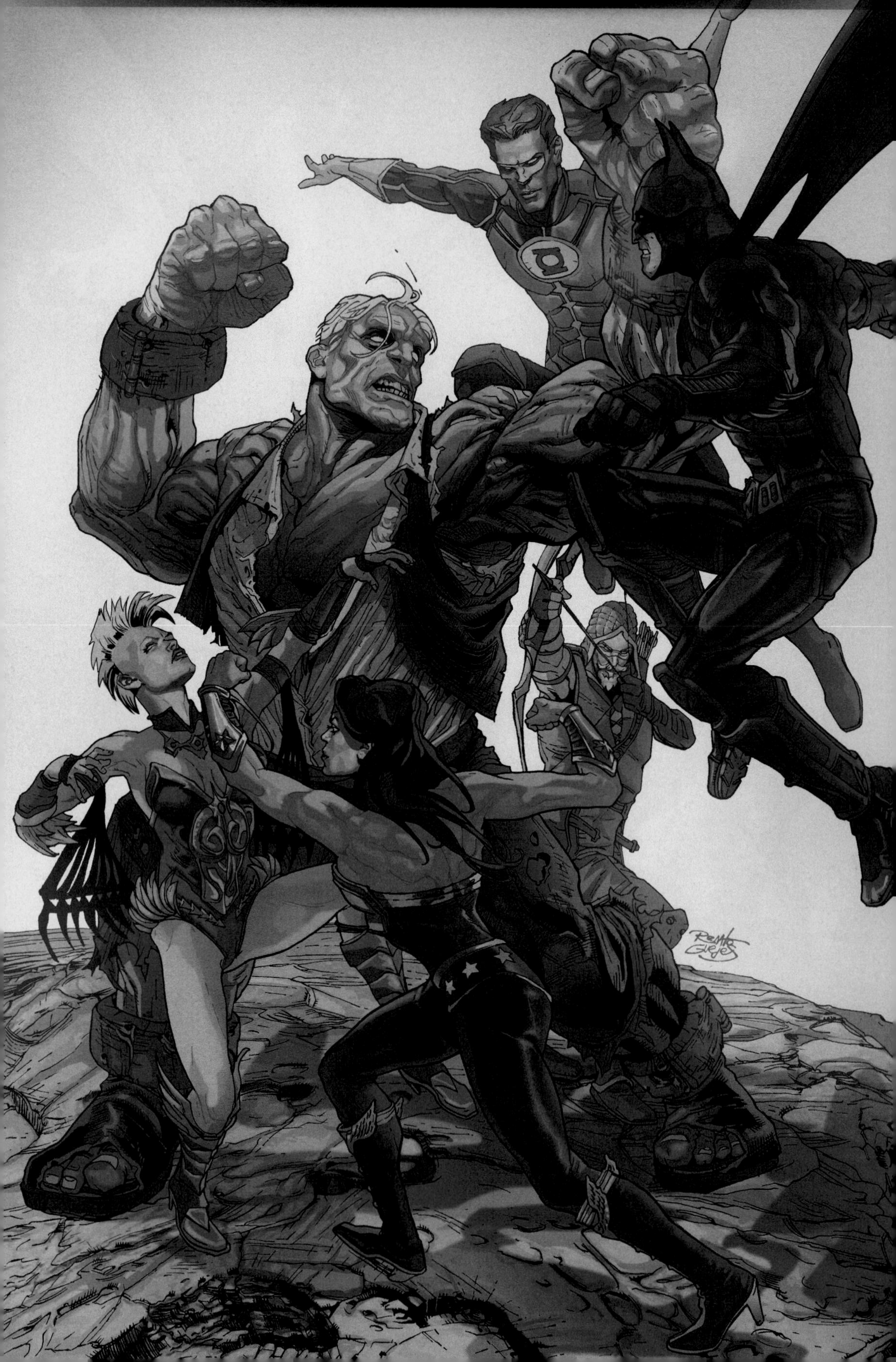

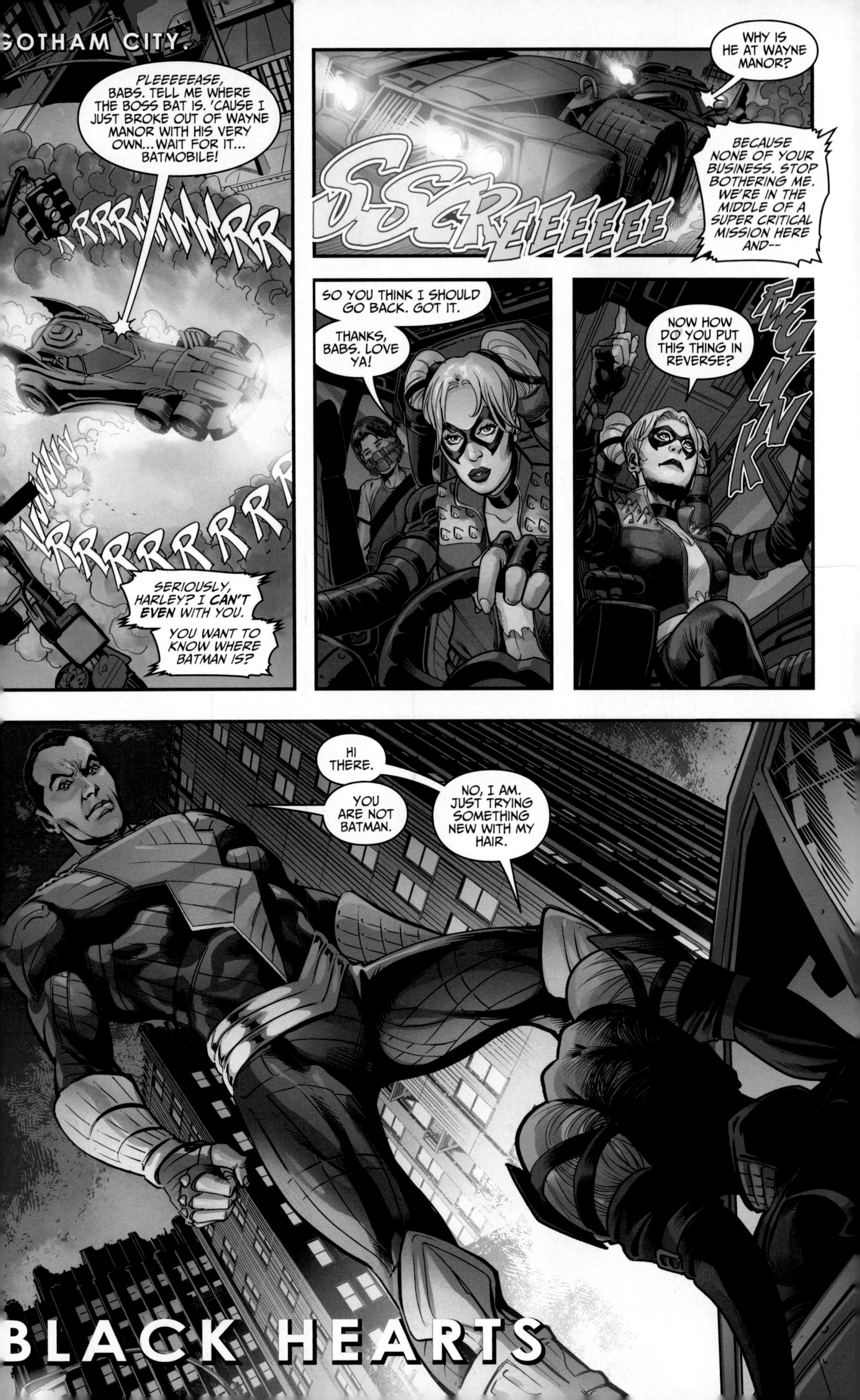
GOTHAM CITY.
PLEEEEEASE, BABS. TELL ME WHERE THE BOSS BAT IS. 'CAUSE I JUST BROKE OUT OF WAYNE MANOR WITH HIS VERY OWN...WAIT FOR IT... BATMOBILE!
SERIOUSLY, HARLEY? I **CAN'T EVEN** WITH YOU.
YOU WANT TO KNOW WHERE BATMAN IS?
SSCREEEEEEE
WHY IS HE AT WAYNE MANOR?
BECAUSE NONE OF YOUR BUSINESS. STOP BOTHERING ME. WE'RE IN THE MIDDLE OF A SUPER CRITICAL MISSION HERE AND--
SO YOU THINK I SHOULD GO BACK. GOT IT.
THANKS, BABS. LOVE YA!
NOW HOW DO YOU PUT THIS THING IN REVERSE?
HI THERE.
YOU ARE NOT BATMAN.
NO, I AM. JUST TRYING SOMETHING NEW WITH MY HAIR.
BLACK HEARTS

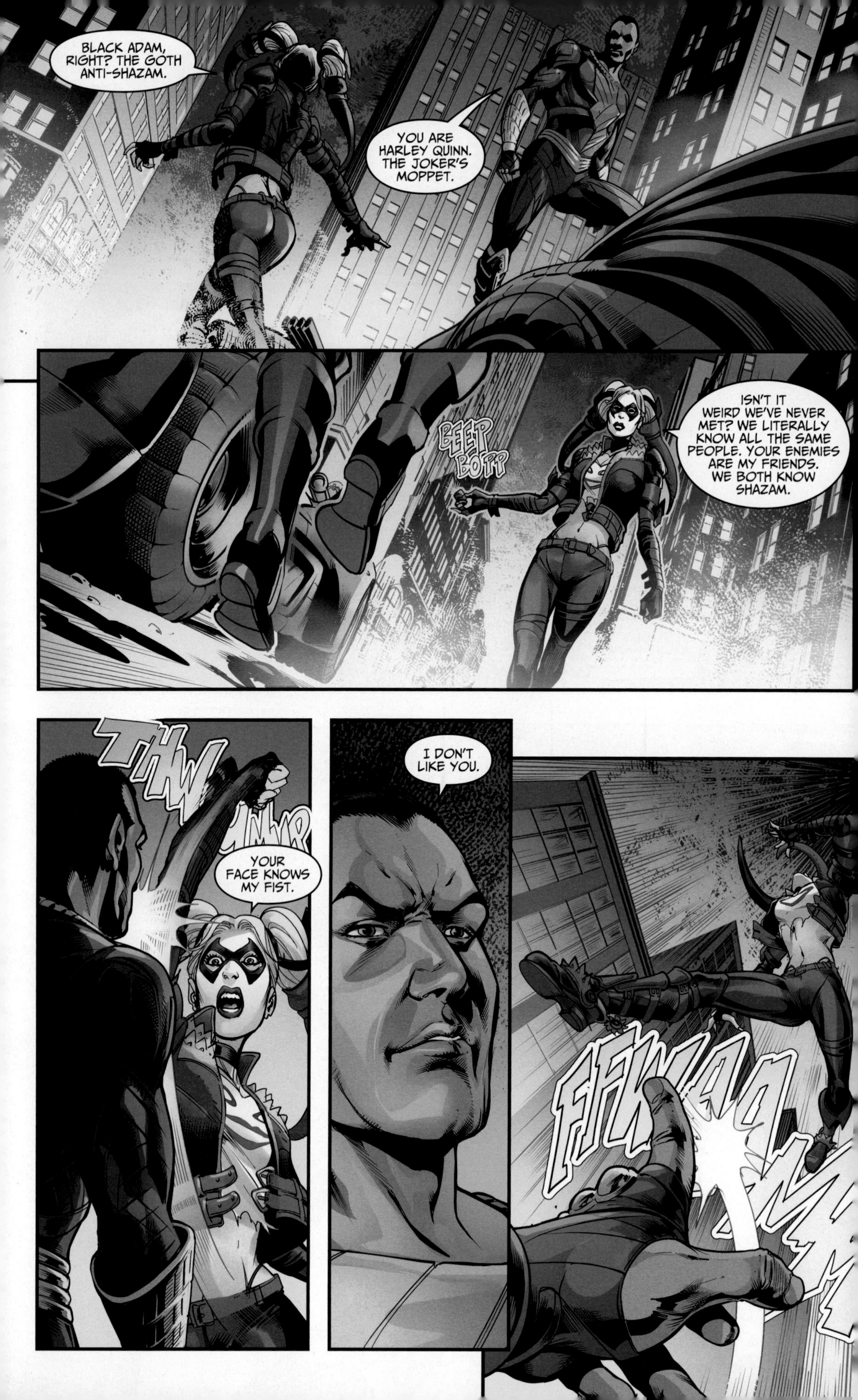
BLACK ADAM, RIGHT? THE GOTH ANTI-SHAZAM.
YOU ARE HARLEY QUINN. THE JOKER'S MOPPET.
BEEP BOPP
ISN'T IT WEIRD WE'VE NEVER MET? WE LITERALLY KNOW ALL THE SAME PEOPLE. YOUR ENEMIES ARE MY FRIENDS. WE BOTH KNOW SHAZAM.
THWAMMR
YOUR FACE KNOWS MY FIST.
I DON'T LIKE YOU.

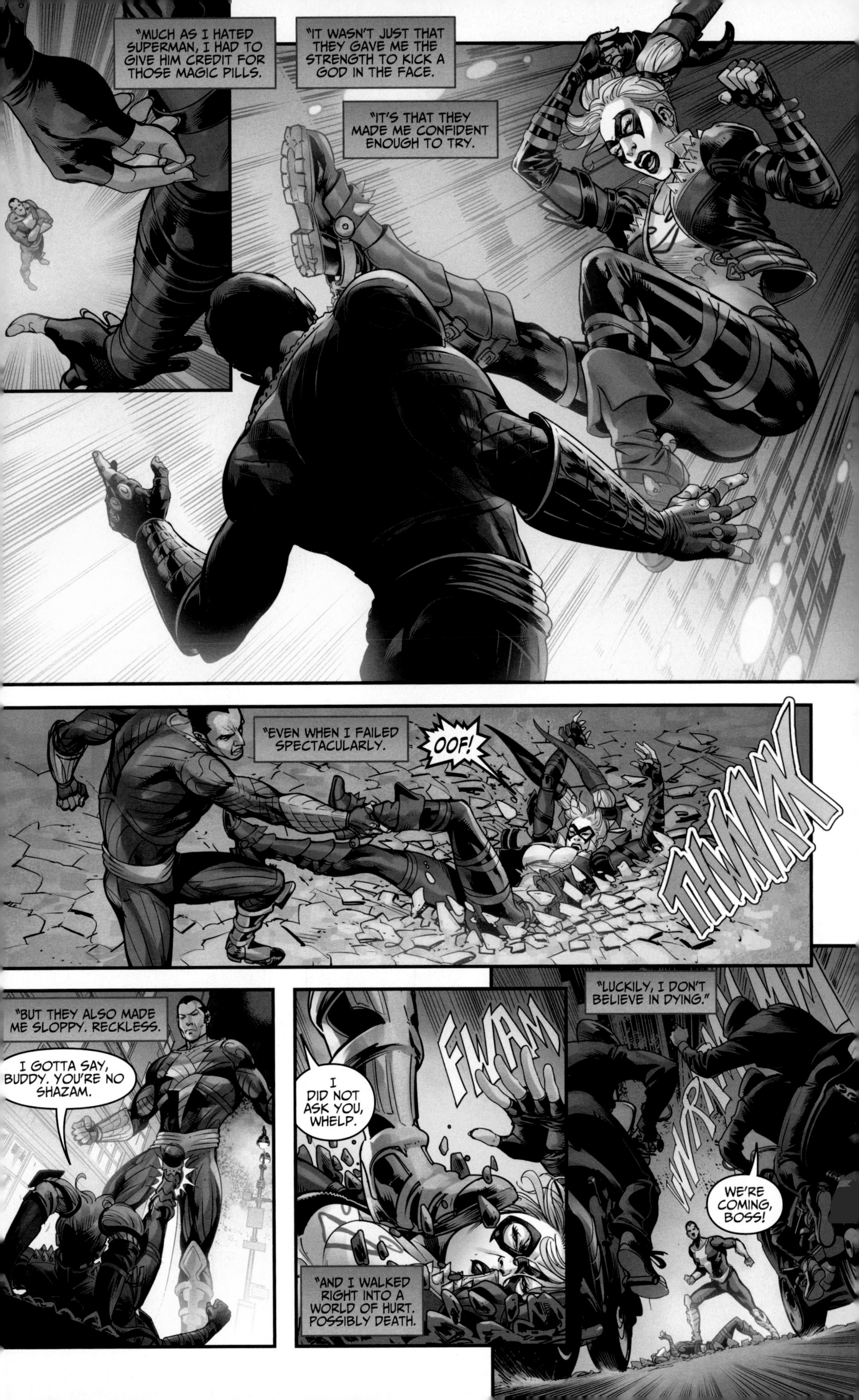
"MUCH AS I HATED SUPERMAN, I HAD TO GIVE HIM CREDIT FOR THOSE MAGIC PILLS.
"IT WASN'T JUST THAT THEY GAVE ME THE STRENGTH TO KICK A GOD IN THE FACE.
"IT'S THAT THEY MADE ME CONFIDENT ENOUGH TO TRY.
"EVEN WHEN I FAILED SPECTACULARLY.
OOF!
THWAKK
"BUT THEY ALSO MADE ME SLOPPY. RECKLESS.
I GOTTA SAY, BUDDY. YOU'RE NO SHAZAM.
FWAM
I DID NOT ASK YOU, WHELP.
"AND I WALKED RIGHT INTO A WORLD OF HURT. POSSIBLY DEATH.
"LUCKILY, I DON'T BELIEVE IN DYING."
WE'RE COMING, BOSS!

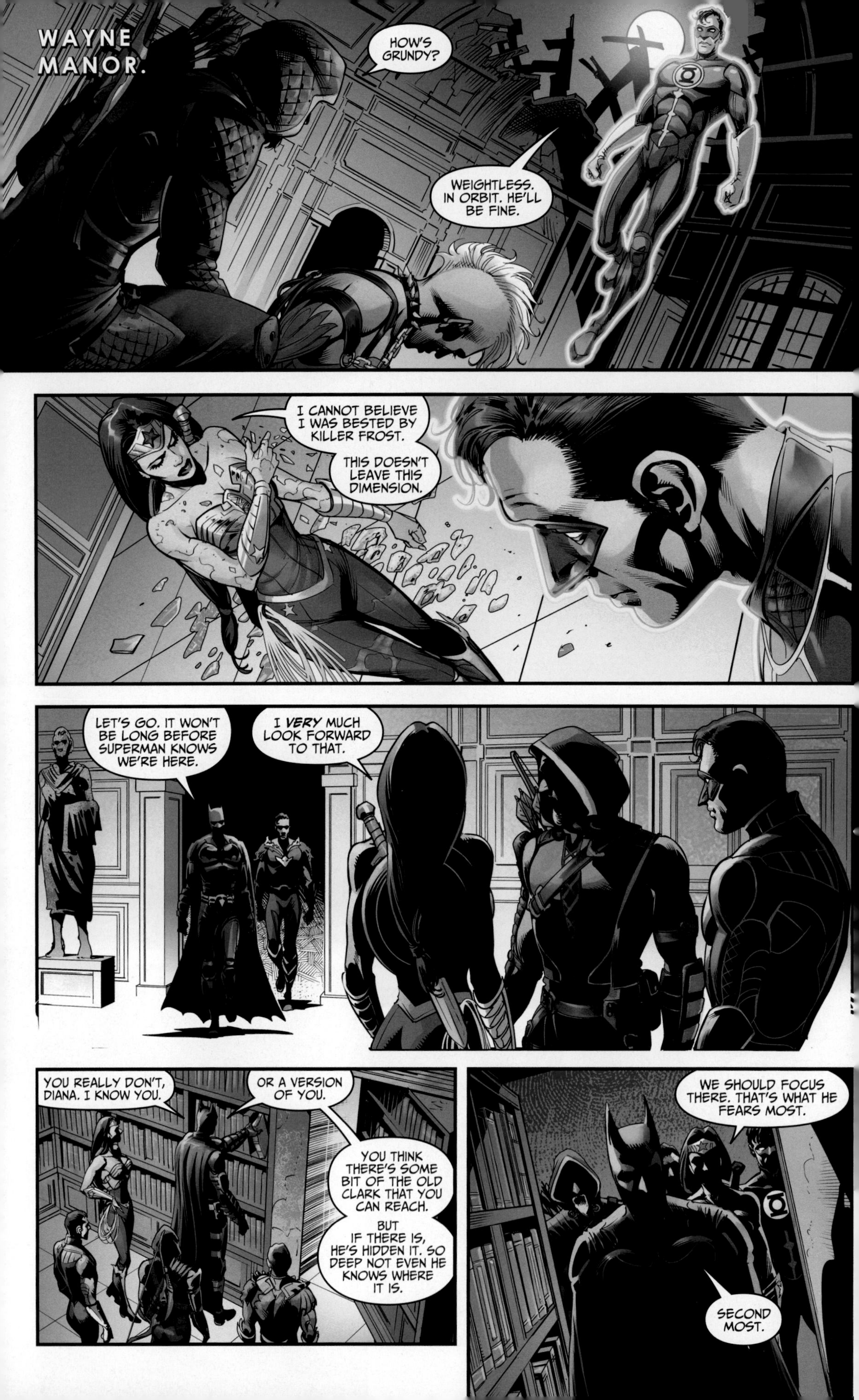
WAYNE MANOR.
HOW'S GRUNDY?
WEIGHTLESS. IN ORBIT. HE'LL BE FINE.
I CANNOT BELIEVE I WAS BESTED BY KILLER FROST.
THIS DOESN'T LEAVE THIS DIMENSION.
LET'S GO. IT WON'T BE LONG BEFORE SUPERMAN KNOWS WE'RE HERE.
I VERY MUCH LOOK FORWARD TO THAT.
YOU REALLY DON'T, DIANA. I KNOW YOU.
OR A VERSION OF YOU.
YOU THINK THERE'S SOME BIT OF THE OLD CLARK THAT YOU CAN REACH.
BUT IF THERE IS, HE'S HIDDEN IT. SO DEEP NOT EVEN HE KNOWS WHERE IT IS.
WE SHOULD FOCUS THERE. THAT'S WHAT HE FEARS MOST.
SECOND MOST.

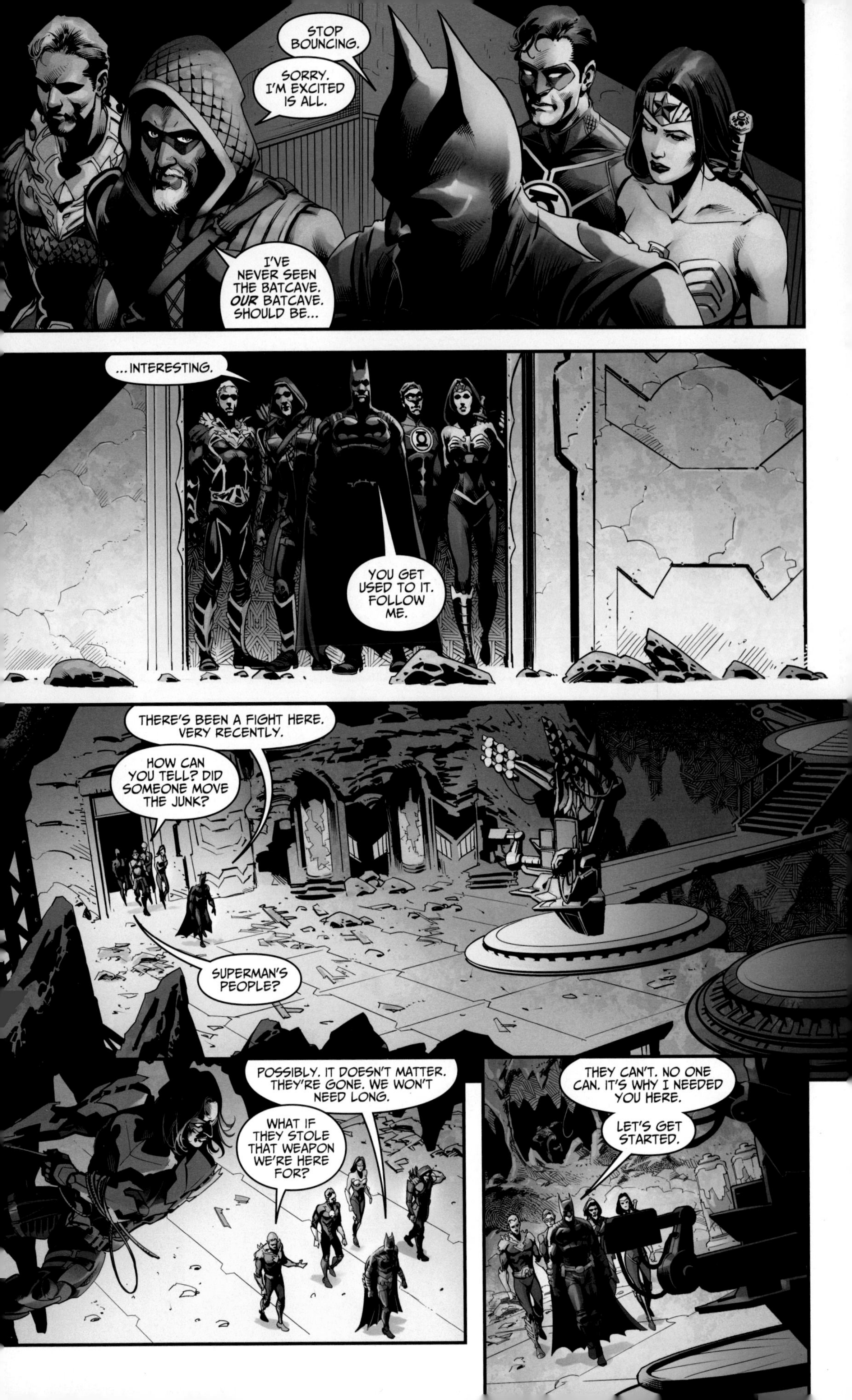
STOP BOUNCING.
SORRY. I'M EXCITED IS ALL.
I'VE NEVER SEEN THE BATCAVE. *OUR* BATCAVE. SHOULD BE...
...INTERESTING.
YOU GET USED TO IT. FOLLOW ME.
THERE'S BEEN A FIGHT HERE. VERY RECENTLY.
HOW CAN YOU TELL? DID SOMEONE MOVE THE JUNK?
SUPERMAN'S PEOPLE?
POSSIBLY. IT DOESN'T MATTER. THEY'RE GONE. WE WON'T NEED LONG.
WHAT IF THEY STOLE THAT WEAPON WE'RE HERE FOR?
THEY CAN'T. NO ONE CAN. IT'S WHY I NEEDED YOU HERE.
LET'S GET STARTED.

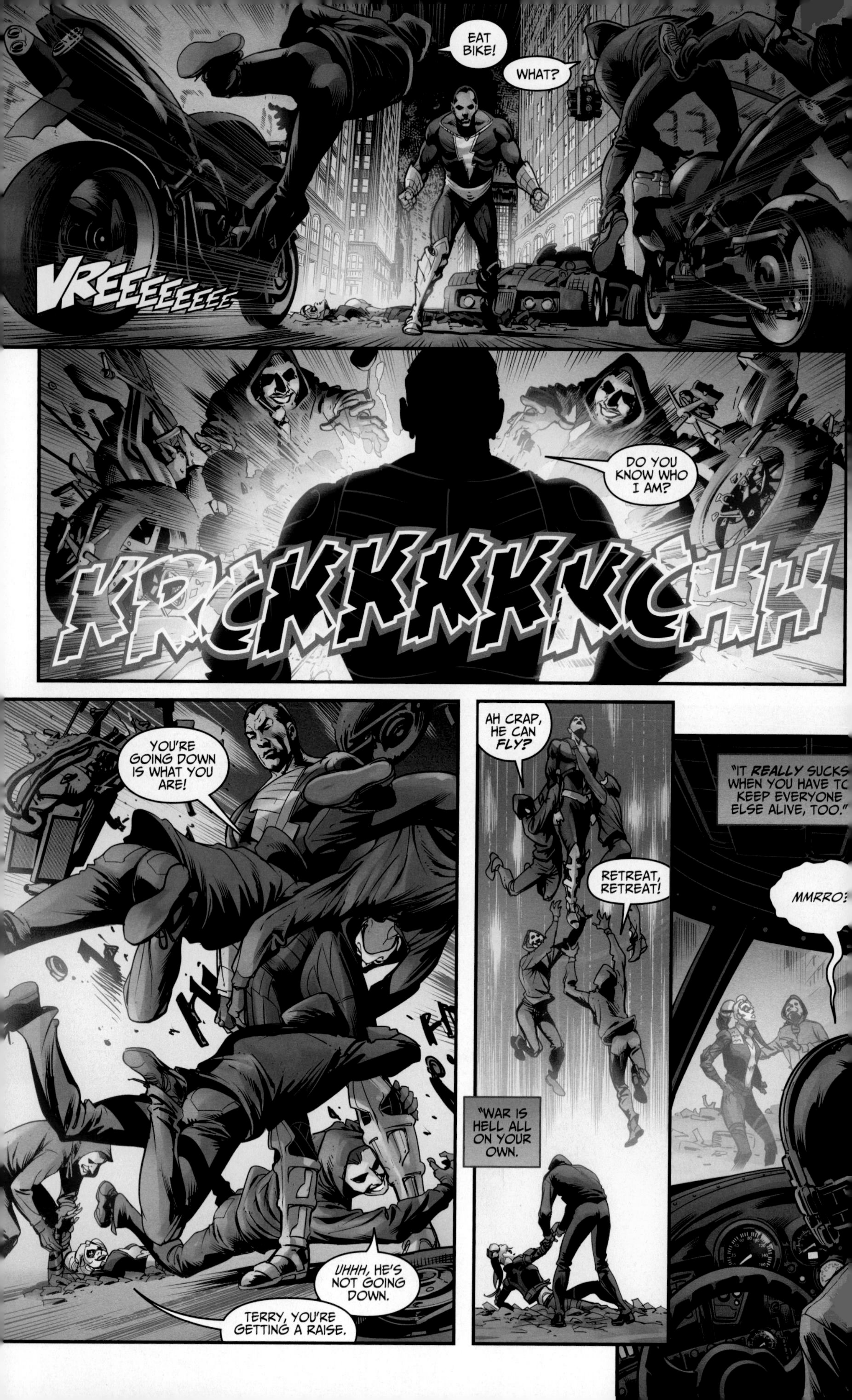
EAT BIKE!
WHAT?
VREEEEEEEE
DO YOU KNOW WHO I AM?
KRRCKKKKKCHH
YOU'RE GOING DOWN IS WHAT YOU ARE!
UHHH, HE'S NOT GOING DOWN.
TERRY, YOU'RE GETTING A RAISE.
AH CRAP, HE CAN FLY?
RETREAT, RETREAT!
"WAR IS HELL ALL ON YOUR OWN.
"IT REALLY SUCKS WHEN YOU HAVE TO KEEP EVERYONE ELSE ALIVE, TOO."
MMRRO

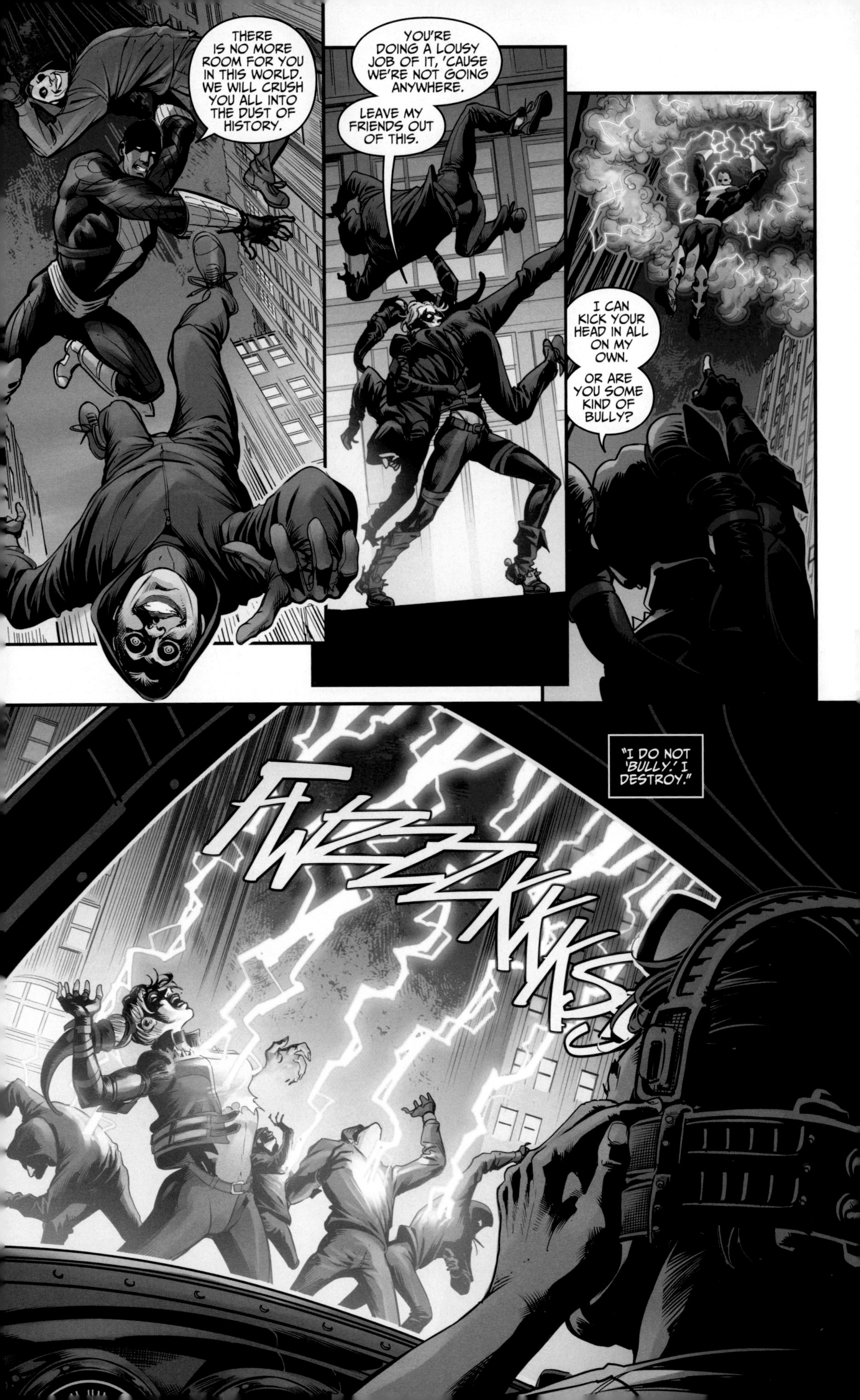
THERE IS NO MORE ROOM FOR YOU IN THIS WORLD. WE WILL CRUSH YOU ALL INTO THE DUST OF HISTORY.
YOU'RE DOING A LOUSY JOB OF IT, 'CAUSE WE'RE NOT GOING ANYWHERE.
LEAVE MY FRIENDS OUT OF THIS.
I CAN KICK YOUR HEAD IN ALL ON MY OWN.
OR ARE YOU SOME KIND OF BULLY?
"I DO NOT 'BULLY.' I DESTROY."
FWZZZKKKSSSS

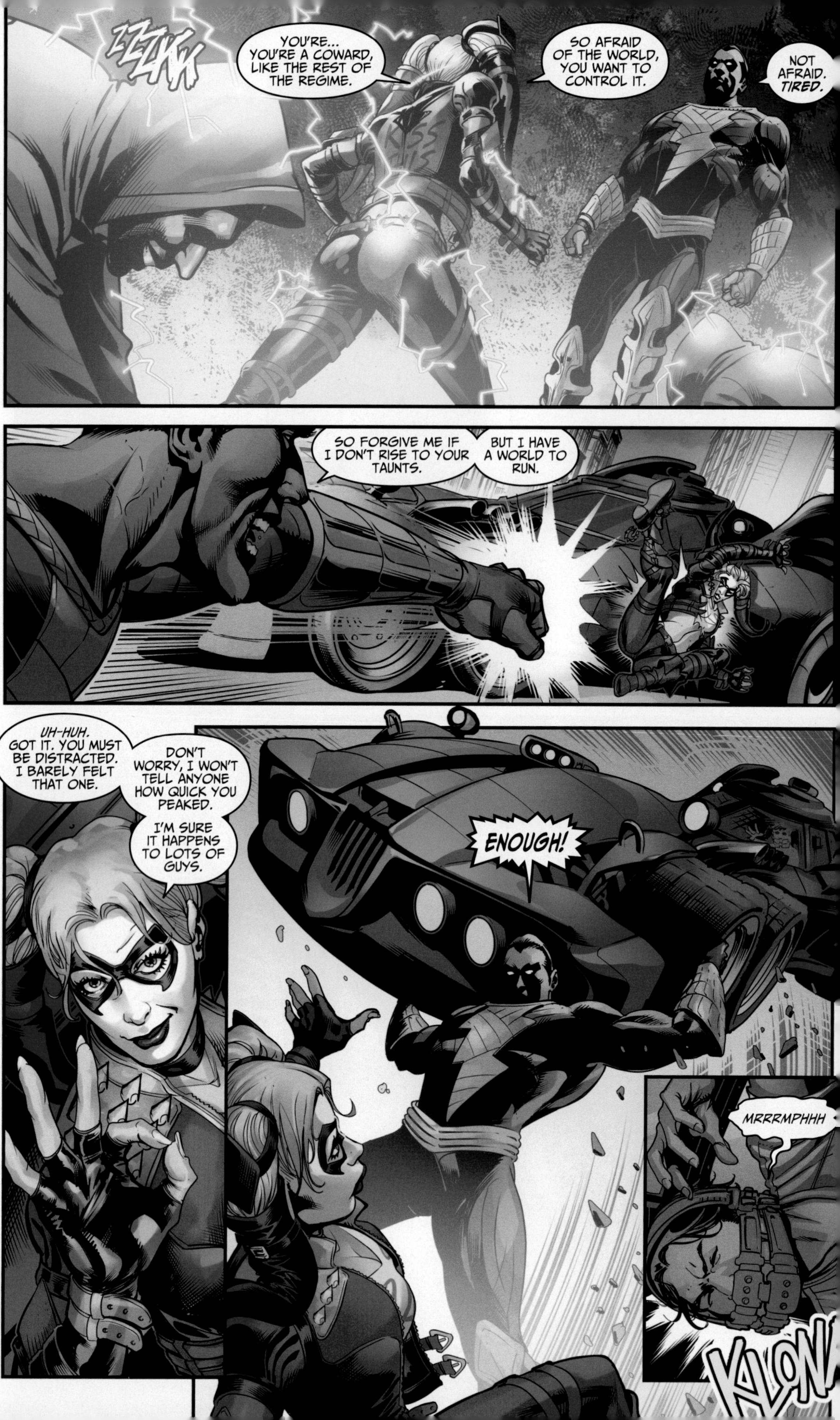
ZZZKKK
YOU'RE... YOU'RE A COWARD, LIKE THE REST OF THE REGIME.
SO AFRAID OF THE WORLD, YOU WANT TO CONTROL IT.
NOT AFRAID. *TIRED.*
SO FORGIVE ME IF I DON'T RISE TO YOUR TAUNTS.
BUT I HAVE A WORLD TO RUN.
UH-HUH. GOT IT. YOU MUST BE DISTRACTED. I BARELY FELT THAT ONE.
DON'T WORRY, I WON'T TELL ANYONE HOW QUICK YOU PEAKED.
I'M SURE IT HAPPENS TO LOTS OF GUYS.
ENOUGH!
MRRRMPHHH
KALONK

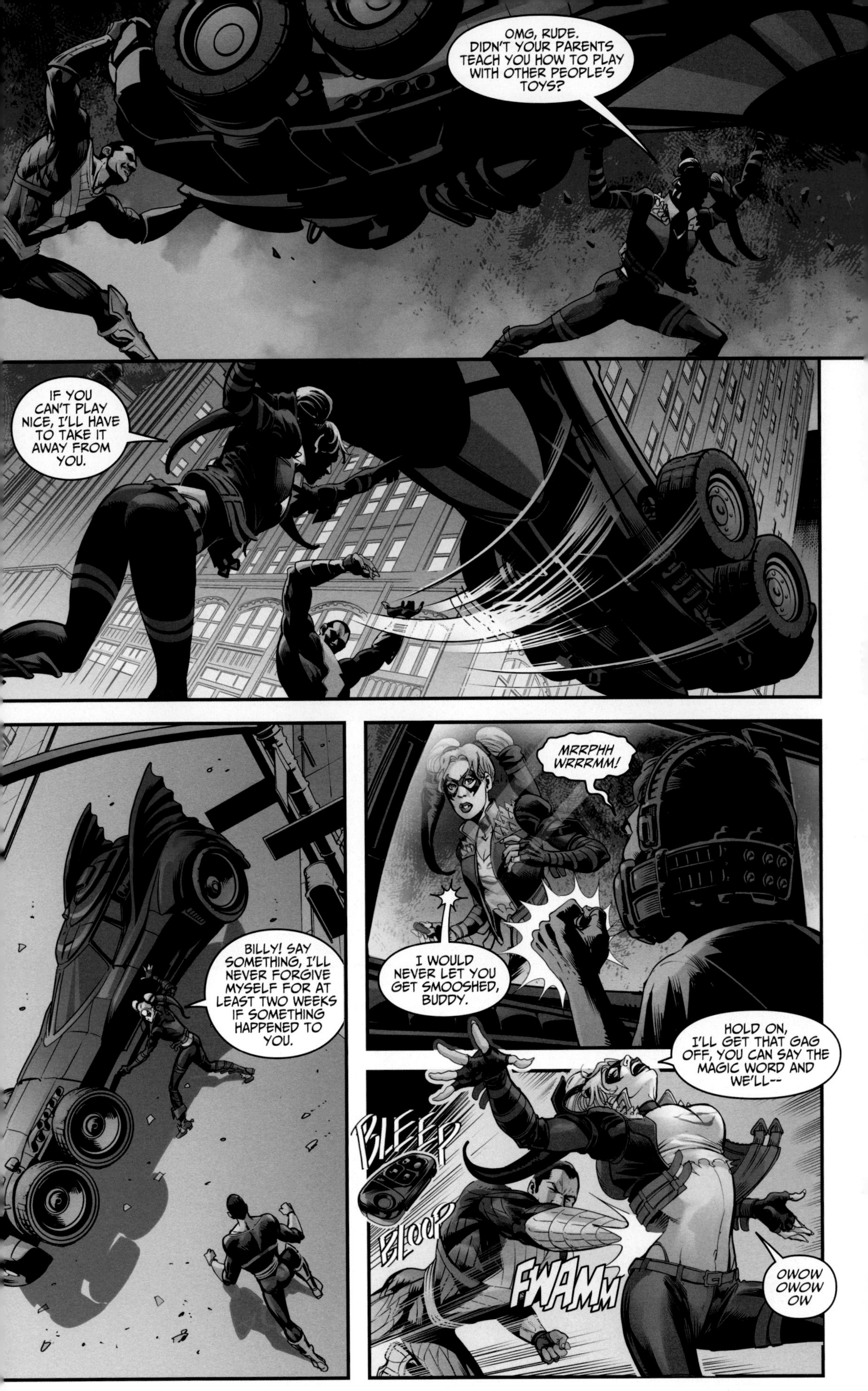
OMG, RUDE. DIDN'T YOUR PARENTS TEACH YOU HOW TO PLAY WITH OTHER PEOPLE'S TOYS?
IF YOU CAN'T PLAY NICE, I'LL HAVE TO TAKE IT AWAY FROM YOU.
BILLY! SAY SOMETHING, I'LL NEVER FORGIVE MYSELF FOR AT LEAST TWO WEEKS IF SOMETHING HAPPENED TO YOU.
MRRPHH WRRRMM!
I WOULD NEVER LET YOU GET SMOOSHED, BUDDY.
HOLD ON, I'LL GET THAT GAG OFF, YOU CAN SAY THE MAGIC WORD AND WE'LL--
BLEEP
BLOOP
FWAMM
OWOW OWOW OW

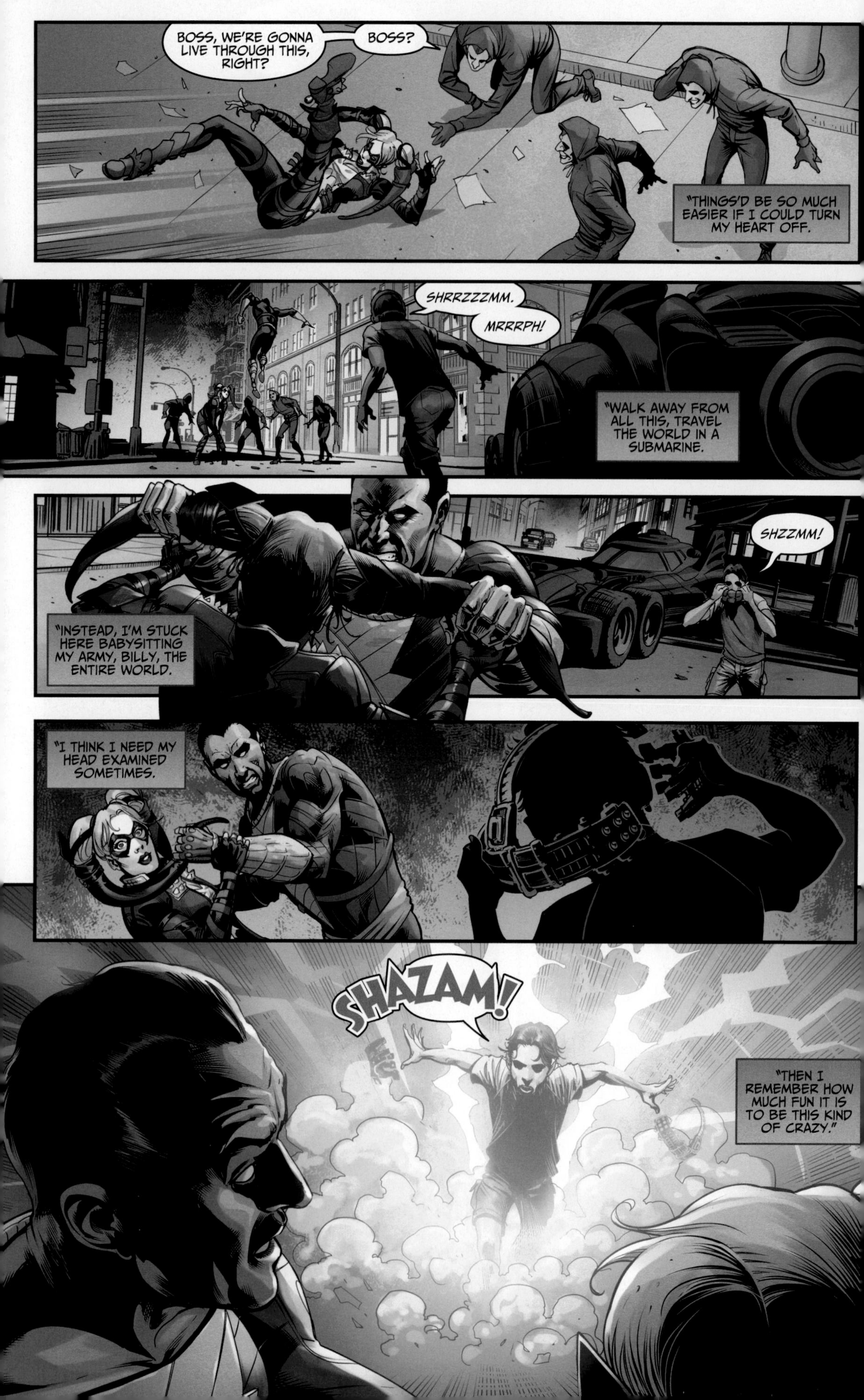
BOSS, WE'RE GONNA LIVE THROUGH THIS, RIGHT?
BOSS?
"THINGS'D BE SO MUCH EASIER IF I COULD TURN MY HEART OFF.
SHRRZZZMM.
MRRRPH!
"WALK AWAY FROM ALL THIS, TRAVEL THE WORLD IN A SUBMARINE.
SHZZMM!
"INSTEAD, I'M STUCK HERE BABYSITTING MY ARMY, BILLY, THE ENTIRE WORLD.
"I THINK I NEED MY HEAD EXAMINED SOMETIMES.
SHAZAM!
"THEN I REMEMBER HOW MUCH FUN IT IS TO BE THIS KIND OF CRAZY."

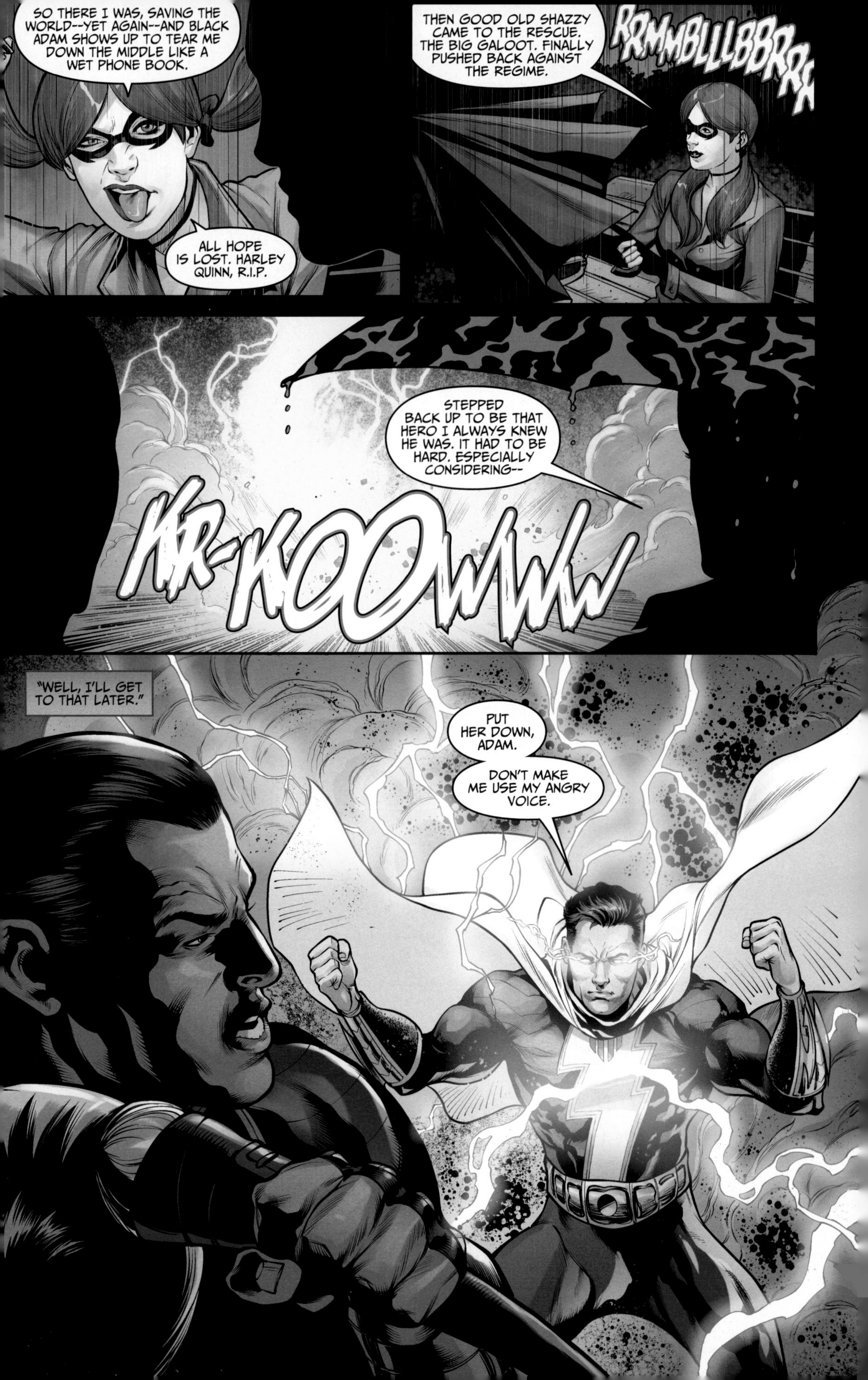
SO THERE I WAS, SAVING THE WORLD--YET AGAIN--AND BLACK ADAM SHOWS UP TO TEAR ME DOWN THE MIDDLE LIKE A WET PHONE BOOK.
ALL HOPE IS LOST. HARLEY QUINN, R.I.P.
THEN GOOD OLD SHAZZY CAME TO THE RESCUE. THE BIG GALOOT. FINALLY PUSHED BACK AGAINST THE REGIME.
RRMMBLLLBBRRR
STEPPED BACK UP TO BE THAT HERO I ALWAYS KNEW HE WAS. IT HAD TO BE HARD. ESPECIALLY CONSIDERING--
KR-KOOWWW
"WELL, I'LL GET TO THAT LATER."
PUT HER DOWN, ADAM.
DON'T MAKE ME USE MY ANGRY VOICE.

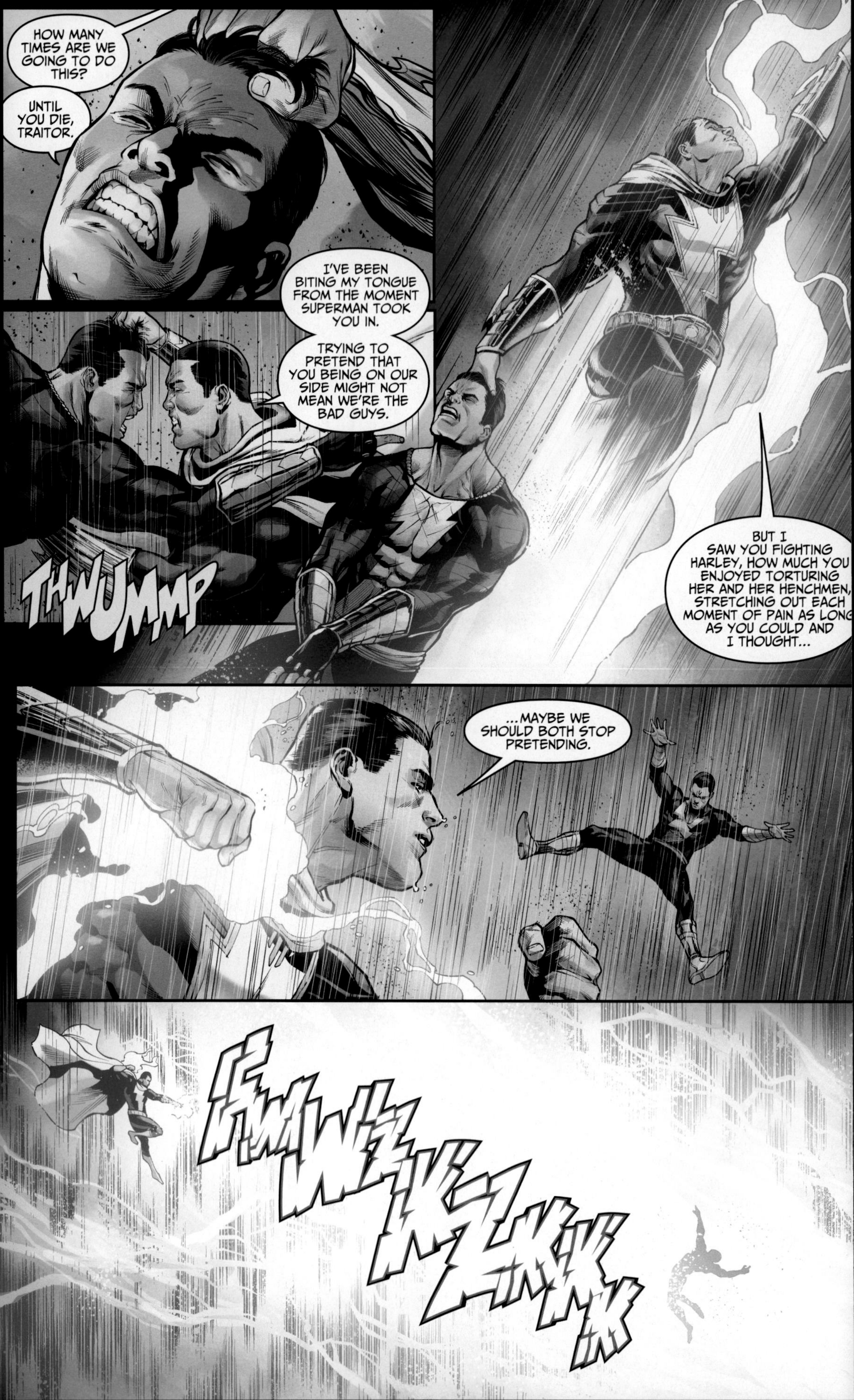
HOW MANY TIMES ARE WE GOING TO DO THIS?
UNTIL YOU DIE, TRAITOR.
I'VE BEEN BITING MY TONGUE FROM THE MOMENT SUPERMAN TOOK YOU IN.
TRYING TO PRETEND THAT YOU BEING ON OUR SIDE MIGHT NOT MEAN WE'RE THE BAD GUYS.
THWUMMP
BUT I SAW YOU FIGHTING HARLEY, HOW MUCH YOU ENJOYED TORTURING HER AND HER HENCHMEN, STRETCHING OUT EACH MOMENT OF PAIN AS LONG AS YOU COULD AND I THOUGHT...
...MAYBE WE SHOULD BOTH STOP PRETENDING.

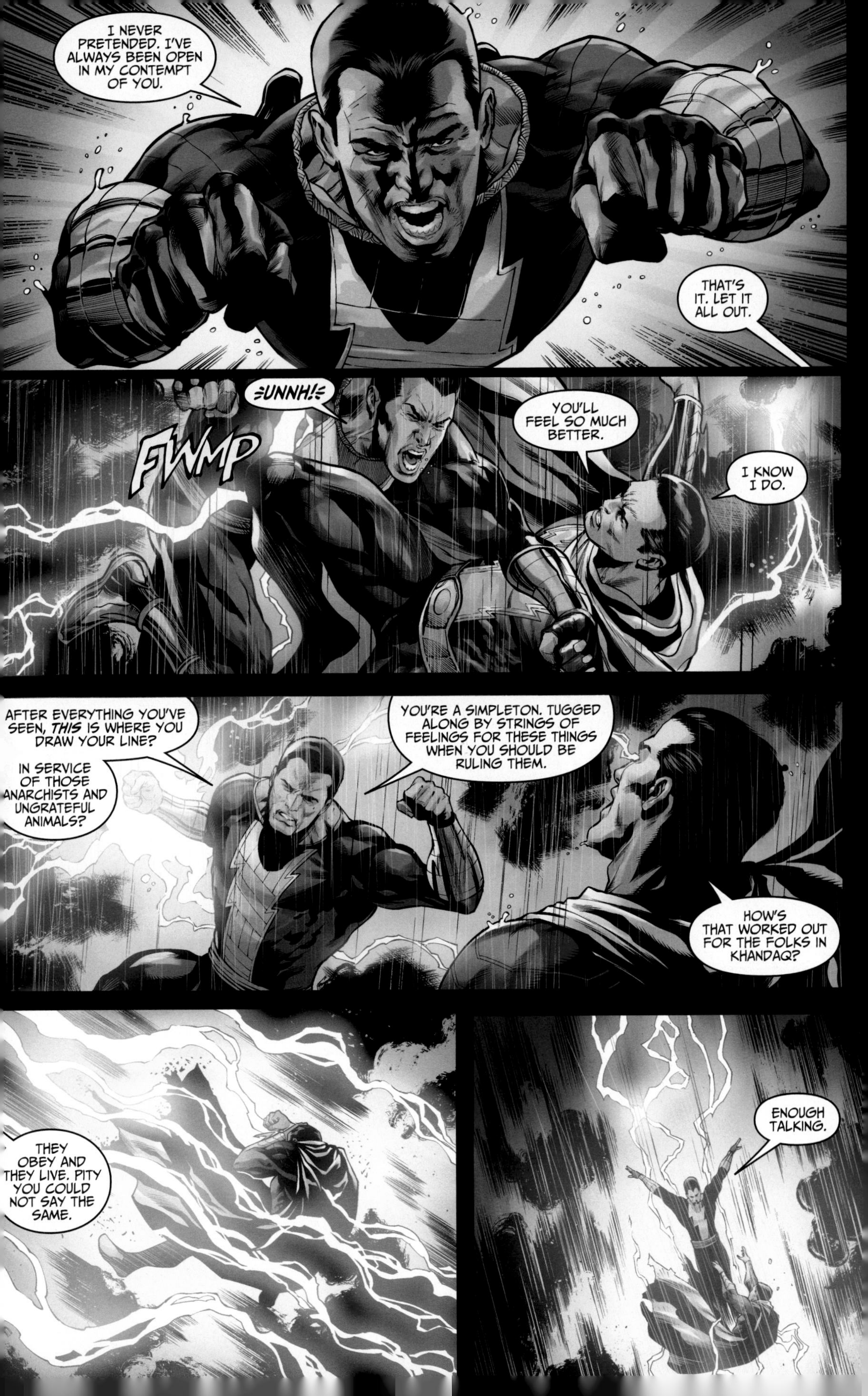
I NEVER PRETENDED. I'VE ALWAYS BEEN OPEN IN MY CONTEMPT OF YOU.
THAT'S IT. LET IT ALL OUT.
UNNH!
FWMP
YOU'LL FEEL SO MUCH BETTER.
I KNOW I DO.
AFTER EVERYTHING YOU'VE SEEN, *THIS* IS WHERE YOU DRAW YOUR LINE?
IN SERVICE OF THOSE ANARCHISTS AND UNGRATEFUL ANIMALS?
YOU'RE A SIMPLETON. TUGGED ALONG BY STRINGS OF FEELINGS FOR THESE THINGS WHEN YOU SHOULD BE RULING THEM.
HOW'S THAT WORKED OUT FOR THE FOLKS IN KHANDAQ?
THEY OBEY AND THEY LIVE. PITY YOU COULD NOT SAY THE SAME.
ENOUGH TALKING.

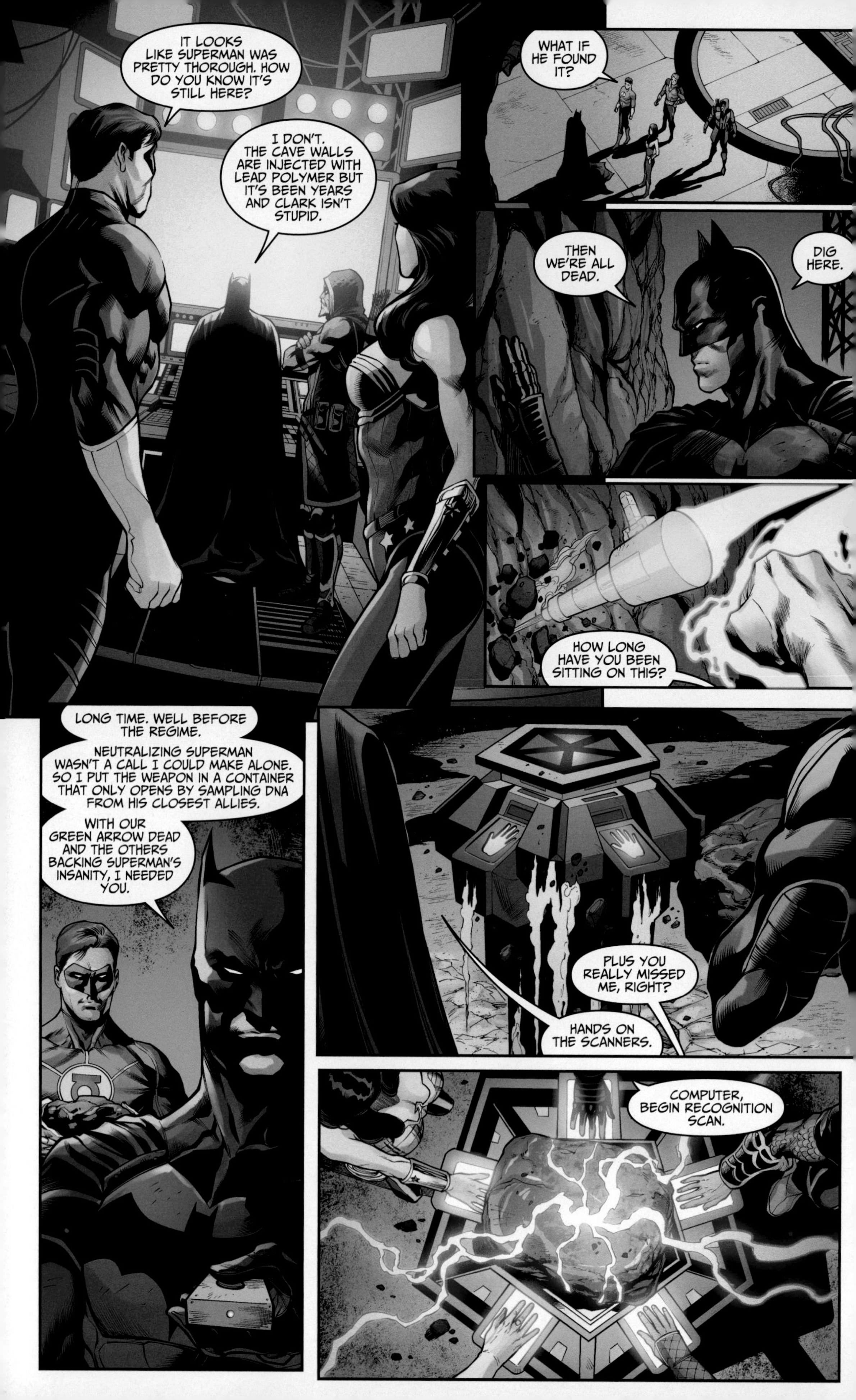
IT LOOKS LIKE SUPERMAN WAS PRETTY THOROUGH. HOW DO YOU KNOW IT'S STILL HERE?
I DON'T. THE CAVE WALLS ARE INJECTED WITH LEAD POLYMER BUT IT'S BEEN YEARS AND CLARK ISN'T STUPID.
WHAT IF HE FOUND IT?
THEN WE'RE ALL DEAD.
DIG HERE.
HOW LONG HAVE YOU BEEN SITTING ON THIS?
LONG TIME. WELL BEFORE THE REGIME.
NEUTRALIZING SUPERMAN WASN'T A CALL I COULD MAKE ALONE. SO I PUT THE WEAPON IN A CONTAINER THAT ONLY OPENS BY SAMPLING DNA FROM HIS CLOSEST ALLIES.
WITH OUR GREEN ARROW DEAD AND THE OTHERS BACKING SUPERMAN'S INSANITY, I NEEDED YOU.
PLUS YOU REALLY MISSED ME, RIGHT?
HANDS ON THE SCANNERS.
COMPUTER, BEGIN RECOGNITION SCAN.

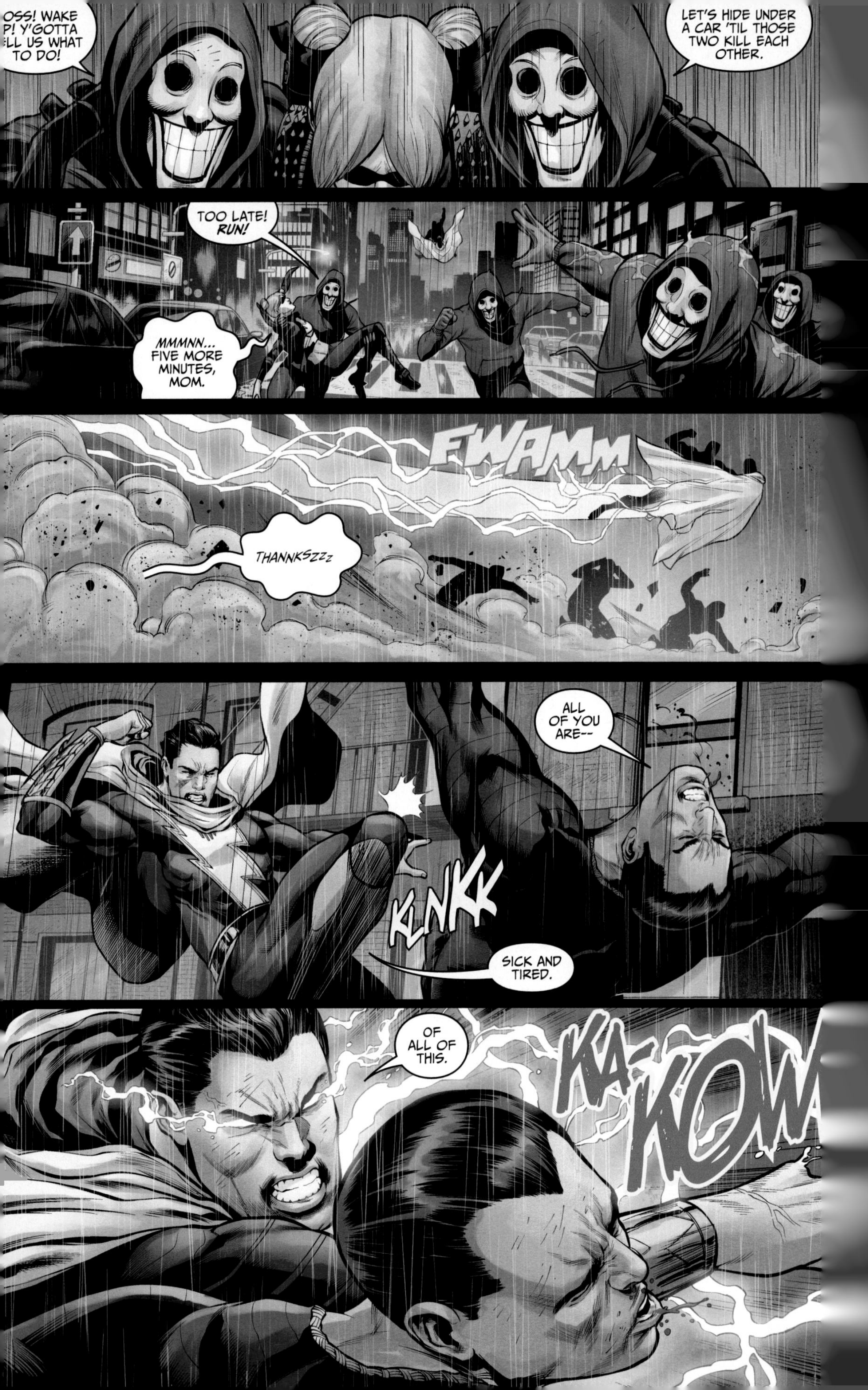
OSS! WAKE
P! Y'GOTTA
LL US WHAT
TO DO!
LET'S HIDE UNDER A CAR 'TIL THOSE TWO KILL EACH OTHER.
TOO LATE! RUN!
MMMNN... FIVE MORE MINUTES, MOM.
FWAMM
THANNKSZZZ
ALL OF YOU ARE--
KLNKK
SICK AND TIRED.
OF ALL OF THIS.
KA-KOW

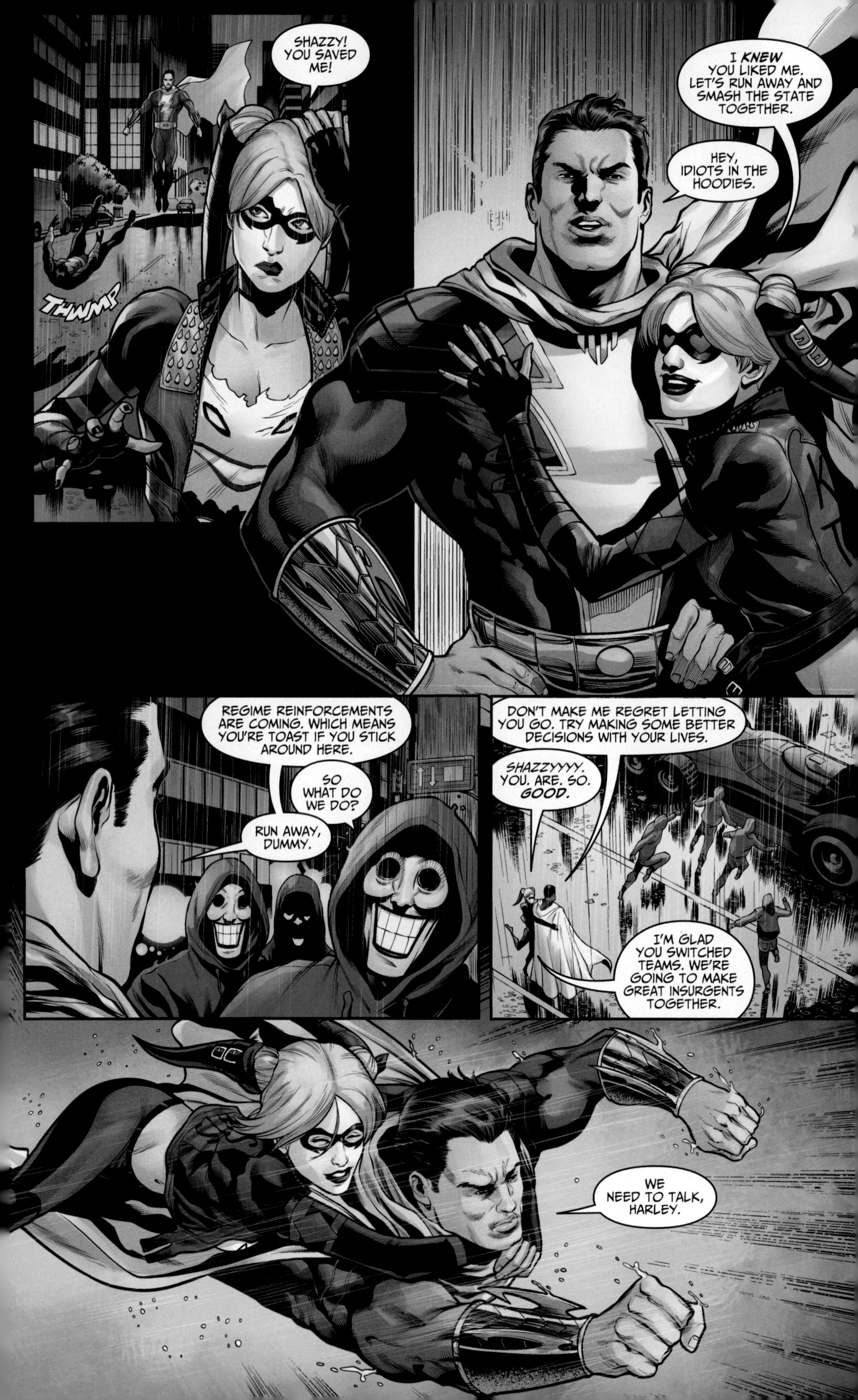
SHAZZY! YOU SAVED ME!
THWMP
I KNEW YOU LIKED ME. LET'S RUN AWAY AND SMASH THE STATE TOGETHER.
HEY, IDIOTS IN THE HOODIES.
REGIME REINFORCEMENTS ARE COMING. WHICH MEANS YOU'RE TOAST IF YOU STICK AROUND HERE.
SO WHAT DO WE DO?
RUN AWAY, DUMMY.
DON'T MAKE ME REGRET LETTING YOU GO. TRY MAKING SOME BETTER DECISIONS WITH YOUR LIVES.
SHAZZYYYY. YOU. ARE. SO. GOOD.
I'M GLAD YOU SWITCHED TEAMS. WE'RE GOING TO MAKE GREAT INSURGENTS TOGETHER.
WE NEED TO TALK, HARLEY.

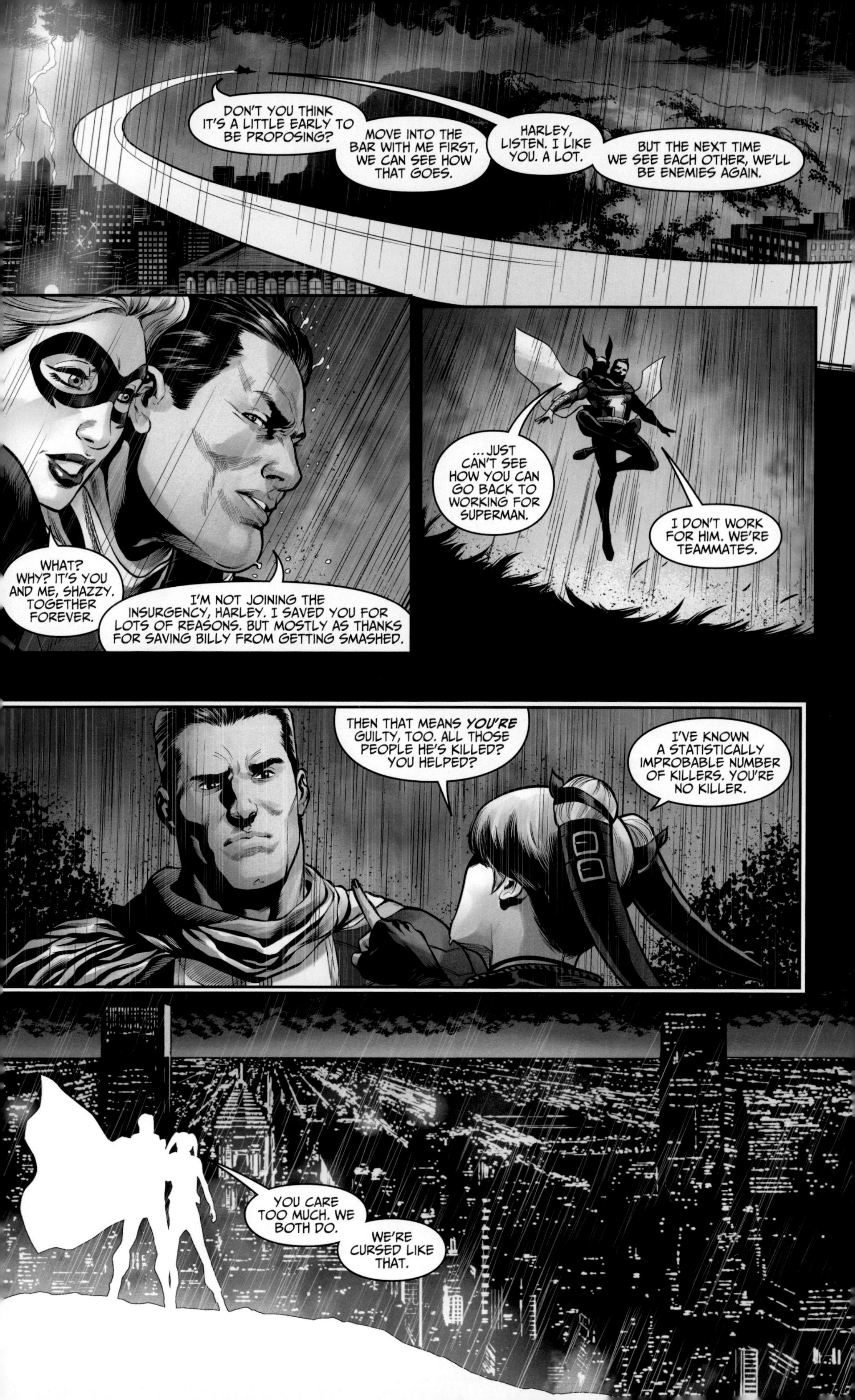
DON'T YOU THINK IT'S A LITTLE EARLY TO BE PROPOSING?
MOVE INTO THE BAR WITH ME FIRST, WE CAN SEE HOW THAT GOES.
HARLEY, LISTEN. I LIKE YOU. A LOT.
BUT THE NEXT TIME WE SEE EACH OTHER, WE'LL BE ENEMIES AGAIN.
I'M NOT JOINING THE INSURGENCY, HARLEY. I SAVED YOU FOR LOTS OF REASONS. BUT MOSTLY AS THANKS FOR SAVING BILLY FROM GETTING SMASHED.
WHAT? WHY? IT'S YOU AND ME, SHAZZY. TOGETHER FOREVER.
...JUST CAN'T SEE HOW YOU CAN GO BACK TO WORKING FOR SUPERMAN.
I DON'T WORK FOR HIM. WE'RE TEAMMATES.
THEN THAT MEANS *YOU'RE* GUILTY, TOO. ALL THOSE PEOPLE HE'S KILLED? YOU HELPED?
I'VE KNOWN A STATISTICALLY IMPROBABLE NUMBER OF KILLERS. YOU'RE NO KILLER.
YOU CARE TOO MUCH. WE BOTH DO.
WE'RE CURSED LIKE THAT.

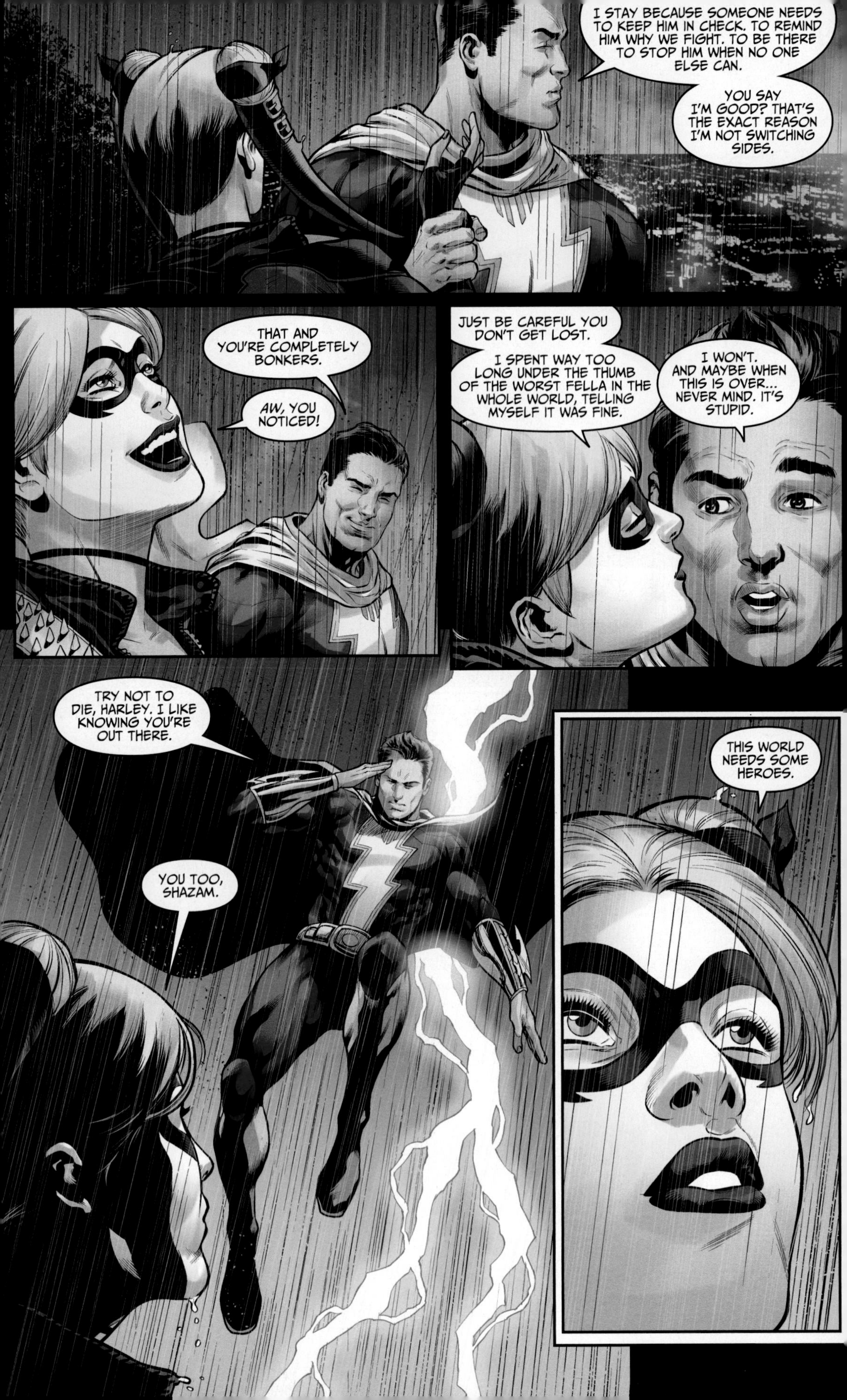
I STAY BECAUSE SOMEONE NEEDS TO KEEP HIM IN CHECK. TO REMIND HIM WHY WE FIGHT. TO BE THERE TO STOP HIM WHEN NO ONE ELSE CAN.
YOU SAY I'M GOOD? THAT'S THE EXACT REASON I'M NOT SWITCHING SIDES.
THAT AND YOU'RE COMPLETELY BONKERS.
AW, YOU NOTICED!
JUST BE CAREFUL YOU DON'T GET LOST.
I SPENT WAY TOO LONG UNDER THE THUMB OF THE WORST FELLA IN THE WHOLE WORLD, TELLING MYSELF IT WAS FINE.
I WON'T. AND MAYBE WHEN THIS IS OVER... NEVER MIND. IT'S STUPID.
TRY NOT TO DIE, HARLEY. I LIKE KNOWING YOU'RE OUT THERE.
YOU TOO, SHAZAM.
THIS WORLD NEEDS SOME HEROES.

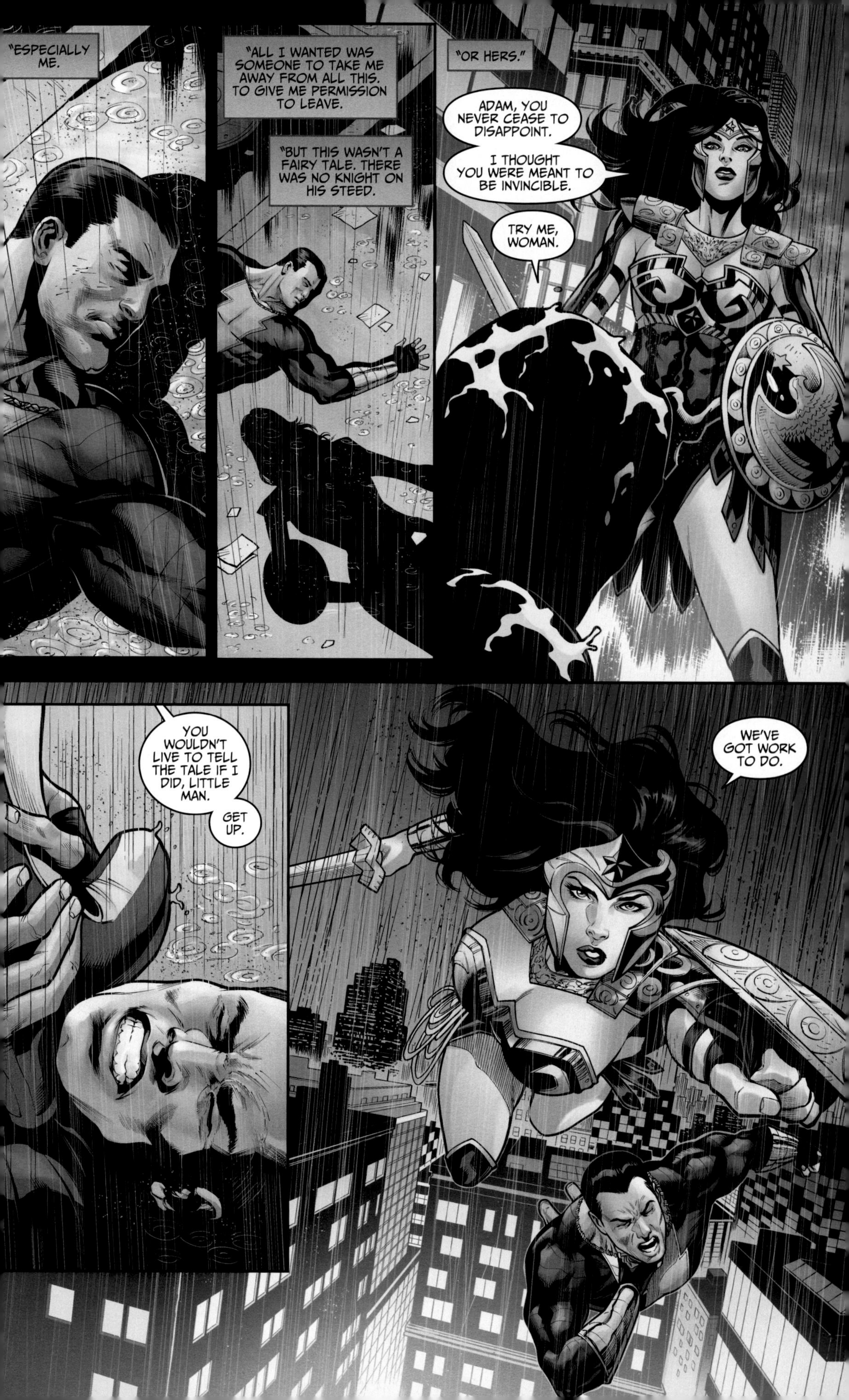
"ESPECIALLY ME.
"ALL I WANTED WAS SOMEONE TO TAKE ME AWAY FROM ALL THIS. TO GIVE ME PERMISSION TO LEAVE.
"BUT THIS WASN'T A FAIRY TALE. THERE WAS NO KNIGHT ON HIS STEED.
"OR HERS."
ADAM, YOU NEVER CEASE TO DISAPPOINT.
I THOUGHT YOU WERE MEANT TO BE INVINCIBLE.
TRY ME, WOMAN.
YOU WOULDN'T LIVE TO TELL THE TALE IF I DID, LITTLE MAN.
GET UP.
WE'VE GOT WORK TO DO.

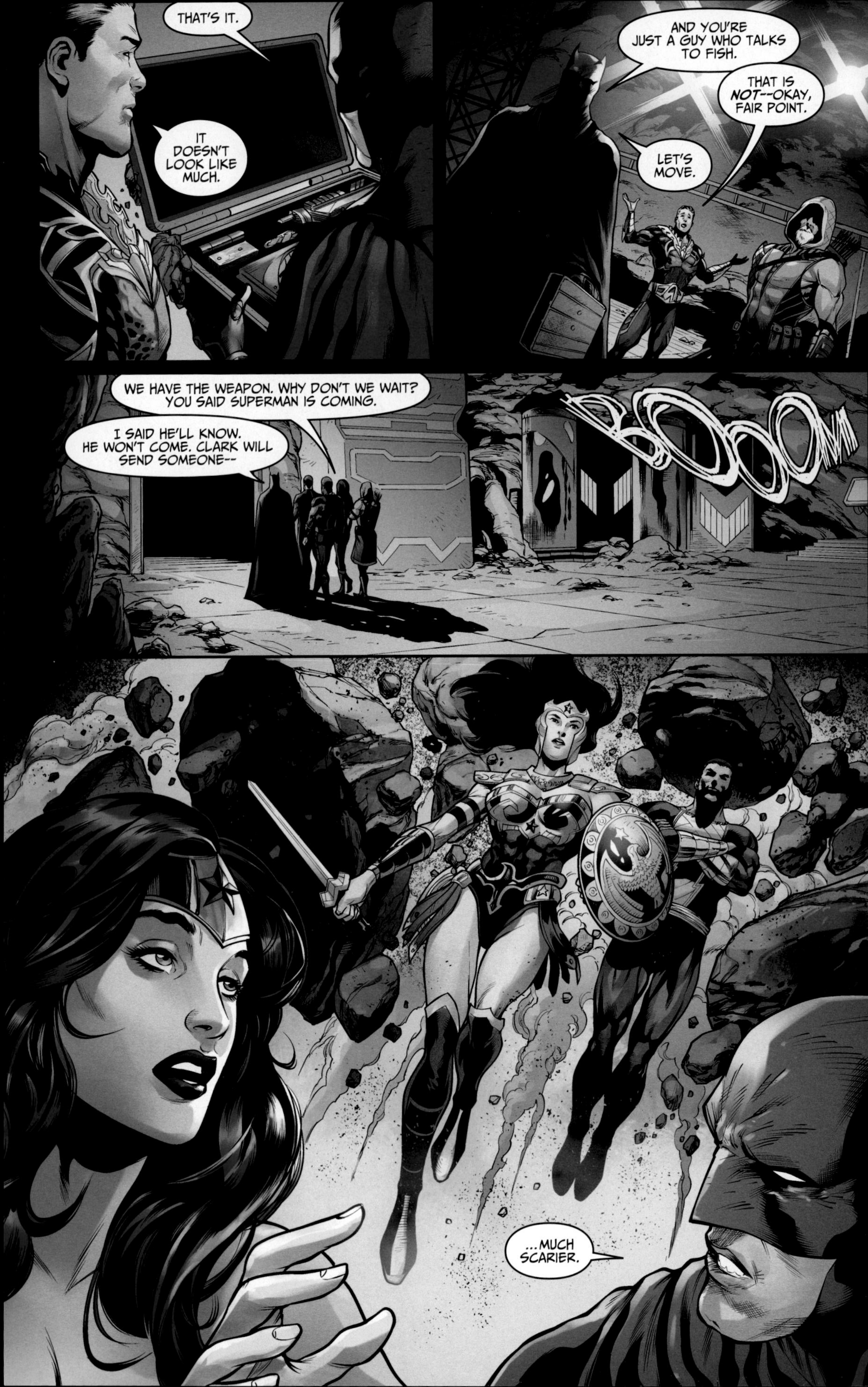
THAT'S IT.
IT DOESN'T LOOK LIKE MUCH.
AND YOU'RE JUST A GUY WHO TALKS TO FISH.
THAT IS NOT--OKAY, FAIR POINT.
LET'S MOVE.
WE HAVE THE WEAPON. WHY DON'T WE WAIT? YOU SAID SUPERMAN IS COMING.
I SAID HE'LL KNOW. HE WON'T COME. CLARK WILL SEND SOMEONE--
BOOOOM
...MUCH SCARIER.

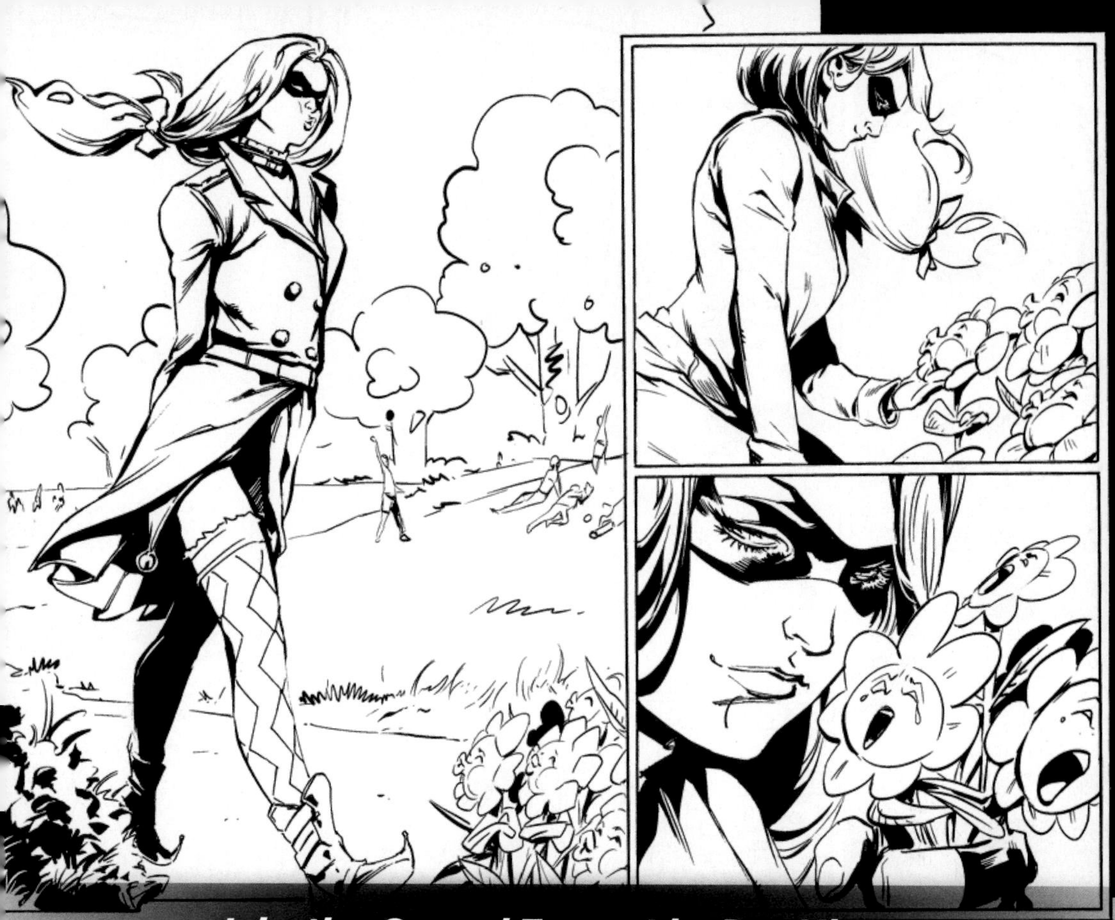

Injustice Ground Zero art by Pop Mhan

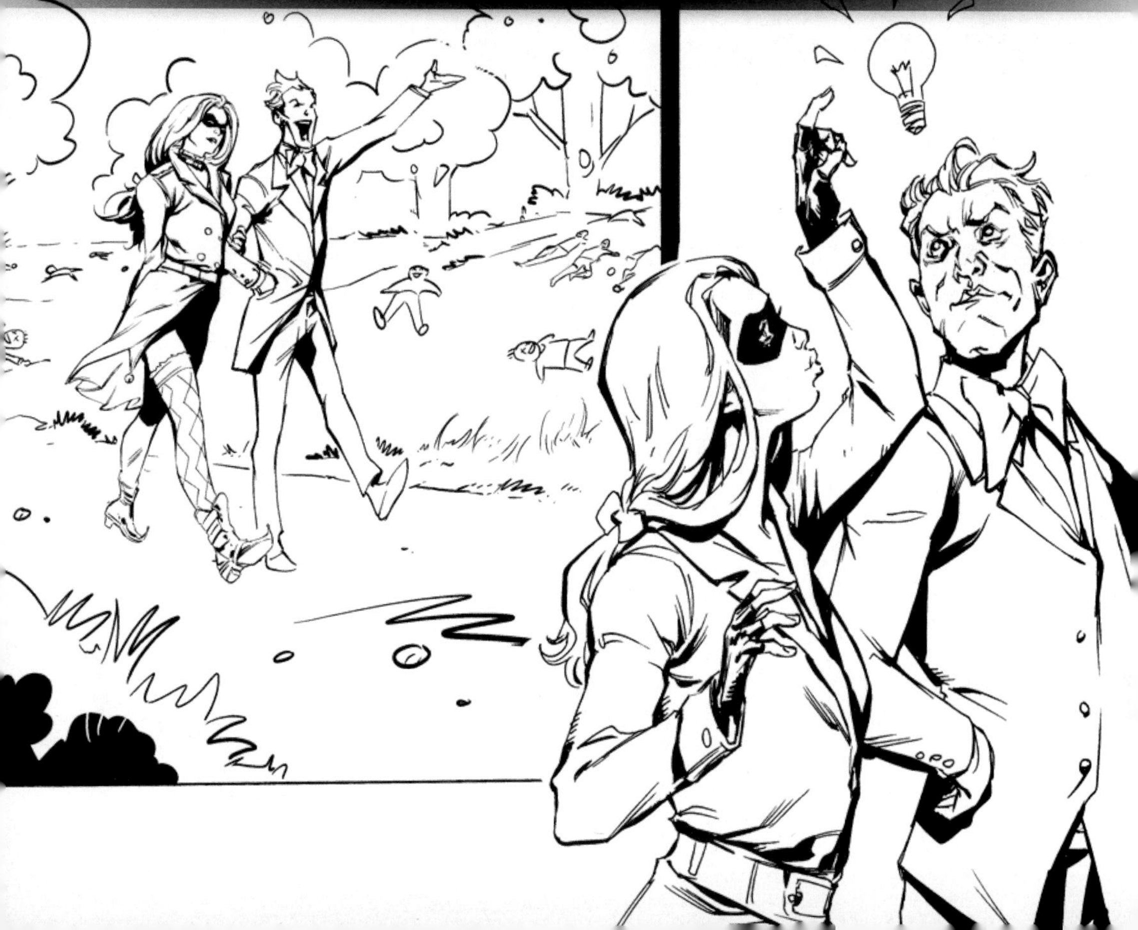

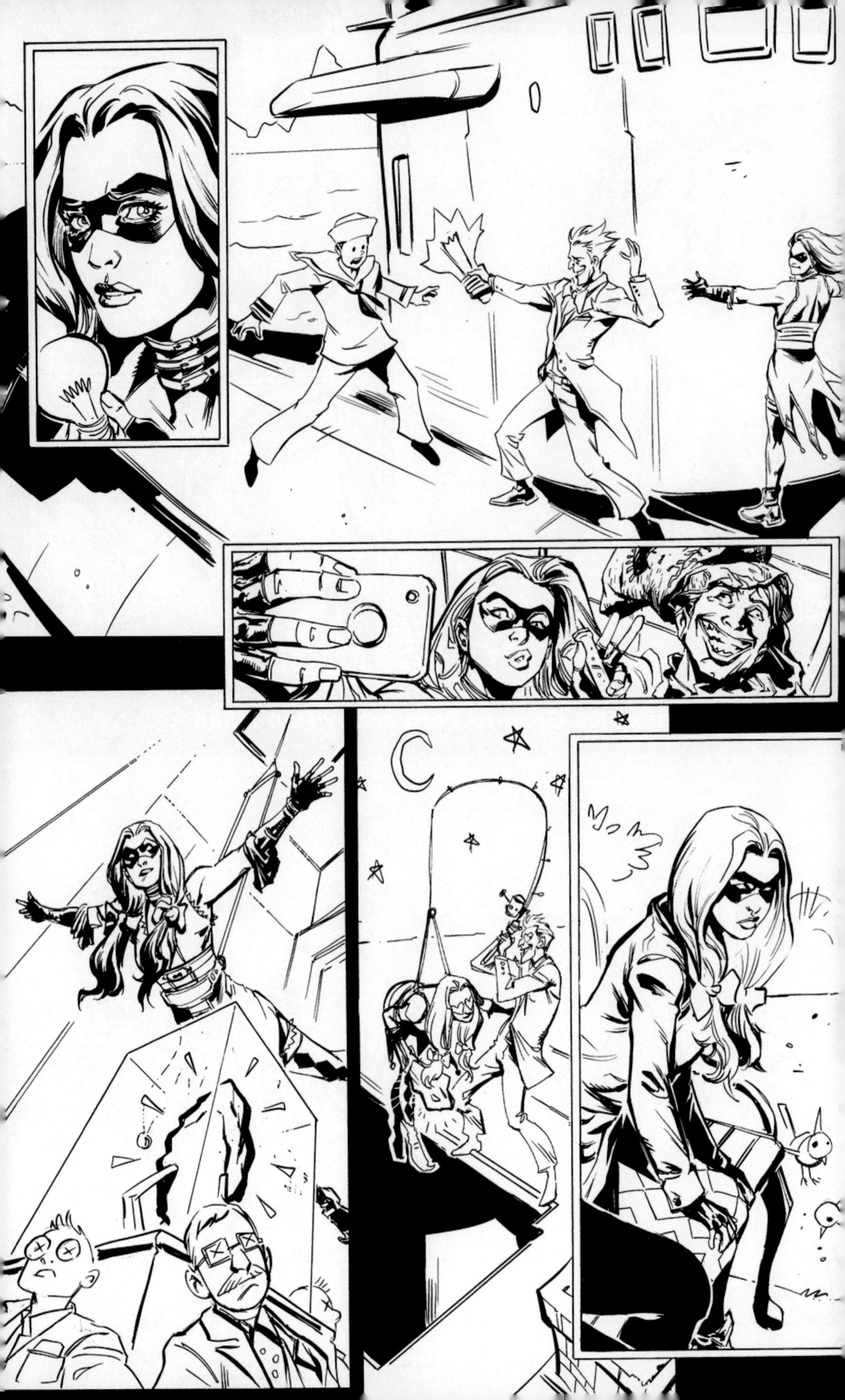

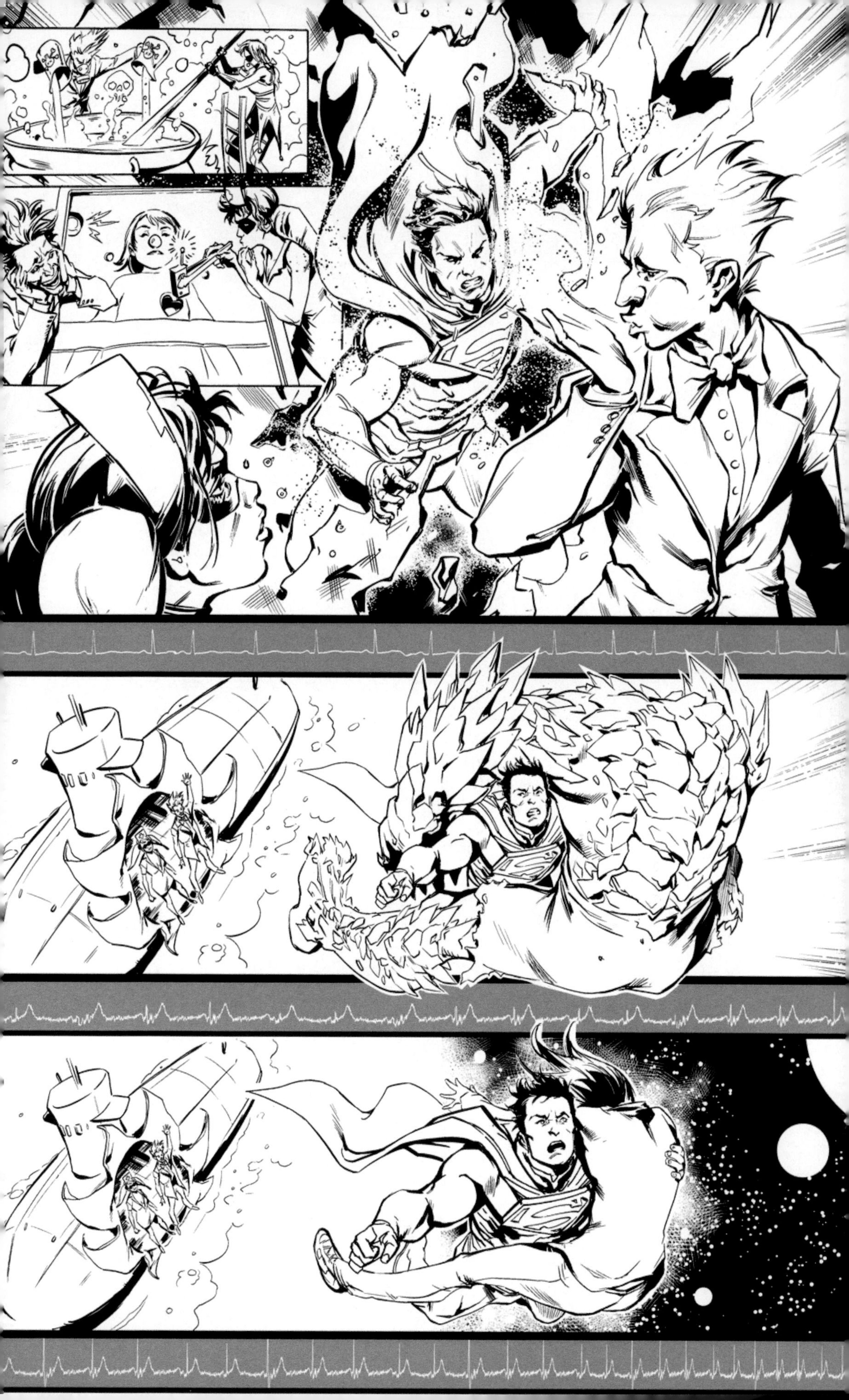

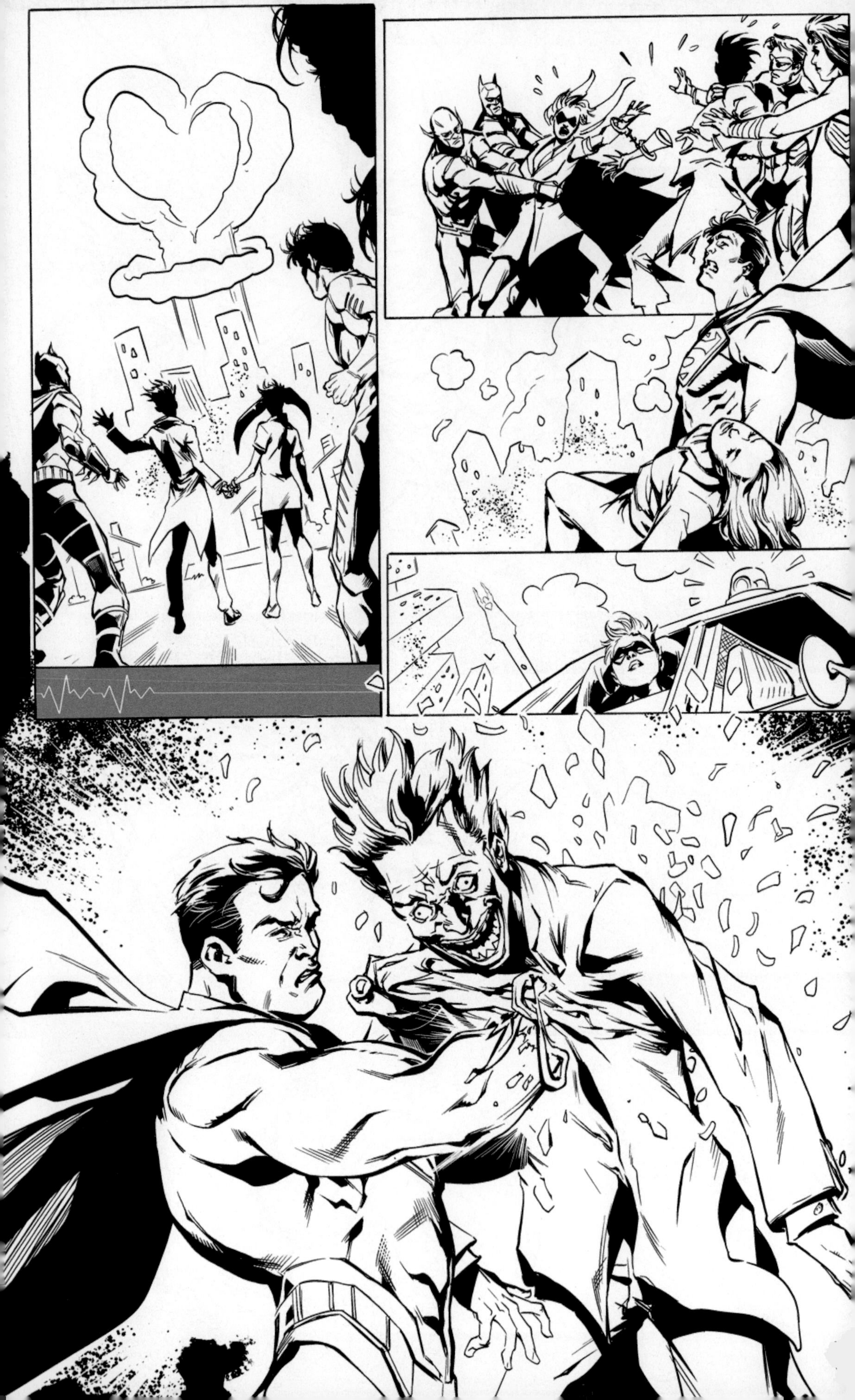

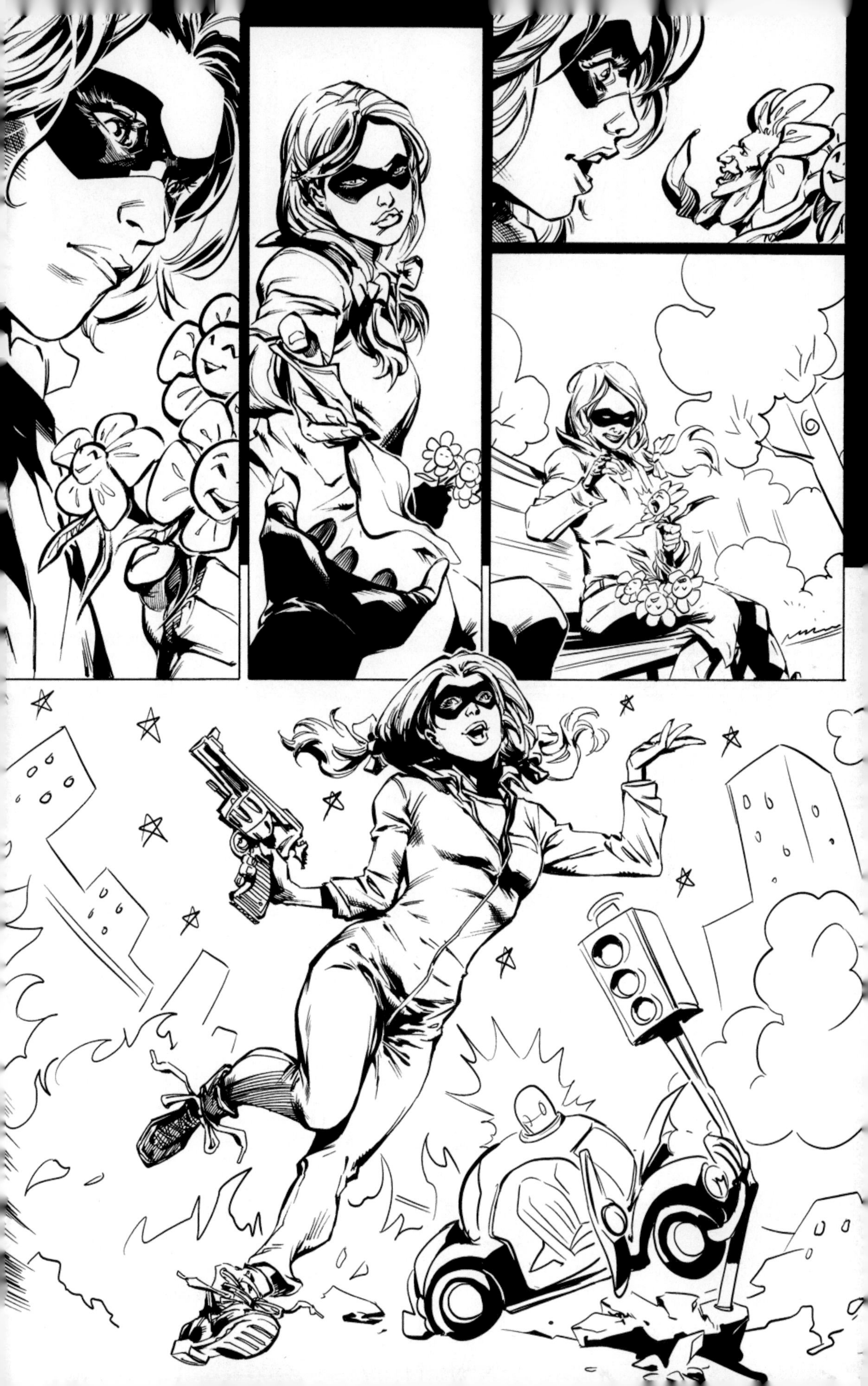

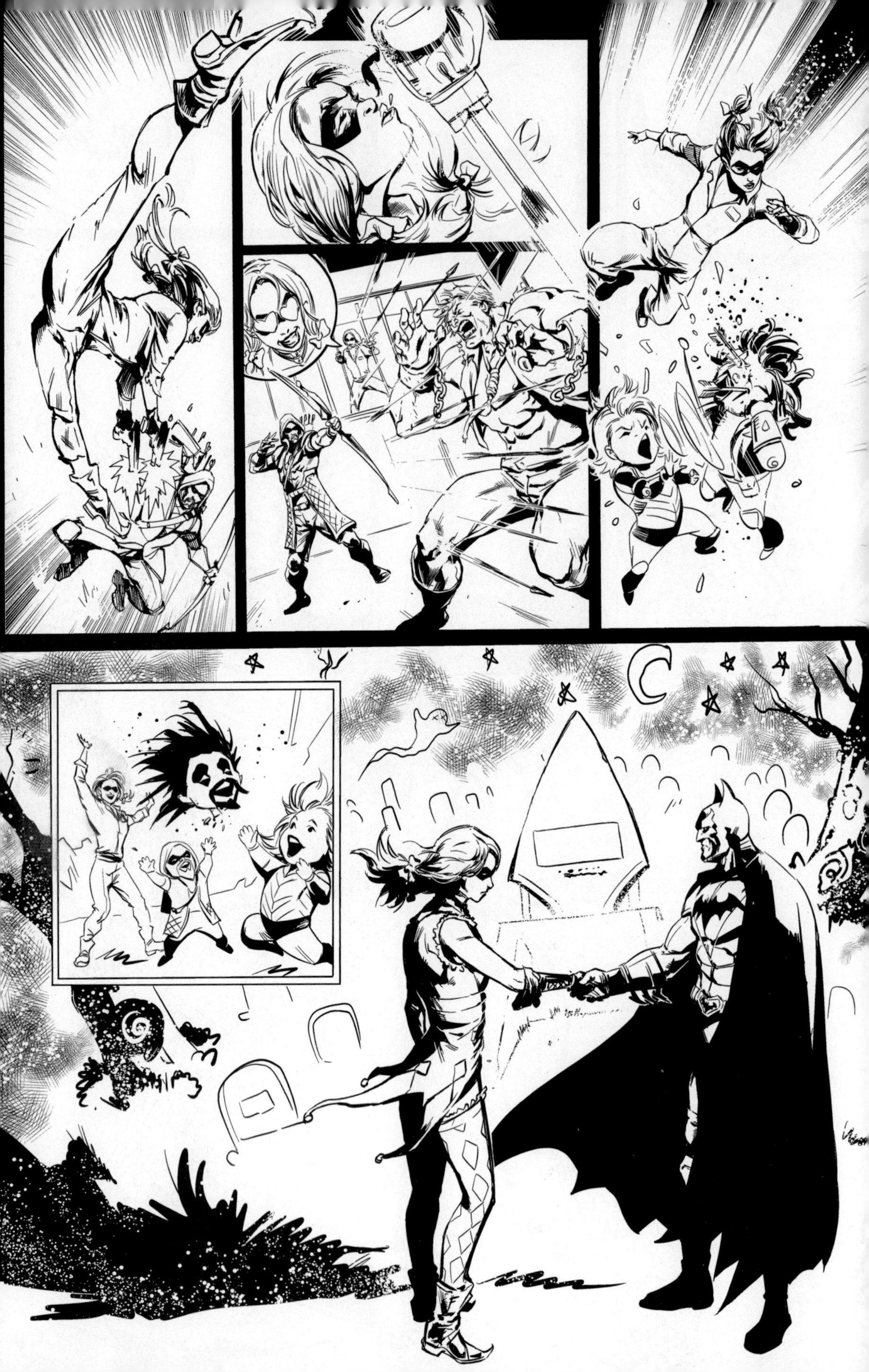

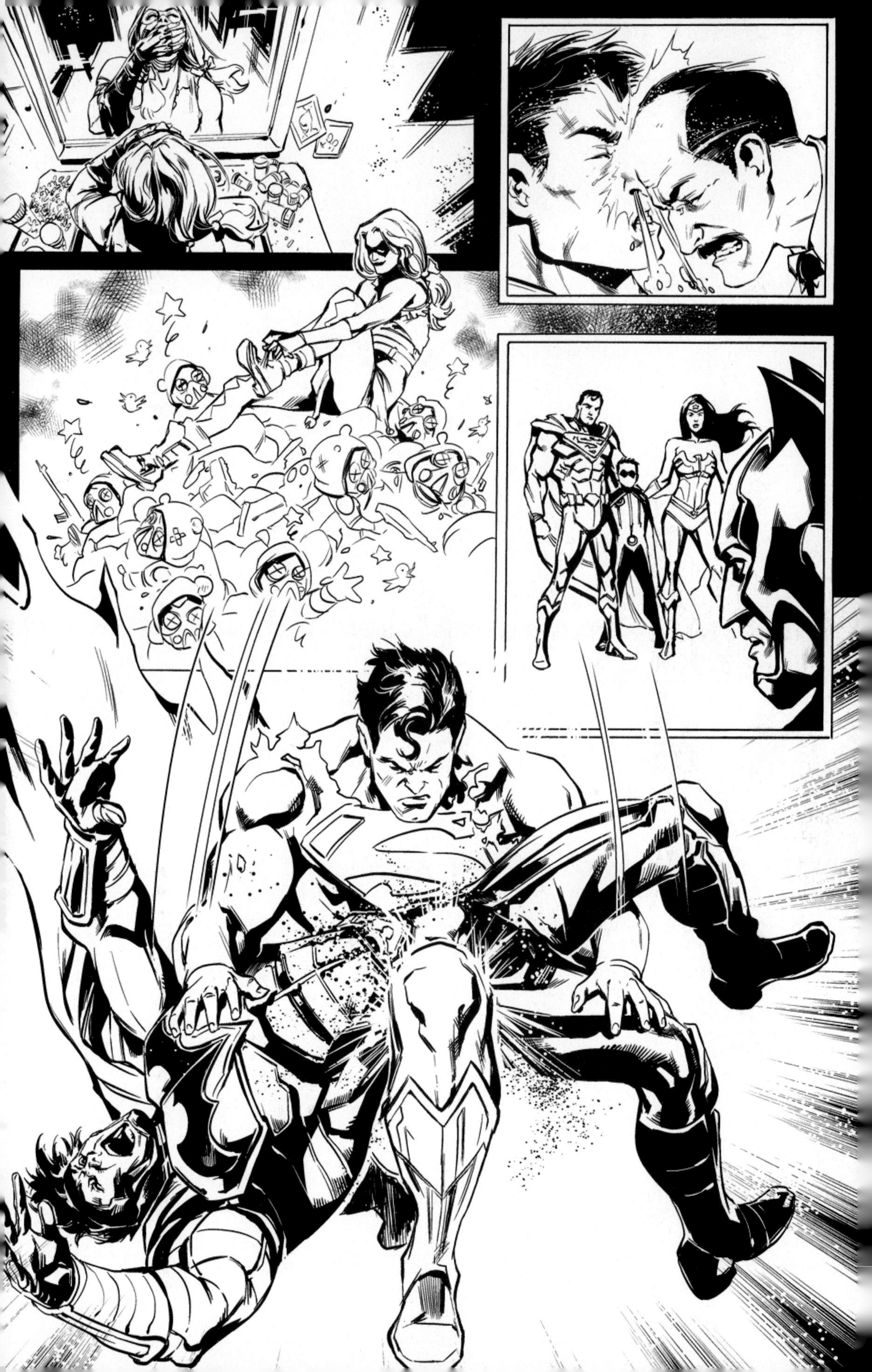

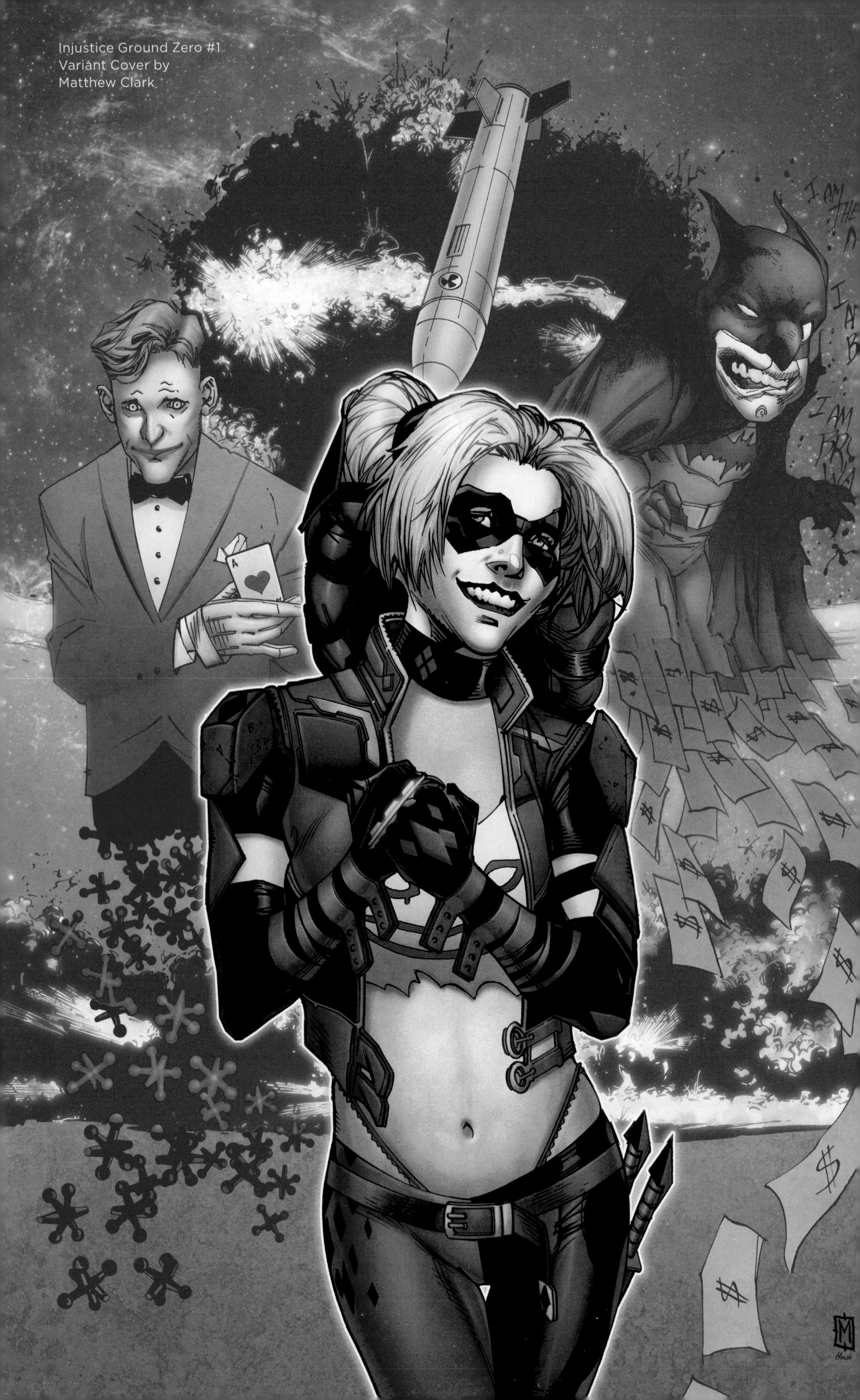

Injustice Ground Zero #1
Variant Cover by
Matthew Clark